Also Exclusively Available on Amazon.com Paperback & E-Book Part 1 (A

& Stopping Over 100 Terrorist Attacks while Tracking & Locating UBL O

is the shocking book that elements within the British Goverment tried to st

Ordering the British SAS to Locate & Destroy my Operational Panasonic Toughbook Laptop...

My Friends, Brothers in Arms in the SAS never completed that order...

Exclusive & Never Released; Evidence, Documents , Witness Statements, 3000+
Photographs, Video footage, Testimonies, Audio Recordings, Original Book
Manuscript (Copyright 2003) Including; The 6 highly controversial detailed,
omitted (Legally Advised Too) Chapters of this book, which have all been recorded
copied & lodged with a British Solicitor for safe keeping & will be released if
elements within the British FCO/Government challenge the content and facts
within this manuscript or if elements within British Government Departments,
Agencies or anyone else try to discredit the Author in any way or the Author dies
from anything other than nature causes. "All" the co-operating evidence will be
un-reservedly released, made public. I have also been encouraged by people &
friends in America aware of the enormous number of photographs & images to
publish an exclusive photography book covering the subjects within this
manuscript, I will endeavour to do this...

"The Truth always comes out in the End".

"Watch out for the Imminent Exclusive Iraq, Syria & Kurdistan Photography
Book followed by the Explosive & Shocking International Documentary based on
All Books & Work covering 2002 - 2018."

After a former British Police Officer of 16 years, interviewed DS Terry Benton of the British Metropolitan Police, Benton Confirmed that the Police Confiscated/withheld from British Court the Operational Diaries & Intelligence reports of Anthony Malone, Detailed in the Official Chain of Custody Evidence Document which DS Terry Benton again withheld & handed over to members of British Intelligence. This Evidence is Damming to elements within the British Government & Police, their interference in the Rule of Law & British Justice System, Perverting the Course of Justice & by withholding Key Evidence & Perjury by serving Police Officers! Time will clear Anthony Malone's Name! Where are these Diaries, Intelligence Reports, Black Book & 200+ Documents now...

Only Police DS Terry Benton can answer that question...

People will be held Accountable!

British Parachute Regiment Cap Badge. American 101st ABD "Screaming Eagle"

"Rendezvous With Destiny"

Book Content Includes

Hunting International al-Qa'dia Terrorists & Operating Behind Enemy Lines

****

Iraq Kurdistan Syria Afghanistan Libya SA, Europe. 2001 - Present (18 Years)

****

The Hezbollah, Haqqani, ISIS, AQI & Taliban Connections "Project Cassandra"

CIA - DEA - DIA-DOD - FBI. "Al-Qaeda & Terrorist Funding"

****

The Secrets of the $1.3 Billion, al- Madina Bank Scandal Lebanon. Hezbollah, "Uday, Qusay the sons of Saddam Hussein, the Bin Laden family & several infamous other people HVTs all banked & held multiple accounts at the banks"& Other International Banks connected; HSBC, Barclays & RBS

****

International Terrorist Networks & Groups, Interconnected & Work Together

****

The Real Killer Elite, 101st Airborne Division who Killed Saddam's Sons

****

CIA $1.2bn & $200m Iraqi Gold in a Bunker in Lebanon Being used by Terrorists to help fund their Syrian, Iraq, Afghan War

****

Target Packages Sent to Washington DC for Urgent Approval

****

Terrorist Weapons, Ilegal Arms Deals, Surface to Air Missiles

****

Meeting the Head of Syrian Intelligence in Damascus

****

Extensive Covert Network & Task Force of NOC assets, Including former British & American Special Forces, CIA & Senior Sources within Hezbollah & Several other Terrorist Orginisations informants that Anthony Stephen Malone Personally Cultivated & Handled for over 15 years! Working alongside & being Tasked (Offical Top-Cover) by American Intelligence Agencies, helped to stop Countless Terrorist Attacks & Acts!
(See Detailed Synopsis at Rear of Book)

****

Over Eight Years, agents working out of a Top-Secret DEA facility in Chantilly, Virginia, used Wiretaps, Undercover Operations, NOC & Informants to Map Hezbollah's illicit networks, with the help of 30 U.S. & Foreign Security Agencies.

****

2018 London has a Hezbollah Problem...

****

Maj. Gen. David H. Petraeus Cites Highs & Lows of Iraqi Deployment

****

Al-Qaeda, ISIS, AQI International Terrorist Network

****

British Secret Intelligence Service MI6 / Colonel Bob Stewart MP

****

Kurdistan

****

Terrorist Attacks Stopped on American & British off Duty Soldiers in Cyprus.

A True British & American Patriot From an Old Military Family, Anthony Malone was "Sold down the River & Betrayed by British Intelligence because he Became too Influential and Powerful across Europe, Middle East & Asia" (Confirmed by Former Senior Members of the British SAS)

Anthony Stephen Malone; Former Member of Britain's Elite Parachute Regiment

4th Generation Soldier

MilitaryAdviser: Africa, Central America,Middle East, Afghanistan

Special Political/Security Adviser: CNN, SKY News, Sunday Times, Telegraph

Director, NGO International Security/Intelligence Organisation (DSSI Ltd)

BEFORE Embarking on the Prologue, readers may benefit from a brief familiarisation with the maps and photographs of Iraq, Syria, Lebanon and Kurdistan. There is also a comprehensive Glossary and Specialist Equipment list with notes sectioned at the back of the book. This is not an "action book" the objective of this book is to give the reader good background knowledge and understanding of what it is really like to live and operate in Syria, Kurdistan and Iraq, it incorporates my story and the facts, data can be used as a reference book for future use. There is detail of the history of places and countries to help the reader gain an understanding of the real situation on the ground across this part of the Middle-East. I have included some of the data and information on terrorist networks so the reader can gain an overview of how these networks are interconnected between geographic countries and a sense of how they function and operate...

Knowledge is power; After disrupting and stopping over 100 terrorist attacks and actions; I thought it about time I shared some of my knowledge. My objective is to save lives... I also felt that some truths needed to be told, this was done so people know the facts and hopefully the past mistakes of the British Government in Iraq, Syria and Afghanistan will not be repeated again, given the fact American, British troops are being deployed again to the Middle-East 2018/2019...

DEDICATION

"This book is dedicated to all the members of the Armed Forces, CIA, "Brothers in Arms". who have given their lives for freedom while serving in Kurdistan, Iraq, Syria, Lebanon, Afghanistan and Libya". I would like to say thank you to all members of 101st Airborne Division "Screaming Eagles" & General David Petraeus, General Michael Lennington, General Joe Anderson. It was an honour spending time with my fellow Airborne Brothers, "It was Emotional Gentleman". A Special Mention to the bravest man I ever know, had the honour to work with & call a friend; Major Bevan Campbell. RIP Brother. "We saved a lot of lives & We found, HVT #1, Bin Laden... Rest easy Soldier until we meet in Valhalla!". Below "In honor of those members of the Central Intelligence Agency who gave their lives in the service of their country."

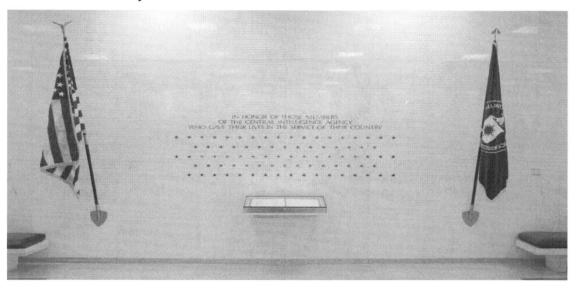

Major Bevan Campbell in Afghanistan (See Bevan @ Back of Book)

"I am not a hero, but I have had the honour to walk alongside men and women who are"

Author's Note

Because of political consideration and to protect some individuals privacy, I have changed or omitted some identifying details of this book. This personal account of the major events, places, military operations in Iraq, Afghanistan and Syria, are based on facts,operational journals and photographs by the author, all facts and opertional time lines are accurate, military names have been changed due to ongoing operational circumstances and to protect the identity ofIntelligence and Special Forces Task Forces, (The Activity's/Grey Fox/Task Force Black), personnel. Certain details about locations and after events have been changed due to the British Government "official secrets act". I have also changed some names and identifying details in this book. Because there is no standard transliteration from Kurdish, Persian, or Arabic into English, I have generally chosen to spell words as simply as possible and according to how they are pronounced. I have spelled people's names according to their personal preference.

In the words of Napoleon Bonaparte " A man is not a man unless he has served in his countries military, experienced his freedom taken from him and imprisoned, looked death in the face".

Whatever one's view on the US and UK's decision to invade Iraq in March of 2003, one incontrovertible fact is that it continued to rage at a deadly ever increasing pace, withtens of thousands dead and no let-up in sight, the nightmare of yet another all-out bloody civil war, proxy war looming on the horizon between Iraq, Kurdish Peshmerga and Iran, not forgetting ISIS and AQI. Much ink along with blood has been spilled explaining and analysing the coalition's presence in that troubled country, but very little has been heard from those who were actually sent in to do the job... though for various official reasons, of course, military personnel cannot divulge their action or even opinions.

Good thing Anthony Stephen Malone is a civilian...

Anthony Stephen Malone @ New York Visiting Ground Zero.

Straight to reality...

Executed - Slaughtered Iraqi Family, Mosul

We turned into the dark and foreboding street where the house was located, a crowd of onlookers had gathered over the road, emotions were running high, any spark could ignite a violent riot, there were several old cars and an ambulance parked outside the house. The convoy of American Military Police Humvees stopped outside the dwelling, an immediate cordon for protection was set up. I stepped out the lead Humvee taking a moment to observe my surroundings and the increasing number of on lookers, I moved towards the entrance of the two storey house. Stopping suddenly, I was hit by a sweet smell, this sickening scent I had come across, many times in the past during operations across Africa; it was the smell of death, rotten and decomposing bodies. I looked at Jane who had joined me at the entrance, I told her to wait by the Humvees, knowing what lay ahead of me, she looked at me puzzled, she asked what was wrong, I told her in a low voice you don't need to see this, somethings can not be unseen. My gut instinct was telling me that this was going to be a bad one. "my gut instinct is never wrong". I escorted Christina into the house, people were stood around no one was talking, the look of

11

shock, horror and disbelief was on all their faces. I noticed thick claret and the trails of blood, leading from the garden, along the corridor floor through the kitchen, blood and splash marks ran up the walls, I noticed a smeared bloody hand print across a fridge door, the smell was horrendous, I had to put my hand over my mouth and nose. We entered the hallway an Iraqi man was just standing there in shock, looking into the main room ahead, crying, weeping with his head in his hands. We moved silently past him, the floor was a good two inches think with dark blood, it was like walking through a thick slush. We slowly, apprehensively, moved into the room. The horrific sight that lay before me was both stomach-churning and sickening, an enter Iraqi family, six in all had been slaughtered. Women, children, young men, all had been shot at close range. The body of a young woman with the back of her head missing was hunched over a chair, in a last desperate effort to protect her beautiful little girl, who must have only been about six years old. The little girl had been shot in the face at point blank range. Empty AK-47 brass cases littered the floor. This gruesome sight made me feel sick. The other bodies also had gunshot wounds to the head and body. The enter room was covered in blood and claret, it was even dripping from the lights shade hanging from the ceiling. The bodies had been there for around four days, the heat of the days had made all the bodies swell up and erupt, body fluids covered the furniture and floor. I tapped Christine on the shoulder, time to go, we had seen enough, there was only death here. We exited the building and found a strip of green grass by the side of the house, others soldiers were hunched over a low wall being sick... we both were shocked at what we had just witnessed. I rubbed her back, taking in a breath of fresh air, she looked at me, her eyes filled up a little, I nodded, I knew what she was thinking. There were no words for this. Christina straightened up and composed herself as her soldiers moved towards her, she gave them orders to carry out. We moved back to the Humvees after a few moments. The rest of the convoy had arrived "J" was giving them orders to reinforce the cordons now at each end of the street, he broke away and looked at us, I said it's a bad one, they asked how bad, I answered the worse I had ever seen, he just stopped and looked at me, this shocked him and the other soldiers around him, they all knew I had been around, there was not much I had not seen. Christine said she needed forensic photographs of this crime scene, the military needed to have them for evidence. I said to Christine give me five minutes and I will go back in and take the shots, I knew that the young soldiers may find this a difficult task. She looked at one of her men, without hesitation he said no, I'm not going back in there, he had already walked in and seen the stomach-churning sight from the end of the corridor at a distance. "I respect a man who has the guts to say no in company that was there that day". After five minutes I put some vic's menthol rum under my noise and put some blue plastic gloves on from my medical kit, I made my way into the house. 20 minutes later I emerged, I had got what Cristina had needed. That room and the children's bodies would haunt me afterwards for a very long time. Intel came back to me at a later date, the family had been massacred by the local insurgency/terrorists. I wanted the reader to read this account early on, so they can steady and compose themselves before they read this raw and shocking manuscript.

"The above iniquitous, sickening and deeply disturbing incident in Iraq strengthened my already steadfast resolve. I made it my personal mission and duty tostop terrorists from carrying out such stomach-churning evil acts against defenceless children and families". This and similar incidents led me to expand my Taskings, I was asked and become an Offical Embeded Photographer for 101st Airborne Divison. My Photographic Everdence was to be used to highlight Murders, Massgraves and War Crimes. This evidence has also been used as reference by the United Nations and other agencies.

Background

Formerly a member of the UK's Elite Parachute Regiment and now a key player in an elite, non-government private contracting firm providing SWAT, Intelligence, protection and political consulting services and with over eighteen years' experience in special, unconventionaloperations in the Middle East, Afghanistan, Balkans and Africa, Malone entered Iraq prier andthen with the invasion force in a supporting role. His actions there included, extracting international journalists from Iraq prior to the start of the Iraq war to supplying specialised medical equipment and supplies to Iraq children'shospitals, "Anna" and later also included assisting coalition forces on raids on HVT# "high value targets", along with working in conjunction with US military intelligence and forming target packages for Washington DC and "SOF" Special Operations Force, targeting al Qaeda.Terrorists,insurgent training campsand theirsafe house across Syria, Iraq, Iran, Afghanistan, Cyprus, Europe and exposingtheir illegal arms and re-supplyroutes into Iraq from Saudi Arabia, Syria, Iran, Afghanistan and China, Russia. Malone also covertly helped multiple international agencies to locate, find and get released Westerners who had been kidnapped across the Middle-East and Africa by terrorist groups. Every hostage recovery Malone had worked on or been involved in resulted the recovery of the hostage alive! Another important fact is that Malone and his entire teams, network had never lost one man or asset in the entire time of working Across the Middle-East and Africa. Not many team leaders or organisations can state that!

Working alongside US and UK military intelligence, the US State Department and such agencies as CIA, CSA, FBI, French DST,Britain's MI6, MI5, as well as specialised groups like Taskforce 20, 121, 626, Taskforce 7 and Task Force Black "the activity" and future ultra-secret Task Force 6.8 named after the book of Revelation 6.8. which first located UBL Osama bin Laden in Pakistan and other High Value Targets... Malone and his firm also liaised with senior UNand several International Special Counter Terrorism Task forces at times. Malone's evidence and photographs were used to help prosecute war crimes and bring killers and terrorists to justice. Malone's first epic book "Honour Bound Rogue Warrior Part 1", about Afghanistan is now referred to and called the "Honour Bound Report" in UN circles!

Combat Patrolling with 101st ABD Mosul Iraq, Looking for Bad Guys.

Malone spent many years in Iraq and (elsewhere in the region) doing the jobs he was contracted to do, fulfilling his obligations but growing steadily impatient with what he considered ever-increasing neglect and mismanagement by the coalition forces – including their post warplanning, and deployment of ill-prepared raw recruits, who had nocultural understanding of the people who they would come into contact with.They had also been deployed with insufficient ceramic plates for personal body armour and dangerously low suppliers of ammunition. Not forgetting the early old snatch Landrovers with very little armour plating which lead to the deaths of so many British soldiers with other far reaching fatal consequences... These were but two of the many glitches in the supply chain suffered by British units. As well as the insufficient consideration of the human and physiological toll on returning British and American soldiers with PTSD"would this be Britain's Vietnam, and Americas Northern Ireland",

When Malone returned to the Britain in 2006 to conduct refresher, recruit fitness training with 63 SAS, Malone was staggered by the rampant ignorance and misperceptions about what was really going on in the ground in Iraq, Syria and Afghanistan. He was determined to tell some truths that people might find hard to swallow...

Good thing Anthony Stephen Malone kept a comprehensively written and in-depth photographic journal of all countries of operation...

Hunting Saddam & Sons. General David Petraeus, Colonel Joe Anderson, Anthony Stephen Malone

His meticulous notes, kept on a continuous basis during his entire stay in Iraq, Syria and the Middle East, have been reconstructed here from the elaborate encryption system Malone used to prevent anyone other than him making sense of his recorded thoughts and experiences. Accompanying them are the staggering and breath taking 3000+ photographshe took while during operations, which bring the war home in a way that even dedicated viewings of the nightly news will not have done for those who were not there and who wish to know: what was really going on in Iraq, Syria?

Military Planning Brief; Endless Missions, Going after Saddam!

Malone also shares explosive new detailed information about his meeting with the feared head of Syrian Intelligence attheir Damascus Headquarters and about other such incendiary scandals, including;"**The British Foreign Office, MI6 Extracted, Interviwed, Moved Saddam's military scientists, covertly out of Iraq and into Beirut, Lebanon ("Phoenicia Hotel") and Southern Cyprus ("Golden Bay Hotel") before the war (Leaving their children behind at an Iraqi orphanage to be used as leverage) and the fact they then confirmed, that Saddam did "Not" have WMD..."** but he did have battlefield chemical weapons before the war! Also the explosive International al-Madina bank affair in Lebanon, $1.4 billion international scandal, he provides behind-the-scenes revelations about the key figures in Governments, the Global illegal daily dealings by the key strategic players pulling the strings. It also revels all the links to International Terrorists organisations, including;The family of Osama bin Laden, Saddam Hussien Iraq, his sons and the shadowy world of the Russian Mafia, black illegal arms deals and the links to Columbian, Mexican drug cartels. Malone can reveal what no one else can, because he was Adnan Abou Ayyash's "the owner and chairman of the bank", senior "IIO", International Intelligence Officer, in charge of liaising with "all" governments and global intelligence agencies. (See official document). His investigation took him to several countries, which included Iraq, Saudi Arabia, Jordon, Lebanon, Turkey,Cyprus, Egyptand across Europe and not forgetting Singapore and South Africa. During his investigation he was methodically hunted by three hostile Middle Eastern Security Service and their Secret Police. He uncovered and witnessed on mass-scale how Syrian interference and security services, tried to cover up the al-Madina bank scandal,keep the Lebanese people caged, using terror, assignation and torture as their tool and how the late Rafiq Hariri,Lebanon's former Prime Ministerand close friend of Adnan Abou Ayyash, was a shining light and guardian for the people of Lebanon until his devastating assignation by a massive car bomb in Beirut on valentine's day 2005.Malone's loyalties and strict code of ethicswould be tested to breaking point and all would end in a dramatic emotional climax and several months in one of the most dangerous and notorious prisons in the Middle East, "the Lebanese lion's den", were Malonewould be surrounded by the very top al-Qa'dia, Hezbollah terrorists and Iraqi Saddams secret police and Afghan Haqqani insurgents and Commandersthat he and the US Government had beenhunting...

Mission Background

"I pour out the wine of my oblivion
Bitter it is, and thus it pleases me.
For this bitterness is the zest of my life" "Omar Khayyam"

The day started just like any other in Cyprus, a beautiful sunrise painting the sky with warm golden hues as darkness slipped away. I could feel the sun's warmth on my face as I walked along the golden sand, a sole wanderer, listening to the symphony of waves breaking over rocks in the cove and collecting driftwood for the eveningsopen fire.

I strolled into town for my morning coffee, the wonderful, spicy aroma of Turkish cardamom wakening my senses. As I relaxed, enjoying my view over the harbour, my Thuryia satellite phone rang out. I picked it up, looked at the display, "Unknown International Number" I answered, it was Paul, an old friend of mine from Africa, I had advised him in the past on his projects, and work in South and West Africa, I was now advising him as a friend on a present task, investigation that he was working on. He was heading up the investigating in Lebanon, off the Bank of Al-Madina scandal. On the behalf of, Dr Adnan Abou Ayyash, the chairman of the bank, he had just lost $1.4 billion dollars. Paul was responsible for the Investigation and recovery of the money and assets. I was using my international human resource network, and contacts in the intelligence community to help him, guide him and keep him out of trouble. This was not an unexpected phone call, he often asked me for advice on sensitive matters. He had just found evidence of Iraq, oil for food program,illegal black market arms deals,

Russian mafia, and Columbian drug cartel linksand international money laundering for terrorists organisations, and groups during his investigation into the Al-Madina banks business dealings, I said, "is that it?"laughing, he asked could I check some data out though my St Petersburg FSB (Russian Intelligence), and Central American DEA (American Drug Enforcement Agency) contacts. I agreed, my friends and contacts owed me a few favours; I told him to send me what he had, by secure means. The conversation ended with a, "Stay safe", speak later. The phone rang again, I thought Paul had forgot to ask me something, I looked at the phone display.To my surprise the Sunday Times popped up on my caller ID. It could only be Adam, journalist extraordinaire, my good friend and on occasion employer. I answered and his cheerful voice boomed across the line, "I've got something I'd like you to have a look at." This was not an uncommon question, so I asked what it was. He gave me a quick run down, "I can't really talk over the phone. Why don't you come to London for a quick meeting?" I paused, a bit reluctant to leave my peaceful island for the hustle and bustle of London. I had come to Cyprus, semi-retired six months earlier.The volume of carnage and killing I had witnessed in and across Africa had taken its toll on me, I needed time to heal and become a civilian again. It's very easy to fall, as some people do, into the trap of becoming emotionally cold and thinking a war zone is home. The golden sun drenched beaches of Cyprus were a world away from the blood stained streets and blood curdelling shrieking screams of terrorist massacres in West and East Africa. Lives had been saved but at great personal lost...

I was again lost in thought, sitting, watching the stunning sunset that night,brilliant shades off oranges and deep reds filled the sky.I mulled over the idea of working in the Middle East again.The aroma off the red wine I was drinking was enchanting, along with the peaceful sound of the sea, washing over the golden sands just feet away. The heat of the day was replaced by a sweet scented easterly breeze from the mountains, I could hear the flames of the open fire dancing and crackling in the background, I moved inside. Curiosity got the better of me, as it would so many times in the future. I called Adam. I was booked on the British Airways flight the next afternoon. Little did I know that one meeting would turn into a four year ordeal that would take me across several Middle Eastern countries and into the depths of the most dangerous places and peoplein the world, Iraq, Afghanistan, al-Qa'ida.

Britain, London was typically grim and grey. A light rain fell as the plane touched down at Heathrow Airport. After 30min I was ushered into a waiting car and on my way to the Sunday Times headquarters on Pennington Street.On arrival I was shown upstairs to a boardroom,Adam walked in, a friendly hand shack and down to business. He and the Sunday Times were interested in putting together an investigative mission and team,going into Iraqlooking for interesting stories, torture chambers, mass graves, weapons of mass destruction; the usual. He needed advice on organising the operation to maximizeits success. As we talked, it became apparent that if they were serious, I would have to become a part of the task and take over the operational and planning roles. They were talking about putting a team of people, behind enemy lines, to visit and investigate enemy locations that the "SOF", Special Operations Forces would also be hitting and taking out, I thought for a minute, the room went quiet, you could hear a pin drop, "from a hand grenade". I had never even heard of anything like this before. I had just semi-retired from operations, "the sharp edge of things"six months prior, I had no major commitments, just a little consultancy work for my long term friend Paul, on the Lebanese al-Madina Bank. "I had no idea that the Sunday Times Iraq task and the al-Madina bank investigation were going to come together and collide head on with spectacle international fallout and consequences with myself in the middle, putting me at the forefront of the west's fight against international terrorism and al-Qa'ida, as well as involving myself in the dark side of international dirty politics, cover-ups and counter intelligence, black Ops, where black is white and white is black, where deceit and betrayal are a daily occurrence depending upon the leader and the countries politics of that day. As a result of this all the International intelligence agencies, CIA, FBI, CSA, MI6, MI5, Task force 7, DST, Interpol, and the UNCounter Terrorism Section, "CTS", "There to take an interest and be involved in what I was doing in all avenues off my life" At this point of my life my name was unknown to the public I was the grey man! (That was about to change forever...) I thought I had time to play with, over the next few weeks this task for the Sunday Times sounded unique... sure, why not? Logistics took over, ground rules, requirements were put into play, a hotel suite for planning booked, intelligence meetings arranged with my MOD contacts, expenses up front and operational equipment for team members was put into motion. All was agreed. I made a satellite phone call, my planning team and operations manager would be flying into London within 24hrs.

I emerged from the meeting surprised at what I had just been asked to plan and carry out. I had flown to London for the day, in the suit I was wearing, without so much as a toothbrush and now I was planning a Civilian Special Forces"CSF"operation behind enemy lines. I knew I was embarking on new territory. The planning was a mission in and of itself, let alone entering a country on the brink of war searching out its most guarded secrets. Yet, with my experience in the Middle East and other countries, I suspected what Iwould findwould surprises me, and I knew the truth had to come out. Nothing could have prepared me for what was in store for myself and the rest of my team members.

Operational Planning

"Freedom suppressed and again regained, bites with keener fangs than freedom never endangered"

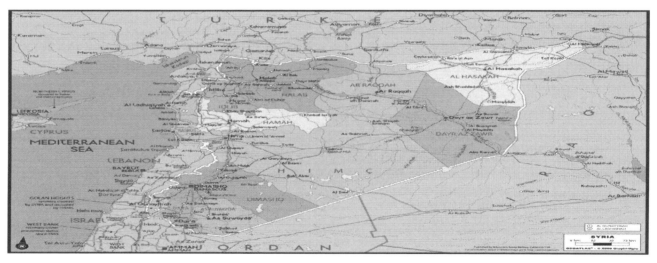

Planning phase of the operation. One day later, the entire team gathered in a hotel suite overlooking the Thames River and Tower Bridge. We got down to business. Our timeframe was tight, we were civilians, breaking new ground, about to plan an impossible mission into a hostile country and execute a mission within two weeks. From experience this kind of operation, mission should take three months to plan and prep. I had two weeks, "it was do able", The Tasks were divided and briefs carried out every six hours. The team worked 24/7 to complete all tasks. Rox, my intelligence officer,worked with his contacts in both military and intelligence circles, compiling current reports on all military, political and geographic aspects of Iraq. Updated reports were formed on al-Qa'dia, they were known to be operating and had training camps in Iraq. As well as what WMD materials we might encounter. There was mounting British intelligence that pointed to Saddam acquiring components of nuclear materials, (Russian U-235 weapons-grade uranium), by way of Djibouti. Our own intelligence HUM-INT Human Intelligence in Iraq had passed on intel about a uranium mine in western Iraq. Our sources had also indicated that Saddam had his sciences research and developed blister agent, this was to be confirmed when a platoon, friends of mine from the US 101st Airborne Division, were infected in southern Iraq. Sharpie, my operations manager,kept up to data with all incoming intelligence via a make shift ops room hub in the hotel suite, he also sourced military pilot charts, satellite imagery, (US Falcon view) and archaeological maps; he had set up an official map room for the task; and supervised all business details, off shore accounts, confidentiality agreements, security clearances etc. I was the team leader on the ground, responsible for identifying locations, planning the logistics of the actual task, briefing the boys on the team and overseeing all other details of the mission.Reading material was very important at this point, all team members studied, T.E Lawrence, Seven Pillars of Wisdom. This is still one of the few books which is invaluable to read and this would enable the reader to start to understand the customs, mannerisms, mentality and culture of the Arabs of the Middle East. The second book which influenced a major part of the planning stage of the operation was, Wilfred Thesirer, Arabian Sands, this is a classic, the people who have read these books will understand the value of them. Three years later the British and the US Government list these books as essential reading for troops and officers serving in the Middle East, including Iraq and Afghanistan. It is shame that they didn't start their troops reading such works, gaining cultural understandingand sensitivity prior to the wars in Iraq and Afghanistan, this could have saved lives.The full kit list was compiled for each member of the team, picked for ability and endurance. Key items included, GPS 12XL (Global Positioning System), Atropine injections (anti-nerve agent), Nato, silver compass, Tactical Surefire torch with weapon attachment, F1 and spider knives, LeatherMan tool to remove computer hard drives, black fire retardant Kevlar jackets, Taser and Breitling Emergency watch (with built-in dual frequency personal locator beacon PLB). Detailed MOD werelaminated and satellite imagery of all operational areas were studied by all team members. Scaled down mini versions to be carried on each team member at all times, locations were never marked on any maps, they were memorized just in case we were caught by the enemy. "maps were to be hidden inside the back of our combat vests". The car kit included: Marina communications equipment, spare car battery for charging the communications equipment, thuraya sat phones, night vision equipment; sledgehammer andbolt cuter (to enter locked locations, buildings and rooms), heavy chain to pull equipment out of buildings; black 50 meter rope for abseiling, heavy duty cargo/equipment straps, (2ton) for towing; orange markers to indicate friendly call signs to Coalition forces aircraft; U.N.-issue Kevlar flack jackets, tested for 7.62mm rounds. My contacts in Syria and Lebanon sourced the weapons and special equipment that were on my list, AKS's, AR-15's, 203, Glock 23, wing master shotgun, (short) and crates of ammo. 5.56mm for the M16's, 0.40mm Smith & Western for the Glocks, (0.40mmhas a lot more stopping power than a 9mm), 7.62mm short for the AKS's and specialised customised armoured piercing rounds for the shotgun. All weapons had already been field tested by my friendly call/signs, and where waiting in a safe house to be picked up on route, close to the Iraq border. This was set in place to cut down on the Syrian Secret Service taking an interest in my teams as they crossed the Syrian border from Lebanon. A cover story was put into place and all relevant documents ID and specialised maps, books were sourced and acquired. Stanfords book shop in Covent Garden, London is one of the best map shops to source specialised maps and books, on travel and Middle East history; this is a valuable source of literature. Our cover stories wereput into place. Archaeology students, one of my contacts sent me letter heads and letters of introduction from the archaeology Unit from one of the UK's topuniversities. My team was now an international authorised archaeology team, travelling around the Middle East visiting historicalsites. I have a fond interest in archaeology, anything that is old and historical, so this was a big plus for me. I had already visited the Middle East with regard to sites of interest, this would help my cover story and make it even stronger. When I was later being questioned and interrogated my cover story was floorlessand backed up at every stage.

Al-Qa'ida. and International Terrorism.

"Pray tell the purpose of a sinless live"(Omar Khayyam)

The changing face of International terrorism, hit home dramatically on September 11, 2002 in New York. The shock wave of that attack and military, security after effect can still be felt and seen today. The world changed on that day. The 7th July 2005 suicide attacks in London was Britain's wakeup call... Suicide bombers brought death, chaos and destruction to central London. It was a savage reminder that al-Qa'dia still represents the most potent threat to Western security and stability with continuing blowback. It had had a devastating and lasting impact on western civilization. I have been involved in counter terrorist operations for many years, from the streets of Northern Ireland fighting against the IRA's "dirty war", to the jungles of the Africa continent, conducting covert operations. Terrorism and the terrorist always had the same M.O. "modus operandi", whether domestic or foreign, they used violence and intimidation to further their cause. Until now. al-Qa'ida was changing the face of terrorism and taking it to the next level. Their members are not just people who fight with AK-47s, they are Bankers, Judges, policemen, politicians, international businesses. Their members are in every walk of life and money has never seemed a problem to them. After the devastating attacks on the US on September 11, 2002, the US Government made the command decision to take the fight to al-Qa'ida. TheirNo 1 target was the leader of al-Qa'ida, Bin Laden who was being harbored by the Taliban in Afghanistan and Western Pakistan. (Malone's future Task to find Bin Laden by American Intelligence is another epic story...) The American Government wanted a regime change in Afghanistan. After the biggest covert SOF's operation and a massive full scale military overt campaign, the US with the help of the Northern Alliance and my friends, commanders in the Afghan, Panjshir valley based Mujahideen, got their wish. The horrific reign of the Taliban was over and al-Qa'ida, its leader Bin Laden, where held up at their last retreat the mountainous, cave area of Tor abora, after blanket bombing of the area, and an undulating barrage of rocket and gun fire, it was realised that Bin Laden, had escaped with his followers through the caves and mountain tracks, over the border area and into Pakistan. Some say he was helped by the ISS, Pakistan's Security Services(I confirmed this years later when talking to senior Al-Qa'dia commanders in Afghanistan). Al-Qa'dia, from this point started to grow on the world stage, both tactically and strategically. Their use and manipulation of the internet, worlds media, helped bring their fight, terrorist activities into the spot light and to the attention of the world. There's not a news station around the globe today that does not show or cover the story every time al-Qa'ida,the Bin Laden family or now ISIS release one of their trade mark famous and notorious video tapes, via al-jazeera or other social media platforms. Al-Qa'dia and ISIS have taken terror to a new level, when they started posting on the internet, pictures and videos of their hostages being beheaded, this struck fear into the hearts of many people around the world. Whatever your view, one thing is certain, al-Qa'ida's campaign of fear is very well thought out and executed using western technology to achieve their aims. To fight this new generation of terrorist, the Governments of the world will have to think outside of the box and forget about their conventional ways of dealing with them. The much spoken blow back affect is well underway in Iraq, Syria and Afghanistan, thousands of insurgents are being well trained and supplied to fight the coalition forces. They are gaining valuable combat experience. If you look at the standard of the attacks on the collation troops from the late 2003, to present, the advancement in the combat effectiveness of the daily attacks has reached a 100% fatality rate, from the 5% or 8%, in 2003. Now all the attacks are carried out with military planning and precision, with deadly effect. Western intelligence need to look at how and why that is... how is that possible... who is teaching and training the terrorists... (During a future Tasking for American Military

Intelligence, I submitted a report to my Afghanistan area handler Walter, This pin pointed compounds in Iran being used to make shape chargers and sophisticated IEDs that were being sent into Iraq and Afghanistan to be used against, kill American and British, coalition forces and soldiers).

There are also many similarities from the attacks on coalition forces in Iraq, Syria and Afghanistan, to the M.O. "modus operandi", of the IRA in Northern Ireland. Some military experts say too familiar. I.E.D.s, "Improvised Explosive Devices, homemade mortars, ambushes, snipers, kidnappings, bombings, executions. The British military has been fighting an unconventional war "dirty war", on the IRA for years. The British wakeup call was when the IRA bombed CanneryWharf, in London's docklands. A massive bomb ripped through the buildings in the area. There was destruction and mayhem. The same kind of wakeup call hit the US on September 11th. The area and subject on people's minds should be where are all these terrorist/insurgents going to go when Iraq, Syria, Afghanistan eventually calms down, Europe, America…? The fight has taken a new turn, with Britain sending in thousands of troops again to fight the terrorists in Afghanistan, who are growing stronger and more vicious by the day, the Taliban/insurgents/ISIS are not a rag-tag outfit, they're hardened battle aged men, with over 30 years of insurgency fighting experience. They first fought the Russians and won, then the Americans, now the British. As it stands, the British have sent in, ill-prepared troops, with a shortage of basic equipment, and ammunition, they were like lambs to the slaughter. You don't see the politicians from Whitehall patrolling the roads of Iraq, Syria or Afghanistan, they are toobusylistening to their ill-advised, British Government advisers, who are a world away from reality. (I had it confirmed at a later date some of these top paid government advisers had never set foot in the Middle-East?). The alarming thing is how strong will al-Qa'dia and other terrorist groups be in the future and where will there next big attack be... it is not a question of if, but when... The suicide attack in Manchester, England on the music concert of American singer Ariana Grande killing 22 and injuring 59 was the most deadly attack in Britain in a decade. Terrorist commanders had been talking about hitting a music concert in Manchester, Britain for years, British Intelligence had been warned years before...

Middle East Updates and Preparations

"Once in awhile a man arises boasting;
He shows his wealth and cries out, "It is I!"
A day or two his puny matters flourish;
Then Death appears and cries out, "It is I!" (Omar Khayyam)

Since the dawn of time astrologers have proclaimed that four cities were bore under the sign of revolt, Samarkand, Mecca, Damascus and Palermo, and their words are true! These cities have only ever submitted to government through force and mass bloodshed. They follow the straight path only when it is traced by the sword. The history of the conflicts of the Middle East, past and present, should speak volumes to the leaders of today. There has very rarely been peace throughout these mystic lands.

That morningI received a letter via Paul from Adnan Abou Ayyash, authorising myself to investigate the Al-Madina banks illegal activates and follow any leads. This was the first of many letters and later personal private meetings with Adnan Abou Ayyash.

Adnan Abou Ayyash, is a man of small stature, he is a quiet shy man by nature. In private he is a softly spoken, family man, who always tries to help the people who surround him. He holds duel Saudi Arabian and Lebanese passports.

He was a close friendto King Fadi and is a close friend and confidant to King Abdullah of Saudi Arabia and in so is protected by them politically. He is an engineer by trade, he owes his millions made in his engineering projects, due to his friendship with the king. He spends his time flying in his private jet between Riyadh and Jaddah, overseeing engineering projects. Adnan Abou Ayyash brought the Bank of al- Madina for his brother to run. Over time I would become part of Adnan's trusted inner circle, and it would be myself who would intervene to keep him personally safe when an international contract was put out to kill him. He was moved under my instruction to the royal palace in Riyadh for his personal safety and protection.

The Abou Ayyash family acquired shares in the al-Madina Bank in 1984. The purchasers were IbrahimAbou Ayyash and Adnan Abou Ayyash. The latter brother had graduated from the University of Texas at Austin in 1974. While studying there, he became a close friend of Nasser Rashid, a Saudi engineer who became consultant to the Saudi royal family for all their construction requirements in Saudi Arabia and to a certain extent abroad.Adnan Abou Ayyash went to Saudi Arabia directly after graduating from the US. He started working with the Rashid Engineering Consulting Company, and by the early 1980s had become a junior partner in the enterprise as well as the acting General Manager. During the period 1974-82, Saudi revenues increased exponentially and the construction boomed. The Rashid company prospered immensely, supervising billions of dollars' worth of construction works. By 1982 Adnan Abou Ayyash had over $300 million of private wealth. This would turn into billions of dollars by 2003. He remained reclusive and lived modestly in his private villa in Riyadh. Ibrahim Abou Ayyash, the brother who followed in the business affairs of the family in Lebanon, adopted more overt attitudes to living. He was a spendthrift, and within a circle of close friends lived the life of the wealthy and famous. Little did Adnan Abou Ayyash know about the illegal dealings going on within the bank. Adnans bank was building strong ties to international organised crime, ties were made between Russian mafia and Columbian, Mexican drug cartels. Saddam Hussein and his son's money was also filtered through the bank from the Iraq oil for food program. Illegal arms deals to Saddam's Iraq were also brokered through the bank. Large donations of money where also given by the al-Madina bank to the head of Syrian intelligence and terrorists front companies controlled by (Hezbollah). The funds were used to buy military equipment in Europe and the US. An example off this was the specialist military night vision goggles that a convicted terrorist tried buying for one of thefront company based in Lebanon.

British banks were also involved. HSBC, Midland,Barclays off shore, as well as banks in France, and Dubai. Millions of dollars had been funnelled to these banks from the bank of al-Madina over time. The bubble would burst, it would just be a question of time. The scandal would be who was being paid off, bribed, blackmailed, and assassinated. Who were the key members of the Lebanese and Syrian Governments and intelligence, security service, covering up and protecting the people involved, turning a blind eye for personal profit, lying, blocking any investigation into the bank "Pandora's box" but who would take the lid off? Well that would be me in the future when my work with American Intelligence and the Director of the Bank of al-Madina became the same Task...

My plan was to finish the Task for the Sunday Times within 2-3, weeks, then meet up with Paul in Saudi Arabia or Lebanon and assist him on his task. My advanced party hadorganised, sourced and servicedthe Jeeps and car kit, then placed them at our mountain safe house in Lebanon, "the only relatively neutral country close to theatre". The two GMC jeeps, with Arab number plates, lovingly known as Victor One and Victor Two, these were heavily armoured with Kevlar, doors, roof, floor, back of all seats, equipped with state of the art communication equipment. This equipment would enable 24/7 contact with our Ops room in Cyprus, directly from Victor One, even once inside Iraq. A communication's check on distance confirmed Brazil could be reached directly from Elite main operations room in Cyprus. A crucial point as our Marina radio communications provided the only civilian radio frequenciesnot disrupted during the war. Our backup communications, the Thuraya satellite phones,were immediately compromised due to their usage by the Coalition forces and built-in GPSs (these were turned off and only to be used in extreme emergency situations only).

"Both paradise and hell are in you", (Omar Khayyam)

Some off the more specialised equipment was sourced and acquired in London, flown by courierto Lebanon from Heathrow by British Airways. On arrival full testing and training was carried out. All team members went through an intense refresher course in specialist skills: combat medic, communications, night navigation, weapons, nuclear biological and chemical (N.B.C.) warfare, small arms recognition, and refresher training, weaponry stoppage, firing, striping and assembling for both the AK-47/AKS (Iraqi Forces) and M16 (203) assault rifle with 40mm grenade launcher (US Forces). Combat refresher skills were also carried out using the Glock 19, 23 and Sig-Sauer pistols. All were likewise trained on skills specific to the job, basic Arabic, specialised communicationsatellite equipment, locations of emergency safe house and manned relay stations in Syria and Lebanon were memorized and computer hard drive removal was carried out by all team members, all were required to memorizeall information, no notebooks or ID tags were to be taken into theatre (Iraq or Syria).

Personnal Weapons, AK47, Glock, MP5.

Final Preparations

"Arise, we have eternity for sleeping!" (Omar Khayyam)

Sharpie and I flew back to Cyprusabout a week before the war to finalize infiltration and extraction routes and put in place emergency medical evacuation plans. My favourite was the speed boat, put on 5 hours stand-by notice, to take friendly call signs from northern Syria to southern Cyprus. "A little known fact" I was informed of by my intelligence officer - there is a very small British satellite base located in the South of Cyprus Island, it has a small slip of sandy beach/ I was told that if things went pear shaped, get to and land on that beach, it is classed as British sovereignterritory and would be a safe location.I was told it would cause a cluster fuck in international paper work and only use it as a last "ace card".We also popped back up to London to finalize the digital video and camera equipment (Nikon) allowing me to film the mission from beginning to end and we were ready to go. We headed to Lebanonto meet up with the rest of the teamto go over all last minute points, administration and checks. A list of inspiring and mood changing music was made on the flight over, I was going to pick up some CDs from the Virgin mega store in down town Beirut, The list comprised of classics groups like the Rolling Stones, ACDC, Guns and Roses, Bob Dylan, Dire Straits and the Animals, 60s sounds were a must for this mission... It's funny how I can relate a song to every war zone, intelligence tasking and mission I have been on...

Beirut, Lebanon

" We are the pawns, and Heaven is the player;
This is plain truth, and is not a mode of speech.
We move about the chessboard of the world.
Then drop into the casket of the void." (Omar Khayyam)

Returning again to Beirut was surreal. The city has always enchanted me even from the first time I strolled along the sea front, Corniche.The basin that surrounds the airport is beautiful at night. City lights dancing and reflect on the calm Mediterranean water stretching from Junieau to the end of the Corniche. Contrary to common belief, the city is quite beautiful, modern hotels and office buildings form the solider, down town, intermingle with French colonial architecture and the local population struts down the street Parisian-style. Only when ambulances race by with a deafening scream and soldiers run past with M16 assault rifles, car bombs shattering the nights tranquil scene, do you remember that you are in the Middle East and a country that has survived over 18 years of blood fuelled sectarian massacres and relentless killing as well as the internal carnage offcivil wars.

Lebanon, Beirut

"Lebanese background"

To even start to understand the Middle-East, a person has to know and understand its' history, Lebanon is a great example of knowing your history of a war torn country before you set foot in it. To all reading this book, knowing your basic history of all your countries of operation could save your life, it did mine many times...The spark that ignited the war occurred in Beirut on April 13,1975, when gunmen killed four Phalangists during an attempt on Pierre Jumayyil's life. Perhaps believing the assassins to have been Palestinian, the Phalangists retaliated later that day by attacking a bus carrying Palestinian passengers across a Christian neighborhood, killing about twenty-six of the occupants. The next day fighting erupted in earnest, with Phalangists pitted against Palestinian militiamen (thought by some observers to be from the Popular Front for the Liberation of Palestine). The confessional layout of Beirut's various quarters facilitated random killing. Most Beirutis stayed inside their homes during these early days of battle and few imagined that the street fighting they were witnessing was the beginning of a war that was to devastate their city and divide the country.

American University Beirut, Lebanon

Despite the urgent need to control the fighting, the political machinery of the government became paralyzed over the next few months. The inadequacies of the political system, which the 1943 National Pact had only papered over temporarily, reappeared more clearly than ever. For many observers, at the bottom of the conflict was the issue of confessionalism out of balance of a minority, specifically the Maronites, refusing to share power and economic opportunity with the Muslim majority. The government could not act effectively because leaders were unable to agree on whether or not to use the army to stop the bloodletting. When Jumblatt and his leftist supporters tried to isolate the Phalangists politically, other Christian sects rallied to Jumayyil's camp, creating a further rift. Consequently, in May Prime Minister Rashid as Sulh and his cabinet resigned, and a new government was formed under Rashid Karami. Although there were many calls for his resignation, President Franjiyah steadfastly retained his office. As various other groups took sides, the fighting spread to other areas of the country, forcing residents in towns with mixed sectarian populations to seek safety in regions where their sect was dominant. Even so, the militias became embroiled in a pattern of attack followed by retaliation, including acts against uninvolved civilians. Although the two warring factions were often characterised as Christian versus Muslim, their individual composition was far more complex. Those in favour of maintaining the status quo came to be known as the Lebanese Front. The groups included primarily the Maronite militias of the Jumayyil, Shamun, and Franjiyah clans, often led by the sons of *zuama*. Also in this camp were various militias of Maronite religious orders. The side seeking change, usually referred to as the Lebanese National Movement, was far less cohesive and organised. For the most part it was led by Kamal Jumblatt and included a variety of militias from leftist organisations and guerrillas from rejectionist Palestinian (non-mainstream PLO) organisations. By the end of 1975, no side held a decisive military advantage, but it was generally acknowledged that the Lebanese Front had done less well than expected against the disorganised Lebanese National Movement. The political hierarchy, composed of the old *zuama* and politicians, still was incapable of maintaining peace, except for occasional, short-lived cease-fires. Reform was discussed, but little headway was made toward any significant improvements. Syria, which was deeply concerned about the flow of events in Lebanon, also proved powerless to enforce calm through diplomatic means. And, most ominous of all, the Lebanese Army, which generally had stayed out of the strife, began to show signs of factionalizing and threatened to bring its heavy weaponry to bear on the conflict.

Syrian diplomatic involvement grew during 1976, but it had little success in restoring order in the first half of the year. In January it organised a cease-fire and set up the High Military Committee, through which it negotiated with all sides. These negotiations, however, were complicated by other events, especially Lebanese Front-Palestinian confrontations. That month the Lebanese Front began a siege of Tall Zatar, a densely populated Palestinian refugee camp in East Beirut; the Lebanese Front also overran and levelled Karantina, a Muslim quarter in East Beirut. These actions finally brought the main forces of the PLO, the Palestine Liberation Army (PLA), into the battle. Together, the PLA and the Lebanese National Movement took the town of Ad Damur, a Shamun stronghold about seventeen kilometres south of Beirut. In spite of these setbacks, through Syria's good offices, compromises were achieved. On February 14, 1976, in what was considered a political breakthrough, Syria helped negotiate a seventeen-point reform program known as the Constitutional Document. Yet by March this progress was derailed by the disintegration of the Lebanese Army. In that month dissident Muslim troops, led by Lieutenant Ahmad Khatib, mutinied, creating the Lebanese Arab Army. Joining the Lebanese National Movement, they made significant penetrations into Christian-held Beirut and launched an attack on the presidential palace, forcing Franjiyah to flee to Mount Lebanon. Continuing its search for a domestic political settlement to the war, in May the Chamber of Deputies elected Ilyas Sarkis to take over as president when Franjiyah's term expired in September. But Sarkis had strong backing from Syria and, as a consequence, was unacceptable to Jumblatt, who was known to be antipathetic to Syrian president Hafiz al Assad and who insisted on a "military solution." Accordingly, the Lebanese National Movement successfully pressed assaults on Mount Lebanon and other Christian-controlled areas. As Lebanese Front fortunes declined, two outcomes seemed likely: the establishment in Mount Lebanon of an independent Christian state, viewed as a "second Israel" by some; or, if the Lebanese National Movement won the war, the creation of a radical, hostile state on Syria's western border. Neither of these possibilities was viewed as acceptable to Assad. To prevent either scenario, at the end of May 1976 Syria intervened militarily against the Lebanese National Movement, hoping to end the fighting swiftly. This decision, however, proved ill conceived, as Syrian forces met heavy resistance and suffered many casualties. Moreover, by entering the conflict on the Christian side Syria provoked outrage from much of the Arab world.

Despite, or perhaps as a result of, these military and diplomatic failures, in late July Syria decided to quell the resistance. A drive was launched against Lebanese National Movement strongholds that was far more successful than earlier battles; within two weeks the opposition was almost subdued. Rather than crush the resistance altogether, at this time Syria chose to participate in an Arab peace conference held in Riyadh, Saudi Arabia, on October 16, 1976.

Israeli-Palestinian fighting in July 1981 was ended by a cease-fire arranged by U.S. President Ronald Reagan's special envoy, Philip C. Habib, and announced on July 24, 1981. The cease-fire was respected during the next 10 months, but a string of incidents, including PLO rocket attacks on northern Israel, led to the June 6, 1982, Israeli ground attack into Lebanon to remove PLO forces. Israeli forces moved quickly through south Lebanon, encircling west Beirut by mid-June and beginning a three-month siege of Palestinian and Syrian forces in the city.

 Throughout this period, which saw heavy Israeli air, naval, and artillery bombardments of west Beirut, Ambassador Habib worked to arrange a settlement. In August, he was successful in bringing about an agreement for the evacuation of Syrian troops and PLO fighters from Beirut. The agreement also provided for the deployment of a three-nation Multinational Force (MNF) during the period of the evacuation, and by late August, U.S. Marines, as well as French and Italian units, had arrived in Beirut. When the evacuation ended, these units departed. The U.S. Marines left on September 10. In spite of the invasion, the Lebanese political process continued to function, and Bashir Gemayel (see pic) was elected President in August, succeeding Elias Sarkis. On September 14, however, Bashir Gemayel was assassinated. On September 15, Israeli troops entered west Beirut. During the next three days, Lebanese militiamen massacred hundreds of Palestinian civilians in the Sabra and Shatila refugee camps in west Beirut. (Some of the text above is from my friends book, Pity the Nation by Robert Fisk) a must read for an in depth understanding of Lebanon.

Down Town Beirut City   Catholic Church Beirut City

Lebanon Today

Civil war erupted in Lebanon in 1975, largely the result of tensions between religious groups, worsened by the influx of Palestinians. Each group in Lebanon had its' own soldiers. But now Lebanon has made progress toward rebuilding its political institutions and regaining its national sovereignty since the end of the devastating 16-year civil war in October 1990. Under the Taif accord - the blueprint for national reconciliation - the Lebanese have established a more equitable political system, particularly by giving Muslims a greater say in the political process.Since December 1990, the Lebanese have formed three cabinets and conducted the first legislative election in 20 years. Most of the militias have been weakened or disbanded.

The Lebanese Armed Forces (LAF) has seized vast quantities of weapons used by the militias during the war and extended central government authority over about one-half of the country.
Hizballah retains most of its weapons. Foreign forces still occupy areas of Lebanon. Israel maintains

troops in southern Lebanon and continues to support a proxy militia, The Army of South Lebanon (ASL), along a narrow stretch of territory contiguous to its border. The ASL's enclave encompasses this self-declared security zone and about 20 kilometres north to the strategic town of Jazzine.

As of December 1993, Syria maintained about 30,000-35,000 troops in Lebanon. These troops are based mainly in Beirut, North Lebanon, and the BekaaValley. Syria's deployment was legitimized by the Arab League early in Lebanon's civil war and in the Taif accord. Citing the continued weakness of the LAF, Beirut's requests, and failure of the Lebanese Government to implement all of the constitutional reforms in the Taif accord.In 2005 Damascus withdraw its troops from Beirut.

I had flown into Beirut from London Heathrow. My No. 2, (seconded in command), in Lebanon, 'Chief,' picked me up at the airport in his Black Range Rover with a big beaming smile on his face, the job had begun. After a quick stop off at the virgin mega store down town Beirut, to pick up some CDs, we were on route to the safe house. Our safe housewas located in the northern mountains of Lebanon overlooking the Mediterranean Sea, (Hezbollah terrorists country) were the dominate force in this area.We would go totally unnoticed up here. It was dark when we pulled up outside the safe house, it was an eerie sight, surrounded by dark broken bombed out buildings, shutters hanging from broken windows, no light other than a bare bulb and the ghost like glimmer from the cities distant lights below us on the mountain. On entering again the safety of this old building, memories came flooding back of voices and passed missions, I reflected for a moment. Faint light from outside was reflecting off the dusty clear plastic which covered the rooms furnishings, dust filled the air as I pulled the plastic off a large round table which was to become our map table. The team carried all the bags and equipment into the safe house. I moved alone outside, in the quiet of the evening, as I stood on the shadowy bullet riddled balcony looking out to sea, a moment of reality passed. The past two weeks had been a constant go and this was the first time I had stopped to reflect upon the task at hand. The reality of planning and executing a civilian Special Forces operation hit me and would soon be rammed home to all involved. Then I heard the rustling of more plastic,Sharpie had pulled the plastic dust sheets from the other large tables, he was moving around the tables setting out maps andgoing over notes, maps locations and the final details of the task.The team worked well together, we all paid attention to detail. A little wooden log burner was lit in one room to give us all some warmth during the night. No bright lights, I wanted our presence here kept to a minimum. I only allowed the small fire due to me knowing that the area was safe, but even then I was always careful. Past experience had always made me think and plan, "expect the worse, when you're least expecting it..."

Military Intelligence, Green light

An Intel report had come in over the wire, it was an update, from London, It was March 20th 2003, it contained the following. At 1930hrs local Iraq time, five MC-130 "Combat Talon" transport planes from the US. Air Force's 352nd Special Operations Group had lifted off from a runway in Constanta, Romania. The first three specially modified transport planes held members of the 10th SFG, (A), the last two were loaded with members of the 3rd Battalion, SFG (A). All were now part of the same task force, the "Combined Joint Special Operations Task force-North, " or CJSOTF-N. For security the planes split into two groups and flew different routes. The first three Talons flew a tedious, low-level, three and a half hour rout, nicknamed "Ugly Baby",north along the Syrian-Iraq border before banking east and into the northern tip of Iraq. The three planes were cross-loaded with half of the members of five ODAs (Operational Detachment Alpha or A-teams) on each plan, and half of a B-Team, or ODB, on each plan, along with the B-Teams communication augmentation and equipment. Altogether, there were about sixty A-team operatives and fourteen to sixteen B-Team members. If one of the birds went down, only part of each A-Team and a part of the B-Team would be lost. This was standard SF SOP, (standard Operating Procedure).CJSOTF-N was code-name Task Force Viking. Their motto was "concede nothing". They would live up to their name in the weeks to come. One of the transport planes was seriously hit by Iraqi AAA, "Anti Aircraft Battery", so it turned from Syria airspace, over Sinja mountain range, northern western Iraq over forty holes and gashes where in the fuselage, the aircraft had to divert from the mission and make an emergency landing at an airfield in Turkey, luckily there were no fatalities on board. This was the start of the major side and deployment of SF Task force in Northern Iraq.

This report confirmed other timings and that the US and British military were starting their major operations inside Iraq. Coalition forces SF were already on the ground in Iraqand had been for some time. This latest deployment meant that a major military push was just days away.Sharpie looked at me "We're at the point of no return, mate. The coalitions military war machine was now in full swing, "from the Intel reports I was getting at regular intervals, it was obvious that they were now committed to the invasion and removal of Saddam's regime, "Failure for us was not an option."I'm on it, all was in hand, I had planned all to this point with surgical precision, I told him, let's leave it for the night, it was getting on to 4am in the morning, time to get head down."Sharpie is a man who works till the job is done and is very loyal, larger than life, with a colourful background, he is a very measured man. I am lucky enough to be able to call this man a close goodfriend". We both smiled and I pulled out a sleeping bag. "Looks like you get the flea-infested blanket tonight." We laid back on our beds talking, then out of nowhere a large chunk of plaster and paint came down off the ceiling, it landed on sharpie chest, he jumped up with a string of words... and looked over at me, I just burst out laughing he has covered in yellow dust like paint, his expression was not amused, which made it even funnier, fuck it was funny... he stood up and brushed himself off and laid down again, I thought it best that I didn't wind him up, the room and outside was dead silence, then after about a minute he started to laugh. Good job really because about 20 second later it happened again, the laughing stopped and the air went blue, I had to sit up because I was laughing so hard, sharpie shouted out do you think it's funny, I waited then answered fuck "ya". After awhile he settled down and the rest of the night went without incident. The next day I drove into Beirut, a contact of mine had arranged a meeting for me in the Iraq Embassy, I was to meet the Iraq ambassador to Lebanon.Nabil Abdullah al-janabi and his aides. It was more of a meet and greet, my contact was very well respected and he thought that my knowing them now could help me in the future. He was so right...

On arrival at the Iraq embassy my contact and friend was greeted warmly, people were shaking his hand,and asking how he was. "my friend was an old war hero of the Lebanese civil war", he was respected and known where ever he went in Lebanon. We were respectively ushered into an office and asked to please take a seat. There was a large old solid wooden desk, and behind it hanging on the wall was an oldeerie black and white framed photograph of Saddam Hussein, in military uniform. I looked at it for awhile, the moment felt a little surreal.We talked and took tea "chai" the ambassadorNabil Abdullah al-janabi and histop aidescame in, after warm greetings I was introduced. Theywere keen to know my thoughts on the US and the war that was about to happen, these people actually thought that the war was not going to happen, what planet were they living on. They had total blind faith in their leader Saddam Hussien. This was to be theircountries' undoing. The ambassadors aids told me that all the visasI required would be done and they would ring me when I could pick them up. My thoughts were to use my local contacts to pick up the visas (You don't walk into an enemy house twice for tea!). We said thank you, gave ourfarewells and left. What surprised me was the Iraq Embassy was running as normal, no sign of unease, even though their country was on the brink of war. The remaining team member flow into Beirut.Sharpie returned to Cyprus to lead up the 24hr manningof the Operations room. My contacts in Syria and military were kept upto speed, the mission was moving forward and "H" hrs was approaching. Adam was looking a littlenerves and apprehensive, I looked at him, I asked him "are you cool", he answered, always. I told the boys to have a few hours down time, try and rest, have some food and water pipe, but stay in contact just in case we get a fast ball and have to move out quickly. Everything that needed to be done had been done, all vehicles and equipment had been serviced, checked and double checked. I went for a walk with Adam, down to Batron High Street. On the way we passed an old women dressed in traditional Lebanese clothing, she was cooking bread in the outside oven of her little ran down one bed room house. In a lot of the countries of the Middle East, bread and food are cooked and prepared in an outside oven area. We made our way to a little known café just off the high street, I liked it here, away from prying eyes, a place where only the locals used for their morning coffee. By now it was late in the afternoon, the café only had one old man sat in the corner, reading the Lebanese Daily Star newspaper and puffing on a well-used water pipe, the smell of the "tufa" apple tobacco was prominent, it smelled good.I ordered two glasses of white arak, which is an aniseed alcohol drink which is served in a little glass, with a splash of water. I knew that this café had its own still out the back to make itsown arak, abit like the old moonshine and speakeasies of America. I told Adam to drink it, this would chill him out, it worked well. I offered him one of my Montecristo No 3 cigars, he reached over the table accepting one. After lighting it, he puffed on it afew times and you could tell he was enjoying it, I ask if he was enjoying that mighty fine cigar there, he answered, "ya", I said good "it could be your last"... Adam froze nearly chocking for a split second, he looked over at me, calling me a Bas***** we both laughed, that one liner would stay with us both for a very long time.We sat talking about Lebanon and the history, culture of the Middle East. The conversation turned towards, Samarkand, the Sec of the Assassins, I had studied a lot of the history and politics of the Middle East, to understand the present, you need to look into their history and the rich culture of these people, their day to day mentality is very different to ours in the west, once you understand this, you can only start to understand the people and their old school ways.Adam had set a meeting up for me to meet Maria Coburn another journalist for the Sunday Times. Maria was spending alot of time in Iraq, Bagdad and was concerned about her and friends safety in Baghdad once the war started. I had extracted VIPs and persons of interest from war zones in the past and the Sunday Times wanted me to setup and put a plan to extract Maria from Iraq, Baghdad if it became toodangerous for her. Danger never stopped Maria doing her job, she was one of the best journalists I had ever met, she was very matter of fact and straight to the point. She loved her work. Maria was a veteran of wars in Iraq, Chechnya, Sierra Leone and Kosovo. She lost her eye to a grenade attack in Sri Lanka. She was named Best Foreign Correspondent twice at the British Awards and won the Foreign Press Association's Journalist of the Year award. I considered it an honor to be asked and trusted with her safety, it was the eve of the Iraq war. We met in Beirut for morning tea the next day. Maria told me her plan and the stories that she was going after in Baghdad. I just sat and listened, she asked my personal opinion about a few points, then exchanged notes. We put a plan in place if she needed to be extracted from Baghdad, if it happened it would be a "hot extraction". RV points were agreed west of Baghdad. We exchanged sat-phone numbers and I said to Maria I am on the end of a phone if you need me. We left the meeting at that.We would speak on the phone but that would be the last time I would ever see Maria Colvin alive again... Maria went to the airport and flew back into Baghdad that afternoon. That afternoon I also meet Jon Swain, the celebrated foreign correspondent immortalized in the film The Killing Fields, Jon had been with the Sunday Times for 35 years' service. Jon Swain, whose real life experiences were portrayed by Julian Sands in the Oscar winning 1984 film, was a legend. Little did he know, but Jon was one of my inspirations in my taking up photography and my publishing my own Combat Photography Book "Honour Bound the Photography Collection" in the future. The Sunday Times had asked me to meet Jon and give him an update on Intelligence and the fast changing situation on the ground across Iraq. I agreed and met Jon Swain in his room at the world famous Phoenicia Hotel, Beirut. Time was ticking on so I made this a quick meeting with Jon. I gave him an update on the ever changing situation on the ground, showed him some military maps and pointed out the areas of interest in South Western Iraq. We talked briefly about Saddam and his torture chambers, Chemical weapons and HVTs High Value Targets... Jon asked my opinion on afew subjects. After a good all round informative meeting we shook hands and with a stay safe I left the luxury of the hotel and discreetly headed north back to my mountain safe house in Hezbollah ran territory.

Marie Colvin & Remi Ochlik Died Homs, Syria, February 2012 . Colvin, of the Sunday Times, and Remi Ochlik, a French photographer, were killed by rocket fire in the besieged city of Homs, Syria.

I spent the rest of the day checking on my personal kit... I was cut short by a phone call, all hell was about to break loose, it was Rox, my intelligence officer on the other end of the phone...

Compromised

"A drop of water fell into the sea.

Aspeck of dust came floating down to earth.

What signifies your passage through this world?

A tiny gnat appears – and disappears."(Omar Khayyam)

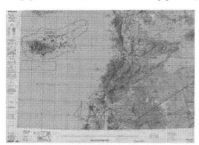

All was going too smoothly. Our intelligence was so good we had the timings of the first coalition air strikes going into Iraq. The first warning flags went up when Rox, in London, began hearing reports of a special operation team in Lebanon, planning to go into Iraq as the war started. The rumour had also gotten to the Lebanese, Syrian and Iraqi security services. We had a leak, butwhom? Initial security checks on all the team members had come up clean. I fired local names back to one of our friendly call signs who was senior in the intelligence community, I asked him to dig deep. An answer came back within hours; one of our team members had an international black market arms dealer,with extensive Middle Eastern connections gunning for him, (later we found out that this was also a former member of MI6). When our visa request was faxed to Baghdad, one name on the list was highlighted and marked as a spy. The entire team was then compromised. All three authorities in our operational area had our operational namesand were told to arrest and detain us on sight. Within six hours, we were receiving calls from multiple sources advising us to abort, extract by boat, keep clear of airports and return to a safe country, the entire mission had been red flagged. Unexpectedly the following events would dramatically shape the next ten yearsof my life and change my strong personal views and challenge my deepest beliefs... The War on Terror was about to become personal.

Against the odds

"Use your enemy's weight to bring him down.
Hind amongst his hordes.
Strike your enemy, put fear in his heart, and then melt away."
(Gengus Karne)

Time to reassess the operation. Conference calls were held and all parties made aware of the situation. At this point, the Sunday Times decided to officially terminate the operation and stand the team down. Unofficially the Sunday Times still supported us with logisticsand I was told to continue.The safety of their personnel was of paramount concern and Adam was quickly taken and flownback to the UK. Adam was panicking as a friendly call sign dropped him off at the main airport on the out skirts of Beirut, my intelligence sources had told me to fly him out within 2hrs and he would be ok, then the window would be closed for him. He made it to Beirut's main airport, in just over an hour he called me from the toilet of the plane, he was taking the long way back to London, just to be safe. He sounded so relived to be on the plane, he rang me again when he was in the air (Adamwas out and safe).

"Failure is not an option."

"What candles may be held to speed them all?
Not in the hands of boys, but in their eyes
Shall shine the holy glimmers of good-byes." (WILFRED OWEN) "Anthem for Doomed Youth"

"Failure is not an option." Sharpie's words echoed through my head. I could not let this go, not in the final moments, not after coming so far. I made the command decision to stand down most of the team and all the Lebanese friendly call signs, only the communication relay stations were kept on line, I continue on my own. I contacted the rest of the international contacts and my intelligence officer by conference call, briefed them on the situation and asked for volunteers, "I kept my old international contacts separate to the rest of my Lebanese team, looked like my security measures paid off this time". I was told later that the boys looked around at each otherduring the conference call, I had backed my boys play many times in the past, no matter what. Now was their time to back my play. Their loyalty was second to none. I had passed my "Para Reg", Parachute Regiment training, (Britain's Elite Airborne Forces) with most of these guys, the few that were not from the UK were from SA, South

Africa, I had worked the most dangerous combat zones across the African continent, Nigeria, Sierra Leone, Angola, I had fought side by side with them, trust was not a question with these guys,we were like blood brothers, (brothers in arms), the harder it was the more they wanted to have ago and soldier on, regardless of the risks. As I had hoped, everyone was on board. As one voice after the other echoed down the speaker phone line"we're in, what do you need" all was now in place, secondary specialist equipment was now en-route to my new RV, points in Syria. I had to assume that my original plan and RV points had been compromised so I changed all locations. Friendly call signs were being briefed on my immediate needs and my ETA into Syria. I filled then in on the details, new plan of action and the overview of the situation. The enemies security services, (Iraq and Syria) were looking, for a group of four man,foreigners, travelling in two vehicles. The enemy's security services would not be looking for a lone male student, travelling by himself, touring archaeological sites... This was defiantly a "doable plan". I had always kept my Hum-Int network, intelligence connections and contacts completely separate from all other areas of anytask or mission, operation. Everyone was on a need to know. I always kept it like this, from past experience, good Op-Sec Operational Security had kept me alive; "I always hold an ace card". This was to be proved very important after one of the Lebanese team members was picked up and interrogated by the notorious Syrian/Lebanese Security Services, he had just told them enough to stop them beating and torturing himanymore with an electric cattle prod, it did not matter, all my plans RV points and routes had changed and my local contact did not know enough to compromise me or my network.My International contacts had got him released and local contacts were now looking after him in another county.

En-RouteSyria

"Oh, what a tangled web we weave,
When first we practise to deceive!" Walter Scott, Marmion,VI, introduction, st. 17

A green light across the board on the mission went out, "we had a go", Sharpie changed my personal radio call sign to "lone wolf". I made a run for the Syrian border within an hour. If the security services were to find out I was on the move, the task would be finished before it began. I slipped by the sleepy border guards easily with my new ID, Lebanese passport and driving licence(a friendly c/sign had dropped them to me in Tripoli, Lebanon, en-route. I had ordered them the week before),I thought they would come in useful. Even the Syrian border guards who took an interest and wanted to look over my equipment, were dealt with quickly or should I say "US green backs", Mr Benjamin,

$100 bills, saved my ass more times than Nato, 5.56mm, (one thing in common with all low paid border guards all over the world, they're easy to bribe). I continued across northern Syria, Passed the château, Hamra, a city well known as a terrorist safe area, up and passed Aleppo after a quick stop at a safe house in Raqqa (To be future ISIS Capital) for chai/tea and kebab with a local friendly intelligence contact. "Places and locations in Syria I stayed and visited during operations and tasking included; Hadida, Snoon, Homs, Hama, Ldlib, Reyhanli, Aleppo, Azaz, Al Bab, Manbij, Kobane, Ain Issa, Suluk, Ar Raqqah (Future ISIS Capital City), Ratla, Madan, Deir ez Zur, Markadah, Aaloua, Al Hasakah, Al Mnajeer, Qamishli, Tel Hamees, Jaza, Al Haul, Al Maabadah, Rabia, Faysh Khabur, Al Mayadin, Al Bukamal, Palmyra (Tadmor), Jayrud, Damascus, Jdaidit Yabws, Merom Golan, Daraa, Nassib, Imtan."

I moved onto Al-Hasakah, 30KM from the Iraq border, then down to the area of Al-Hauland its village which over looked the notorious western border area of Iraq. Aided by night vision and excellent Intel coming in every Hour, I followed a small dirt smuggling path towards my RV Western area. Al-Hauleast area was my target, a small village not on the map. Darkness was setting in as I approached the village from the West, an uneasy feeling of being watched came over me.I pulled off the track about 2KM short of the village, climbed some high ground, observingthe village through my night vision, all seemed quiet, the village dogs were roaming around, the flickering of candle light from the windows of houses was just visible in the distance. The sight of a light in a certain window and the dogs at a certain place meant all was ok. My gut instinct told me all was ok.I stayed in position and watched quietly for another hour. Then moved back carefully to my 4x4, I stopped short and sat for 20min in darkness watching my 4x4 and the area around it just in case I had been made or located. As I pulled into the village square, I noticed a new British military Landrover parked next to an old wall and partly hidden under some old tarpaulin (cover from the air) I parked up behind it. This none descript village was the same as hundreds of villages I had passed though on travels across the Middle-East, four main mud brick building, with a hand full of smaller out buildings in turn partly surrounded by an old mud wall, some lazy nocturnal skinny chickenswere walking around and a donkey was in a fenced area to the side of one of the mud houses, these house are normally one big main room, people eat, sleep and live, all their worldly belongings are in this room in homemade wool bags hanging from rusty nails in the walls. A voice called out to me, a familiar voice puffing on a cigar, a thin tail dark figure was lent against the outside of one of the mud houses I moved closer "salaam aleikum", I answered "wa aleikum as-salaam" there was complete silence, the voice spoke again "you took your time getting here" it was a friendly voice from a long time ago. Stevey boy was an old friend, still kind of in the British SF side of things.

 Elite Team Member in Iraq

 He said his boys had seen me from their OP, Observation Post on the high ground about 2k away, overlooking the border area and the village they had radioed aheadon my ETA, (some things don't change). They knew it was me by the way I had moved and also watched the area. We moved inside, the room was dark and dingy, an old gasoline lantern was sitting on an old Iraqi army ammo create in the corner of the room, this gave the room ashadowy warm glow, the rough texture of the mud bricks that the building which made up the walls could be seen flickering in the dim light. As I walked into the room we were joined by the village elder, after shaking hands and formal greetings, the three of use sat on some cushions on the floor, which lay on some old red Persian carpet, Stevey informed me that this village was still a trusted safe place, they had been using it for the past four weeks, with no problems, they had been operating out of it using it as a forward operating base/post, no-one ever came out to the village, it was tooisolated, this put my mind at ease. A young boy came in with a plastic tray in his hands and an AK-47 slung over his back. On the tray were chai cups, little glass tumblers, the three of us drank chai, (tea), smoked Cuban cigars and talked about a variety of topics for about an hour.The old man got up and left the room, wishing us goodnight. I was then informed by Stevey that I had left in my wake, a trail of carnage, 3 country'ssecret service agents had been trying to find me, (apparently the head of the Syrian secret service was well pissed off, I had made him look like a "Muppet" (when I personally met him weeks later, he informed me that I was a hard man to catch).

Iraqi Border

"…war began, that is, an event took place opposed to human reason
and human nature. Millions of men perpetrated against one another
such innumerable crimes, frauds, treacheries, thefts…
incendiarisms, and murders, as in whole centuries are not recorded
in the annals of all the law courts of the world, but which those who
committed them did not at the time regard as being crimes".   Leo Tolstoy, War and Peace

My British friendly call/sign was an old friend from way back, he was a former member of 42 commando, he had also completed the rigours all arms "P" company,"Para company" and received his parachute wings at Brize Norton. We had also been together when presented our French parachute wings in southern France. He was a good man, who knew the score,with a lot of combat experience, one I could trust, he was very old school. I had bailed him out of major problems in Africa, when a unofficial mercenary job went belly up. Now it was my turn to call in an old favour (ace card)to help me out. I knew better than to ask him what he was doing here or who he worked for... whatever it was it was unofficial... Contrary to common belief, the British SF had multiple specialist teams working in the north West of Iraq working as part of the (activity) the old grey fox boys. Task force 121, a joint US and British Elite Task force "activity" This would later become "Task Force Black" in Iraq. Elite members picked from SF units and specialised teams, all team members have specialist skills ranging from multi lingual, to explosives and demolition, surveillance, and counter surveillance are also an important asset which most team members have.

Task force 121 and 626, as well as the British Task Force 7, had been set up to hunt down Saddam Hussein and Al Q terrorists. As well as high level targets around the Middle East. The SF teams in the background played a major part in the down fall of Saddam and the Baath party. I had been given the heads up on a rough idea of their A.O, "Area of operations" and an overview of what was going on. After a quickpersonal update on life, down to business, I showed him the areas of interest I was going after, he got his map out, this was a surreal moment, we didn't just have the same MOD maps, we had the same areas of interest and some of the same locations and away points saved in our GPS 12XLs, we looked at each other and smiled, he commented that my intelligence contacts were still as good and accurate as always. We compared notes, I took note of the other areas of where the other SF teams were operating, I thought it a wise idea to stay clear, I did not want a friendly fire incident. The British are good at not shooting at friendly call signs, the Americans were and still are the opposite. In the first gulf war the US military killed more British soldiers than the enemy in combat, in so called friendly fire incidents, when the American A10 (warthog), Tank buster military aircraft, opened fire on one of the British APC's, armoured personnel carrier,this is just one example.

My British Friendly call sign filled me in on what was happening along the Syrian border area, he and other SF teams had been monitoring a lot of trucks coming over the border from Iraq into Syria carrying a lot of things of interest, their orders were just to observe, he said at the rate that these trucks are moving every night, there will be not a lot left in Iraq. He was hinting that the trucks where full of military equipment, I asked how many trucks, he and his teams in OP's (observation posts), had countered 58 Trucks, with Iraqi and Syrian military markings just over the past 4 nights, the Syrian border guards don't even search them, they just let them straight through, every time, its organised at a high government level. Looks like the Government in Damascus is hiding a lot of Saddam's Military equipment. An interesting fact about all these truck convoys was that all the soldiers in the convoys spoke Russian!

In the future, Former US Deputy Undersecretary of Defense for International Technology Security John Shaw. Contended Syrian Chemical Weapons Iraq's Missing WMDs. A wide-scale smuggling operation of Iraqi chemical and biological weapons, together with related components, from Iraq to Syria took place in the weeks before the March 2003 US operation in Iraq. He detailed that the Russian "Spetsnaz" (Special Operation Forces) had organized large commercial truck convoys for CBW removal; whatever CBW was not buried in Iraq was put on those trucks and sent to the Syrian border. The goal of the clean-up was "to erase all traces of Russian involvement" in Iraqi CBW programs, and it "was a masterpiece of military camouflage and

deception." We were on the ground and witnesses to the above! What the Russians could not put on the back of trucks they buried large containers in Iraq and Syria. Fast forward to 2018! Some of these Battlefield Chemical Weapons have been used in Syria against Syrian Civilian and Kurdish targets by Hezbollah/Iran backed groups and Syrian military forces! The target packagers that Anthony Stephen Malone worked on with American Military Intelligence, included, some of these locations in and across Syria, Lebanon! (Interesting fact, Hezbollah Underground Bunkers in North Eastern Lebanon... What is in them, American $, Money, Iraqi Gold 200M$, Battlefield Chemical Weapons from Iraq and Syria!). Importent question, will Hezbollah use some of these Chemical Weapons against Israel and Western Targets in the future... Could these Battlefield Chemical Weapons be given to other terrorist groups by the Iranian backed, trained group Hezbollah! Importent Fact; Cyprus is 45 min away from lebanon in a boat!

Back to 2003,

The other area of major interest was the tunnel complexes under the Sinjar Mountain range, the SF boys had found a massive amount of weapons there, new SA7, Surface to Air missiles, military explosives, new AKS assault rifles, ammo, and new military communication equipment, with Jordon, and Saudi Arabia stamped on the side ofthe boxes. These kind of arms and equipment cashes where to pop up all over Northern Iraq. In return for his update I filled him in on all the IntelI had received from my London contacts. He looked at me surprised; when you're in the military, information always goes up the chain of command, to operational HQ, it is very rare that information comes down to the men on the ground. He asked what my plan was, using a pen I pointed to an area on the map, he smiled, he had heard rumours about the area that I was interested in, he told me that his Intel had informed him that this was an old army base, now it was disserted, I smiled, my intelligence says that it is of interest, he looked at me, "enlighten me", what I said next made him look puzzled, I informed him that some off Saddam's top scientists had been paid and helped by the British to get out of Iraq, and now were staying at the Golden Beach Hotel in Cyrus. He looked at me, how the fuck do you know that, I informed him that I had contacts at the base in Cyprus, this was the HQ for British military intelligence for the entire Middle East, he smiled, (he said retired in Cyprus my ass), Stevey boy smiled. Let's go and have a look, call it old fashioned curiosity. That makes two of us. As we were talking my sat-phone went off, an SMS had come in from London, it read " Tactical Military Air strike can be organised in front of your border location to neutralize enemy passions to facilitate movement, and help you cross safely", My friendly call sign back in London had been following my movements, via my operations room in Cyprus, he also had just spent time on board, and he was good friends with the Commander of the HMS Ark Royal, the British aircraft carrier, which was then situated in the Gulf. "this was being used as a forward Special Forces deployment base. This location was also my emergency medical helicopter evacuation plain. This was also my tactical pick up if I found High Level Targets, or information. I showed Stevey the message, he smiled and said that's handy, if we ever need a tactical air strike I know who to talk to. Officially I never met up with or spent time with any serving or former SF teams In Iraq or surrounding countries, this sort of thing is frowned upon by the British pencil pushers and red tape inventers back in London, unofficially this is how the British intelligence gain some of their most valuable information on the ground, military contractors, PMC are used all the time. "the door swings both ways" any idiot who says it doesn't is just naive or has their own hidden agenda! After a short talk about RV points and tactical plans, I was on my way with a parting voice saying, "remember you were never here", something I was growing accustomed to. I was in two worlds now, one being total deniability. I did not exist. The ultimate grey man "Expendable". We had agreed that I should make my way across the border alone, this was because the Syrian border was now the most monitored and military satellite "Falcon View" photographed area in the world. I fixed an inferred strobe to the bottom of my jeep, this could not be seen with the naked eye, only when observing it though specialised military night vision equipment can it be seen, the other SF teams in the area had been informed by radio that a lone friendly jeep was making its way across via a certain route. The strobe was to ID me, this was for pure safety, so a friendly SF sniper team would not engage and take me out. I would go across the border being lit up like a fucking Christmas tree lol that was so not tactical... But stopped me being shot by my own side.

It was time to go, 0200am, I made my way out of the village, and down the track towards the Iraq border, all the jeeps lights including victor 1 break lights were turned off, using a hidden switch under the dash board, using night vision to drive I pulled up 1KM short of the border, I could see the strobe flashing under the jeep as I moved on foot to the crest of the high ground. The silence that surrounded me was defying, not even the sound of wild dogs, which I had grown accustomed to, a penetrating nothing, dead silence, nothing there, just a big open space.To my front was a plan full of shadows. It was a bright star lit night, only the moon for company. I waited, watching for over 30mins, no movement, it was safe to cross. I moved back to Viktor 1 and moved slowly, coarsely over the border.I knew that there was a mine field to my left and right, a small track separated then, just big enough for a single truck to get across. I was on an old smuggling route that few knew about. I had seen this on past tasks and knew it was very much still in use, I just prayed I did not meet anyone or anything coming the other way, now that would have been emotional... 20 minutes later, I had crossed the border. Insertion successful, I had penetrated Iraq. I removed and turned the inferred strobe off. Time to get to work...

The Western Desert of Iraq "No Mans' Land"

"Far-called, our navies melt away;

On dune and headland sinks the fire:

Lo, all our pomp of yesterday

Is one with Nineveh and Tyre!"   Rudyard Kipling, from "Recessional"

Ten kilometres behind enemy lines, I hid emergency supplies in a ravine under some rocks, recording the GPS location, day sack with water, food, map,silvercompass, Spare weapon AR15 (The serial numbers had been filled off to stop identification, this was common practice with all my weapons in Iraq and Afghanistan) and a few boxes of ammo, spare ID documents,friendly country passports with $1000, etc, Rendezvous Point 1 (RV1) complete. If the worst were to happen and I was compromised or got ambushed,split from my friendly C/Signs, I would make my way back to this point. Daylight was breaking, time to find some cover and get my head down.(I had been on the go over 60 hrs without any real sleep), it is best and safer to travel at night in the desert and rest during the day. I found a culvert under some high ground, put the desert camouflage netting over the Victor call sign, set up an covered observation point (OP) and waited until dark before I moved out. That day went without incident, only the distant pounding of the Iraq republican guard could been heard and seen in the distance by coalition air strikes.

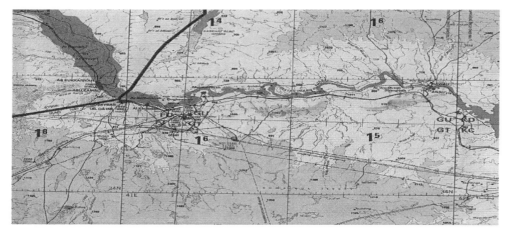

The western desert changed by night, it became an eerie silent shadowy plain. Before moving out, I checked the route aheadand found the area mostly flat, with approximately 10 to 15 kilometres visibility in front. I moved out up to the RV point where I was to meet up with my friendly C/Sign, we had exchanged Intel and found that we were both now interested and heading for the same target, so I tagged along with the team. A flicker of light on the horizon drew my attention. I checked navigational bearings and realised that the light had come from the direction of one of my target locations. The location, an old underground military complex, had been reported abandoned by Iraqi authorities. My Intel told me otherwise and the lights seemed to confirm that suspicion. I made my way to RV 2,I briefed by friendly C/Signs on all I had seen, they had five hrs to kill before they had to be anywhere, "what the hell, we were all queries" I left my Victor One at RV2 as did my friendly call signsand we moved forward on foot to observe. "Five of us were in the team at this point". On observing the activity to my front, the count was five enemy soft skinned vehicles and about 20 troops armed with AK-47s and 3 PKMs. The troops were scattered around an open space between three buildings, some casually chatting around a fire built in an old oil drum, others sleeping inside or under vehicles or open structures. To our amazement there was no sentry post and no one on watch. We set up an OP in a small ravine and observed the enemy for about 60 minutes. We moved a full 360 degrees around their location. (CTR),"close target recce". They had no tanks, armoured vehicles or heavyweaponry. It looked like a platoon strength group, but what were they doing there? What where they guarding?

The silence was suddenly broken by the booming thunder of air strikes about 5km away. The camp became a buzz of activity, bodies running in every direction. Instantly, we had an excellent diversion enabling us to take a closer look at the base and buildings within. We moved quickly on the target as the air strikes got closer. Two friendly call signs approached the closest building while threeheld watch from the high ground. We had our com's headsets, to alert us of any danger moving towards us, but with all of the confusion, it was not hard to slip into the base undetected.

Upon entering the building, we immediately realised that we were at an entry point to a major underground complex. We swept and cleared the surface rooms from left to right finding boxes of documents, maps on the walls, Saddam Hussein'scalendar and two very old computers. The towers of the computers were opened, hard drives extracted and placed in the day sack with all of the files to be examined at a later date. We moved deeper into the complex, following a hallway to a small stairwell, our entry to the below level facility. As we descended, we could hear the ruffled sound of human movement. It was coming from behind a set of massive red rusty steel doors lying at the end of a long corridor large enough to fit a vehicle. As we moved forward, we could hear the muffled sound of a generator, we observed conventional Russian made short-ranged, multi-rocket systems standing inside large Air shafts that went up to the surface. The weapons were surrounded by boxes marked with a red triangle with a circle in the middle indicating chemical weapons. To the left of the boxers where a pile of long green hardened plastic boxers, marked with black stencilling in English, Surface to Air

Missiles, (See Photographs) "what the hell had we walked into?!" Large green boxes of new anti-personnel and anti-tank mines were stacked high in another room. I noticed the stamps on the side of some other wooden creates, "Saudi-Arabia and China".Other boxes had France stamped on the side. It was ever clear that many countries had been breaking UN Sanctions by supplying Saddam's Military with Arms and explosives. I would later find a warehouse south of Mosul city, full of aircraft and "new" anti-tank missiles also from France and other countries... At this point, a thundering explosion shook us, all power went out, the air filled with dust and survival instinct kicked in. We made our way back to the surface, all hell was breaking loose and we were caught in the middle of it. The republican Guard located 4KM away was being attacked by several US apache helicopter gunships. Rockets and 30 calibre tracer rounds were filling the sky, going off in all directions and the air strikes by the coalition fighter aircraft were coming in too close for comfort. (I was to find out latter that what started this immense firelight was that a British SAS team had been mistakenly dropped off by Chinook helicopters, right in the middle of the republican guards position by accident and all hell had broken lose). The British Special Forces team had been in such a rush to get back onto their helicopter, they had left most their specialist equipment behind, including; a jeep, quad bike, surface to air, anti-tank missile and a laptop!!!! I would speak to my good American friend and Brother in Arms, Colonel Michael Lennington at a later date about this, when he recovered them from the locals and I helped to return the Laptop which was "Top Secret" to the British Government (This caused great embarrassment to the British Government given the fact that all this equipment had been destroyed by an airstrike!!).But at least it did not fall into enemy hands! Theorder cameover the coms for all team members to pull back immediately to RV2 via the same entry routes. As the team withdrew, I brought up the rear with the evidence, paper work, computer hard drives in my day sack on my back. I stopped briefly to pan my camcorderaround, I was stood in the middle of the best fire work show on the planet, also the most deadly. Then a group of Iraqis soldiers appeared out of nowhere. I hit the ground as the others moved out. The Iraqis advanced. The RV point lay less than a kilometre away, if the Iraqis made it over the skyline, the team would be in full view across the flat ground. Sitting ducks, waiting for slaughter.

I broke cover, firing a bust of Automatic AK-47 fire into the area off the Iraqis soldiers, I got their undivided attention;they wildly returned fire, they followed me. Moving quickly south, away from the rest of the team and RV point. My plan was to circle backroundlater.A message came over the coms, the team was now safe, what was my "sit-rep"I thought, pretty fucked, I answered OK, I'll touch base latter, I am heading off by myself. "Good luck, Stay Safe" come over the coms. I observed the area, unable to get back to Victor 1, and RV 2. my friendly C/Signshadnow escaped and were headingtowards the Syrian border area, they had been re-tasked. They had been ordered to move to another enemy location to help another British military patrol who had come into contact with the enemy. "Most of the official intelligence that the British SF were getting about enemy positions on the ground was bad". (The fact that multiple Special Forces teams were being dropped in the middle of enemy forces locations, that were supposed to be clear... proves my point!) The dim light was filled with flashers from the muzzles off weapons, the air was filled with the smell of cordite. "this occurs when hundreds of rounds of ammunition are fired in the same area".

Gunships on Mission.

The red hot empty brass casings were falling like rain,bouncing off burning enemy vehicles, from the US Apache helicopter gunships (Above) flying overhead, they were firing bursts from their .30 milometer cannon with deadly aggression into Iraq enemy positions. Amongst all the chaos and activity, I moved quickly and quietly over the terrain, a sole individual trained to take advantage of confusion and obtain a few crucial minutes to evade and escape. "This is when your training takes over" and the real sense of urgency sets in.Lady Luck provided me with an assault rifle to my front,I knelt down on one knee and extracted the magazine from the weapon, I checked the magazine, it was full, I placed it in my side pocket, "always acquire extra ammo when you can", the last thing you ever need is a dead man's click, "when you run out of ammo" "where are friends and bullets when you need them lol".I continued through the outskirts of the camp. Suddenly, a tremendous explosion and fire ball went up behind me to my left, "fuck I thought, there goes Victor 1", now I am on foot, suddenly a force from nowhere sent me hurling back into a pile of rocks and knocked the wind out of me. A split second went by before I realised what had happened. "I had just been shot""definitely having a bad day".

I took a quick look around and saw nothing. There was shouting in Arabic directly in front of me, time was of the essence. I tried to move to my feet, but a sharp pain crippled me. The rounds had hit my chest. I put my hand inside my vest, Luckily the rounds had not gone though, there was no blood; my Kevlar vest had stopped it from penetrating. The voices were getting closer; I had to get out of there. I put down cover fire and moved away as fast as possible. The day sack weighed heavily on my back and was slowing me down. I knew I had to stash it to get away with my life, so I moved down a ravine until I came across a small, cave-like hole in the ground only about two feet wide, another gift from Lady Luck. Without a second thought, I shoved the day sack and Kevlar vest in and took the GPS location. The vest was heavy, so no need for it, I needed to move low and fast!

"Time to get out of Dodge city". The pain at this point was severe, but the only thing to do was to soldier on and keep pushing forward. All the talk of no pain no gain, and pain is all in the mind, is bullocks, if you're in pain you know it. I made my way to the crossroads on the map, 10km south, using my silver compass.Tabbing, making my way cross country, diving for cover every time anapproaching vehicles' head lights swiped across the desert's floor, the night sky was lit up with red and green tracer, fire fights where going off in all directions, burning oil wells where lighting up the horizon. A few hours later I arrived at the cross roads.There was an array of buildings on the right hand side and what looked like a truck or van sitting outside. I quietly made my way forward, to my amazement, the keys were in the ignition. The buildings seemed to be deserted, It look like it was being used for cross border smuggling, with all the fighting going on everyone seem to have gone or were in hiding.I left $500, under a rock, next to the doorway, (the old battered rusty pickup, with no glass in the windows was worth that), I checked the rear view mirror as I drove toward the Syrian border expecting hostiles, but no-one emerged. My concern now was, did I have sufficient fuel to get me over the Syrian border. The area of the Syrian border was disserted, no one was in sight, no sounds, no dust from approaching vehicles or anything, it seemed very eerie, surreal. I made my way forward and crossed over the Syrian border illegally again.

Injured and in hostile Syria

About 30km inside of Syria I left the truck under a bridge outside a small village and waited using some rocks as cover, I patiently watched and waited for one off the small local vans which the locals use as a bus to come alone, you can spot these along way off, they normally play loud Arabic chart music, have Christmas decorations covering the front windscreen, and dash board with flashing lights. One approached, I flagged it down at the side of the road, it pulled up in front of me, with a cloud of desert dust flowing it. The side door opened, a volley of voices fired out at me, "Salam Malakcum"I answered "Malakcue Al Salam, "Aleppo"""Ner"I got in, passed $2 forward, the driver smiled at me, he was happy with this, I was on my way to Aleppo, with two chickens, six people and a goat to keep me company, I was wearing my brown Arabic clothing and head dress, it was not clean but helped me to blend in. The bus interior was some sort of surreal Christmas card, full of old people, animals and adorned with lights and tacky decorations. I sat back in my seat and sighed, "Whatever happened to a two week job?". All my extensive training and people telling me,"no pain, no gain", and "mind over matter". When you're injured and in a lot of pain it goes out the window, you're just left... with "pain". I took a careful account of my body before drifting off to sleep. The pain in my stomach was intense, but I would survive.

The bus stopped only once for about ten minutes, I got off, went to the outside toilet.I called the Ops room on my satphone, letting them know I was alive and well. I could not get through, my sat phone was playing up on me. I found out later while spending time with the US Special Forces Task force, (Pathfinders, 101st Airborne), that they had electronic counter measures on top of Sinjar mountain, these where responsible for disrupting all communications and GPS's in the area, (the GPS where reading totally wrong locations, some were 40KM out, the US did not change the counter measures until several weeks later).Seven hours later after passing through several dusty towns and across a river, I arrived in Aleppo.

Aleppo (Halab)

An Example of a Burqa, worn by alot of Middle-East women in Aleppo

Aleppo going back to the early 2nd millennium BC, competes with Damascus on being the oldest inhabited city in the world. It appeared in the Hittite archives in central Anatolia and in the archives of Mari on the Euphrates. Aleppo (Halab) was the capital of the Amorite kingdom of Yamkhad, in the middle centuries of that millennium. It was the focus of the Hittites in their overthrow of the Amorite Dynasty, in 1595 BC. In about 1000 BC, Northern Syria was taken over by the Sea Peoples; however Aleppo remained a small Neo-Hittite state. From 800 BC to 400 BC, the Assyrians followed by the Persians were in control of Syria. In 333 BC, Aleppo was taken over by Alexander the Great, and was kept under the Greeks for 300 years in the form of the Seleucid Empire. During this time Aleppo was an important trading city, between the Euphrates and Antioch.

In 64 BC Pompey brought Syria under Roman domination. It remained under Roman control in the form of the Byzantine Empire until 637AD, when the Arabs took over. In the 10th century Aleppo was taken over by the Hamdanids who made it virtually independent until 962 AD when it was retaken by the Byzantine Empire. In 1098, it was circled by soldiers from the First Crusade who could not conquer it, but paralyzed its commercial power. It was besieged again in 1124 by another Crusade, and then taken over by Zengi and his successor Nur al Din. Saladin then took over and at his death the Ayyubid dynasty was perpetuated in Aleppo. At the Mameluke period, trade was diverted from Aleppo to the North in Antioch and to the South through Palmyra.But when the Mongol Empire broke up and some converted to Islam, trade resumed through Aleppo. The Ottomans later took over, but by that time Europe had redirected its trade through sea routes to India and China. During World War I, Aleppo's trade rose with the arrival of Armenian refugees, who fled the Ottoman massacres. But after France had given Antioch to Turkey, Aleppo lost its Mediterranean outlet.In many ways Aleppo is a nicer and more relaxed city than Damascus, and it's a wonderful place to spend a few days. Using the historic Baron's Hotel as your base, explore the souqs (covered market), the citadel with its famous gateway, and the main mosque. The small ruined church of St Simeon, just outside Aleppo, is well worth a visit for its windswept peaceful location on a remote hilltop, with the ruins of St Simon's pillar in the centre. On my arrival at the buses station located in the old part of Aleppo town, I moved into a taxi to the ChamPalace. Ten minutes later "I was checking in to the ChamPalace, the nicest hotel in Aleppo" The Cham Palace Hotel caters to Western businessmen, which would allow me to blend in, minimizing my risk of being spotted by the Syrian secret service. I stayed for 3days and a local friendly call sign hooked me up with some medical help. The Kevlar plate had done its job, the bullet didn't penetrate, but I hadn't gotten away that easy. I had blood was coming out from every hole. The docconfirmed my suspicion; I had internal trauma and bleeding. No cure, other than the one thing I did not have, time.

He patched me up the best he could gave me some pain killers and then I was on the move again. My team had to be reassembled to go back in, recover the Bergenand check the remaining locations.

Updated intelligence identified a new RV point,a small town in north Eastern Syria close to the Iraqi border. The area was Kurdish, reportedly friendly and a main smuggling route for people and arms from Iraq into Syria. Perfect, except that everyone had underestimated the rapidly changing political climate in Syria. En-route, one team member was pinged detained and questioned by the authorities. The country was too hot and the risks too high; I made a quick risk assessment with my Intel Officer and called total index on the task. The risks had become too high. I stood the team down and dispersed all members back to safe countries - the mission was over, at least for the original team.

With total determination, I continued on alone again; Phase Two of the task was now beginning. The task had become too high risk, so I cut all ties to parties to even up my odds, back to basics. Airborne initiative and experience took over, Misinformation was put out; word came back to me,many weeks later, that I had ironically spent a good deal of time on a beach in Turkey... Only my Ops room and Intelligence officerRox knew my true whereabouts, back on track to a GPS coordinate within the Western desert of Iraq. "noman's land".

Qamishli

"There are three types of people in Iraq, enemy, coalition forces and embedded journalists. Anyone found not fitting into the last two categories will be classed as the first." Donald Rumsfeld??

I arrived that night at the Sahara Hotel, a well-known stopover point for those crossing the Iraqi border by illegal means. Two nights, maybe three, enough time to arrange a backup supply of ammo and magazines to be dropped just inside the border. Much to my surprise, amidst the typical dodgy Arab male clientele, I spotted a mysterious female alone in the lobby, watching the war live on the SKY TV. I observed her while taking my Arabic breakfast.

Curiosity got the better of me after a day and I approached her cautiously, light casual conversation over the news, Jane was an American freelance photographer, travelling with Robert, a war-experienced,well-known author [This call sign on their way into Iraq would become unfriendly after drawing the Syrian security services to them and visiting the US Embassy in Amman,]. They were at the Sahara with common intentions, to get across the border, by any means necessary.After talking to her for a short time, she told me of their plan to cross the Syrian Iraq border area, I pointed out that the areas that she was thinking about were one big mine field. She looked lost in thought.Her friend she was travailing with was known for taking life threatening risks with his own life, to get to where he wanted to be with no regard for other people's safety, Jane seemed unsure and nervous about this. She knew a lot about her friend's past that made her feel even more unsafe and insecure.

She made a decision to ditch him, he was a liability to her and was putting her at risk. She gave him misinformation and he was gone within 2 days. I found out at a later date that he had put myself at risk, during this time. The golden rule of operating in any hostile environment is cut anything lose that causes you problems or is not essential and draws attention to yourself. Unnecessary risks are unacceptable.

The war was in full force by now and Syria, the worldwide focal point. Pressure was being put on the government to seal its borders with Iraq, cutting off the sole escape route for senior Baath party officials as well as major smuggling routes for illegal arms, equipment, money and stolen archaeological treasures. The Western border and desert were becoming increasingly dangerous. Intel update from London was that American Apache helicopters were patrolling the border at night, backed up by specialist sniper teams, under orders to take out anything crossing into Syria on illegal routes.

Journalists were being found and executed and I was told that there was a 90% chance of being taken out, killed if a crossing was to go ahead. All covert entries had become nearly impossible.

At this point, I made a command decision to get out of Syria. I made a call on the sat-phone, I organised a jeep, it would be with me at my location in 24hrs, Yet, travelling alone would now be a hindrance to completing the task. My Intel had also told me that the Syrian secret service were looking for lone males, anotherlittle known British SAS operation had gone pear-shaped on the other side of the border and a few soldiers were on foot, known to be escaping an ambush. Travelling alone at this point would draw too much attention, so I decided to test Jane as an operative/asset. After all, what could be more natural than a man and a woman travelling together? [Not to mention, I could pass as being security for a journalist when stopped by normal Coalition Forces once in Iraq, this would help me blend in.]

I watched her carefully in all situations, below her sweet, nice, exterior lay an aggressive animal instinct with a wild attitude. I was really interested in testing her discreetly (she could talk the talk but could she walk the walk), with map reading and physical training skills, the basic skills and instinct were there,(a diamond in the rough), while keeping her up to speed on certain low levelintelligence from my contacts in London and developments on the ground. She completed all tasks professionally. I also noted that she was good at working in hostile situations and calming them down. She possessed all of the qualities of the two best female operatives I trained in Africa and the extremes of both the best and the worst. She was funny and intelligent yet could be very cold, aggressive and professional, even mercenary when required. She was fiercely independent and determined to achieve her goals, yet a good team player. And she had a hell of a temper yet could be a ray of sunshine on a dark day. With a little training would be a hell of an asset. Just what I needed to help me get out of Syria quietly. Beyond that, I could see that she was also a very genuine person. One of the moments that stood out at this period of time was when she was taking photographs of some children, she made the children feel so at ease and happy, there was an inner glow, warmth from her that all around could see, though she never could understand this. (See Photographs) She didn't realise at this point, but I had done a lot of voluntary worked with children with behavioural problems in the past, this enabled me to see that she was not using her job as cover, but she was who she stated and that she really did care about her work and the people around her. Over the next coming months she would win my respect and admiration for saving my life, but she wouldn't see that for our friendship was to be tested to extreme by the people who surrounded us and the severity of their political situations.

After her crash course on the AK-47 and some basic on the ground training, I checked out the jeep that had arrived, GMC, all ok, I moved locations to a little known hotel outside of Qamishli, past the run down airport, "you can get a flight from the airport to Damascus for $20, you fly in an old one engine plane, not great and I don't think it's very safe but it's doable", 2KM on the left past the airport, was the hotel. This hotel was under suspicion by US military intelligence for being a safe house for Al Q, and later it was to be used as a staging post for the insurgents in Iraq. It was worth the risk, I wanted to stay there for one night and have a look around, my instincts were right, the new hotel complex was very isolated, nothing around or overlooking it, it was almost empty. After checking into the hotel, Jane crashed in the room, sorting some kit out. I had a walk, around the area, discretelytakingphotographs and notes, (the relevance of this hotel would not become clear until I was to meet up with the US J2 Intelligence officer in Basra, Iraq). I found two dug in mostly buried lorry containers surrounded by freshly planted trees, they where looked by two heavy chains and padlocks. I walked back into the hotel, I could hear shooting, an old man who I found out later was the owner, was shouting at the desk clerk for letting us, two westerners, stay in his hotel.

I sat out of sight in the dining area, listening to their conversation. The hotel was all new, brand new, and very out of place, it also had internet access and international phone access. "it was a good place for the Iraq insurgency to stay and plan their attacks on the coalition forces".

I made my way back to the room, told Jane the rest of the day was down time and that it would be an early start, 5am. I spent the rest of the day getting intelligence updates from the UK and keeping up to speed on the ever changing turbulent political situation in Iraq and Syria. I knew that we were safe at the hotel, if they killed us it would have drawn too much attention to the hotel. I used the hotel switchboard to make two subtle phone calls out talking about how nice the hotel was.

5am the next morning, it is warm, but cooler at this time of the day, when trailing long distances across deserts it is wise to get an early start. I drove across the open desert area on the only road in the eastern side of Syria, passing though several little villagers, scattered along the route, the black smoke off the burning oil fields on the left spiralled up and across the sky for miles, the Iraqi army had blown up and set alight as they retreated north. As the coalition fighting cut though their positions.This was a sudden sobering reminder off the war that was raging little over 20KM away. On towards Del al Zor.

Del Al Zor

Del Al Zore is located on the banks of the Euphrates River, it is the main crossing point across the river in Eastern Syria; it is an isolated town, located in the middle of the desert, with little outside influence for decades. It is also where a little out of town to the west lies the location of where thousands of Armenians where massacred, by the Turks, a generation ago, men women, and children. The skeletons off their bodies can still be seen when the wind blows strongly along the dusty desert valleys, ask any Armenian and they will tell you about the holocaust that the Turk's conducted on the Armenian people. Many people in the west do not even know that it happened. The Turks try to bury it in history.De La Zore has two old stone bridges, which are the only way of crossing the river, these are manned by the Syrian secrete police 24/7, to the south of the river is the town itself, to the north is open country, a lot of wild dogs in packs can be found roaming this area. The main illegal smuggling routes from Iraq to Syria are located here, a lot of the Art and historical artefacts which were looted from the Baghdad museums found their way to this area, a mud brick house with a 200 year old painting hanging on the wall and antique lion heads outside the front door are testament to this.

After a drive though the old part of town and finding ourselves being surrounded by an angry mob banging on the doors and trying to open them, rocking the jeep side to side and chanting death to America, it was time to leave. My American friend had drawn a lot of attention. On the way out of town I had a run in with the Secret police, $100 and a pack of cigarettes later and it was time to leave this place behind. I would advise no westerners to visit this area, I would class it as being hostile. (insurgent country). It would become an ISIS strong hold in the future.

Four hours later out of nowhere, heading towards Palmera, (Tadmore). I slowed down as I passed, a set of buildings on the left hand side of the road, three mud huts, with a sign outside, it read in English, "Baghdad Café", I needed a break, what the hell, 15min to stretch my legs would not hurt, I pulled up in front of the main door, I told Jane to stay in the jeep while I check it out, all was ok. I left the jeep infront of the road side café, so it was in full view at all times. The kids in these settlements will strip your jeep of bags and equipment in minutes, if it is not locked or bolted down, they will have it away. This was a "dear diary moment", the Baghdad Café was a relic of the old tourist, (not terrorist), industry. It was in the middle of nowhere, just a ran down building. Painted in white and light blue, with a piece of wood with welcome painted on it in red, sticking out the ground. It had postcards and a little Sylvania shop inside, all this is very surreal. It was completely deserted, A word of warning, do not use the toilets in places like this and never drink the water, unless it comes from a bottle that is sealed, it's the quickest way to get very bad stomach bugs. A young boy came out, I ordered some drinks. After a glass of chai and a short walk around the area to the front of the café. Time to get back on the road.

Ancient ruined city of Palmyra, (Tadmor).

After three more hours on the road, only two old cars passed us going in the opposite direction, no other life was to be seen. Through the scorching blistering heat of the midday sun, an old battered rusty sign appeared on the side off the road, 20KM, to the Ancient ruined city of Palmyra, (Tadmor).

When ISIS emerged as a major terrorist group in the future Palmyra would be one of their strategic locations in Eastern Syri. A little known fact as I was driving through Palmyra, I noticed the little cafe just of the small squire that marks the centre of town. This cafe had been a meeting point for Al-Qaeda and Hezbollah commanders for many years, the rooms upstairs are used as meeting rooms and safe house. After a quick stop to get a few photographs as holiday snaps/intelligence, we drove out of Palmyra on the only road. This little town would hold great tactical and strategic value in the war on terror in the future.

■ ■

Tadmor (in Arabic تدمر), the famed Palmyra of Antiquity, is a small city of central Syria, located in an oasis 215 km northeast of Damascus and 120 km southwest of the Euphrates. It has long been a vital caravan city for travellers crossing the Syrian desert and was known as the *Bride of the Desert*. The Greek name for the city, *Palmyra* (Παλμυρα), is a translation of its original Aramaic name, *Tadmor*, which means 'palm tree'.

The city was first mentioned in the archives of Mari in the 2nd millennium B.C. It was another trading city in the extensive trade network that linked Mesopotamia and northern Syria. Tadmor is mentioned in the Hebrew Bible (Second Book of Chronicles 8.4) as a desert city that is fortified by Solomon. The city of Tamar is mentioned in the First Book of Kings (9.18), also fortified by Solomon. This is traditionally read (see Qere) as *Tadmor*, but may refer to place near the Dead Sea. (*Tadmor* is the name of Palmyra in modern Hebrew.)

When the Seleucids took control of Syria in 323 BCE, the city was left to itself and it became independent. The city flourished as a caravan halt in the first century BCE. In 41 BCE, the Romans under Mark Antony tried to occupy Palmyra but failed as the Palmyrans escaped to the other side of the Euphrates. The Palmyrans had received intelligence of the Roman approach. This proves that at that time Palmyra was still a nomadic settlement and its valuables could be removed at short notice. Palmyra was made part of the Roman province of Syria during the reign of Tiberius (14–37 CE). It steadily grew in importance as a trade route linking Persia, India, China, and the Roman empire. In 129 CE, Hadrian visited the city and was so enthralled by it that he proclaimed it a free city and renamed it *Palmyra Hadriana*. Beginning in 212 CE, Palmyra's trade diminished as the Sassanids occupied the mouth of the Tigris and the Euphrates. Septimius Odaenathus, a Prince of Palmyra, was appointed by Valerian as the governor of the province of Syria. After Valerian was captured and killed by the Sassanids, Odaenathus campaigned as far as Ctesiphon (near modern-day Baghdad) for revenge, invading the city twice. When Odaenathus was assassinated by his nephew Maconius, his wife Septimia Zenobia took power, ruling Palmyra on the behalf of her son, Vabalathus. Zenobia rebelled against Roman authority with the help of Loginius and took over Bosra and lands as far to the west as Egypt. Next, she attempted to take Antioch to the north. In 272, the Roman Emperor Aurelian finally retaliated and captured her and brought her back to Rome. He paraded her in golden chains but allowed her to retire to a villa in Tibur, where she took an active part in society for years. This rebellion greatly disturbed Rome, and so Palmyra was forced by the empire to become a military base for the Roman legions. Diocletian expanded it to harbor even more legions and walled it in to try and save it from the Sassanid threat. The Byzantine period only resulted in the building of a few churches and much of the city was in ruin.

The city was taken by the Muslim Arabs under Khalid ibn Walid. Under the Umayyads, two Qasr al Heirs were built. In the 16th century, the intimidating Fakhredin al Maany castle was built on top of a mountain overlooking the oasis. The castle was surrounded by a moat, with access only available through a drawbridge.

Archaeological teams from various countries have been working on-and-off on different parts of the site. In May 2005, a Polish team excavating at the Lat temple discovered a highly-detailed stone statue of the winged goddess of victory "Nike".

Isis first would capture Palmyra, once a Silk Road oasis that boasted some of the best-preserved ruins of antiquity, in May 2015.

Militants would rampaged through the city's museums and ruins, blowing up the 2,000-year-old towering Temple of Bel and the Arch of Victory along with other priceless artefacts. ISIS would also kill Khaled al-Asaad, a leading archaeologist.

ISIS would also destroy the tetrapylon, a collection of monumental pillars on a raised platform near the ancient city's entrance, and part of the facade of the Roman theatre, where musicians from St Petersburg's Mariinsky orchestra had performed at a victory concert. I would never get to see Palmyra again in its complete form...

Damascus

On to Damascus, it is hard to say what is the most amazing sight in Syria. The ruins that map human history in toppled stone? The church where St. Paul converted to Christianity? Or maybe it is the Saudi tourists who put aside their puritanism for a beer, or a sloppy snowball fight in the mountains above the desert here?

To the United States and Great Britain, Syria may be a threatening place, where terrorists and their training camps are welcome and democracy is not. But to Arabs living under more authoritarian governments, it is a nation of relative tolerance, beaches and mountains, good food and cheap shopping. It has become a vacation spot for more and more visitors from elsewhere in the Middle East.

Around the region, in fact, Arabs are visiting other Arab countries in such numbers that they are more than making up for the loss of Americans and Europeans after the Sept. 11 terror attacks in the United States.

Thanks to that new and growing trend, and despite the Iraq war, tourism in the Middle East as a whole grew faster than anywhere else in 2003, according to the United Nations World Tourism Organisation. In the near future ISIS would put an end to all this...

"There is a proverb in Kuwait that asks, `If you have soup, why put it in someone else's bowl?' " said Assad al-Fadli, 34, a Kuwaiti who packed his family in their car in late January to drive 900 miles for a five-week winter vacation in Syria. "It should go in the family bowl."

As the proverb suggests, part of the reason for the trend may be Arab pride. Mr. Fadli, for example, is furious over the war in Iraq and is less inclined to spend his money in the United States. He said he was visiting his brother in Kansas City on Sept. 11, 2001, and was so afraid of reaction against Arabs that he stayed indoors for 20 days.

Arabs also have trouble these days getting visas to visit Europe and America. At the same time, the Arab countries have improved what is known in the industry as the "tourist infrastructure," loosening visa requirements and making it easier and more comfortable for visitors to travel to their countries and stay awhile.

"The borders are open more," said Rok Klancnik, a spokesman for the World Tourism Organisation. "There are better airports, better hotels. This is an unstoppable development."

It is probably no coincidence, but the countries doing best are also the ones with a more relaxed attitude toward alcohol, women and fun.

Tourism in the United Arab Emirates — which has been aggressively trying to transform itself into the Middle East's commercial, shopping and tourist hub — grew by 32 percent in 2003, according to the United Nations.

In Lebanon, the most laid-back of Arab nations, tourism grew by 14 percent, as it did in Bahrain. In Egypt, hit hard by the terror attacks in the United States but long accustomed to Western tourists, tourism grew by 13 percent in 2003.

The numbers for Syria, right next door to the violence in Iraq and Israel, are more erratic but still show growth. In January 2003, just before the war in Iraq, tourism was booming at 35 percent over the previous January.

From February to July — the war and its immediate aftermath — tourism dropped to almost nil. But since then it has grown at a rate of 11 percent over the same period last year. Nine percent more Arabs — about 70 percent of the two million or so tourists here — visited in 2003.

Syria is hardly a den of vice, but it is an avowedly secular country where most women walk around without veils and various sects of Islam and Christians live in tolerance. (The situation was worse for Syria's Jews, most of whom have left for Israel).

Alcohol is freely available, which a 40-year-old Saudi businessman, who would only give his name as Nasser, acknowledged was one lure for his countrymen.

But he noted that alcohol was available elsewhere in the Middle East and so was not the main reason he comes to Syria to "relax" as he put it, for several   days every month.

"There is everything here," he said. "There is atmosphere. There is the sea. There are mountains.

But most important, there are the beautiful faces here. God is beautiful, and he likes beautiful things."

Nasser did complain that good hotel rooms were scarce and expensive, and that there were not enough attractions for children, as in, say, Dubai. Saadalla Agha al-Kallaa, the nation's tourism minister, said Syria knew that it needed to compete and had been expanding hotel rooms and had recently begun a marketing campaign aimed at other Middle Easterners.

For the stray Western tourists, even for Americans, Syria is still welcoming and just as beautiful and fascinating as for anyone else. There are 3,000 archaeological sites and major shrines for Christians and Muslims.

Still it is not the proverbial day at the beach: Syria is a police state, which can be a little unnerving, though the upside is that tourists are perfectly safe. There is no specific State Department warning to Americans against going to Syria, as there are for Saudi Arabia and Yemen.

But it is difficult to ignore that Israel bombed here just last September. Syrians are also quite angry at the war in Iraq and the fraying relations with the United States, and it shows.

"If an American citizen wants to stop by the cafe, he is most welcome," said Faraj Sharaf al-Din, 32, who works in the Baghdad Cafe, a tourist stop in the desert along the road to ancient Palmyra. "We are so tolerant. But of course we have to keep up the fight if we are forced."

For historically minded Americans, at least those who like their nation's current place at the top, Syria is also not heartening about the nature of power. Greeks, Romans, Byzantines, Umayyads, even the French, passed through Syria, and none are still here.

"Nothing lasts forever," said Ibrahim Kassem, 62, who has been a tour guide for three decades at the ruins of Palmyra, itself the seat of a small empire two thousand years ago. America, he said, "will not be the last."

"Nobody knows what will happen, what will be."

Damascus appears on the horizon as you drive out of the heat of the desert on the Tadmor Road. It feels surreal to be in a city from spending hours driving though the mostly flat golden deserted desert. On entering Damascus a decision on where to stay had to be made, I needed somewhere that was low-key, and a place where westerners would not look out of place, we found the perfect place in the "lonely planet guide book of Syria", a backpackers hotel come hostel, perfect, we would blend in here. "The lonely planet guide books on all the countries in the Middle East are a very good sauce of information, from where to stay, on low budgets, places to see, things to do, where and what to eat, embassy locations and good information on where government visa's and documents can be organised". I made the carrying of one of these SOP, "standard operating procedure" when operating in the Middle East, it can cut down on so much time when you're on the ground. The place where we would spend the next few days, was an old known gem of a place, used by my contacts in the past. Located right in the heart of the city.

Only afew days needed in Damascus, I needed to pick up a new passport from the UK embassy, receive some money through the Foreign Office, had a quick check up on my stomach at the red crest hospital. This all was pretty straight forward. It was now midday, the Embassies were now closed, "the Embassy in the Middle East only open for a few hours on a morning, four to five days a week, if you have to visit them, get there early, 0830am is a good time. They normally close at midday. A key thing to remember is that anything in the Middle East takes three times longer to do than in the West. If you're in a rush, take your time, people in the this part of the world never rush. After checking into the hostel, dropping kit off and a much needed hot shower, I made my way to the Red Crest hospital. My sources had told me that they was a friendly call sign there, a Dr who could speak good English, and would look after me, he had helped some of the British boys who had been injured on the Iraq, Syrian border and cut off from there command, with no means ofcommunication with their HQ, "inner sanctuary", they had made their way to the hospital. It was an unofficial safe location, where contact and help would be. As soon as the Dr was made aware that I was British and injured he took me aside and into a private room, he looked me over, no real long term damage, just a lot of internal bruising, he gave me some shots, pain killers, I told him I was passing a lot of blood, "you have to take it easy, you need time to heel", I said I would try to, he told me that two other British men had been here to see him, with gunshot wounds and similar injuresonly a few days before, he looked at me, " I will make sure there are no forms or records of your visit here", I said thank you. He asked did I need the Embassy Regional Security Officer to be informed or pass a message to him of my arrival, I told him no I would make my way there in the morning, I told him that they should be expecting me. My friendly call-sign had given them heads up on my arrival. I thanked the Dr, and slowly walked out into the midday sun, I did not feel well, I sat on the wall next to the hospital, I suddenly felt very sick, I spent the next ten minutes being ill, it felt like an hour. I got a local taxi back to the hotel, I put the sat-phone under my pillow and slept straight though undisturbed until the next morning, I was totally exhausted.

I woke up the next day, at 0700am, Jane was already up, her bed had not been made yet, I sat up, she came in with a bag ofwonderful smelling fresh bread and water, "I thought you could do with some breakfast", thanks. She went on to tell me that she had been up half the night trying to keep me cool, I had a fever, that explained why I was feeling weak, I said thanks for looking out for me and the food is good. We talked for awhile over Arabic coffee, slowly eating the rest of the bread. Time to make a move, I wanted to be at the Embassy for 0830am, I had business to take care of.. After a quick shower, I told Jane I would be back in few hours, then we could have a walk around town, I wanted to visit the Soaks, Caravanserai, and Mosque. I had also been told that one off the best places to get water pipe was at a cafe called "studio one".

I arrived at the British Embassy, "Embassy Britannia", as the doors were being opened, the security around the area was tight. When I got in, I asked for the main clerk, I explained I had a new passport waiting and that I was also to pick up money. She looked at me for a second, then she directed me into a private both. After afew minutes an middle aged man well-dressed came in, he asked how I was, I said ok, "you have some friends looking out for you", he gave me a form to sign, then gave me some money in local currency and informed me my new passport would be arriving by diplomatic pouch within the next two days from London. He told me to call back then, he asked was I sure I was alright and did I have somewhere to stay, "ya I've taken care of that".

I made my way back to the hotel, I found Jane sat by the water fountain in the front meeting area of the hotel reading her book and sipping chai. "all done, do you fancy a walk", we strolled in to the centre of town, I had time to kill, I could do nothing until my passport arrived. I had read a lot about the souq and bazaars of Damascus, now I had the time to experience them first had. This would be a great time for reconnaissance and gathering local intelligence for a later intelligence task! I knew that there were Terrorist HVTs Commanders hiding within the old quarter, old part of the city... Time to do the whole tourist photograph thing...

The Souq of Al-Hamidiye.

The souq of Al-Hamidiye. In 1260, 1300 and 1400, Damascus fell three times in the hands of the Mongolian and Turkish conquerors, but the invasions in spite of their violence, do not last a long time. The remnants of would be conquerors are visible in the many souqs, bazaars. The souq of Al-Hamidiye in Damascus is one of the most beautiful and oldest souqs in the Middle East. "it is a good example of old meets new". The widening narrow alley ways, with their cobbled floors and high walls are the hall mark of Damascus, the locals in theirtraditional dressset up there stalls along the outside of the alley ways. Fragrant and colorful aromas fill the air. The piles of bright reds, yellows, oranges fill the stalls of the spice merchants. A sweet smell familiar from ones childhood directs you to the sweet stall, piles made up in pyramid formation mark the white frosted sticky sweets. Other stalls sell house hold goods, water containers, brass pans, cooking oils. Others merchants sell Persian silk in vibrant blues and greens. One can get lost in this lavernath of dark mysterious alley ways.

The stalls and shops for gold, silver, are all kept in one area of the souq, there is another area for the stalls and traders to sell brass, it's quite methodical if you think about it, there are certain areas in the souq for buying different categories from different merchants. There is a little known café just down the road called "station 1" its sells great water pipe, and the local food is outstanding. It's a local evening meeting place for the students from the local university.After hours of walking around talking to the locals, and endless cups of chai and greetings, we headed back to the hotel.

Adam, had been hard at work booking false flights for me to Rome and Paris, this was to throw the Secret police off my scent. It had worked well in the past...

I could feel the net closing around me, my Intelsources were telling me that I had to pull something special out the bag to deal with this, that is what I did, I was informed by friendly call signs that I would not be allowed to leave Syria alive. Someone from within an International Intelligence Agency was tipping of someone in Syrian Intelligence. (I had my suspicions it was a rogue member or asset of British MI6, could be the same one that rumbled my team in Lebanon?). I was being hunted, everyone thought that I was in the North of Syria or sat on a beach in southern Turkey.Damascus was the last place anyone would look. The only thing that I could do was the one thing the head of the Syrian Secret Servicewas not expecting, it was also the most dangerous and even by my standards, totally off the charts option.

Meeting the Head of the feared Syrian Security Services

"There is such a thing as legitimate warfare: war has its laws; there are things which may fairly be done. And things that may not be done. He has attempted (as I call it) to poison the wells".

John Henry, Cardinal Newman, Apologia pro Vita Sua, 1864

I decided one morning to go and personally see the head of the feared secret police himself at his HQ, in Damascus. I told Jane over breakfast "felt like a last supper" one morning what my plan was and that if I was not back within 6hrs, to make her way to the border and get into Jordon asap.

Before I left I took my watch off and left my personal items in the bedside draw, all I took was money for the taxi, the cloths I was wearing and myself. There was a good chance that I would not be coming back. This meeting was ether going to kill me or get me out of Syria. I flagged down a taxi on the street, I told the driver the address, he looked at me, cold faced, he asked in broken English"are you sure", "yes". The Syrian secrete police struck the fear of god into its' own people, their tools of control and manipulation, were brutal beatings, bloody torture, rape and long imprisonments, or if you were lucky, execution, a bullet to the back of the head. The Syrian people have good reason to fear them. The taxi driver, pulled up at the bottom of the road. He was too scared to go any further, he was sweating "he did not want to be here". He pointed and motioned over to a set of buildings, I paid the driver and stepped out of the car, he was gone in a flash. I was stood alone at the end of the road, dust blowing around me, looking over at the menacing old dark buildings.

I started to walk over, I was thinking that this might not have been a good Idea after all. I got to the large metal grey gates. My mouth was dry, I went over to the Guard box. There were Syrian Officers standing around, in theirstandard grey shirts, suites and ties, several were sat drinking Chia, I greeted them and ask to speak to the general, I said he was expecting me. They looked at me and then at each other, I wasshown a seat in the outside guard room, I handed one of the officers my business card through a small hatch in the steel gate he took it and walked over to the main building, the Syrian guards sat looking at me. I felt like the first westerner they had ever seen, they offered me a cigarette, I accepted. About five minuteslater, two large middle aged men dressed in grey suites stepped in through the steel gates, they said, follow me in English. I walked with them, towards the main building, we walked past several BMWs 5 series and Mercedes S class, all Black with blackened windows. I was escorted into the lift area, the lift was not working, there was some building work going on, around the bottom floor. I was shown to a stairwell, up three flights of stairs and down a long dark corridor, there wereprison cells both sides of me, some of the doors where open, I discreetly glimpsed in as I past, the cells where dimly lit, there were dirty, one cell had a metal bed frame with no mattress just metal springsand four sets of handcuffs one on each corner, there was a large car battery "used for electric shock" outside one of the cells. I heard a scream from the end of the corridor from one of the cells that had a closed door. It suddenly hit me.This was where the Secrete police brought their victims for torture and interrogation. The dirt was not all dirt, it was blood, splattered up the walls and ceiling, the smell confirmed it, I had smelt this many times in the past, blood and flesh have a bitter sweet smell. I noticed a bloody drag mark across the floor, a body had been dragged across the floor from one cell to another. Bare electric cables hung from the ceiling, old dirty light bulbs flickered giving the whole corridor an eerie dark ghost like look and feel. At the sight of this, I thought to myself that I was totally fucked, what the hell, I thought if you fuckers want me, here I am. I was guided up another set of stairs and we exited into a brightly lit corridor, painted bright white. It was fresh paint, the smell was strong and blinding to the eyes, it took a moment for my eyes to adjust to the new light. A sharp contrast to the flickering dull light of the dungeons and torture chambers. I was told to wait here, in the corridor outside of a wooden door with a black plastic chair off to one side. I stood there for what seemed to be an eternity. The door opened, one of the men stepped out, "come inside". I walked in slowly, the room was again very well lit and bright, again a total contrast to the dungeons I had walked though. Large windows at one end of the room with golden curtains either side allowed the sunshine to beam in. The room was well furnished and clean, large western style pictures hanging on the walls. Cream leather chairs and a glass coffee table were positioned in the centre of the room. There was an over-sized dark wooden desk off to one side, behind it sat a small frame of a man, black hair and moustache, very smart in appearance, "I was glad I had worn a shirt". He looked up at me and motioned the other men to leave the room, he told me to sit down motioning to the leather seats. I sat down trying to be calm. I noticed the hidden CCTV cameras, we were far from alone. He finished the paper work he was reading, placed the documents carefully into a tray, then he walked slowly over and sat opposite me. After a moment "he asked" do you take chai, I answered, "yes please", trying to be composed and polite, I knew in the back of my mind that this is the one person that can have me taken out, killed in a heartbeat. He was not what I was expecting and I don't think from the way that he looked and reacted that I was what he was expecting ether. We silently looked at each other for a second, again trying to weigh each other up. He asked how I was and how I was enjoying my time in Syria, I said I like the country, there was a knock at the door, a man came in and handed him a file, it looked like the British yellow pages. He looked through it, why did you come here? I said I had heard that his people were looking for me, if there was a problem, I thought it better to came and speak to him in person. He looked at me, I looked straight back at him, my balls had just hit the floor, but I was not going to give him the satisfaction of mentally getting the better of me. "You have seen a lot of my country". The file he had in his hands that he was browsing though was about me. He had a list, a report of almost everywhere I had been, photographs of me and who I was with, and copies of E-mails that Jane had sent back to state side. He smiled, he told me he was educated in the UK, at Oxford university. I smiled, that's a good university. He stroked his dark moustache and asked who else knew that I was here... I said confidently," as a total bluff" The

British and American Embassies. He pondered for a silent moment, how did you find Iraq, I said I had not been there yet..."yet", but when the war was over I might visitBaghdad. He laughed. What do you want, I want to go to Jordon, why, just travailing around, my cover story would not work on this guy, "I want for me and my travelling companion to leave Syria". Will you return, "No". "Good. I will give you 24hrs to leave, never to return. Is this acceptable?" I answered "yes". He said after 24hrs your safety is not guaranteed in Syria, it can be a dangerous place.... I have work to be done, have a safe trip, the general stood up, shook my hand, shouted one of the men into the room, "he's free to go", the men looked puzzled, even not happy. I was escorted out.

The large grey metal doors slammed closed and bolted locked behind me.I was stood by myself again on the dusty silent road.I had just done one of the most outrageous things in my life and I was still alive. The words "it's been emotional", spring to mind.I walked down to the end of the road and flagged down a taxi, back to the Hotel, "I needed a drink".I got back to the hotel, Jane was chilling, out reading and talking to the locals, I gave her a smile, "all ok" I went in and grabbed my phone, there was a message from the UK Embassy, my passport had arrived, I put my watch back on, grabbed my wallet, and headed straight over, I got there just as it was closing, the security recognised me and let me straight in,after a quick conversation with the desk clerk. She went away and came back with a plain brown envelope in hand, my new passport. I got back to the hotel, checked out and moved myself and Jane to Meridian Hotel, "on route I briefed her on what had happened and timings". I had time for one night's stay, I had 24hrs to leave, I booked us both into rooms, and dropped the kit into my room, I had some lose ends to tie up, I told Jane I would meet her by the pool in a few hours, I remembered from past visits that the Meridian Hotel had a high speed internet connection, "very rare in Syria" I needed to spend two hours on it. I had to get hold of Adam and get him on a plane, to meet me in Jordon, I wanted a personal update from his side. I touched base with Rox and my Intel people, as well as my British friendly call signs, finally I had a good 30min chat on the sat-phone with Sharpy, back at Cyprus HQ. After spending over three hours on the net and phones, receiving updates and confirming my next movements with HQ, I went down to the poolside bar to relax. "I needed that drink", it had been an emotional day.

The rest of the day was down time, I need the rest.

Final Attempt

"Utrinque Paratus"
"Ready for Anything". Latin; The motto of the Elite British Parachute Regiment.

0600am the next morning. Armed with $900 bribe money, I was to make my final attempt at a Syrian border crossing. Two incredibly confused secret service agents stood at the door of the Meridian Hotel in Damascus as we jumped in the Victor call signand made my way along the long dusty highwayto the southern border withJordan. Sunset fell and the night grew dark as the border guards held my freedom in their hands. After about three hours wait, I was told to move the GMC into a compound area, where we waited, joined by some armed guards. They quickly looked over and searched the GMC, they had no real interest in it,I broke the ice with some cigarettes, the guards, brought some chai over, we sat talking, trying to stay cool, I knew that if I get refused passage, I would send Jane on to Jordon by herself, I on the other hand would be totally fucked. My only option would be, let Jane take the GMC, and I would make an illegal border crossing the next night, this was not a very good option. I had a little faith in my meeting with the head of their intelligence/ secret police in Damascus, I was a headache for him and money/bribes given to the guards was going to help. The phone rang in the compound, I held my breath, were the Syrian intelligence going to nail me to the wall.

After six hours wait, we were silent my mind was racing 100 miles an hour, as we finally drove slowly into Jordan. The immigration offices on the Jordanian side were quiet at 2am, and we breathed easily with warm smiles and hellos from the Jordanian border guards. I laughed in relief at the giant Red Bull advertisement in the mini market, we loaded up on Pringles, biscuits and iced coffee. On our way again, this time to lap of luxury, a well-deserved break at the Hotel Intercontinental in Amman.

Jordon Amman

"Never has a sunrise looked so beautiful,
Than through the eyes of freedom regained". "SA"

To my total amazement, my new friendly call sign appeared by the swimming pool the following early the morning wearing her standard operating procedure (SOP), a red-hot pink string bikini, that she had carried through the torture and torment of Syria. "A true dear diary moment". I found out later that she had been a top end cover model before she had become a photographer. Still the stunning blonde Californian bikini clad babe was a surprise! The American military were going to love having her around, great for moral. Jane would in the future earn the respect from soldiers and officers alike across the American military due to her time spent with them and the fact she made the effort to talk and listen to young soldiers on the ground in Iraq which was a dangerous war zone. But at that moment we both needed a little pool time.

After carefully talking things through with my intelligence people, I made the decision to help and look after Jane to get some good photographs in Iraq. All was fair, she hadhelped me and was a great cover to move aroundSyria. I was going into Iraq, I know the clearance and Intelligence contacts I had would make for good access for photographs for her and travelling with a female would look more natural, then a lone male. My Intel people thought it was a wise idea too. Even from a pure safety point of view for her, she was going to go in anyway, she did not have any contacts, or support in country, I know that I would be able to open some safe avenues for her in Iraq, the last thing I needed on my mind was a dead American photographer. Too many good photographers had already been killed in war zones over the past few years, some had been my close friends.

Time to reassess, re-supply and plan the next phase of the operation. I allocated a four day turn around and back into theatre. I arranged for a friendly call/sign to pick up my jeep and have it serviced, as well as re-supply the car kit. This was done in 48hrs. Though some time had passed, there was still no information coming out of north western Iraq,I knew that the day sack and follow-on locations were still intact, due to people I knew monitoring the locations using satellite imagery (American Falcon View). Despite all normal regulations, we acquired press passes from the Jordanian authorities with nothing other than a sweet smile and a kind word (your mission if you care to accept it).After this and her role in adding movement and escaping Syria, there was no question in my mind as to my decision to add her to my team for the travelling into and around Iraq.I used the time in Jordan to establish communications with my intelligence officer in London.Several international conference calls and a full intelligence update/brief was given, the next phase of the mission was ready to start.

Adam, was flying in for a two day turn around, I was looking forward to hearing what he had to say about the situation and what was really going on behind the scenes in London. He was due to arrive at 0600am local time the next morning, I had arranged to meet him at the old ruins in the old city ofAmman, at 0900am. Lots of entry and exit points and very public. I have used this location in the past for meetings. He was to ring me when he was clear of the airport and on route, to confirm timings. The next morning was bright and sunny, the first morning of freedom was amazing, the sun seemed brighter and warmer, the smell of the fresh morning coffee smelled better than ever. Adam called me from the airport, he was on route to his hotel. We arranged to meet at the meeting point, the location at the ruins of the old city was pre-arranged.I arrived early and had a coffee from a vantage point which over looked the area, always best to check if the area was being watched by any bad guys, I was not expecting any trouble. One hour later I was standing on the steps of the entrance to the old ruins. The sun has high in the sky and the heat of the day was kicking in. A group of foreigner tourists passed me taking photographs as they walked, I turned away to avoid my face being in their photographs. The situation made me smile thinking about it, just because you're a little paranoid doesn't mean they're not out to get you! This place seemed so normal, just every day normal, it suddenly hit me that I had been living in a very strange environment the past few weeks. I spotted Adam as he got out a taxi 100meters away, he was wearing light brown pants and a white shirt, his black sunglasses gave him away as a tourist. I walked towards him, we shook hands and smiled, "it's good to see you".We walked over to a coffee shop on the corner, not many people around, so we sat outside. I briefed him up on all that had happened. "he realised that I was lucky to get out of Syria", I informed Adam that I had secondedJane into the team, she would be good to use as a second photographer and she would be a good cover in "country", Iraq.

There was an element of trust there with Jane but by no means absolute. She needed a ride in to country, I needed a good cover. "the door swings both ways". Something didn't fit with a lot that Adam was telling me, my gut instinct was telling me something was wrong. I decided to test him that night, I needed to know if he really had my best welfare in mind, Syria still played on my mind and I knew that someone had tipped of the Syrian Secret Service! Not everyone wanted me to succeed... After a few drinks at the bar that night, I dropped it into conversation to Adam, that I was thinking of ending the task and walking away. He did not look too pleased. I called it a night, said I was tired and wishing them goodnight and I left Jane and Adam to finish off their drinks.

I was sat in my room talking to Rox, on the phone, getting intelligence updates and telling him on the timings for me going back into Iraqwhen there was a knock at my door, it was Jane. I answered, she walked in, she could see I was working not sleeping. I asked "what's up",The warning bells went off, after Jane had told me, what Adam had just said to her, "Adam had told Jane to sleep with me if she had to and do anything to keep me on task" he had promised to help her in her photographic career. I viewed this as a pretty low thing to say and do, it just proved to me that he was desperate to take the credit for the task I was doing or was there more to it. This was when I started to distrust Adam and his intentions, he was a good man but there were unseen players, pressures and politics at play. I had already told them straight back at Sunday Times London HQ, that if I find anything of Tactical or Strategic interest, I would hand it over to military intelligence. If they were willing to fuck me over at this point, god knows what they would do if I handed them anything of great importance. I told Jane thanks for the heads-up and information. I bid her good night. I never let Adam know that I knew. I wanted to see how certain things panned out.Unbeknown to everyone at this point I was already hooked in to American Military Intelligence and had been feeding them intelligence reports. Adam phoned his forgery friends the next morning back in London, he informed me that ID documents could be made and sent to me, BBC etc, he thought this would be useful. I never took him up on his offer, for two reasons. The first, I always use my own trusted contacts, second this sort of action was not above board for a journalist.I got Sunday Times ID, organised, from the Amman press office, I showed my letter head from the Sunday Times, Adam was shown this and was OK with it. I was marked down as a "Special Adviser" Photographer. It mimicked the official ID I had received from the Sunday Times, "Special Adviser". Adam left that afternoon, to fly back to the UK. I found out later from his boss that he had flown out of his own back, the Sunday Times did not now he was coming out to meet me... there was another side to all this that I was told when I met the editor of the Sunday Times, when I eventual got back to the UK.The rest of the day I spent checking kit and looking over the victor call/sign. All was ready to go, I told Jane to have some down time and an early night, we would be setting off early the next morning.

Iraq Border

0400am. A long, hot drive in the GMC across the Jordanian desert brought usto the border of Iraq. The expected checkpoints were non-existent and the border to Iraq shockingly unassuming. After attempting to cross into Iraq numerous times from Syria, I blew through the Jordanian border and actually had to seek out border officials to stamp our passports.

Entry into Iraq the second time around was surreal. The border was a virtual ghost town other than a few American troops and budding Iraqi entrepreneurs vending the only gasoline for miles. I drove past H3-H2,along the same route SpecialForces took during the early stages of the war. H3 was the location of the enemy air field, the British and Australian SAS, had covertly made a hole in the Jordanian border near trig point 2648, in the middle of the desert and slipped through undetected at nightand attacked, held the Iraq air bases in the days prior to the official start of the war. They had gone back to the tactics used by David Sterling, the man who first formed the SAS regiment back in World War Two. Land Rover Jeep formations, in a spear head formation they had drove over the desert and air filed at high speed and fought through the enemy capturing and destroying enemy locations. These raids were carried out in true SAS fashion and style, captured on specialised night vision camcorder equipment. The trail of destructionSF left in their wake was phenomenal, a virtual road map of its own.The highway was littered with burned out skeletons of vehicles, scarred by Apache gunship fire, all major bridges had been taken out by special forces using specialisedshape charges. (See Photographs)

After navigating my way past Ar Rutbah, H2 and H3, though the mine fields, insurgents illegal check points, blistering heat of the south west desert of Iraqand along the way, giving a stranded Iraq family with three young badly dehydrated children, water, food and towingtheir car 60KM to the next safe village, it was a good start to the day. During the next few hours I drove past the scenes of some of the locations, aftermath of the early battles of the war. Burnt out Iraq tanks still smouldering with chard clothing and body parts legs and arms, a headless burnt torso was off to one side, others were scattered over the sand. A large group of American vehicles way out on the horizon to my left, this marked the spot to the track entrance to Saddam's uranium mine. I thought it best to give it a wide berth at this point of time. My Intel had informed me to leave it alone. I emergedthrough the afternoons scorchingheat at a point where the only main road is met by the river road, marked by a crossroads, I stopped to re-fuel victor one;all seemed quiet no one around. I grabbed my AK-47 and vest, thentook the short walk to the high ground. On the left, there was a pile of stones, this was where the British SAS, ill-fated mission Bravo Two Zero, "Andy McNab", had made it to, in the first gulf war, the small pile of stones was all that marked the spot, he had told me about it when we had met drinking. I stayed five minutes there in respect of the boys who did not make it back from that mission. Time to go, a dust cloud was approaching, the first sign of a dust storm is a red cloud in the distance, it moves very quickly, you never want to get caught out in the open when it hits. I found myself finally in Al Qa'im, "Husaybah" After a 1,000 mile detour, I was finally on the Iraqi side of this infamous border. Prior to the war, Al Qa'im was a stereotypical border town with minor smuggling of arms and people the southernmost crossing into Syria. The war, however, turned the town into an international hotspot forterrorists and was a known insurgent safe haven. Making headline news on several occasions, when an underground oil pipeline blown up by unknown forces, (some weeks later I meet the US rangers who blow it up by accident lol). Thearms market had expanded tenfold and large terrorist training camps to the north of the river at trig point 1135, (this was confirmed by the Operation Snake north of Rawahover the bridge from Anah). Over 30 international terrorist were killed, their origins were of a wide variety, including, Lebanese, Saudi Arabia, Iranian, Afghanistan, Syrian and European. (See Photographs)

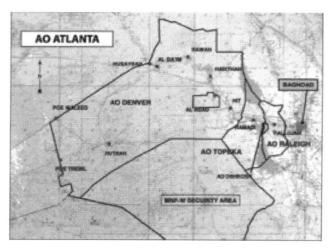

As I drove slowly watching, observing everything with detail,I moved forward through the townsensing something familiar, something not quite right. The penny dropped, the downtown market had the same look and feel as the arms market in Harare,Zimbabwe, down to the clapped-out,old vans cruising up and down the high street. A quick stop for an ice cream with chocolate chip and a spare AK-47 with sixspare magazines and I was on our way.

Idrove through town to the crossing point into Syria and laughed in disbelief at the proximity of the border that had eluded us several times. Istopped the vehicle just short of the Syrian buildings, beyond the destroyed, abandoned Iraqi checkpoint and left the vehicle ready for escape. A couple of photos would have to be taken as a keepsake. All of ten seconds passed when Jane shouted to get my attention, a truckload of Iraqis brandishing AK-47s and RPGs, were coming our way. Given the history of the place and sinister stares on their faces, I jumped into the driver's seat and left in a cloud of dust...

I made my way to the outskirts of the town and happened upon a U.S. army convoy. Three heavily armoured Humvees, with several armed troops, were parked next to an old school, the officers meeting with new Iraqi police officials. As we would see, many times to come, the soldiers drew their weapons as we pulled the GMC in front of the first Humvee, then stared in amazement we hopped out with a friendly hello. The last thing in the world they expected was a British bloke and a blonde American chick cruising the Iraqi countryside in a GMC Jimmy with Arabic plates.

I had a quick chat with the commanding officer and agreed to follow the convoy out of town to get some on the ground intelligence.(See Photographs) Maps on the hood of victor 1, and a vague nod in the direction of a close phosphate plant sent me on our way. (heads up on the location of the Saddams uranium mine and disused railway? was motioned).

The LT also pointed out the locations on the map of the pontoon bridges and crossing points over the Euphrates River. It was mentioned that not many people know that they were there, (this would prove to be valuable on the ground Intel)I pulled out some cold sodas from my cool box and gave them to the boys in the Humvees, after a dusting off, chat and stay safe, I drove off in the direction of the complex.

Military and Industrial Complexs

Myintelligence from HQ told methat four Special Forces teams, (the activity), had raided the plant afew hour prior,all the people and employees/security had been arrested and taken away in a military convoy, the official Military line was that not a shot was fired, the amount of empty bullet casings littered the approach road, they made a distinctive sound when driving over them, on turning into the vast outer complex, the walls of one of the smaller compounds, (guard rooms), had been hit with a mass of .50 calibre heavy machinegun fire.The clean up teams were not there yet, a perfect place to have a bit of fun. I drove towards the main plant.

Iraqi Complex After Firefight

The main plant emerged from the dusty skyline, looming structures rotting with rust and eerily quiet. The gates were open and the few straggling Iraqi employees gave us no notice; they were too busy looting the inner gate house. I drove slowly through the facility and picked a place to begin our exploration. Underground storage, new trains and cars, "on the rail line that according to the UN was not in use", enormous holding tanks dripping with fresh water, seemingly abandoned, yet we found new office structures, electricity on and day old bread and a cold cup of tea on the desk. The office doors were locked, but a swift kick I gained access and provided me with several current log books and a couple of Saddam Hussein calendars.

I walked around taking "photographs" of the new rail cars that were located on the supposedly disused rail track that led to Saddam's secret uranium mine. After a sweep of the area I decided to make a move, back to victor 1, I had about three hours of daylight left, Anna children's hospital was my next target. I had some much needed special medical supplies to drop off at the Anna children's hospital, my intelligence from London had informed me that this hospital had been ran-sacked, and was in a bad way, they had no supplies for the local kids. I was carrying a lot of spare medical supplies and I was going to get to the hospital before darkness, the location of the hospital in Anna was still hostile, Insurgence where still fighting in the area. And reports had come in that the insurgents were mounting illegal check points at night. I slowly snaked my way through the roads and tracks towards Anna, passing a battalion of burnt out Iraq army tanks "T64", body parts and charred, smoking clothing scattered all around, an APC, was burning feistily to my left, this battle had

just happened, the road had entry, splash marks and craters from where the US apache gunships had strafedand churned up the road, the black smouldering skeletons of destroyed enemy vehicleslittered the sides off the road and surrounding area.To my amazement a T72 main battle tank had been blown upside down on to the side of the road. There was no glory here, the enemy did not know what hit them. The Apache helicopter gunship is the most devastating fast attack helicopter in the world and it had left a shadowy trail of devastation and death through this earth scorched location. The trail of destruction left by the SOF teams was very prominent. Saddam's covert underground communications lines had been blown up,craters, scorched earth and the residue of C4 "plastic explosives" indicated this on several occasions, as well as the shape charge explosions that had taken out all the bridges in the area, the SOF must have totally disrupted the enemy. No wonder reports of all hell breaking loose on the Iraq army side had come back over the intercepted communication networks...

Anna, Children's Hospital

I started to enter Anna at last light, there is only one main road into the town from the west. It's an eerie road, the mist coming over from the river gave it a ghost like appearance; there were large mounds of earth on both sides of the road. Iraq machinegun positions were still intact, situated on top of these prominent mounds. Something did not fit, it looked wrong, I slowed down to a crawl;all windows of the jeep were down. I listened to the sounds of the coming night. It was absolute silent, not even a sound from animals, not even a howling dog in one of the wild packs that roamed these parts...Then suddenly several figurersappeared on the sky line of the mounds to my left, I could not make them out, they moved closer, all were carrying AK-47s, they were dressed in Iraqi army uniforms, I remember thinking "fuck me" as I moved my personal weapon close to me, "this is going to be interesting". The shadowy silent figures moved closer to my open window, I greeted them, in Arabic, they stood around the jeep looking at us and at each other. I asked directions to the hospital, they seemed very relaxed, almost pleased to see us. One of them jumped in and showed me the way into town, he directed me to the police station. I was greeted by the chief of police of Anna, he was also dressed in a military uniform. After a short talk over chai, I explained that I had some specialist medical supplies for the children's hospital, I had brought these in Lebanon, Syria and Jordon. He sent for a teacher to take me to the hospital. He was pleased to have me in his town. He told me he did not want any US military in his town, he could run his own town without outside interference. I agreed and with a shake of hands and goodbyes my jeep was escorted to the hospital. On arrival in the hospital grounds, there were a group of twenty armed men in a variety of clothing, all brandishing AK-47s, they looked on as the main Dr of the hospital came out, we talked, then he shouted for some help and we unloaded the boxes of medical supplies into the hospitals storage room.

On entering the hospital it was in a mess, it had been looted and ransacked, the store room was empty. They didn't even have the very basic of supplies. The boxes of supplies I had brought would give them a life line. Antibiotics, wound dressings, IV's, syringes, tablets, creams, medical instalments, etc.

I had been told by my Intel people back in London that this place was in bad shape, my friendly call/signs knew me and knew that I would take the time and get some much needed supplies to them. The Dr's were happy that they now had supplies to treat the local people and children. The Dr's also insisted that we spend the night in the hospital, they said it was safe.

I spent most of that night being shown around the little hospitaland talking to the local people and the Dr's, after many cups of chai, it was about 0300hrs, I was shown to a private room and fell fully clothed onto the bed,I fell asleep before my head hit the pillow.

I woke the next morning at day break, after a quick wash in ice cold water, "good for wakening up", I said my goodbyes to the Dr's wishing them the best, after an open invention back at anytime, I drove out of Anna.

Next stop, Haditha on the Euphrates River.The Euphrates and the Tigris are the life lines to the people of Iraqo

The Regime of the Tigris and Euphrates Rivers

Rivers in any country in the world, especially war zones are always a good form of emergency extraction. You can always find a boat of some sort on every river bank. My advice to anyone operating in war zones, learn about your rivers... The headwaters of the Euphrates are the Murat and the Korasuyu (Karasu) in the Armenian Highland of Anatolia. They join to form the Euphrates at Keban, near Elazig, forming a deep gorge. The river breaks through the Taurus Mountains and descends to the ancient kingdom of Commagenes. With the Mediterranean only 100 miles to the west at this reach, the Euphrates continues south and southeast into a relatively barren part of Syria, where the cultivable floodplain is no more than a few miles wide. Ample rainfall in the northern reaches of both these tributaries allowed the creation of major cities in ancient times.

 Euphrates River Iraq

From its confluence with the Al-Khabur down to Abu Kamal, the Euphrates flows through a broad agricultural region. Below the border with Iraq, the river once again narrows to an alluvial strip between limestone escarpments. Below Hit, the river begins to widen and irrigation increases.

Just south of the river below Ar-Ramadi lie Lakes Al-Habbaniyah and Al-Milh, both of which are large depressions. At Al-Hindiyah the river splits into two branches, Al-Hillah and Al-Hindiyah, each of which, over the centuries, alternately has assumed importance. Below An-Nasiriyah the river flows into marshes and then joins the Tigris at Al-Qurnah to form the Shatt al-'Arab.

The Tigris, rising in a small mountain lake, HazarLake, southeast of Elazig, and fed by a number of small tributaries, drains a wide area of eastern Anatolia. After flowing beneath the impressive basalt walls of Diyarbakir, it receives the waters of the eastern Al-Khabur near the Syrian border at Cizre (Jazirhe-a-bin-Omar), entering Iraq a few miles beyond at Faysh Khabur.

Near Mosul the Tigris passes the ruins of two of the three ancient Assyrian capitals--Nineveh (Ninawa) and Calah (modern Nimrud)--on its left bank. The ruins of the third capital, Ashur (modern Ash-Sharqat), overlook the river from the right bank farther downstream, between the left-bank junctions with the Great Zab and the Little Zab. During flood time, in March and April, the two Zabs double the volume of the Tigris.

The Tigris reaches the alluvial plain near Samarra`, the capital of a great empire during the 'Abbasid period (AD 750-1258). In Baghdad and its environs, artificial embankments line the Tigris, as well as districts occasionally threatened by the Euphrates and the DiyalaRiver, which joins the Tigris just below the capital. The Shatt al-Gharraf is the main line of the Tigris.

The regime of the Tigris and Euphrates depends most heavily upon winter rains and spring snowmelt in the Taurus and Zagros mountains. The Euphrates traverses a considerably greater distance than the Tigris from its mountain basin to the point where it meets the Mesopotamian alluvial plain at Ar-Ramadi. On its long, gently sloping route through Syria and northern Iraq, the Euphrates loses much of its velocity and receives only two tributaries, the Al-Balikh and the (western) Al-Khabur, both of them spring-fed and entering from the left. The Tigris, in contrast, flows down the edge of a long, multi channelledcatchment basin and is fed by four strong tributaries, the Great Zab, Little Zab, Al-'Uzaym (Adhaim), and Diyala, all of which derive their water from snowmelt in Anatolian, Iranian, and Iraqi Kurdistan. The precipitous flow of its tributaries makes the Tigris more susceptible than the Euphrates to short-term flooding and brings its annual flood period a month earlier.

As it reaches the Mesopotamian alluvial plain above Samarra`, the Tigris is a bigger, faster, more silt-laden, and more unpredictable river than the Euphrates at the corresponding point, Al-Fallujah. This character is expressed in the Arabic name Dijla, meaning "Arrow." The mean annual discharge of the Tigris is estimated at 43,800 cubic feet (1,240 cubic meters) per second, and the silt load at approximately one ton per second. These estimates are roughly twice those calculated for the Euphrates. In flood time the two rivers together carry as much as three million tons of eroded material from the highlands in a single day.

The Tigris and Euphrates make habitable and productive one of the harshest environments in the world. The region has a continental subtropical climate, with extremes of heat in summer and cold in winter, as well as great diurnal variations. Rainfall is scanty. In the higher elevations, where the rivers have their upper courses, winter winds are light and variable. Much of the precipitation falls as snow, which can lie in some places for half the year. During winter, the mean temperature in the mountains is well below freezing, so that agriculture comes to a halt and communications are restricted. With the melting of the snow in spring, the rivers are in spate. The mounting volume of their waters is augmented in their middle courses by seasonal rainfall, which reaches its peak between March and May. In the lower courses of the rivers in the alluvial plain, rain can be torrential in winter but usually does not exceed 8 inches (200 millimeters). Rain is a welcome supplement to irrigation, which since ancient times has made possible the region's legendary agricultural richness.

In the Mesopotamian plain, the most characteristic climatic feature is the extreme heat of the summer, with daytime temperatures rising as high as 140 F (60 C). Often, there are drops of 40 F (22 C) from day to night. Humidity in most areas is as low as 15 percent. Dust storms, which occur throughout the year, are especially frequent in the summer. Most wind-borne dust consists of particles of clay and silt mixed with minute fragments of shell, which are from a remnant dune belt that has been formed from abandoned irrigated fields and dried-up marshes in the area between the two rivers. Only occasionally are there true sandstorms, bearing material from the western desert.

Oak, pistachio, and ash forests covered the mountains and foothills through which the upper Tigris and Euphrates pass. In the steppe zone between the mountains and the Tigris, some vegetation can flourish year-round, but the growing season in most nonirrigated areas is quite brief; the wildflowers and other plants that appear in spring die off in the heat of May and June. In the driest zones, camel thorn and prosopis are the dominant shrubs. The densest communities of plants are to be found along the rivers and in the marshes. Various reeds and the narrow-leaved cattail are abundant, and the giant mardi reed, which reaches a height of up to 25 feet, has been used as a versatile construction material since antiquity. The Euphrates poplar and a species of willow grow in small belts beside the rivers and canals; the poplar provides strong timber for construction and boat building, as well as handles for tools. The date palm is indigenous to the region. Five-stamen tamarisk and mesquite form thickets along the lower and middle courses of the Tigris and its tributaries, up to an altitude of about 3,300 feet. Licorice is sufficiently plentiful to allow exports.

Warning Locally Resident Wildlife Iraq

Wild pigs are common in the marshes. Jackals, hyenas, and mongooses are to be seen along the rivers in southern Iraq, and a large variety of Indian jungle cat reportedly still inhabits remote tamarisk thickets. Lions can be sighted along the Tigris. Foxes, wolves, and gazelles are common in the alluvial plain, and some of these range as far north as central Anatolia. Among the smaller animals are several species of gerbil, the jerboa (desert rat), hares, shrews, bats, the hedgehog, the river otter, and the Buxton's mole rat, which covers the entrance of its riverbank burrow with a mound of clay.

Locally resident birds include babblers, bulbuls, scrub warblers, sand grouse, crows, owls, a variety of hawks, falcons, eagles, and vultures. In spring and fall, many birds migrating between Europe and Asia--such as pelicans, storks, and various geese--fly along the rivers' courses, and the marshes provide a breeding ground for some migratory species.

There are several kinds of viper and a small cobra, as well as a variety of nonvenomous snakes. Lizards can reach lengths of nearly two feet. Frogs, toads, and turtles abound in the rivers and marshes. Among the freshwater fish of the Tigris-Euphrates system, the carp family is dominant. Barbels weighing as much as 300 pounds (136 kilograms) have been recorded. There are several varieties of catfish, as well as the spiny eel. Some saltwater species--including anchovy, gar, and sea bream--range upriver at least as far as Basra, and the Ganges shark has been known to reach Baghdad.

Also spelled MuradRiver, Turkish Murat Nehri River, the major headstream of the Euphrates. In antiquity it was called Arsanias. The river rises north of Lake Van near Mount Ararat, in eastern Anatolia, and flows westward for 449 miles (722 km) through a mountainous region to unite with the Karasu Cayi and form the Upper Euphrates near Malatya.

Haditha

Haditha FOB Forward Operating Base

Highway 12 exit, Haditha, the location of the major hydraulic dam providing energy to the entire region. I made our left hand turn and ran into our first American vehicle checkpoint (VCP). Heavily manned with at least50 troops, 3 M1 Abrams, 4 Bradleys and 2 Humvees, Crazy Company had a strong show of force due to recent hostility and a mile-long line up of civilian vehicles. After the initial shock wore off, the soldiers were friendly and cooperative, so we hung around in the hope of some action. The checkpoint yielded results, two enormous bags of Iraqi monopoly money, [the final remnant of the ex-leader's image], a couple of AK-47s and a live goat in the boot.

Found in the back of an Iraqi man's car...

Moments later an old rusty lob sided Iraq car pulled up at the check point, after afew moments the occupants of the car were on the ground, spread eagle being covered/guarded by US soldiers.The US Capt. called me over, not a word was said, we looked at each other, then I looked in the boot, 15 sold gold bars, gleaming in the sun. Jackpot, Saddam's gold, what a find, it was funny hearing him report that on the radio.It was moved to HQ. (See Photographs) The soldiers were not happy because every bill of Iraqi and American money had to be counted and spoken for. There were two black bin bags full of bills lol...

Example of Saddam's Gold Bars

Downtown hostile, the insurgency had learned new skills, trip wires attached to a hand grenade and telegraph post, a photograph of Saddam glued to the post, when the soldiers took the photo off the wood it would detonate the hand grenade, and kill the solider. The US soldiers were ordered by their HQ to take down these photograph, they were booby-trapped. The whole set up looked too familiar to me. I recognised it from my days fighting the IRA, terrorist organisation in Northern Ireland.Ijoined the convoy back to HQ. 50km south of Haditha.One glance and my instinct and gut feeling told me to stick around, the place had all of the hallmarks of a FOB Forward Operating Base (Special Forces forward deployment location), proper vehicles, weaponry and morale. I would later be proved right as the patrols went active well after midnight and tracer rounds lit up the sky, as the bad guys were being hunted down.

An evening patrol followed a welcome swim at the damand a hot meal. The night time, more serious, body armour was put on and we accompanied the Captain in his personal Humvee. We set up a checkpoint on Highway 12 and sat under the bright with stars, checking out the night vision scope while the cars lined up. My friendly call sign Jane had a warm welcome by the soldiers, the tank commander was all too happy to give her a spin in his A-2 tank over the sand dunes (See Photographs) and the sentry likewise with his 50 cal belt-fed machine gun.Jane found out first-hand what it was like to have the firepower of a .50 calibre belt fed machinegun in her hands.

Al Asad Air Base

Al Asad, located 7km south of al Fallujah, nicknamed, "Little Baghdad Airfield", Iraq Air force Base, 100km west of Baghdad's main airport. At least 50 Russian Migs(Jet fighters), Armed with rocket and fuelled,surrounded the outer desert area of the main airbase, the jet fights were in excellent condition, half buried, abandoned, never used in the war…(I was Photographed in the cockpit of one of the Migs). An ejection handle was kept as a keep sake. HQ bollocks, red tape, picked up some medical supplies and a hot meal then back to crazycompanies HQ, fired upon by unfriendly Iraqi AK-47 fire on my way back in,I gave the US commander a bottle of black label whiskey, to share with is men, an open invite was given in return, "If you ever run into trouble you know where we are, just call for help". Across the river and into harm's way.

The WesternDesert makes up the land between the Syrian border and the Tigris river valley is a virtual no man's land. Acres of harsh, scorched terrain and hidden secrets. An anonymous landpeople enter, especially during the war, and do not return. Not manyU.S. troops nor Intel came out of this area, almost total silence during the actual war, hostile territory, journalists and photographers had disappeared and been executed in this area! Appropriately, it was in this area that our targets and locations lay.

I entered cautiously, crossing the Euphrates and leaving the safety of the U.S.base, the final bastion of friendly forces we would see for hundreds of miles.The light hearted attitude of the past few days was replaced by a tense awareness and the hairsstood up on the back of my neck.The Intel brief the night before by the US Intel stated that this area was still very hostile, the U.S. didn't send patrols into this area because of the hostility and insurgent/guerrilla movements, unless they were in large numbers. The Job had just gotten real, we were now in real harm's way. I placed the AK-47 at the ready with a full 30 round mag in place at my feet,8 spare magsin my vest, in case we needed to shoot our way out of ahostile area or situation. My emergency grab bag with extra ammo, grenades and water was always behind my seat just in case I had to leave my 4x4 in a rush. Insurgents are operatingopenly in the west of the country, they were manning illegal vehicle check points. Bad news if we were to come across them, aggressive negotiations would have to be used, shoot first ask questions later. Large numbers of people were being caught out by these, the insurgents would just drag the people out the cars and execute them at the side of the road, with a bullet through the back of the head. Bodies of men, women and children had already been found by the American military. Dismembered bodies had also been reported, insurgents leaving bodies with the severed head placed on top of it as a warning to other people. You had to be switch on all the times when driving, constantly looking for insurgents and IEDs. Time to get our game faces on!

Iraqi Elite Republican Guard Training Camp, Western Desert

I had drivenfor a few hours into the desert when across the windshield I spotted a discreet sand embankment paralleling the road. I decided to follow it a bit further and came upon a deserted entrance, marked only by a burned out guardhouse full of bullet holes. A smile played across myface as I read the white spray painting on the side, 'The Whack Shack.' Someone had been here before us. The US Rangers had been through this area in force, aSOF, recognisance search and destroy platoon, I recognised the style of spray paint, it had been on the destroyed enemy machine gun bunkers on top of the Dam at Hadetha, and the tell-tale art work was on APC's, and T72 tanks that I had driven past over the past hours. The SOF teams were sent out in front of the main coalition force tolocate, contact and destroy enemy passions and locations, there where fast, mobile teams, who travelled in Humvees and even sometimes Land Rovers, which are heavily armed, with heavy machineguns, rockets and anti-tank missiles. They moved through enemy locations leaving death and destruction behind them. "Rangers Lead The Way".

The entrance was deceptively modest; the complex covered a massive 12 square kilometres. Targeted destruction along the drive in confirmed our suspicion that we had stumbled upon something big. As I drove slowly and carefully deeper into the facility, I knew trouble was looming. There was activity around a small cluster of buildings in the distance, we were about to meet unfriendly enemy call signs. Armed Fedayeen/insurgentsstood in their places, stunned, without even time to raise their weapons before I sped past. I pulled a 180 degree turn in the centre of the complex as Jane hung out the window taking photographs." Not wise looking back at it lol". Up close and personal, we could see a major, organised smuggling operation being carried out. In their distinctive all-blackgarb, the Iraqis were loading large cargo trucks with crates of ammunition, weapons and explosives, hiding it below bags of grain and produce. This was where the insurgency was equipping itself with the ammo and mines that they were to use to make IED's to kill our troops.(I made a mental note to tag this location and have it blown off the face of the earth in the near future).

I drove about 600 meters past the set of buildings and pulled over to the side of the road, the Iraqi men had not followed us, yet. I hung a left and drove toward another set of buildings, I used them as cover. I noticed a mine field to my left, I kept it between us and the insurgents, my left flank was covered, theyknew it was there, they would not risk cross it, and if they came after victor 1, I would see them coming. I waited 15mins at the ready, no sign of the insurgences, AK-47 at the ready. It turned out the insurgents were more interested in quickly moving weapons, mines and artillery rounds, they knew that time was running out for them to move the weapons. It's amazing that Coalition forces hadn't even searched the whole area. This was going to prove to be a very bad and costly mistake, this area and complex would arm the Iraq insurgency with IEDs for attacks on the coalition all over Iraq over the coming years.

The sheer size and capacity of Saddam's Elite Republican Guard facility was staggering, small arms training ranges, Nuclear Biological and Chemical (N.B.C.) warfare training buildings,New discarded N,B,C EQT and manuals, littering the floor, international shippingcreates with France and Germany clearly marked on the side. Assault courses, living quarters, the list of facilities was endless.I pulled up around the back of the buildings, among an array of ammunition and ordinance which was scattered everywhere, high explosive and armour-piercing rounds. Over the next few minutes I quickly searched the buildings to check for booby traps, all was clear. Walking into one of the buildings, we were met by a massive room full of new wooden boxes full of new ammo, there was millions of rounds in this room, no wonder the insurgentswere not wanting us on the camp. At this point while Jane was taking photographs for evidence, the names and makes of the new ammo and equipment was clear;France, Germany, Saudi Arabia, Yemen, China to name a few. These were clear breach of the U.N. sanctions...

A vehicle was approaching, time to leave, in a split second we were in V1 and speeding away from the armed insurgents, for safety reasons the search of the camp would have to wait. On leaving the camp some discreet cover was noticed, it was fast approaching last light, V1 was pulled up in the cover and a (O.P.) observation post was set up, to observe the movements in the camp. After about 30 minutes all was quiet, the Iraq trucks had left the camp and the darkness had crept in over the desert and the ghost like camp. There was dead silence, not a sole in sight.

Terrorists/Insurgent Illegal Smuggling Routes

"To those who have fought for it, life has a special flavour
That the protected will never know" (Motto of theUS Special Operations Association)

I moved away from the O.P. and observed movements and lights about 40k to the east. Suddenly the dead silence was broken, there was anoutburst of small arms fire, followed by controlled bursts from a belt fed 50 cal. heavy machine gun. The sky and the darkness were lit up withthe thundering sound of a fire fight in full progress,with all the thrills and spills,red and green tracer cutting through the cool night air. The sound of Ak-47s and amass of small arms fire replied and instantly silenced by the god like thundering sound of the awesome50 calibre belt fed heavy machine gun(targets will fall when hit).At this point IinformedJane that there was a contact between our American friends and the Iraqi insurgents. The firefight going down on the horizon was great, the red tracer was friendly forces (special forces patrol), the green was Iraq, the distinctive sound that both of usknew all too well was the AK-47s. Just a split second after this a motorcycle pulled up outside the main entrance to the camp, the lone man dressed all in black,waited to see if all was clear. A minute passed then he fired up into the air a green flare, in response to this action the sky to the left and right of our position was filled with flares, suddenly the little dirt track that ran parallel to us became a flurry of Iraqi 4x4s (we were observing a well-organised insurgency weapons re-supply and ammo run). We watched in anticipation, we knew that if we were spotted then the Iraqs would have shot and tried to kill us. We were observing their entire operation in secret, we followed all movements and I noted all key points. This went on for about 2hrs, then just as it started, it all stopped and there was an eerie silence all around us. The rest of the night went without incident.At first light I made a command decision, the sheer volume of arms, mines and explosives in the republican guard camp was staggering, it would supply the Iraq insurgency for over six months. I could not allow the insurgents to move it all and use it against our coalition troops, there was only one answer, "blow the lot up". This was not a small decision. I was about tocross the line big time, the decision was made, I advised my friendly call sign about what I was going to do and my reasons behind it, I took full responsibility for these actions. I slowly made my way back into the camp, my AK-47 at the ready. All was dead quiet now, it was about 0430am, I pulled Viktor 1 up at the side of the main buildings. I searched the location on foot, cleared all rooms (did not want any surprises). All was clear, I knew that the insurgents would be back anytime. With no time to spare, I set up the Explosive charge and poured petrol though the rooms and connected all the arms dumps surrounding and close buildings, just to make sure the lot went up. Timer lit and we left, I got about 1KM away before it blew, the fire ball and thick black smoke filled the morning air. Mission completed. The insurgents would not be using any of the equipment, weapons, mines and ammunition against our troops now. The location and intelligence would be passed on to"DJ" G1 intelligence officer at 101st Airborne Division Head Quarters (HQ), I told the G1 intelligence officer of what I did, (off the record). There was not a problem. HQ, tasked a company of infantry to deal with our intelligence and Republican guard training camp clean-up. Me being subtle as always, in the future I would walk into the American operations room at D-Main and place a wooden box of specialist ammo which I had taken from the arms dump, it had marking on the side, Saudi-Arabia... one of Americas so called allies had been double dealing under the table... You could have heard a pin drop in the ops room... (It was a good result all round). I got 100 cool points for my actions, even if it was a little close to the mark! I would later look at my handy work via American satellite imagery, Falcon View. I had wiped out an entire area, local intelligence Hum-Int would later also confirm that I even managed to catch a few Iraqi insurgences in the blast radius... (This was one of many locations I would be blowing up over the coming years in order to save American and British soldiers lives!)

"Never Leave an Enemy Strong Hold Intact..."

First light broke at around 04:30. After a quick area sweep, I checked the map and we were on the move again moving on a northern bearing. Our Intel officer had informed me that there was a friendly airbase at a location on route (the home and HQ of the Apache battle group for Northern Iraq, the scalpel blade of the US army), the GMC rolled up to the front gates, the US soldiers on guard duty pointed their weapons at the approaching 4x4, the heavy machine gun was shouldered ready to fire into use if we were unfriendly. From the actions of the soldiers they were expecting trouble, rumour had it that local insurgents were planning an RPG attack on the base that day. I stopped the GMC short of the main gate, I and Jane got our hands in full view at all time. There was a moment of tension, (the tension was broken by a how's it going lads, we've just driven up from the south, anything happening up in this part of the world) the tension was broken and the lads just looked at the both of us, with a smile, their minds were racing, who the hell are these two, and where have they come from, it was a surreal moment, We stood chatting to the troops for about an hour, exchanging information, I left with a see you later and "Stay Safe".

On way out of town, I stopped at the local petrol station for much needed refuelling. For the largest oil producing country in the world, fuel in Iraqwas a rare commodity at this time. The station was obviously demarked by a two-mile long queue of local cars. Two American Bradleys and 15 troops stood guard against common squabbles. An Iraqi officer approached, local school full of munitions was on fire.

After a chat and soda with the US troops, Viktor was fully fuelled with spare on the back.

Next stop on the road, Tikrit (home town of Saddam himself),

Tikrit, Birth Place of Saddam Hussein

Saddam Hussein was born on April 28th, 1937, in the village of Owja on the outskirts of Tikrit, Iraq, a city northwest of Baghdad. As a young boy, Saddam was raised by a maternal uncle, in the town of ad Dawr, a mud-brick village on the banks of the Tigris river. Saddam Hussien's parents had been simple farmers, but his uncle, an officer in the Iraqi Army, gave him a glimpse of a life other than that of a humble peasant. He greatly influenced the young Saddam and instilled in him a deep passion for politics and the military. Tikrit had always been Saddam's base of power, "a local lad come good", his birthplace held a special meaning for him, and was also part of his full name, as is custom in Iraq: Saddam Hussein "Husayn" al-Tikriti. This connection to this place was a part of his very identity.

In his younger and teenage years Saddam moved to Baghdad, where he joined the Arab social Ba'ath Party when he was nineteen years old. The Ba'ath party was new them and set to overthrow the nations' Prime Minister, Abdul Karim Qassim. As he entered his early twenties, Saddam was very ambitious and daring when younger. In later years, cunning with an iron fist, would be added to that. He knew he did not want a life as a poor peasant, or farm worker. The only way he could see at avoiding this happing was by the use of force. In 1959, when he was just twenty two, Saddam was involved in a brash coup attempt, the attemptto assassinate the Prime Minister failed, Saddam was shot in the leg by the Prime Minister's bodyguard, but fled with his life. Showing a great flare and talent for evade and escaping he fled to Syria. He would use this same flare many times in the future. He would even try this in the future when cornered and captured by American soldiers on intelligence from Kurdistan!

Saddam Hussein's Presidential Palaces Tikrit

I arrived at a small US Army HQ, our first venture into one of Saddam's old presidential palaces on the banks of the Tigris River, our meet was with an officer there.I spotted CIA operatives walking around,a group of large plain green and red containers, they caught my eye, they looked familiar. I had seen the same set up in Afghanistan with the 5th Special Forces group. These containers housed portable fixed wing router aircraftand a strategic and technical operations room. I had spotted one of the specialist aircraft at Mosul Airbase. I had seen the CSA "Central Support Agency " operating alongside the DEA "Drug enforcement Agency" in Columbia, against the ongoing fight with the Columbian drug cartels. It was a big tactical decision to have a CSA "Central Support Agency" location set up in northern Iraq. It was more of a strategic placement, maybe the CSA where keeping tabs on and hunting targets in the countries next to Iraq. The special containers also housed state-of the art electronic countermeasures and their satellite computer networks, including drone Command and Control.Afterexchanging contact data, satellite numbers, Intelinformation, a report on AQI and terrorists coming over the border from Syria, Iran; a well-deserved brew inside the CSA HQ.Ihad a wonder and found Jane talking to one of the US 4ID officers, by the side of an armoured Humvee, he seemed upbeat, he asked how I was. I answered good, Jane had been telling him of some off the things that had happened to us on our travels in Iraq, he said "You guys are very different to anyone else around here". Over time we would build a "solid, good reputation with the men on the ground in the US military" and we would help them in some seriously sensitive operational areas! We walked pastone of Saddam's son's palaces, with a hot brew in hand. I gave the palaces a once over, the entry point for the cruise missile that took it out was in plain view (a photo was taken as a keep sake).Nice stop, but priorities lay further north

Jacuzzi in the Peach Orchards of Tikrit.

I made my way up the dangerous dusty, highway paralleling the TigrisRiver. The blistering desert heat was unbearable. My friendly C/Sign Jane was going down with bad heat exhaustion after 3hrs of travelling in this unbearable heat,my target destination could wait. I had studied maps and satellite imagery of the area, as I did with all areas I operate in and committed key points to memory. They was a river close by,I broke off the main road, blasted through some dusty little villages at much to the interest of the local farmers, found my perfect oasis, a makeshift Jacuzzi in the middle of a peach orchard. After 30 minutes of cool water going over Jane, she cooled down and came round, I told her not to worry, it happens to the best of us. Sun stroke andrelentless desert heat has killed a lot of good people each year in these parts of the world. A shamack or a head scarf, with a neck cooler/scarf, are a good way of keeping cool, only wear light cloths and drink a lot of water, at least 4 LTS a day.

Comfortably clean and cool, I threw on some horse beats for the drive. The desert scenery flew by as dusk fell:American troops rolling through townson patrol, handing out food, candy to the local kids;brightly burningfires at nearby oil fields; Bedouin Sheppard's herding their flocks to evening shelter. The flat desert plains had not so much as a hill or culvert to give us protection for the night, so I continued driving. I remembered fromstudying the map that there was a SF Base and palace about 6km north next to the oil pipe line. There was an area of sand dunes before the base. Not safe to be driving about after dark, "Ali Baba and his fortyThieves", on the move, but that's why I have a good 4-wheel drive and mylittle friend the AK-47 (accept no substitute). I finally found a safe place 400 meters off road between some sand dunesand got our heads down for the night under the silent starlit Iraqi sky.

Morning came and Iwoke with flies covering us, hundreds of them, crawling over every inch of us, our sleeping bags and the jeep; left open to air out overnight. After shaking all the flies and bugs off, Jane finally sat on the hood of the jeep to write in her journal (See Photograph) and have her morning brew, coffee,"she was a Tasmanian devil without it".

While I cleaned and oiled the weapons and looked over the map and planned the day's agenda, routes. I had locations to hit and another American airbase to visit.

Balad home of (JSOC-Joint Special Operations Command).

One of the Task Forces Operating out of Balad at that time was Task Force Back.

Following the toppling of Saddam Hussein's regime in Iraq, 2003 an SAS Squadron was assigned to a joint US/UK group of Special Operations units operating in the country, known previously as Task Force 145 (TF-145).

Eventually renamed to TF-88, this cream of Western Special Operators consisted of several elements:

- TF Black - - made up of an SAS sabre squadron, supported by a Company of SFSG (TF Maroon). Some SBS operators are thought to be attached to TF Black.
- TF Blue - US Navy SEALs from DEVGRU (Seal Team 6)
- TF Green - 1st Special Forces Operational Detachment - or 'Delta Force'
- TF Orange - signals intelligence gathers from the ISA

Elements of the 160th Special Operations Aviation Regiment (SOAR), US 24th Special Tactics Squadron, aircraft from the UK's 7 and 47 RAF Squadrons, along with a RAF Puma flight, provided specialised air support for TF-88. American military intelligence operatives alongside the UK's Joint Support Group, elements of MI6 and the SRR are believed to have been attached to the Task Force to provide intelligence support. 18 UKSF Signals and their US equivalents (Task Force Orange) provided signals intelligence (SIGINT) capabilities to the task force.

The primary role of TF-88 was to hunt down senior members of Al-Qaeda operating in Iraq. To this end, the Task Force had several successes including the killing of Al-Zarqawi. In response to a spate of kidnappings involving Westerners, TF-88's remit expanded to include countering this threat.

TF-Black was based in headquarters known as 'the Station', within Baghdad's green zone.

Task Force Black Operations

- In July 2003, an SAS team performed a close target reconnaissance of a residence in Mosul, thought to contain Uday and Qusay Hussein, Saddam's sons. British commanders pushed for the SAS to raid the house but are denied. A combined force of US Delta Force and the 101st Airborne eventually attacked the building and killed Uday and Qusay.

- Operation Marlborogh
  In July 2005 an SAS sniper team neutralized an insurgent bomb squad before they could reach their targets in the city.

- In March 2006, in a bloodless operation, the SAS rescued British activist, Norman Kember, and 2 Canadians who had been kidnapped in Baghdad
  more info: SAS rescue Norman Kember

- September 5th, 2007 - A 30-man SAS team assaulted a house that intel had pinpointed as the location of a senior Al-Qaeda figure. The mission was a success but sadly it costs the life of one of the SAS assaulters.
  more info : SAS soldier killed in mass raid on Al-Qaeda chief
  (Times Online report)

- March 26th, 2008 - 1 SAS soldier from Task Force Black is killed during an operation against insurgents in a town in Northern Iraq.
  more info : 'Ambush' that left SAS trooper dead
  (BBC News Report)

As with its other commitments such as counter-terrorism and training, the SAS rotated a squadron into Task Force Black on a 6-monthly basis.
The unit changed names at least once, becoming known at some point as Task Force Knight (TF-Knight). The British contingent of TF-88 ceased operations in 2009 due to the British military's withdrawal from Iraq. The SAS squadron committed to Task Force Black was subsequently deployed to Afghanistan, significantly boosting the UKSF presence in that theatre.

I would work in the future, with "EH" "T" "S" "V", E was SAS Chief of Staff in Kabul, Afghanistan, we would work very closely together on locating Terrorist Training camps and HVTs including; Senior AQI Commanders and Taliban Leaders... But that's another story covered within my first book... (See witness, legal statements at back of book).

After checking my maps, GPS and conducting some advanced weapon drills with Jane, she had to be able to defend herself if things went bad. (See Photo below) We made my way out into the Western desert of Iraq, to hit and check multiple targets, the first was a mass grave site, al Hatra, the local Ba'ath party had killed another family, children and all, the people in the village said that they knew nothing (too scared to say)I moved on.

Jane Weapon Drills

(I was to witness in a blood splattered room, with several coups, the horror of what the Ba'ath party did to families they did not like, they killed tortured and mutilated many children and young women, sometimes even worse).
I came across a small dirt track that seemed to lead to nowhere, only marked as an old army complex on our map. From past experience what we found out on the ground was very different to what was marked on the map. I investigated and made my way up the endless dust track that seemed to lead us to nowhere, the track was well travelled with large craters every few feet, movement was slow. Suddenly

the track became smoother to travel on, this struck us as strange, we continued. A few minutes passed, then out the blue,movement in the distance. I stopped and observed through the binoculars, a US sentry post with a heavy machine gun about 400 meters to my front. Idrove up slowly observing all around us at all times. There was a moment of tension as Ipulled up just short of the entrance.We both de-bussed and walked towards the soldiers, (this was now routine for us),after a brief chat with the soldiers on the gate and showing them ID,I drove into the military complex.

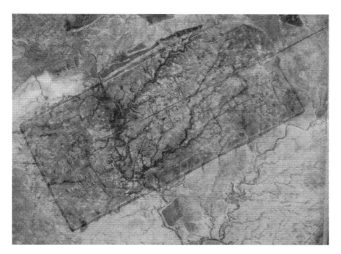

I had come across two ammunition complexes, (Jaguar north and south See Photographs), over 300 over and underground bunkers full of ammo of every kind and calibre, RPG, rockets, aircraft missiles, hand grenades, a massive selection of new mines of every kind and tank rounds.(See Photographs)

There were also mortars with a large selection of rounds, the list was endless. All this was just sitting there in the words of a US Officer 'there were billions of rounds here'.I had a quick drive around investigating some of the locations, several of the bunkers were totally full with the new plastic mines from China andother new equipment of all shapes and sizes, anti-personnel and anti-tank mines littered the entrance to one bunker. I cleared a safe path before we entered, double checking for booby traps.Suspected countries of origin included China, France, Germany, Saudi and Yemen, to name a few. (Were these countries in breach of UN sanctions..?). The mines looted from this location would turn up all over the area in the months to come, the insurgents would adapt a deadly new way of using land mines to kill coalition troops. They would strap and hang the mines from under low bridges, the passing military convoys would detonate them when passing, this was a very crud, but very affective new form of IED; it was having deadly affect. The US Government had given the order down to the military commander on the ground that most of the weapon storagefacilities and complexes, "1000s of then in all" were not to be blown up in controlled explosions, but to be left to give back to the new Iraqi government and the new Iraqi army when it had been formed. This was a massive mistake. The US army did not have enough boots on the ground to guard all the ammo and weapon storage facilities. The insurgence and al-Qi'da were literally just helping themselves, they were treating these complexes like their own personal supermarkets. Only here, instead of buying food, they would pick up 100mines, 100 RPG and so on."M.A.G." The Mine Advisory Group, was working to try and make some of these weapons storage facilities safe. A lot of children had been killed by "UXO" Unexploded Ordinance.An English Gentleman called Ian, a retired British military officer was working on one of these sites called Jag north; he was helping clear the local area of UXO and was doing a great job helping the local children. Teaching them what UXO is and how dangerous it was.

 **Anthony Malone @ Jag North**

MAG (Mines Advisory Group)

MAG (Mines Advisory Group) is one of the world's leading humanitarian organisations MAGclear the *remnants of conflict* from some of the world's poorest nations, they*educateand employ* local people and *help provide solutions* for those trapped by poverty and economic devastation through no fault of their own. Operating since 1989 and having worked on a variety of conflict-related projects in around 35 countries, MAG is also co-laureate of the 1997 Nobel Peace Prize, awarded for their work with the International Campaign to Ban Landmines. MAG helps build futures for people affected by conflict by providing local know-how, physical clearance, education and working with local partners to rebuild communities. MAG help provide solutions in both clearance and mine risk education and use a variety of methods to remove the threat of poverty and economic devastation through education, employment, metal detecting, minefield marking, sniffer dogs, large machinery, new technologies and much more. Landmines and UXO restrict people's access to education and healthcare facilities, as well as to clean, safe water and land for cultivation. They hinder links between villages and restrict local trade. In addition, fear of death or injury has a negative impact on those who live, work and grow up amidst the danger of a contaminated environment. By reducing landmine and UXO contamination MAG addresses these obstructions to long-term and sustainable development.

MAG's community liaison teams work closely with 'at risk' communities to find out how the landmine and UXO contamination is affecting their daily lives. With this information they can then choose the most appropriate response. Their expert technical staff are best placed to know which method suits which terrain, but they do not do this in isolation: the anticipated impact of the work are determined in conjunction with the local community, partner NGOs and national or local authorities. MAG has been operating in the heavily mine-affected north of the country since 1992. During the recent conflict our efforts were concentrated on delivering vital services in Government of Iraq territory, particularly in the areas surrounding Mosul and Kirkuk. MAG work here significantly reduced the threat to both resident and transient populations, and has supported both rehabilitation and development initiatives. In the past two years alone, MAG have cleared more than one million landmines and items of unexploded ordnance, freeing several million square meters of land for use by the local population. Currently MAG have some 700 national and international staff working in the seven northern governorates. This staffing comprises 21 Mine Action Teams, providing a highly responsive and mobile clearance role, 10 Community Liaison/Mine Risk Education teams, 2 midi-flail machines and operating teams and 4 Mine Detection Dog teams. Although the current security threat has impeded some activities.

RIP Ian (MAG)

MAG remain operational and able to deliver much-needed clearance and development services. Our threat management is continually reviewed and refined. BeneficiariesVulnerable populations, including Internally Displaced People and refugees, as well as other agencies implementing humanitarian, reconstruction and development projects have all benefited from our work in Iraq. The futurewhere security allows, MAG will continue to develop our programme throughout all seven northern governorates, and continue to support the building of a national clearance workforce, I stopped for a chat and hot brew (tea) with the Captain in charge. He gave me the run down on MAG's operations in Iraq. After a good brief with the Captain and Ian, and a tour round some of the facility,light hearted conversation (banter) followed. With smiles and a hand shakewe were on our way, it was time to push on and recce the area of myday sack, I wanted to revisit this area for many reasons.I left the complex behind and made a note of the location so I could return at a later date to have some fun and investigate. The entire area was crawling with US troops at this point.Another investigation team looking over another mass grave created by the former Bath party, I made my way past their location, my instinct told mewhat they were going to find, "more mass graves".

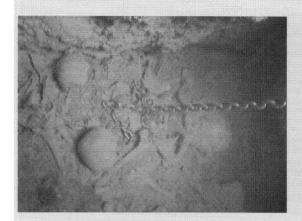 

I headedup to the high ground, I needed an overview of the whole area,as I made my way cross country to the high ground the size of the military presence in the area was all too visible; this was not what I was expecting.US troops and vehicles covered the entire area. I noted the position of anO.P."observation post"that was watching meon the high ground adjacent to us, it was manned by two US soldiers. After a quick assessment of the area it was clear that location was now of high value to the Americans.Briefly a moment was taken to confirm compass bearings of the dusty track running along the twisting dried up river bank which ran silently through our location of interest.Looking down on the area where I was shot was a strange feeling, it was both a reality check and humbling. I was glad that lady luck and my angel were with me that day.

The military activity was to intensifyin this area, it would also become an insurgent and ISIS strong hold in the future.I pushed on north to 101st Airborne (Air Assault) Divisional, HQ's, D-Main, located in Mosul Northern Iraq. The drive up was eerie, passing on the way more burnt out vehicles, T54 tanks and BMPs, there were scattered and burnt out skeletons of anti-air craft positions, (AAA batters), there was also otherremnants of the war just scattered.

The route up through the desert was like a ghost town, dead man's land, the futile efforts of the Iraq army against the might of the US army was evident all around us, (it seemed so pointless, what a complete waste of human life).I thought of David and Goliath from the bible at this point (the unnerving thought of this was that the underdog won)..?

I arrivedat US Military HQ, D Main Mosul. In the middle of the afternoon it seemed cooler up this part of the country, the heat was not as intenseas in the south of the country.Upon arrival I was introduced to M ajor Kate, he was the public relations, Media Officer at D Main.

One hundred and fifty-eight soldiers reenlisted on July 4th, 2003 at Saddam's Palace in Mosul.

He is a large sprit of a man, 100% US Airborne through and through. We stood chatting for awhile, he gave me the run down on the camp area and all that was going on, my reputation had preceded me, and word had got around the senior US commanders that I was a good covert asset to have around.

The above viwe is from Saddams balcony as the sunsets over the river and Mosul, Iraq. By Author.

The city of Mosul is predominantly Kurdish but has a substantial non-Kurdish minority. This minority consists of Iraqis sympathetic to the Saddam Hussein regime. The Iraqis as well as both Kurdish factions are Sunni Muslims. Although the Kurds and Iraqis share a common religion they have little else in common and are frequent adversaries. After the deployment of US forces in 2003, militant members of both the PKU (Patriotic Union of Kurdistan) and the KDP (Kurdish Democratic Party) were suspected of reprisals against Iraqis in Mosul. Mosul has a rich ancient Assyrian history, Mosul is a historically important trade centre linking Persia and the Mediterranean. In the 8th century, Mosul became the principal city of northern Mesopotamia under the early Muslim Abbasid dynasty. In the Ottoman period it was one of the provincial seats of administration. The largest city in Iraqi Kurdistan, Mosul is predominantly Kurdish with a sizeable Turkomen minority. The Yazidi sect is most numerous in the surrounding mountainous area. Mosul also has the largest number of Iraqi Christians of any Iraqi city, including Nestorians, Jacobites, Catholics and Chaldeans. There are churches in Mosul that are historically and culturally important for several of these Christian sects. When ISIS took over the City of Mosul in the future after the so called Iraq army just dropped their weapons and ran away back to Baghdad. ISIS had rounded up raped and executed or beheaded, thousands of women and Kurdish and Christian families. The mass graves found around the city are evidence of this...

Mosul City

Mosul [Arabic: 'al-mawsil] was the location of the headquarters of the Iraqi Army 5th Corps and the 16th Infantry Division of the Iraqi Army 5th Corps. The territory of modern Iraq is roughly equivalent to that of ancient Mesopotamia, which fostered a succession of early civilisations. The history of Mesopotamia began with the civilisation of the Sumerians around 5000 BC in the southern region of Iraq. In 2371 BC, King Sargon Of Akkad asserted control of the region and established the first Assyrian dynasty. The Assyrians ruled the region and expanded its' territories to include modern Turkey, Iran, Syria and Israel. The Assyrian empire reigned until the fall of its capital Nineveh (modern day Mosul) in 612 BC. Mosul is Iraq's third largest city, with approximately 665,000 inhabitants as of 1987. It is situated some 400km north of Baghdad situated on the west bank of Tigris, and close to the ruined Assyrian city of Nineveh. Many of the people of Mosul and its environs are Assyrians, though they are not the Assyrians of old. The city is sometimes described as the Pearl of the North. It differs considerably from the other cites of Iraq in its architecture: marble is ubiquitous, especially in frames of windows or doors. The city has kept an oriental character that Baghdad has lost: its older part is preserved, with its tortuous streets. There is an old centre to Mosul with narrow, shady alleys of mud-plastered houses but much of the city consists of prosperous looking suburbs with large, square concrete houses surrounded by walled gardens. Some of them are extravagant mansions with dramatic balconies and plastered entrances.

In approximately 850 BC, King Assurnasirpal II of Assyria chose the city of Nimrud to build his capital city where present day Mosul is located. In approximately 700 BC, King Sennacherib made Nineveh the new capital of Assyria. The mound of Kuyunjik in Mosul is the site of the palaces of King

Sennacherib and his grandson Ashurbanipal. Probably built on the site of an earlier Assyrian fortress, Mosul later succeeded Nineveh as the Tigris bridgehead of the road that linked Syria and Anatolia with Persia. Assyria took its name from its chief city, Assur, on the upper Tigris. Lying north of Babylonia, on the great trade route of the Fertile Crescent, the country was frequently invaded from the north as well as from the south. Constant warfare made the Assyrians fierce fighters and traders who passed their way were forced to pay them tribute for protection. The Assyrians had long been under the control of Babylon and had absorbed Babylonian culture. Like the Babylonians they were Semites and their language was almost identical with the Babylonian. From the Hittites of Anatolia they learned the use of iron and developed powerful weapons to build up a military state. From them they also acquired horses and were the first to use them in war as cavalry instead of for drawing chariots. Assyria's greatest period of expansion took place as the power of the Hittites and Egyptians over Syria and Palestine gradually weakened. The Assyrian King Tiglath-Pileser III (745-727 BC) took Damascus, in Syria. Sargon II (722-705 BC), most famous of Assyrian kings, made Palestine an Assyrian province. His son Sennacherib (705-681 BC) conquered Sidon, in Phoenicia, but Tyre resisted his assault. Esarhaddon (681-668 BC) conquered Egypt. Ashurbanipal (668-626 BC), the last of the great Assyrian kings, subdued Elam, east of Mesopotamia, and extended the empire to its greatest size. Roads were built to enable the Assyrian armies to subdue rebels quickly. A highly organised mail service carried messages from the court to faraway governors.

North of Nineveh, Sargon II built a palace far surpassing anything seen before his day. It covered 25 acres (10 hectares) and had nearly 1,000 rooms. Near it stood a seven-story ziggurat temple. Sennacherib put up three magnificent palaces in his capital at Nineveh. The Babylonians had covered their brick walls with glazed brickwork of many colours, but the Assyrians faced theirs with delicately carved slabs of limestone or glowing alabaster. Colossal human-headed winged bulls or lions, carved in alabaster, stood guard outside the main gates of palaces and temples. The Assyrians produced little literature, but in great libraries they preserved copies of Babylonian and Sumerian works. They worshiped the old Babylonian gods but gave their own god, Assur, first place. After the death of Ashurbanipal in 626 BC, Assyria's enemies joined forces. In 612 BC the Babylonians and Medes completely destroyed Nineveh. Six years later the Assyrian Empire collapsed.

By the 8th century AD Mosul had become the principal city of northern Mesopotamia. The city was an important trade centre in the Abbasid era, because of its strategic position on the caravan route between India, Persia and the Mediterranean. Mosul's chief export was cotton and today's word muslin is derived from the name of the city. In the 13th century, Mosul was almost completely destroyed by the Mongol invasion, but rebuilding and revival began under Ottoman rule. Mosul was once a walled city, and the remains of part of the city wall are still in existence at Bash Tapia castle, on the western bank of the Tigris. Mosul has an oil refinery; its productivity in the 1980s was hindered by the Iran-Iraq War.

The population of Mosul is principally Kurdish, but with a large minority of Aramaic-speaking Christian Assyrians, and a smaller minority of Turkomans. An ethnically diverse city, Mosul has the highest proportion of Christians of all the Iraqi cities and contains several interesting old churches, including the Clock and Latin Church, which contains some fine marble and stained glass. The Chaldean Catholic Church of Al-Tahira was built as a monastery in AD300 and became a church in 1600, when various additions were built. The Prophet Younis Mosque is one of most famous mosques in Mosul, northern Iraq. It is situated at the left bank of TigrisRiver on a hill called " Prophet Younis Hill" and the other name is "al- Tawba Hill." It was named in this way due to "younan Bin Matty " and the story of the whale that was mentioned in AL-Quran and the Bible. Younis, the prophet who in disobeying God's command, was punished by being thrown into the sea and swallowed by a whale. After spending many nights inside the whale in earnest prayers, God forgave him. His shrine is situated on a high hill in Mosul (NehnevaProvince), 450 km northern Iraq. Pilgrimages and visitors flock to it from everywhere. The shrine and the mosque have undergone certain changes. New houses, watering places, blue glazed-brick buildings and a limestone minaret have been built. An intensive campaign to develop and upkeep the shrine started in 1989. It intended to modernize the shrine service facilities in a way that would suit its religious and historic status, such as electric, health and mechanical systems, decorating walls with inscription, gypsum and Quran chapters, covering arches and support them with iron frames. The mosque walls have been covered with marble and the ceiling with brick and supply it with modern light and air conditioning systems. The mosque is one of the sacred places in Ninevah where people and monks visit in certain occasions. It was first an Asserian temple, afterwards the place changed to became a place for fire worshipers, then a monastery, and a church, finally it became an Islamic mosque. In one of the rooms inside the mosque, there is the prophet Younis' shrine. On the walls of the room one can see the whale bones. The conic brass domes of the mosque can be seen from the outside. A winged statue is situated near the mosque, which is the sign of the Asserian civilisation that was found through excavations during restoring the mosque. Besides, there is a well-known as "Prophet Younis Well " where he bathed after the whale released him.

Remembering Our Fallen Brothers in Arms

Remembrance Service for Members of 101st Airborne Division "Air Assault" D-Main Mosul, Iraq. By Author.

Maj. Gen. David H. Petraeus Cites Highs and Lows of Iraqi Deployment

Maj. Gen. David H. Petraeus, commanding general, 101st Airborne Division (Air Assault). Photo by Sgt. Robert Woodward, USA. Talking to the Military Times.

FORT CAMPBELL, Ky., March 17, 2004 - Home along with his soldiers after a one-year deployment in Iraq, the commander of the 101st Airborne Division (Air Assault) called the division's experiences in Operation Iraqi Freedom "a roller coaster" of highs and lows.

Since the first elements of the division began leaving their sprawling post that straddles the Kentucky-Tennessee border north of Nashville in February 2003, Army Maj. Gen. David H. Petraeus said they experienced amazing high points in Iraq.

Division troops engaged and killed Saddam Hussein's two sons, Uday and Qusay, in Mosul, and also captured Asa Hawleri, third in the terrorist group Ansar al-Islam's chain of command. They played a peacekeeping role, presiding over the first elections in post-war Iraq and helping to rebuild the country.

But contrasting these high moments were some tremendous lows, Petraeus said, particularly the loss of 60 division soldiers in Iraq. "There is nothing tougher than the loss of a comrade in arms. There really is not," the general said.

Petraeus said his own personal low of the campaign came the night of Nov. 15, when 17 of his soldiers died in a collision of Black Hawk helicopters.

"The loss of 17 soldiers in one night when two helicopters collided over Mosul was just a blow beyond belief," he said. "It's like losing 17 children. It's almost beyond comprehension -- a terrible, terrible blow to the organisation and the individuals in it."

Two months earlier, the division had experienced another devastating tragedy, this one alleged to have been inflicted by one of its own. Sgt. Hasan Akbar allegedly threw a grenade into three tents housing members of the 101st's 1st Brigade Combat Team, killing two officers and wounding 14 others. Akbar's trial is set to begin July 12.

Petraeus said the attack, launched just as the division was preparing to move north into Iraq, could have zapped his soldiers' resolve. Instead, thanks to the "tremendous response" by leaders within the brigade, Petraeus said it served as an inspiration.

"After every death came the question, what would that soldier have wanted us to do?" he said. "And the answer was to ensure that his death was not in vain and to drive on and accomplish the mission."

The morning after the Black Hawk tragedy in Mosul, Petraeus said, a young soldier in the headquarters provided similar inspiration. As he left his morning update session, struggling to think about anything but the loss of 17 soldiers, the soldier grabbed him and said, **"Sir, that just gives us 17 more reasons to get this right," Petraeus recalled.**

"I drew an awful lot of strength from that particular soldier that morning," he said.

Not all the division's highs and lows in Iraq were so profound, but they, too contributed to the day-to-day roller coaster effect of the deployment, Petraeus said.

In addition to the 101st's successes during the operation - from deploying to the theater in record time to successfully carrying out its warfighter role against a variety of enemy threats - the division's soldiers performed equally well in their peacekeeping role.

After the division blanketed Mosul with four infantry battalions to establish order, soldiers presided over Iraq's first postwar elections last May. Iraqis in Nineveh province elected a provincial council.

Meanwhile, the 101st oversaw the completion of more than 5,000 projects, building or rebuilding more than 500 schools and dozens of medical clinics, opening hundreds of kilometers of roads, reopening Internet cafes and putting an irrigation system back into operation. More than $57 million from Petraeus's commander's emergency reconstruction fund covered the costs.

The people of Mosul are so grateful for the 101st Airborne Division's part in the projects that this week they named a street in the division's honor. "It's wonderful recognition that they appreciate what our soldiers have done for them," Petraeus said.

Yet for every success, Petraeus said, he and his troops struggled with what he called the "man in the moon challenge."

"(The Iraqis) would ask us why we could overthrow Saddam in three weeks and why we could put a man on the moon but we couldn't give them a job right then, right there," he said. "Why we couldn't throw a switch and get the entire electrical infrastructure working again."

Expectations were enormous, he said. "We used to joke that the reward for one good deed in Iraq was a request for 10 more good deeds."

Petraeus said he has "cautious optimism" about the future of Iraq, citing the country's vast oil, water and sulphur reserves, the high education levels among the people, their entrepreneurial spirit and most of all, their willingness to work   hard to achieve their goals.

The caution, he said, comes from the various groups and factions now jockeying for power in the new Iraq. "At the end of the day, there has to be a spirit of compromise that prevails to allow the new Iraq to serve the needs and hopes and dreams and aspirations of all Iraqis, not just one of these particular groups," the general said.

Now that the 17,000 soldiers under his command are back at Fort Campbell, Petraeus said he feels good about the role they played in helping overthrow Saddam Hussein and reestablish peace and stability in Iraq.

"It's the greatest privilege that I can possibly imagine to have served in this division and to be blessed with such a team that we have here, at every single level, from the soldier on up to the division staff," he said. "I think our soldiers should be very proud of what they've accomplished in Iraq, and I think all Americans should be very proud of what our soldiers did."

Maj. Gen. David H. Petraeus stops to pick up a young Iraqi boy when his convoy stopped in Karbala,

Iraq, April 6. Photo by Sgt. Jason L. Austin, USA

CampLeader

CampLeader is located in the 3rd Brigade "AO" area of Operation. Camp Leader features a weight room setup outside their tactical operations centre, including a nacscent leg press machine. Well-wishes from a Clarksville elementary school hang inside the 1-187 Infantry Regiment tactical operations centre. A lot of work is going into making the CampPerformance facilities look and feel like a home, including artwork capturing the spirit of the 101st Airborne Division (Air Assault). CampPerformance offers soldiers a cafe with a variety of both American and Iraqi cuisine,including the Sunday special of a double cheeseburger with fries. Soldiers can also catch up on popular music videos while they dine. Soldiers can catch up with their friends and family over e-mail that is provided in the camp's computer room. What was once nothing more than a boxed collection of books became Iraq's first 101st Airborne Division (Air Assault) library. Chaplain (Capt.) Fran Stuart of Derry, N.H., 526th Forward Support Battalion chaplain, opened the Camp Performance Library Oct. 9, 2003 with a ceremonial ribbon cutting, followed by cake and coffee. The library started with about 200 paperback books in boxes, in sand on the side of the chaplain's tent. Stuart and her sister, Robin, a writer in New York, have worked on the library for several months. They contacted publishers and the New York Public Library, and lobbied them successfully to donate books to the cause. The library's shelves are now loaded with fiction and non-fiction readings, from spiritual selections to a book covering the 75-year history of the New York Giants football team. The chaplain also got help from the R.F. Sink Library at Fort Campbell, Ky. The library includes a reading room with new magazines, CDs and a DVD selection. Steve Wariner, a country music artist, donated several hundred copies of his album "Steal Another Day" for soldiers to grab for free. Camp Strike, my home from home for many months, is located along the west side of the TigrisRiver in downtown Mosul, includes a volleyball court, an outdoor exercise facility and ample internet and phone access to   contact home.

The compound is home to the headquarters company of the 502nd Infantry Regiment. 101st soldiers sit and watch Fox News as they await their food at the Strike Cafe at CampStrike. CampTop Gun was the stomping grounds of 1st Battalion, 320th Field Artillery Regiment. A monument in the Top Gun dining facility was built by 1-320th soldiers in Camp New York, Kuwait. The signs point to the soldiers' hometowns. Soldiers enjoy a Shakira music video at the Redleg Cafe. The "cantina" offers food, convenience store type goods, pool tables and a football table. The Top Gun Internet Cafe centre houses 14 computers from a local connection. The current rate is $3 an hour. In addition to these amenities, every soldier goes to bed at the end of their workday in air conditioned sleep areas. Now compare the American forward operating bases to what the British do for their soldiers... You're lucky if you get a cot and a tent LOL... After a quick brief by Platoon Commander and a night patrol lookingfor insurgents (See Photo, note captured insurgent weapons in photo). Then head down for a few hours then off to CMOC.

Planing, Briefing (Above) before a night patrol with the "Widowmakers"

101st Airborne Division Civil Military Operations Center (CMOC)

The 101st Airborne Division's Civil Military Operations Centre is located in downtown Mosul, situated on the banks of the river Tigrus, in the old grounds of SaddamHussiensPalace. The 101st Airborne Division established a new Civil-Military Operations Centre in Mosul on 21 May 2003 to help coordinate the humanitarian efforts of governmental, non-governmental and private volunteer organisations. A civil-military operations centre (CMOC) is an ad hoc organisation, normally established by the geographic combatant commander or subordinate joint force commander, to assist in the coordination of activities of engaged military forces, and other United States Government agencies, including FBI and department of justice and nongovernmental organisations, regional and international organisations. There is no established structure, and its size and composition are situation dependent. It is a golden rule if you stay there, stay on the top three floors, the insurgents attacks on the CMOC have never hit them as of yet, although when a RPG hits the floor below my room, it's a hell of a wakeup call. "I was on the sat-phone stud on the balcony overlooking the swimming pool one time, when another insurgent attack hit", it was a true dear diary moment.

CMOC

Sumer Group Holdings was the successful bidder for the operation of the Niniwah Hotel in Mosul. An agreement to terms was signed 01 August 2003 and will put $14 million into the renovation of the hotel if it is approved. Sumer representatives are currently working details of the renovation with the Iraqi Board of Tourism. The eight-story hotel, located on the north side of Mosul, was formerly controlled by the Ba'ath party. It features a pool, cabanas, bowling alley, restaurant, conference room and an overlook of the TigrisRiver. It is currently used as the 101st Airborne Division (Air Assault) Civil Military Operations Centre. This whole location would end up being a prison and torture chamber for ISIS in the future... (See Photographs)

In September 2003 soldiers with the 101st Airborne Division (Air Assault) and the 431st Civil Affairs Battalion gave a group of Iraqi orphans a day filled with fun and games at the Civil Military Operations Centre in Mosul. The purpose of the event was for the kids to be able to have fun in a safe environment the "swimming pool", and spend quality time with the soldiers. Soldiers volunteered time and services to help set-up and run different events of the day. Some soldiers also served as lifeguards at the pool. Children from three separate orphanages arrived to participate in the events. Each group was greeted upon arrival and given a gift of a towel with the Screaming Eagle insignia on it. The children then went swimming in the pool, participated in relay races and played games such as pin the tail on the donkey.

Winners of the games got candy and snacks. This was an important break, not just for the children but for the soldiers as well.

The US military confirmed rockets hit the Civil Military Operations Centre (CMOC) office in Mosul late on 18 September 2003, damaging some vehicles and leaving two people slightly wounded. I had been staying there at the time on the 5th floor, I had been returning from a day out on the ground when the RPGs where fired from the other side of the river. As soon as we all heard the sound "a mighty boom", we all knew that the insurgents had fired a few RPGs at CMOC again. CMOC was hit at least twice a week, with RPG or small arms fire. After being there when it was attacked 3 times, I decided to stay at another Military base...

When the Soldiers of 1st Brigade, 25th Infantry Division took over operations in the northern Iraqi city of Mosul from their Stryker brothers of 3rd Brigade, 2nd Infantry Division, many did not expect to see the increased level of combat that has occurred in their area of operation.

Nevertheless, these Soldiers of 1st Battalion, 24th Infantry Regiment, 1st Brigade, 25th Infantry Division (Stryker Brigade Combat Team) have proven their mettle to the insurgents operating in Mosul and demonstrated that they are a fierce and unyielding force. During the second week in November, 1-24 or "Deuce Four" Soldiers executed sustained combat operations on the western side of Mosul. Multinational Forces had seen a recent increase in violent activity during the religious holiday of Ramadan from mid-October through mid-November. Western Mosul is also an area that the MNF had long suspected anti-Iraqi forces were using to launch attacks on U.S. and Iraqi patrols and bases.

On Nov. 10, insurgent activity spiked throughout Mosul. Insurgents were targeting Iraqi Police Stations and other Iraqi Security forces. Immediately responding to the insurgent attacks, Deuce Four and the rest of the Lancer Brigade manoeuvred to take the fight to enemy, launching several coordinated offensive attacks in the most dangerous parts of the city. The fight lasted throughout most of the afternoon of the tenth, and at the end of the day, no police stations were in the hands of insurgents and a restless calm had been returned to the city. The fight continued on Nov. 11, Veteran's Day, 2004. But this time, the Soldiers of Deuce Four had the initiative. They were going into a neighbourhood known for harbouring insurgents and their mission was to kill or capture the enemy in a movement to contact operation.

"Combat Patrolling through the streets of Mosul (Hunting the bad Guys)"

One night I drifted off into a dark haunted, restless sleep. My memories swiftly returned to Iraq, the stifling relentless heat of the day was replaced by a cool distant breeze, the veil of night had drawn over the city, the once busy streets were disserted, a showy figure moved silently, like a ghost in the shadows. A black dog quickly scurried across the road to our front; there were no street lights, just the crescent moon high in the star lit sky, illuminating the eerie streets below. The whole place and surrounding area seemed quiet and tranquil. Suddenly the fragile peace was shattered in an instant by the distinctive sound of AK-47 automatic gunfire, this was a timely reminder of the hidden dangers that constantly surrounded us and the gravity of what we were doing out on the ground in this lawless place. We were combat patrolling through an insurgent stronghold in the old quarter of the ancient city of Mosul in Northern Iraq.

American soldiers had been ambushed and killed earlier in the day, the local atmosphere was a mix of fear, hostility and anticipation, everyone could feel the undercurrent of violence and death, a sense of foreboding had accompanied us on this patrol. I had accompanied the ultra-professional soldiers of 101st Airborne Division on this combat patrol at their request, they valued my combat experience and skills as a fellow soldier and my trade craft as a specialist operator. The soldiers on the ground knew that I had my finger on the pulse of local intelligence; I knew what was going on across their AO (Area of operations). Many soldiers had seen me working closely alongside Colonel Lennington, Anderson and General Petraeus, everyone knew that my access and status was very unusual. They did not buy my official cover as a combat photographer, the fact that I was now carrying an M4 assault rifle and not a camera was a bit of a giveaway, but it was nice to be myself with the military boys on the ground. They liked having me around on live operations; they valued my no bullshit approach to any given situation. It was an open secret about my work and Hum-Int (Human Intelligence) that had achieved outstanding results, including nailing HVTs terrorists in their safe house locations, my unlimited access to intelligence staff and their main hub, operations room at D-Main spoke volumes.

It was obvious to any outsider that I was trusted by the American military at a very high level of Command... Being at headquarters is all well and good, but I prefer being out on the ground at the sharp end of operations. I had no problem in rolling up my sleeves and getting my hands dirty, the soldiers knew this, my patriotic, die hard, can do attitude went down well. (It takes a soldier to know a soldier). We tactically patrolled on into the old quarter of the city, past burned out traditional mud walled buildings which echoed the sounds of war past. The thick mist rolling off the Tigris River gave these streets a ghost like eerie atmosphere and unnerving feel. Slowly and carefully we drove on, observing for possible IEDs and alertly observing all our surroundings, our minds were hyper vigilant and alert, all the boys had their game faces on, this was as real as it gets. Patrolling through the old warren of small narrow streets which surrounded the whole area was like navigating a maze, which was completely deserted, this warren lead to our target location, the old bazaar (market). On our arrival the whole area was deadly silent, no movement or human presence. Empty market stalls lay over turned to our front; on observing my arks of fire I notice that this place was a perfect bottleneck for an enemy ambush from the roof tops which over looked the main bazaar and surrounding area, a well-placed RPG (rocket propelled grenade) from the terrorists would really spoil our day. The drivers pulled the armored Humvees up in staggered formation, with the 50cal roof gunners given top-cover, safety's off and fingers on the triggers, ready to return enemy fire when it came. The remaining soldiers quickly de-bused and moved fluently into all round defense, instinctively observing the rooftops through and over our weapon sights. On this night I was carrying a M4-A2 assault rifle fitted with a M203 40mm under-barrel grenade launcher. In my opinion, the M4-A2 rife fitted with a M203, is the perfect weapon of choice for patrolling these perilous streets and likewise precarious locations, the assault rifle packs enough firepower to deal with most hostile situations encountered in and across this area of operations (See Photographs). The patrol consisted of two armored Humvees, four soldiers in each, eight fighting men in total. We had worked and patrolled together in the past so team work was a given, now we were out looking for bad guys again, we had started to refer to this as "crocodile hunting".

 Author on Patrol Iraq

We were out on this night in the profound hope of finding and eliminating them. We moved forward on foot, we all thought the same thing, it would only take a moment for a terrorist to pop his head over the roof tops and fire off a burst of automatic AK-47 gunfire, "Beirut unload" (See Glossary) in our general direction, for them it would have be like shooting fish in a barrel, it would be hard for them to miss, given the confined space we found ourselves in. Instead of the eagerly anticipated adrenalin fueled firefight, there was unadulterated silence, stillness engulfed us, nothing moved, still no sign of human presence on any level, not even sounds of concealed movement. The only sound I could here was the sound of my own shallow breathing, hand signals were silently exchanged, four men had stayed with the Humvees, two men giving top-cover with the heavy machineguns, one manning the radio, monitoring the radio traffic of activity in our patrol area and the forth was acting as a spotter, watching for any enemy who could appear at any given time. Our four man patrol stealthy patrolled forward deeper into the bazaar area, observing our arcs of fire as we went, we used the sides of the buildings and overturned market stalls as cover as we went forward. We went firm just inside the mouth of the entrance, the patrol Commander had briefed us prior to setting out from the base camp. The plan of action, objective was to smoke out, overtly luring out the bad guys. We were the bait, the patrol Commander had asked me what I thought of the plan handed down to him, my answer was that it sounded like a plan, as long as I could come along, we were all well up for locking horns with the enemy tonight, we all wanted payback for them killing one of our soldiers. Hunting the bad guys was the order of the night, "happy days". We pushed on further into the deserted bazaar; the pending silence was a foreboding statement that something was very wrong and felt out of place. My past experience had taught me that when the local indigenous population disappears, then this is a red flag and a clear indication that something extremely bad is about to happen, normally an indication that someone is about to be shot or blown up by an IED, and the someone is normally us. Now that was a sobering thought. Our weapons were poised and ready to be cycled in a heartbeat, spare magazines were at hand, ready to be slammed into the magazines housing in anticipation of a sustained firefight, the "rock and roll" on full auto was what we all felt was inevitable. The overall plan was to draw the enemy out, then hit them with a wall of sustained fire and fight our way back to the Humvees and their coving fire from the two heavy machineguns. We also had an anti-tank weapon rocket if needed, just in case we needed to level a building.

The actions after contacting the enemy was to drive like a bat out of hell out of Dodge City as the bullets were flying. American intelligence suspected that an insurgent group was located and operating out of the bazaar, our task was to confirm this intelligence, assess their fighting strength and capabilities and fighting numbers. This was a typical "hang out and see operation", unconventional but proven to be very effective when time was of the essences.

American Black Hawk helicopters were cycling high above the city, surveillance eyes in the sky, observing all that was going on, these sophisticated surveillance birds could monitor and track ground movement and zoom in on individuals and targets, weather structure, human or vehicle, they could even ID a car number plate from their orbiting platforms. The only question was would the enemy take the bait; was the animal hungry tonight in this lawless land, because we were... Electronic intercepts had confirmed enemy movement around us, the enemy was communicating with each other via hand held radios and mobile phones, American intelligence intercept technology and capabilities were impressive. Enemy attacks were on the increase. These were the terrorist foundations of what would later become "ISIL" (Islamic State) the seeds of terror by the terrorists were being sown amongst the local population and the simmering bad feelings between the tribes of Sunni and Shia was becoming a problem due to the Iraqi Government in Baghdad pushing the Sunni tribes of the North out of the Iraqi Government decision making. This would lead over time to a bloody civil war which would span Iraq, Kurdistan and Syria in the future, the seeds of conflict were there if one wanted to see all the warning signs. The problem was that a lot of Western politicians would chose not to see or ignore all the warning signs, at their expense. Looking back at the escalation of violence and terrorist activity across the Middle-East the area in which I was operating within would become the heart land of ISIL and ISIS and their future terrorist state.

At the time of this night patrol through Mosul City, regular attacks were being carried out on American and British soldiers every day within the area of operations, resulting in almost a soldier a day being killed or badly injured. A tape was broadcasted by Al-Jazeera which appeared to contain a message from Osama bin Laden calling for the conflict, civil war in Iraq at that time to be used as an extreme justification for more terrorist attacks and operations against the West and Western interests across the region. (Osama bin Laden UBL was already on my to do list, I would get round to him in the future...) It had gotten personal when AQI had killed a close friend of mine, UBL was already dead, he just did not know it yet...). A lot of the insurgents, AQI, ISISacross Iraq and Syria are members of the former army and intelligence structure of Saddam Hussian Iraq, who were ostracized when the American collation and Western politicians did not include them in the new post Saddam Government. This was a big mistake and members of the American CIA spoke out about this, but politicians made the decision to exclude them. As warned by myself and members of the CIA and other special advisers, the ostracized senior Iraq intelligence and army officers would form their own resistance, which in time would become AQI (Al-Qadea in Iraq and then ISIS Islamic State). Regular attacks were being carried out on coalition forces, resulting in almost a soldier a day being killed or badly injured. At this point Afghanistan was also heating up with terrorist attacks there also on the increase. A tape was broadcasted by the Arab news channel Al-Jazeera which appeared to contain more messages from UBL Osama bin Laden (even after his death tapes would surface) calling for the conflict, civil war across Iraq, Syria to be used as extreme justification for more terrorist operations against the West and Western interests across the Middle-East and Europe. Many of the insurgent groups and their Commanders across Iraq and Syria at one time were part of the much feared secrete Iraq police. The fear from these groups of people is so deep routed, even today local people across Iraq, Syria whisper their names in hushed tones when they are talking about them, the days of local people disappearing and tortured bodies turning up by the roadside have re-emerged with a vengeance due to the added dimension of sectarian violence which has fueled the civil war which has in turn helped to form a perfect storm in which Al-Qadea and ISIS have re-grouped and emerged from the ashes of war and formed their own Islamic State which spans and controls large sways of land across North Iraq and Syria.

Even when ISIS was defeated, their fighters and Command and control elements are still in play and continuing their attacks across Iraq and Syria. AQI with help from Afghan elements are growing in strength every day in Iraq. Local Patrols by the Military are still very important to help the locals, but are becoming ever more dangerous due to the insurgency.

Colonel Joe Anderson, Call sign, "Strike Six" the Commander of Strike Brigade, Informing Major S British Parachute Regiment of his field Promotion to Major

Colonel Anderson was walking past Major Kate who called him over and introduced us. Col Joe Anderson, Call sign, "strike Six", the commander of strike Brigade, the second of the three brigades of the screaming Eagles, 101st Airborne, based out of Fort CampbellKentucky. He is known to those around him as "smoking" Joe", when asked Joe explained to me, "that it started as a boxer at west point and continued as a LT and CPT because of my fitness, aggressiveand personality. As a Ranger Company Commander, he had led the Joint Special Operations Task force main effort in "Operation" Just Cause, (B Co, 2-75 Ranger Regiment). "Operation Just Cause was the invasion of Panama, which deposed Manual Noriega in December 1989". He was one of the old school colonels, "we were to get on very well". I asked to speak to the top intelligence officer, he arranged for me to meet up him. "DJ", the G1 intelligence officer. And most senior intelligence officer in Iraq was a former Special Forces commander, he was a highly motivated and intelligent man who was always thinking. His day comprised of briefing Washington and Langley, "CIA HQ" on a daily basis on the updates on the hunt for high level targets, Al Q terrorists and insurgents. All the other intelligence agencies movements, CIA, CSA, Department of justice and all Special operations task forces, 121 and 626, went through him and all reports went over his desk. He was an interesting man to talk to, "think out the box", I told him I was awaiting new Intel on illegal border crossing points, from Syria to Iraq. My Intelsources had data, I needed then to confirm it before I handed it over. I told him I would pass it on as soon as I got it. We talked about the norm, Saddam, WMD, Syria, al-Qa'dia, the norm. He asked did I need anything, yes "a good map of Mosul city", "not a problem, call into the ops room in the morning, there's a map room there they will hook you up." He went back to his desk, there was a Special Operations Task going on, he wanted to keep tabs on it. The uniformity of army Head Quarters worldwide are the same, lots of officers and salutes, this one was different, it had a warm feeling to it. The people were friendly and helpful, after a quick chat with the press officer on what was going on in the area, he asked did we want to stay, sure why not. It was nice to be back in an total military environment again. Crash anywhere down and along that room, I walked over to the room and walked out onto the balcony, I was standing on Saddam's bedroom balcony, in his palace, "I would sleep out here tonight". The view was amazing, it was sunset, the sky was wash of red and yellow warm colours reflecting in the river Tigrus below. "I took a photo to remind me of the view".After a showerand hot meal, I made my way down into the main operations room.Jane was working on some photographs in the Press Office. I wanted to check out what was going on, Multiple SF operations were in full swing, the Military communications links where giving updates and sit-rep, "situation reports" ongoing missions. I grabbed a coffee from the brew area and walked over to the front of the ops room. There was a large map, on the main wall, with locations and areas marked on it. I noticed a lot of SF teams located along the Syrian and Iranians borders. A British officer came over to me. "Hello" it was Major Sherington, an Officer in 3 Para, my old unit. I was told you were around, we talked for awhile, about the war, and how he was finding working with the US, he was running the Tactical Operations room for Col Anderson, "it's a small world", what's new, I told him of what I had been up to over the past few weeks, he smiled, a message came over the Coms, I've got to go, we can talk later.

The US military had just located a group of insurgents on ariver island, 80KM north east off D Main, an US air strike had been called in. Within minutes the Island and the insurgents were no more. A Clean up team was sent to locate and capture any insurgents who may have escaped the airstrike, I went with them. After an interesting few hrs hunting insurgents we flow back to D-Main, grabbed a quick coffee in the operations room and after spending another 20mins studying the maps and getting a feel for the ops room, I retired to Saddam's balcony for the night. The day's dusty heat, had been replaced by a still dark coolness, I drifted off to sleep that night with the hauntingsound of AK-47 gunfire in the distance.

I was woken the next morning by my sat phone going off, it was 0600hrs, it was my Intel source, confirming the Syrian, Iraq illegal crossing points, he gave me the data and timings, five locations in total, he said high level targets. "great, good Intel". After a quick shower and breakfast, I made my way to the operations room, one of the Intel boys was working out some areas on the tactical map on the wall. I asked did he have a minute, "what's on your mind", I told him what had just came in, "DJ" had given his people heads up if I came in. I pin pointed five locations, crossing points, Iconfirmed them using "Falcon View", the timings were set out, 2300hrs tomorrow night was when the crossings would take place, a target package was formed and put on "DJ" desk. The map we were working off was a very detailed map, I asked for a copy of it, "no problems, pull one out the map store". I had no idea that the Intel I had just given would lead to such an amazing result...

My future Airborne Blood Brother, Colonel Lennington, was in the operations room getting an intelligence brief from the "J2" on his "AO" area of operations, this area was all west of the city of Mosul, including Sinja mountain range and the 500 kilometre area spanning the North westernSyrian border. I had a chat with the Colonel, he asked me if I had time to come out with him. Sure why not, within an hour I was on a black hawkhelicopter flying out to Sinja. The Col had overheard me talking to the Intel boys back at HQ, "you seem to have your finger on the pulse around here", I answered"hell ya, I've got some interesting friends, so what you in?" He had cottoned on that I was somehow connected to the military, "I served with the British Para's" he smiled, "that fits" he laughed.We were to become in his words, "blood brothers". We landed in TalaFar air base, this was his centre command point for his area of operations. We went into his op's room and he gave me the run down on what was going on in his AO, I also gave him a copy of all the Intel I had received about the illegal crossing points. As we were talking the officer in charge of his op's room walked passed, "good to see you again, last time was in Afghanistan", the Col looked at me, "you do get around".

After afew hours of hanging out in the op's room, Col Lennington ask if I fancied a ride out to one of the SOF forts, this one was where the "Pathfinders"were located, on top of Sinya mountain. We headed out in a heavily armed Humvee convoy, weapons at the ready, the insurgents were out in force in this area. Sinya and the town of Tala Far are strategic places for the terrorists/insurgents, because of the proximity to the Syrian border, a lot of the guns, explosives, HVT#, come through here on their way to Baghdad, and terrorist training camps scatted across Western Iraq.

"All but one of the Photographs of my friends and their Yazidis families, that I stayed with at Tal-a-far & Sinjar have been omitted from this book out of deep respect".

"The adults were all brutally murdered by ISIS and the children were raped and sold as sex slaves by ISIS Commanders and most later murdered, two took their own life's. I would visit their mass graves in the future... The ISIS Commanders that were responsible for these despicable atrocities were hunted down. "Unconfirmed reports suggests that these perpetrators were killed. The hunt for the leaders of ISIS & AQI continues by members of Task Force 6.8"

Our heavily armed convoy snaked its way through the town, just by the look of fear on the people's faces as we past at speed it was evident that even then the area was in the grip of the insurgents. The convoy climbed up the hillside then through the green valleys of the Sinja mountain range. We pasted the DZ where the SOF had dropped in by parachute weeks before. Then on the skyline was the fort that that the pathfinders and SOF were operating out of. It was totally isolated, not overlooked by anything, the Col radioed ahead for the gates to be opened. (See Photographs)

On entering the fort it had all the hall marks of a major special operations base, creates of ammo, grenades, food, weapons and missiles were stacked in piles, the walls of the fort were armed with Barrett light 50s sniper weapons and belt fed 50caliber heavy machine guns on the turrets. We debussed and went in to meet the lads. After a good chat about op's and life in general, I had a walk around with a hot brew in one hand and an AK-47 in the other. It was good to be in a place like this, there's no HQ bullocks, for young officers trying to get a name for themselves, in aplace like this as in so many Forward Special Operations Base I had been in the past, as long as the job was done everything was ok and laid back.

Col Lennington,came and found me having a play with one of the Barrettlight 50s, .50 calibre sniper rifle, effective range 1800meters, "it was the same as the one I had on past Tasks", he informed me that all Intel had been passed on to his boys, there were sending out a hunter killer team that night to deal with the bad guys. "sounded good to me".It came back to me later that the crossing points for the insurgency my sources had come up withresulted in 18, 4 x 4s, being detained, and a number of high level targets and 28 other men being arrested. "good result" it had kept the pathfinders up most the night. (The HVTs Terrorists would be transferred down to JSOC at Balad airbase, where the Black Site was located and the interrogation of the prisoners would take place).

Suspect Insurgents Being Questioned by American Military

Later that day we moved out to a little house on top of Sinja, where we had dinner and broke bread and ate cooked goat with the local sheiks. The view from the top of the mountain was breathtaking. (See Photographs) That night I went on a raid, Insurgents from Iran were held up and were training in the local school, 16 in total. The raid went in, lighting fast, within minutes all the insurgents were hooded and plastic cuffed and lined up next to a wall. (See Photographs)

Not a shot was fired, "Not bad for three hours work from when the Intel had come in". A lot was found in the school, books and manuals on how to make IEDs, fake documents, money and weapons. (See Photographs) All was sent back to HQ, D-Main, Mosul. I would find out later that some of these men in plain clothes were in fact Iranian soldiers from their Republican Guard Regiment. They had been sending instructors over to the Iraqi insurgency to train locals to attack and kill American and British military personnel...

VIP Protection of local Sheik

On talking to one of the local Sheiks, I had been informed that there were massivetunnel systems that covered the area of Sinja. The US military were aware of this but they did not have the man power to search all of it. I asked Col Lennington about the Electronic Countermeasures I had seen and been show in the fort, "forget you seen that" he smiled. That was why everyone's GPS was off in the area of parts of western Iraq and Eastern Syria.That night I slept on the roof of a Humvee outside the SOF fort, (See Photographs)

There was no room inside, I had a 40 feet drop one side and a minefield the other, the nights sky that evening was totally clear. The stars shone brighter than ever, I looked on as shooting stars flow across and lighting up the sky. Someone else slept on the bonnet and I noticed a pair of US army boots sticking out from one of the windows.The next morning we headed back to Talafar,taking the long way back, the Col wanted to have a look at the oil pumps on the Syrian border, I had told him that a lot of oil was being smuggled from Northern Iraq into Turkey. We had already confirmed the existence of a secret underground pipe line, it had leaked out into Saddam's lake "now Mosul Lake", causing an large oil slick that had covered miles of the lake, the US military had spent thousands of dollars cleaning it up quickly before it could reach the Dam. We were driving along in the Humvee's looking at the oil pumps. To my surprise, the pumps had metal plates fixed on them, saying "made in Sheffield Great Britain", I was floored by this. Britain had been giving Saddam oil pumps... "No-one knew about that".

We continued along a dusty widening track, Col Lenington was chatting away, the driver was watching the track ahead, Col. Lennington took his GPS out of his top shirt pocket, turned it on and held it outside the Humvee to get a good signal. After a few seconds he brought his arm back into the Humvee, his eyes popped out of his head, he shouted stop, the driver slammed the breaks onand skidded to a sudden stop...

The Humvee behind us did the same. Everyone was looking in every direction for bad guys, Col Lennington looked at me "fuck we are in Syria", we had somehow managed to drive over the Syrian border, while exploring the oil fields. we had drove into an area known as a possible mine field, we signalled to the Humvee behind what was going on and to reverse slowly keeping on the same tracks, as not to set of any land mines. Our Humvee did the same.After about five minutes we had reversed back into Iraq, "this was an incident worthy of a dear diary moment". We got back onto the main track, Col Lennington looked at me, "this never happened". This was almost as bad as the time general Petraeus had flown into Syrian airspace on his Black Hawk, with his apache gunship escorting him. That had very nearly caused an international incident, the poor Syrian border guard thought the US were invading Syria through his border crossing point. A five mile no fly zone was put into effect after this incident. Now we had just driven into Syria. "it would be a talking point in private over a cigar later that night". We headed back to base. Back at Talafar US Military base,there was a buzz around camp...

Bruce Willis

Bruce Willisand the Accelerators perform for 101st Airborne Division soldiers in Tal Afar, near Mosul, Iraq, Sept. 25. U.S. Army photo by Pfc. Thomas Day.

Actor Bruce Willis was to perform before US soldiers in Tala Far, northern Iraq and offered $1m (£603,000) to the man who captures Saddam Hussein. I asked the Col about this, he smiled "It's awesome," said Col Lennington. "It's great for morale. "He's a macho actor. Soldiers identify with action movies and action actors. He's a guy's guy.", "a man's man". During an interview Willis said: "Peculiar thing back home is that the liberal media was trying to portray it as a bad war. But being over here just a couple of days, seeing how well our troops and the allied troops are being received here, (I) think the Iraqi people are happy we're here," the Hollywood star said. "Children are being taken care of, starting being inoculated, starting being looked after. Wherever these guys go they get thumbs up. They no longer have to contend with the terrorist leader," Willis said.We're here to support you," the star told troops as he sang a set of blues songs with his band, the Accelerator."If you catch him, just give me four seconds with Saddam Hussein," he said. The night was a major success, all round.
The next day I thanked Col Lennington, told him and his boys to "Stay Safe", "I knew that I would see him again soon". Then I got hooked up outside the TOCand got a ride back to Mosul D-Main then a quick Black Hawk ride to the airfield with Jane.

Christine the Commander of the "MP's" Military Police, MosulUS Airbase

I had been informed that "J" was stationed there, he was now serving with the US military police, he was the bodyguard of Christine the Commander of the American MPs Military Police, who had set up their HQ on the airbase. The helicopter touched down on the Airfield around midday, I made my way into the terminal and got a ride to the MPs HQ. "J" was pleased to see me again, we knew each other'sface and reputationfrom covert African operations. He took me into their Ops' room and introduced me to his commander, Christine was a young but very experienced women, who held the respect from all under her command. We got on well, we were asked to say the night. "J" sorted out a cot for us in the same hut as he was bunked. The commander told me she was going out on night patrol around the city that evening, I could tag along. The flight down to QW was not until the next afternoon so I had some time to kill. Introductions were given all-round and the rest of the squad were briefed. I spent the rest of the afternoon walking around the airfield taking photographs of the day to day life of US soldiers in the field. I also put some time to one side to write and update my journal, it was starting to be quite interesting; I had kept a log of all I had done, seen and experienced. I thought it would be something to look back on over time... 1800hrs, I meet "J" outside the MP Op's room, I had got into the lead Humvee, then for some reason I got out and walked into the Op's room to see and look over the areas of patrol that night. On walking back outside I piled into the second Humvee, the first one had been filled with translators. Only 20minites into the patrol the lead Humvee was hit by an "IED" improvised explosive device and gunfire, it blow the heavy armoured Humvee over the road and onto its' side (See Photograph).

  Simultaneously the terrorists who had detonated the IED had opened up with small arms fire from AK-47s. A shout went over the coms - all units to assist. Within a few minutes there were ten Humvees at the location and a little bird surveillance helicopters cycling overhead, the insurgents had slipped into the night without a trace. Luckily no-one was killed, only the interpreter who had been in the Humvee was jumping up and down on the spot, he did not look very happy, it turned out that it was the third time he had been blown up in two weeks; "he resigned that night". The damaged Humvee was towed back to base with an escort. "J" said "Anth, you're like a cat with 9 lives...You were in that Humvee before we set off", I called that being lucky.We continued on our night patrol through the dark silent streets. After about an hour a call came over the net, the MP commander was called to a house in the east of the city. We were not quite sure what we were walking into or what we were going to find, no information had been given over the radio.My gut instinct; this was bad...

Executed - Slaughtered Iraqi Family, Mosul

We turned into the dark and foreboding street where the house was located, a crowd of onlookers had gathered over the road, emotions were running high, any spark could egnite a violent riot, there were several old cars and an ambulance parked outside the house. The convoy of American Military Police Humvees stopped outside the dwelling, an immediate cordon for protection was set up. I stepped out the lead Humvee taking a moment to observe my surroundings and the increasing number of on lookers, I moved towards the entrance of the two storey house. Stopping suddenly, I was hit by a sweet smell, this sickening scent I had come across, many times in the past during operations across Africa; it was the smell of death, rotten and decomposing bodies. I looked at Jane who had joined me at the entrance, I told her to wait by the Humvees, knowing what lay ahead of me, she looked at me puzzled, she asked what was wrong, I told her in a low voice you don't need to see this, somethings can not be unseen. My gut instinct was telling me that this was going to be a bad one. "my gut instinct is never wrong". I escorted Christina into the house, people were stood around no one was talking, the look of shock, horror and disbelief was on all their faces. I noticed thick claret and the trails of blood, leading from the garden, along the corridor floor through the kitchen, blood and splash marks ran up the walls, I noticed a smeared bloody hand print across a fridge door, the smell was horrendous, I had to put my hand over my mouth and nose. We entered the hallway an Iraqi man was just standing there in shock, looking into the main room ahead, crying, weeping with his head in his hands. We moved silently past him, the floor was a good two inches think with dark blood, it was like walking through a thick slush. We slowly, apprehensively, moved into the room. The horrific sight that lay before me was both stomach-churning and sickening, an enter Iraqi family, six in all had been slaughtered. Women, children, young men, all had been shot at close range. The body of a young woman with the back of her head missing was hunched over a chair, in a last desperate effort to protect her beautiful little girl, who must have only been about six years old. The little girl had been shot in the face at point blank range. Empty AK-47 brass cases littered the floor. This gruesome sight made me feel sick. The other bodies also had gunshot wounds to the head and body. The enter room was covered in blood and claret, it was even dripping from the lights shade hanging from the ceiling. The bodies had been there for around

134

four days, the heat of the days had made all the bodies swell up and erupt, body fluids covered the furniture and floor. I tapped Christine on the shoulder, time to go, we had seen enough, there was only death here. We exited the building and found a strip of green grass by the side of the house, others soldiers were hunched over a low wall being sick... we both were shocked at what we had just witnessed. I rubbed her back, taking in a breath of fresh air, she looked at me, her eyes filled up a little, I nodded, I knew what she was thinking. There were no words for this. Christina straightened up and composed herself as her soldiers moved towards her, she gave them orders to carry out. We moved back to the Humvees after a few moments. The rest of the convoy had arrived "J" was giving them orders to reinforce the cordons now at each end of the street, he broke away and looked at us, I said it's a bad one, they asked how bad, I answered the worse I had ever seen, he just stopped and looked at me, this shocked him and the other soldiers around him, they all knew I had been around, there was not much I had not seen. Christine said she needed forensic photographs of this crime scene, the military needed to have them for evidence. I said to Christine give me five minutes and I will go back in and take the shots, I knew that the young soldiers may find this a difficult task. She looked at one of her men, without hesitation he said no, I'm not going back in there, he had already walked in and seen the stomach-churning sight from the end of the corridor at a distance. "I respect a man who has the guts to say no in company that was there that day". After five minutes I put some vic's menthol rum under my noise and put some blue plastic gloves on from my medical kit, I made my way into the house. 20 minutes later I emerged, I had got what Cristina had needed. That room and the children's bodies would haunt me afterwards for a very long time. Intel came back to me at a later date, the family had been massacred by the local insurgency/terrorists.

"I can confirm that in the future, those terrorists responsible were later identified"

We made our way back to the MP HQ, I showered and scrubbed for over an hour trying to getrid of the smell of death that covered me and my cloths. It would not come off, for many weeks I would suddenly get a scent, smell of death from my kit, that would remind me of that house.

The next morning I was up early, my flight to QW had been moved forward, we had one hour to get our kit together and get on the runway. I said my goodbyes to Christina and "J", "it's been emotional" I said I would be back. Over the coming months, I knew I was going to bump into them again...
The Black Hark swooped in over the airfield, the sand and dust was blown up from the down force of it coming into land...

It was only on the deck for a few minutes, the insurgency were hot in this area now, they were firing rockets at almost all the aircraft landing at the airfield. The Black Hawk quickly lifted off straight up, the doors were left open, the hot air blow in from the engines. After clearing the Perimeter fence andtree line, the pilot banked and we headed due south, onroute to QW, home of the apache battle group and the location of my Victor call/sign. As we made our way to 200 feet, I noticed another Black Hawk and an Apache gunship was escorting us, I put the spear pilot head set onsituated in the back

rack, asked the pilot to adjust Coms and called the Black Hawk over the radio, I got him to fly right next to us, I moved into the open doorand took a photograph of the Black Hawk in flight, over western Iraq. It turned out to be a set of amazing pictures. (See Photographs)

The Black Hark landed at QW 45 minutes later. All seemed quiet here compared to the constant flow of activity over the past few days. After a warm greeting from the soldiers on base I walked into the op's room, sat in the corner with a hot brew and chilled, I had to decide what to do next. A captain came up to me and asked if I was Anth, I looked at him for a second, was I in crap! (I hadn't blown anything up that week) I answered "yes", "I've been told to ask you if you want to come to dinner with the medics later this afternoon at the local village", they were dropping of some supplies. "You can get some great photographs.""Yes, what time?" "We're heading out at 1400hrs"."Ok I will meet you outside the main HQ hanger, sounds like a plan".

This was a village I had wanted to visit, we had flown over it many times. I went to find Jane, I briefed her on the dinner. She was up for it. After a brief conversation with Jane, I made a command decision. London was contactedand a two days head's up was arranged, travel time to complete this was two days outward, two days in London and two days back to Iraq.

The main reason for this was to check with the UKsecurity services thatI would not be in any trouble for the mission that had been completed, also the wake of carnage that I had left behind me, throughLebanon,Syria, Jordanand Western Iraq. And I was aware that the British government did not like former British soldiers becoming too friendly with the US Government or Military"bit late for that" I trusted the Americans a hell of a lot more than the British Government. In the future when it all came out that I had been working and Tasked by American military Intelligence for many years, incompetentelements within the British Government threwtheirdummies out of their cots, at great personal lose to me... all because I did my job, save British and American lives but in the process made elements of the British Government look bad "Muppets..." Obviously I never had the right school tie lol (But that's another epic story).

The call was made to London and flights were booked, the plan was to fly to London for a two day turn around. Arrangements and preparations were made and put into place for our return later that week to Iraq. We were to travel light, clean fatigue without any kit, minimum clothing, no equipment and none of the information that we had.The plan was to return a few days later to complete other tasks, this was told to our friendly call sign in London and was agreed. I wanted to check on the political situation, to cover myself, and my intelligence office had informed me that it looked like I was being set-up by someone, was this the same rogue MI6 officer/asset, who had a personal grudge against Adam, god he was like a dog with a bone... and what did that have to do with me anyway... I wanted his name and to find out what really was going on. The only problem with being out on the ground for long periods oftime, is that, you lose touch with things back in the world. "my gut instinct told me something was wrong" A two day trip back to the UK would confirm what was really happening behind the scenes. "what was waiting for me was not what I was expecting".

Dinner with a HVT# "High Value Target" on the US top ten most wanted list

After making all the preparations for departing the next day, we made my way to meet the medics and go for dinner in the local village close to the river.1400hrs sharp, we meet the medics, outside their HQ, I jumped in the back of the lead Humvee, Jane with a big smile jumped in with the soldiers in the next one. It was a stifling hot sunny afternoon. The column of Humvees made its way out of the camp and on into the dirt track towards the village. On entering the village we were swamped by twenty young children. The Humvees pulled up outside the head of the villager's house. After the formal greetings between the village elders, we unloaded all the supplies, bottled water, blankets, food, toiletries, basic first aid kits and some toys for the younger kids. Two soldiers were left to guard the Humvees, we made our way into the house where the head of the village had prepared a banquet for us, his new found American friends. We sat on the floor surrounded by trays of rice, goat, chicken and fresh vegetables, tomatoes and cucumbers, it was a wonderful colourful spread. There were twelve of us sat around the cloth on the floor, four were US military, two civilians and six Iraqi's. We were sat talking drinking chai, when a middle aged Iraq gentleman entered the room. He motioned to everyone not to stand up, we all gave greetings. The Iraqi men moved over to allow him to sit between them, he was shown a lot of respect from when he walked into the room. The Captain looked over at me and smiled, the penny had dropped, I recognised the man who had just walked in, he was on the top ten most wanted list of the US Government. This was a dear diary moment, the unofficial rule of the medics was they kept politics out of their job, they had known that the HVT# had been staying in the village, but had not reported it. According to the people of the village he was a good man who had always looked after his home village, the HVT# had been born in the village. We ate the food and enjoyed pleasant conversation with our guests. A young boy carried in a hand bowl, it was brought around each for us to wash our hands after the meal, this signified the end of the meal. The HVT# stood up and bided us all good day. He then left the house, we all stayed for about 15 minutes, then we departed the house, on the way back to base, "QW", I thought about what had just happened. I had just been talking to one of the most wanted men on the plant, the CIA and all the joint task forces had put all their resources into finding the top ten and here I was having chai and sharing dinner with him. I put it down as one of those things strange things that happen to me. I gave my word to the Captain that I would not tell anyone about what had happened. It was nice to see that people can be human and civilised, I had witnessedfirst-hand the worse to extremes, it was good to have some positive feedback. The Iraqi HVT would be killed in an American airstrike in the future!

When I got back to base, I visited the engineers/mechanics on camp and asked them to look after my victor call/sign while I was gone, no problems, they said they would check it over and do any work that needed to be done on it.I spent the rest of the night on the phones and internet, prepping for my short trip back into the world and London.

Baghdad to London

I had been given a letter from 101st ABD signed by them that gave me unlimited access to all and any air assets in my area of operation controlled by the American Military.I left country (Iraq) via Baghdad (camp victory), Kuwait, (camp wolf), then onto London, I left our V1 call sign and all our kit and equipmentwith a friendlycall sign in Iraq, (QW). We were on our way backafter being in theatre for 14 weeks; I was going back to the real world…? A phone call later and I had organised military air transport, Black Hawk helicopter from QW(Home of the US Apache battle group) to Baghdad main airport, then after a short chat and soda with the soldiers coming back into Iraq from R&R.We boarded the C130 Heracles military transport plane via the tailgate that was lowered. After quicksafety checks, the C130 taxied down the runway and with a sudden surge of power took off on a steep vertical climb, it suddenly bank to the left pulling a "G" turn, to avoid "SAM"'s, surface to air missiles, if they had been fire at the plane by the insurgency. After some aggressive flying itwas on to camp wolf in Kuwait. The duty driver at camp wolf then dropped us and our kit off at the civilian terminalatKuwait airport, the other side of the airfield.We checked in and it was a short wait. Then we boarded for the long "BA" British Airwaysflight to London Heathrow. I enjoyed the free wine, South African, on the flight. Then settled in and slept most of the way back. The plane touched down at Heathrow in the early afternoon, as we disembarked the plane down the steps it began to rain, "welcome back to England" I thought. After walking through passport control, I flagged a taxi and we were on our way to the Tower Hill Hotel, this was where the planning stage of the operation had taken place in the early stages. On arrival I booked in, I had already booked rooms in advance. I had the same top floor suite as before. Jane moved her kit into her room. I told her to meet me down in the bar in about an hour, she could freshen up, I had some calls to make. I phoned Rox, he was in Whitehall attending a brief by the MOD, Sharpy was calculating and putting together all the Intel together that had come in the past 24hrs, he had sent a update/report to me by e-mail. A meeting was setup for that afternoon with Rox. I also contacted my trusted old MI6 contact, a time and place to meet was arranged for the next morning. The "Union Jack Club". I contacted Adam he was expecting my call, and arranged to meet him under Tower Bridge, next to the Tower of London in two hours' time.After a quick shower, "trying to get the sand out my kit", I put on some jeans and shirt, then made my way down to the bar area, Jane was sitting there enjoying an espresso, "it'snot Arabic coffee but it works". I sat down and ordered one too, I looked at Jane and commented "that she scrubbed up well". I had brought her back with me to the UK because Adam had told her he would use her photographs and notes to do some story for the paper, this would be abig step up for her; being published in an International paper would help her career. She had helped me so I didn't have a problem giving her a helping hand up. She had nothing to do with the tasks I had been working on and I had been very careful not to tell her anything that she did not need to know. Having her around had made my life a little easier, the military in country "Iraq", always liked having a female around, especially a tall long blonde hair, bright eyed, former model form California. She made many a lonely solders day when she turned up on the army bases, with a big smile and a hearty hello, "a little ray of sunshine on a dark day". I told her that I was going off to meet Adam and I would bring him back to the hotel when we had finished our little talk. She had time to go over her notes and photographs I would be back in a few hours. I left the hotel and made my way down to the meeting place I had arranged to meet Adam.

It was outside the Haagen-Dazs ice cream shop, under Tower Bridge, next to the Tower of London. I got there 45min early, I stood under the tunnel that connects the walkways under the bridge. I observed everyone there, the man sat on the bench reading a newspaper, the girl rollerblading along the embankment; all seemed ok nothing out of place. No vehicles were allowed in this area and there were CCTV cameras everywhere. My gut feeling told me it was safe. I walked over to the wall that runs along the embankment along the side of the river Thames and stood there waiting for Adam.

Adam turned up five minutes late with his apologies. I motioned for us to walk alone the embankment. I asked what's happening back here. He went on to tell me what he was thinking aboutand what had been going on including about an incident with John Swain in Iraq. One of the Sunday Times reporters John Swain, famous for finding the "killing fields" in Cambodia (they later made a film about it). He was a gentleman I had enjoyed meeting up with and sharing bottles of red wine with at the Phoenicia Hotel in Beirut Lebanon, had been caught at a military check point in Iraq trying to smuggle out documents about Saddam's WMD. All the documents had been confiscated by the military, Adam went on to tell me the full story. It was unlucky that he got caught, the documents sounded as though they could have been good.

Adam went on that his contract had lapsed at the Sunday Times and he had already contacted a publisher, with regard to printing all the information I and all my sources had collated. I looked at him, he told me there's already a book deal on the table. This was something completely out the blue, we had never discussed this with him at all. I was shocked, he told me that the Sunday Times did not know that his contract had lapsed. So he was free to take all that I had done and achieved, to whoever he wanted.

To say I was stunned at what he was telling me would be an understatement. I looked at him again, so this is not for the Sunday Times, he answered no, there's more money if we take it somewhere else. He also went on and told me he had made contact with MI6 and they did not have a problem with the book as long as they got a copy beforehand of all the information. "I thought for a moment", this was the strangest thing and most dangerous idea I had heard off, it was so far off the scales and out the ball park it was not funny. I had felt that something was very wrong, but I did not know what, "I remember thinking I am so glad that I did not send all the information back to Adam when I was in Iraq" that would have been a global career ending move for me. I asked what would Adams boss "the editor think of this", he said it's not of consequence, it's the way journalism goes. "for some reason I had recorded this conversation, I was now glad I did", I prefer to be open, but sometimes you need to protect yourself. I asked Adam did he knowwhy my team had been compromised in Lebanon. He told me that it was because he had upset a rouge Arms dealer and former MI6 agent. Adam had named him in a story and the Former agent was out for revenge on him at all cost. He had major contacts in Iraq and Syria. And had informed the Iraq "SSS" and the Syrian Secrete Police "SSP", that Adam was a UK spy. This was why when Adams name had been on the visa request list to Baghdad, it had sent the Red flags up and alerted the enemy of our presents in Lebanon. Adam did not have much to say about this topic. He should have told me about this right at the start of the task when I was still in the UK, I would have told him then that it was going to be a problem.I was concerned now at what Adam was planning to do, lucky I was holding all the cards. I realised that the Sunday Times had not been behind me for some time, and as far as I was aware, the project and all that came from it was mine, I had spent a lot of money and invested a lot of time into this, as well as almost being killed on several occasions. I had to double check all that was going on with Adam, I would run it through Rox. For the time being I would keep him on side, I didn't trust him at all now, I hadn't after Jordon but if all this was true then I would cut him loose, to protect all of us. I said Jane was back at the hotel waiting to see him. She brought the stories she has written, with some photographs, you told her you would use them right... Adam said yes. We walked back to the hotel, I left Adam with Jane in the hotel bar, I headed off to meet Rox, I had a feeling that I needed to put some major damage limitation into action.

I met Rox at a pre-arranged meeting place up at St James, there was a wine bar that we both liked. It was a local hang out for the MOD on lunch breaks. I got to the meeting place early, Rox was sat in the corner, sipping on a red wine. The place was dimly light and quiet. I walked over to the table and said hello, Rox stood up "how are you old boy", I am fine, he signalled to the barman to bring another glass of red wine over. "glad you made it back alive", yes, it has been an emotional few months.

I ask his advice, fire away, I went on to tell him everything about Adam and what he had told me. Rox had a frown on his face, his advice was cut him loose, he will cause you nothing but problems and trouble.Deal with the British intelligence, they will look after you. He had warned me that most journalists were like snakes with tits, not to be trusted. Rox also told me to set a meet up with Adam's boss, the news editor of the paper. Tell him everything that has happened, play him the tape, then he will deal with Adam internally and you keep a clean slate. He will actually owe you a favour for this, you would have proved to him that you are a man of your word. Hit him with your hotel bill in London and flights back to Iraq, he owes you that much. We went on to talk about all that had happened, and what my plans were, he told me he had a friend that needed some photographs of certain areas in Northern Iraq, Kurdistan, border areas of Iran, Iraq. Not a problem, I will send them to you when I am out there. Rox was someone I knew I could trust, and he always tried to keep me out of harm's way, and made sure I as up to date on all the intelligence information I needed. I informed Rox that I was breaking contact with my team/Sharpie in Cyprus, this was to protect him from any problems with MI6, Adam or anyone else. I would have to explain this at a later date but the buck stops at me and I was not going to put my friends in harm's way.I was fully aware of the dark side of MI6... A bottle of red wine later, Rox had to get back to Whitehall MOD HQ, he had a Briefing and Government dinner to attend. We walked out onto the street, we had been in there for two hours, we shook hands, "you know where I am if you need me", not a problem. I flagged a taxi and headed back to the Hotel. Rox knew me from the old days of me working as a SWAT Instructor in South Africa, I had flown him out to spend time with the South African Police, Special Task Force!

Adam was just about to leave the bar when I got back, he had arranged for Jane to go into the offices the next morning to go through some of her work with the relevant departments at the Sunday Times. This worked out great, I had meetings in the morning.

I went up to my room to drop off some things and I made a call to the News editor of the Sunday Times, I was put through straight away, he knew that I might give him acall at some point. A personal meeting was set up for the next day at St Catherine's dock, there was a little quiet restaurant we both knew. The time was set 1300hrs.That night Jane was excited about going into the papers offices the next day, it was good to see. But I knew that Adam was doing it just to keep me happy. I would make sure she got something published. She spent most of the night working in her room on the work that she needed the next morning.It was getting late now, I sat in the hotel bar, enjoying a brandy and cigar. Contemplating what had happened that day and my plan of action for the next. I retired to my room about 1030pm, it was going to be another long emotional day tomorrow.The next day I woke bright and early, I opened the big double windows of the room that overlooked some of the oldest buildings in London, fresh air blow into the room, it was a sunny day, I had an exceptional view of Tower Bridge and the Tower of London, the British Flag Union Jack was flickering in the wind, I always feel proud when I see the flag fly "Queen & Country". I sat on the open window sill and noticed on the streets below people scurrying around on the pavement, they looked like little worker ants, on their way to work.

MI6 "British Intelligence"London

I made my way down to breakfast, I had an hour before my first meeting with my MI6 contact "SJ". I had coffee and fresh fruit, (contrary to common belief, I'm not just made of bourbon and bad decisions). I browsed through the mornings' papers, to keep up to speed on International current events. A TV in the bar had Sky News on in the back ground, Jane came down and joined me for breakfast. She had a quick cup of coffee and ask how things went with Adam, I said ok, I didn't want to tell her I was meeting his boss today to blow the lid on what he had and was planning to do. She finished her coffee and headed over to the Sunday Times head office. I told her to "take care and have a good day, I will be back around 1500hrs we can hook up in the bar then", "ok see you later". Even with me blowing the lid on Adam, I knew Jane would be well looked after by the Sunday Times.
I flagged a taxi outside the hotel and made my way to my first meeting, this was to be held at the Union Jack Club, Waterloo.The Officers Club, Army and Navy was my first chose but I wanted to keep this meeting as low key and secure as possible; I knew too many spooks who stayed and met there! I made my way into the club, showing my Military ID, to the doorman on the way in. I left a message with the front desk that a friend of mine was meeting me for coffee and could he be shown to where I was sitting, coffee was organised, I sat waiting for my contact to show.0930am, I was sipping on my coffee when my MI6 contact "SJ", was escorted in by the doorman. We shook hands and sat down, I offered him coffee, he took it Nato style, cream two sugar. He said I have been busy over in the Middle East, my name had come up a few times.He had been keeping tabs on me again. He already knew that I was

getting close to Adnan Abou Ayyash, and that I had used my old network of friends in the Special Forces and the international intelligence community to deal with certain areas of my work. He was well aware that the door swings both ways. I asked him about the Sunday Times, he answered that they had lost a lot of credibility with the intelligence agencies, their basic conduct and that of their people was isolating them. I thought of Adam. The Sunday Times had ran some stories not to certain members of the government's liking.I told him about Adam and what he was trying to do, I gave him the run down on the whole situation. He thought for a moment, "what did I want to do", I told him I was going to cut the Sunday Times lose, over the next few days and that, I wanted to know where I stood with the intelligenceagencies. "SJ", looked at me, my credibility was as good as always and would remain so as long as we continued to have these little chats. Great.I asked do you have a British SOF team In the north of Iraq. Yes there is, part of "the Activity", the Det of SAS, is based out of a little compound on the outskirts of Mosul city. There is also one in Baghdad, based out of the British Embassy. The officer in charge of the Embassy security team is an old friend. I will drop him your operational name "SA", drop my name to him, he will be expecting a call from you. He will assist you. "I asked" if I give him the location of a HVT# and other information, will they be able to quickly and quietly pick him up. "No problems", I also don't want my name on any of the Intel. It would look funny to the US, I don't want to jeopardise my standing with them. "I will give you a F3, classification" (my F1/F3 Classification would later be confirmed for me by Major Daz my Senior British Military Intelligence Contact in Cyprus when we worked together to stop terrorist attacks across the Island on British and American off duty soldiers). SJ looked me in the eyes and reaffirmed to me that no one will have any idea who you are or where the information has come from. "It's a shame, you should get some credit for this.""That's not important to me. As long as the information is used productively. Well until we meet again.""When do you fly out?" "Tomorrow night""How long are you in country for this time?""Not sure, I have some things to take care of."He looked at me and smiled. "You take care out there. Drop me a line when you get back, you know how to contact me." We shock hands and he left.My next meeting was in two hours' time. I made my way to the area of St Catherine's dock, I wanted to grab a bite to eat before my meeting with the news editor. There was a little Starbucks coffee shop in the heart of the docks. I called Rox as I walked over to it, updating him that all was ok and moving forward. He said good, keep me in the loop, speak soon, Stay Safe.I was sat in Starbucks having one of their great chocolate muffins, when Paul rang me, there had been a lot of movement on the investigation with Adnan Abou Ayyash, all hell had broken lose in Lebanon. The Bank of al Madina was in the news again, Ibrahim Abou Ayyash and Rana koleilat had been arrested along with 20 other people by the Lebanese authorities and were being questioned about the illegal dealings of the bank of Al-Madina. Paul went on to tell me about the full run down of the whole episode to date. "it could only happen in Lebanon". Paul had been liaising with my contacts in Lebanon and Europe, I had put my human resources network at his disposal.He was gathering HVT# information on who the movers and shakers were behind the scenes of the bank. The web of lies and corruption was spanning the globe at this point. I advised him on afew areas that he needed to concentrate on and told him I shouldbe clear of the Iraq and Times Tasks shortly, but for him to keep me in the loop at all times. We parted with "it's never a dull day in Anth's world".

I made my way to the restaurant where I was meeting the Sunday Times news editor. It was 1300hrs,we met outside and went in. We took a booth on the left, it was more private. He asked how I was, I said fine. We ordered some drinks, I thanked him for attending the meet. I went on to tell him all that happened and all that Adam was planning. He looked at me. He knew that some things just didn't add up, as far as he was concerned with regards to Adam, they had not added up for some time. I asked him if it was true that Adam didn't have any up to date contract now... he answered, he should have one I will get on to that.. He went on and filled in the gaps that I had, his answers explained a lot. He thanked me for taking the time for coming back to the UK to meet him, he asked where I was staying I told him, I'll pay the bills on that hotel and I will organise the flights back out as well, E-mail me all the details, I will send the tickets to the hotel. He knew that I had just saved him a big problem with Adam, now he could deal with internally. I asked him to keep it as quiet as possible, he knew that I was still operating out in the Middle East. I left the meeting with a hand shake and if you need anything else you know how to get hold of me. I asked him to make sure Jane was looked after and helped regarding her photographs, not a problem.

I walked back to the hotel, with the feeling that I had done the right thing all round.

When I got back to the hotel I e-mailed the Information and bills over to The Times, they were paid and the tickets were booked for the next flight out the next day and delivered to me at the hotel.

Jane was in the hotel bar when I came down from my room, I picked my messages up from reception and joined her, she was happy, the Sunday Times where going to publish some of her work. We had afew drinks to celebrate. She asked how my day was, I answered quiet; I went shopping. "my day had been anything but". I briefed her on the timings and flights, they fitted in with her work well. We had a meal in the hotel that night, it would be the last good meal I would see for awhile.I told her that The Times had paid all the bills, she looked surprised"call it a professional courtesy".

The rest of the night was down time, sorting out paperwork and kit. Adam rang me the next day, he had been sent on a new assignment up in the north of England. I said no worries, we fly out today. Keep in touch Adam said. My actions against Adam some might say were harsh, but I was also keeping him safe. His Rogue MI6 arms dealer and asset of MI6 was still gunning for him and my taking Adam out the equation for awhile might very well save his life... Even after all the head work he was a good man deep down and I did not want him to get hurt (5 countries secret Intelligence services now knew his real name so it was time Adam kept his head down for awhile).

I was woken up by my phone going off the next morning, a voice boomed down the line, it was Rox. He told me to check my e-mail, there had been a big hit by SOF, "Operation Snake" in Iraq.I came down for breakfast late thatmorning, about 0950am, the breakfast was being packed up, I pick up some fresh coffee and fruit and made my way into the bar area, I sat down and started to watch Sky News. Iraq was on the news all channels, Rox rang me again, he gave me an update and copied all to my E-mail, drop account.

Operation Snake

In 2017, Iraqi officials said Islamic State (then the Islamic State of Iraq) was operating multiple training camps in western Anbar province, 47 training camps were operational at that time. Back in the day 2003,Operation Snake, the biggest terrorist camp was locatedin al-amber, north of Anna, Western Iraq (what really happened at snake). Brief given by SOF. Delta force and clean up teams. Apaches had searched using grids over a massive area of the western desert of Iraq. Over 70 international terrorist were killed, their origins were from a wide variety, including Lebanese (Hezbollah), Saudi Arabia,

Iranian, Syrian and Moroccan. This terrorist camp was located and attacked by elements of 101st ABD and Apache gunships operating out of QW. (One Apache was lost during this operation)

Passports and documents of all dead terrorists were found and photographed. This was the first terrorist training camp to be destroyed in 2003, many others would pop up over the next 15 years across Iraq...

Yes. Saddam Hussein's dictatorship provided headquarters, operating bases, training camps, and other support to terrorist groups fighting the governments of neighboring Turkey and Iran, as well as to hard-line Palestinian groups. During the 1991 Gulf War, Saddam commissioned several failed terrorist attacks on U.S. facilities. Prior to the 2003 invasion of Iraq, the State Department listed Iraq as a state sponsor of terrorism. The question of Iraq's link to terrorism grew more urgent with Saddam's links to Al-Qaeda and his determination to develop weapons of mass destruction (WMD) and battlefield chemical weapons, which Bush administration officials feared he might share with terrorists who could launch devastating attacks against the United States. (Battle Field Chemical weapons were found by American forces in Iraq 2003). Some Iraqi militants trained in Taliban-run Afghanistan helped Ansar al-Islam, an Islamist militia based in a lawless part of northeast Iraq. The camps of Ansar fighters, who clashed repeatedly with anti-Saddam Kurds, were bombed in the early days of Operation Iraqi Freedom. In February 2003, Secretary of State Colin Powell told the UN Security Council that Iraq was harboring a terrorist cell led by Abu Musab Zarqawi, a suspected al-Qaeda affiliate and chemical and biological weapons specialist. Powell said al-Zarqawi had both planned the October 2002 assassination of a U.S. diplomat in Jordan and set up a camp in Ansar al-Islam's territory to train terrorists in the use of chemical weapons. Powell added that senior Iraqi and al-Qaeda leaders had met at least eight times since the early 1990s. Czech officials have also reported that Mohammed Atta, one of the September 11 ringleaders, met an Iraqi intelligence agent in Prague months before the hijackings. Al-Qaeda members fleeing Afghanistan have hid across Iran and in northern Iraq after safe passage, escort through Iran. (2010 intelligence report submitted by Anthony Malone detailed several safe house locations and the rat runs/ routes used by senior Al-Qaeda leadership from Afghanistan, Iran, Iraq and Turkey. IED factories in Iran making IEDs and shape chargers that were being used against American and British troops were also confirmed within the highly detailed report). The report was given to American Military Intelligence/CIA (Afghanistan Station) and it was acted upon! (At this point in 2003-2007 British Special Forces and members of the Parachute Regiment were operational and taking casualties across Iraq and Afghanistan, closing down these IED factory was a personal mission for me...

"Iranian missiles and IED's, Improvised Explosive Devices and 'FMSC' (Factory Made Shape Charges), which were being used by terrorists to kill American and British soldiers"

The IEDs being constructed and used against British and American ISAF forces in Iraq and Afghanistan and other areas of operation including Syria have becoming a huge problem. Insurgent IED attacks are killing and injuring more soldiers than any other kind of attack in Iraq and Afghanistan. There have beendaily IED attacks, soldiers have been killed and seriously injured at an alarming rate, (three a day). Some of the shape charges and missiles that are being deployed against American, British and ISAF forces across Afghanistan and Iraq are being made in Iran and Lebanon, at multiple location given the code names 'K1 and K2'. This was the location of two of the engineering factories which have been manufacturing the IEDs and shape charges. Shipments from this factory were of extreme interest to the Americans. I had located the factories and been able to establish the dates and times of the shipments and their routes from Iran into Iraq and Southern Afghanistan. This information had been utilised by the American military and CIA, resulting in drone strikes on terrorist convoys crossing the border from Iran into Iraq and Afghanistan...

Taken by Author during Military Operations with American Military. IED Found in Northern Iraq

Two of the missiles found in terrorist safe houses and weapons storage locations were the Iranian 'Sagger' and 'Arash'. I had seen some of the shape charges that had been made and transported from Iran. The workmanship and engineering was very precise. These IEDs had been used against British and American armored vehicles in Iraq and Afghanistan with lethal results and on one occasion the insurgent IED's had even disabled an American 'Abraham' main battle tank. The Iranian rockets and weapons used by insurgents had also been used to attack British and American bases, not only in Iraq and Afghanistan, but also North Africa. This was not a new development; Iranian rockets and weapons had been found previously in Somalia, Syria, Lebanon (Hezbollah) and Iraq, being used by extreme Islamist groups and other groups backed by Iran. The Iranian rockets had given the terrorist the ability to launch attacks on Western locations and military bases from greater distances. The method of the terrorist attacks in Iraq and Afghanistan had changed. They were no longer 'shoot-and-scoot' attacks, what had evolved was calculated, planned and co-ordinate; multiple attacks were simultaneously unleashed. AQI, ISIS, Haqqani Network, Pakistan and Afghan Taliban had evolved into effective, unconventional, fighting forces...

Update 2018, Members of the so call Iraqi Government have strong links and ties to the Iranian Military, Special Forces and senior members of Al-Qaeda and the Afghanistan/Pakistan Haqqani network. The Haqqani Network is supplying fighters, instructors and sharing intelligence with Al-Qaeda in Iraq. This was confirmed by Anthony Malone after an interview with a senior Haqqani network Commander in Afghanistan! So why are the British Government supporting and helping to finance with aid the Iraqi Government which is running a failed state... Wouldn't British Support and aid be better placed by supporting the Kurdish people in the North of Iraq who were the first people to step up and fight ISIS, International terrorism, when the Iraq army dropped their weapons and ran away from Mosul and the North of Iraq...Come on people wake up, if the Kurdish people of Kurdistan are betrayed yet again... by the British Government maybe the next time Britain needs the Kurds and their brave Peshmerga they will not be there... It's about time Iraq was called what it really is, "A failed State"...

Intelligence source state 100 to 160 former Iraqi army officers with ISIS. The 2003 US led invasion of Iraq led Saddam Hussein to allow foreign fighters to join the resistance against the invaders. ISIS's deputy leader Abu Muslim al-Turkmani was an Iraqi army major.

Once part of one of the most brutal dictator's army in the Middle East, over 100 former members of Saddam Hussein's military and intelligence officers are now part of **ISIS**.

Now they make up the complex network of ISIS's leadership, helping to build the military strategies which have led the brutal jihadi group to their military gains in **Syria** and Iraq.

The officers gave ISIS the organisation and discipline it needed to weld together jihadi fighters drawn from across the globe, integrating terror tactics like suicide bombings with military operations.

The CIA and CENTCOM, JSOC;have been banging their heads against a wall, as they closed down one of the terrorist lines of communication, two other lines of communication would pop up. Terrorist IED and suicide attacks on American and British ISAF troops were at an all-time high. The 'bleed out' of terrorists from the Iraq, Syrian and Afghan wars are on the increase. Many new groups like the Pakistan Taliban and Kandahar Al-Qaeda, the 'Lions of Allah' (Al-Qaeda's equivalent of Special Forces), all handpicked men, were making up small teams of 4 to 6 men. All specially trained and cross trained in covert and overt warfare. (What was disturbing about this was the fact that different terrorist networks and groups were now talking and communicating and sharing fighters and intelligence between themselves, Example; Afghan Haqqani Network and Lebanese Hezbollah who are Iranian backed). They were pooling resources and finances, supporting and facilitating each other. Large amounts of F/F (Foreign Fighters) were being utilised by the terrorist networks, as were suicide bombers and IED bomb makers. Oil, weapons, drugs and kidnapping were now helping to fund a self-sustained very complex terrorist network. Even Al-Shabab and Hezbe-Islam in Somalia were now part of the bigger terrorist network. Somali pirates also provided ships and a means of transport for Al-Qaeda and the Pakistan Taliban, Haqqani Network, ISIS between countries. I knew a lot about all of this and I had included it in great detail in my written reports, which I had previously given to American Intelligence. I also mentioned during my meeting with the Americans, that Al-Qaeda and the Pakistan Taliban/Haqqani network had plans to hijack oil-tankers off the coast of Somalia, pack them with explosives and UXO and then use them as suicide bombs, targeting oil refineries in Saudi Arabia, American naval bases and locations in the Red Sea and the Suez Canal. Al-Qaeda and the Pakistan Taliban were looking at both tactical and strategic targets including the sinking of several oil tankers in the Strait of Hormuz and the Gulf of Suez (see Glossary, Strait of Hormuz attacks). This would disrupt oil shipments to Western countries and in turn would dramatically affect the price of oil... Al-Qaeda planned to disrupt the economies and financial markets of the West. Slowly but surely I was building a picture on how the terrorists moved and operated across their area of operations, which was basically the whole of the Middle-East...

2018... Intelligence and Hum-Int on the ground indicates that ISIS leadership are becoming part of the new Al-Qaeda in Iraq/Afghanistan under the Command of Bin Laden's Son who has senior Haqqani Commanders as his personal advisers...

Back to 2003...& how the future of international terrorism was being mouldered by political events I was caught in the middle of...

Back to Kuwait

The rest of the day was spent on personal administration. We moved to Heathrow Airport,London and bordered the late afternoon flight to Kuwait.

The BA flight touched down at Kuwait Airport in the early morning. After collecting our kit, I headed in to the police office in the arrivals terminal, I asked the duty officer if he could arrange for the duty driver to take me to the other side of the airfield to the US air base, "Camp Wolf, "vehicles are not allowed to cross the runways, so it is along drive round". On arrival at camp wolf's main gate, the police driver dropped us off, I showed ID and got a ride into camp with a patrol of Humvees, they dropped us off at the outgoing military flight terminal. The little hanger was as I remembered it, sand bags surrounding it, with a flurry of human activity. Large pallets of ammunition, were being unloaded, and different groups of troops were being briefed on their movements, manifestsand chalk times. C130

Heracles, and Starlifter military transport aircraft were taking off and landing a short distance away, the noise was amazing. We made my way to the security gate outside the hanger, two US marines were there, one was armed with a 203, "M16 carbon, with 40mm grenade launcher, the other was behind a belt fed "SAW, "section automatic weapon". With a hearty "hello boys" I showed then my flight documents for us and letter from General Pretaeus. They smiled, come on in. I noticed the little stars and stripes flag, fixed to the side of the guard room, it was fluttering in the wind "it looked good".

On arrival at the terminal office, I was notified that the next C130 Hercules to Baghdad was due to take off in two hours, great my timing was as good as always, sometimes you have to wait 24hrs to get a military flight. The hanger was packed and hot, I told Janeits best to move outside, there were a few shade areas out front. I dropped the kit next to a Humvee, I asked Jane if she fancied a cold drink, she looked at me puzzled; there was not a shop around here, "give me 10min". I made my way to the flight line and the administration officers. I asked a Staff SGT, where I could get food and a cold drink, he pointed at a large fridge and a box of MREs in the corner, "help yourself", I grabbedtwo 1LT,ice cold bottles of water out the fridge and put some others back in thefridge, "unwritten rule" and two MREs. chicken, and beef. I had grown accustomed to the Boil in the bag MREs, over the past few years.If there's nothing else, they will do. I took them back to Jane, she smiled, "I was always good at finding things". The chalk commander called us over for a brief with the rest of the troops, the C130 was loading now ready for take-off. We grabbed our kit and made our way to the flight line with the rest of the troops. Something seemed out of place, the line of troops around us, something did not fit, then it dawned on me, most of them did not have a personal weapon, not even a side arm. I asked one of the soldiers stood next to me about this, he told me new troops going into Iraq for the first time, most of them did not have weapons, they would get their weapons in country. I was shocked at this, troops flying over and into a hot combat zone, with no weapons sounded mad, what happened if they crashed, or got a contact as we got off the plane, it sounded mad to me. This was one of many regulations that I could not understand.

BaghdadAirport

The C130 Hercules accelerated off the runway, we were now airborne, next stop Baghdad. The flight to Baghdad was all low level, "hugging the contours of the ground", with plenty of "G" turns to minimizethe risk of being blown out of the sky by S.A.M.s, "surface to air missiles"(See Photographs) fired by the insurgents. Being thrown around the back off a C130 is not a great experience, the younger soldiers,for whom this was their first tour of Iraq, were making full use of the sick bags.For some strange reason I had a craving for a hamburger with cheese... After one last "G" turn and a rapid descent the C130 touched down on the tarmac at Baghdad Airport. The tail gate opened as the C130 stopped next to a set of buildings, the hot desert air rushed in. "Debus".I've never seen a group of young soldiers step off a plane's tail gate so fast, with all their kit "they didn't like the ride". I made my way over to the building marked flight office, I was informed that there was a Chinook helicopter flying out to QW, in afew hours, "great, can you put 2 X Pax on the flight manifest" he looked down the list, "yaI will fit you on", I walked out the office and informed Jane that we were on the next flight to QW, two hours' time. Another two hours to kill, we moved over to where some Military trucks were parked up. I laid down with my back on my kit reading "The history of Baghdad", my black Orkney sunglass shading my eyes from the glaring sun. Two US jet fighters took off from the nearest runway on another combat mission, the noise was deafening, the rouge and whoosh of their after burners kicked in as they accelerated down the run way. I thought to myself "It was another beautiful day in sunny Baghdad". I was growing to like this country and its people.The origin of the name "Baghdad" is under some dispute. Some say it comes from an Aramaic phrase that means "sheep enclosure" (not very poetic...). Others contend that the word comes from ancient Persian: "bagh" meaning God, and "dad" meaning gift. *The gift of God...."* During at least one point in history, it certainly seemed so.

The Capital of the Muslim World, In about 762 A.D., the Abbasid dynasty took over rule of the vast Muslim world and moved the capital to the newly-founded city of Baghdad. Over the next five centuries, the city would become the world's centre of education and culture. This period of glory has become known as the "Golden Age" of Islamic civilisation, when scholars of the Muslim world made important contributions in both the sciences and humanities: medicine, mathematics, astronomy, chemistry, literature and more. Under Abbasid rule, Baghdad became a city of museums, hospitals, libraries and mosques. (Check out the links to the right for the Baghdad Photo Gallery, which has pictures of some of these great monuments).

Most of the famous Muslim scholars from the 9th to 13th centuries had their educational roots in Baghdad. One of the most famous centres of learning was *Bayt al-Hikmah* (the House of Wisdom), which attracted scholars from all over the world, from many cultures and religions. Here, teachers and students worked together to translate Greek manuscripts, preserving them for all time. They studied the works of Aristotle, Plato, Hippocrates, Euclid and Pythagoras. The House of Wisdom was home to, among others, the most famous mathematician of the time: Al-Khawarizmi, the "father" of algebra (which is named after his book "Kitab al-Jabr").

While Europe festered in the Dark Ages, Baghdad was thus at the heart of a vibrant and diverse civilisation. It was known as the world's richest and most intellectual city of the time and was second in size only to Constantinople.

After 500 years of rule, however, the Abbasid dynasty slowly began to lose its' vitality and relevance over the vast Muslim world. The reasons were partly natural (vast flooding and fires) and partly human-made (rivalry between Shia and Sunni Muslims, internal security problems).

The city of Baghdad was finally trashed by the Mongols in 1258 A.D., effectively ending the era of the Abbasids. The Tigris and EuphratesRivers reportedly ran red, with the blood of thousands of scholars (a reported 100,000 of Baghdad's million residents were massacred). Many of the libraries, irrigation canals, and great historical treasures were looted and forever ruined. The city began a long period of decline and became host to numerous wars and battles that continue to this day.

The low thumping sound off a Chinookcame into ear shot, you can always hear them before they are visible, "it is very distinctive". The sound slowly became louder, the Chinook came banking low into view over the airfield, it was banked at 45 degrees, the noise from the pitch of the rotors blades was monstrous, the helicopter was in an horizontal angleas it came into land, then suddenly righted itself, and with a fast change of pitchand pace,landed. The dust cloud of sand that the rotors kick up, rolled towards where I was laid. I sheltered my face with my hand while the cloud passed over me, the deafening, thunderous noise of the router blades started to down pitchand whine down. The tail gate at the rear of the Chinook dropped and twenty armed troops in clean fatigue, wearing desert camouflage uniforms run off, "de-bussed", in to files, straight back for 30 meters, then they filed right onto the flight line and tarmac outside the buildings. They all stopped and gathered outside a hanger, two Humvees and a truck pulled up in front of them, the soldiersspilled into the waiting transport, in a heartbeat, and they were gone. "Hanging around in the open areas of a military base is not a good idea"; the insurgency had a habit of lobbing mortar rounds into the base without any warning. Best to always be around some kind off cover, just in case. "Being wiped out by a stray insurgency mortar round was not a good way to go, you would lose 100 cool points". There's been many a time that I have seen Iraq workers employed by the coalition pacing out the distances between buildings and areas, this is how the insurgency can fire mortars with such accuracy into the base, every time one of these workers is caught another one takes his place.

A flight officer walked over to where I was sitting, "Sir, that's your ride", boarding in ten minutes, I grabbed my kit and shouted to Jane to head over to the back of the helicopter. A member of the flight crewwas stood on the tail gate, he greeted us, pointing to the front area, "find a seat at the front left and secure your kit". The routers of the Chinook started up again, the vibrations echoed through the fuselage. A platoon of pathfinders bordered, theirinsignia on theirshirts gave them away, another group of four plain clothes men got on board and sat opposite me. There browncivilian mountain boots, long hair and rough beards gave them away, as well as their customised weapons and laser sights; they were a hunter killer team from task force 121. We looked at each other and smiled. We were eyeing each other's personal kit up, "you can tell a lot from looking at a person's personal kit, their boots, watch, appearance. All tell, tell signs of a Special Forces operative. The Chinook lifted off, up straight vertically, then a sharp bank to the left and low level hugging the river banks of the river Tigrus, the tailgate had been left down and a tail gunner sat on the end looking for bad guys, the view of the river banks flickered from side to side. The tail gunner got up, strapped himself in, hooked himself on to his safety line and sat with his legs hanging over the end of the tailgate. His mounted belt fed M60 machine gun, held at the ready, this was a reminder that the threat of being shot down was very real. A muffled sound came over the intercom, five minutes to landing. This was the most dangerous part of flying around Iraq and hot zones, landing and take-offare the best time to shoot down any aircraft and the insurgencewhere well aware of this, with the volume of S.A.M.s being fired at coalition aircraft, the insurgency were not short of them.

Al Qayyarah "Qayyarah West"

155

Two minutes later the Chinook touched down at QW,"the home of the apache battle group. We grabbed out kit and made our way to the closest hanger. Which turned out to be the HQ for the black hawk detachment. This was commanded by Richards, she was the only women Black Hawk Commander and had just recently been on the cover of Time Magazine. I walked into the operations room, the Sgt behind the desk looked at me, a voice shouted out, "Hay man you're back"; the boys in the main ops room had recognised me. The Sgt behind the disk had just come into country the week before, he was told that I was an old timer and friend of the Col and I had clearance to be anywhere. He looked abit puzzled. After a quick brew and chat, getting updated with the news on the ground, I asked if there was anyone heading over the main Base HQ, I wanted to call in and say hello to the Intel boys over there and let them know I was back in country. I told Jane to hang out here with the commander for about an hour, "we would bunk down here, this side of the airfield tonight". We pulled out outside the hanger being used as HQ. On the way inside a captain walked out and a "good to see you again Anth" was voiced.

After a chat with the Intel boys and a look at theirupdated operations maps, I made my way over to the engineer's area. They had been babysitting my GMC jeep, they had carried out some work on it and it was running well, just needed a good clean. I acquired my personal weapon that had been put into safe storage. I gave the boys a bottle of Jack Daniels whiskey, for doing a good job. I looked in the back, the boys had acquired a full military tool kit for me and a few extras... "a job well done".

My Little Baby V1

CIA

I made my way to the operations room, I had clearance to use the secure line to Baghdad, I placed a call to a friendly Embassy and asked to be put through to the RSORegional Security Officer "CIA", I gave him a key word, then gave him the GPS location of the day sack. He had already been briefed, he was expecting my call when I was back in country "Iraq". It had already been arranged that aSpecial Forces Team would pick up and neutralize the information in the day sack, it would be copied and passed onto the UK as well. It was the safest and best all round answer. I was to find out what had been in the day sack a few weeks down the line. The information helped to save lives, "I felt happy not giving it to the press" I placed the receiver down, it was done. I drove back around the base to the Black Hawk flight line, refuelling on route. I had the Rolling Stones blasting out from the CD player, the windows wound down, the sunroof back, with the hot afternoon air blowing in. "it was good to be back in Iraq". My gut feeling was that things were about to happen. I choose not to tell Jane on what I had done with the Americans. There were a few marks on her now and my intelligence contacts had told me to lose her over the next few weeks. I had been given afew tasks and areas of interest by my friendly call/signs when back in the UK, so I was going to work on what they required.

When I got back a BBQ was in full swing outside the hanger, fresh salads and beef burgers were on the go. The smell was great, everyone was in a joyful mood, the troops were sat around talking and joking; the rest of the Black Hawks had just come in and landed and settled in for the day. There were no major operations on that night. The rest of the day was spent as down time, cleaning kit and weapons.

In this pleasant environment, it was hard to image that we were all in an active combat zone. I grabbed a cot and slept outside under the stars; that night the hanger was too hot inside. I drifted off to sleep looking at the shooting stars zooming across the sky.I was woken the next morning at 0530am by a Black Hawk helicopter flying overhead.

I got up and went for my morning run down the runway and along the Black Hawk flight line. I ran around the massive craters that littered the far end of the runway, where the US had dropped cluster bombs to close the runways off to the enemy aircraft during the early days of the war. One of the craters had one still in the middle of it, it had not detonated, like so much UXO, it had been tapped off at a safe distance and was waiting to be made safe.When I got back to the hangarJane was digging into breakfast and her much needed and loved coffee lol. I showered and joined her. We were sat talking when a young girl from Intel headed over to us, I stood up to get a refill of coffee - I will be back in a moment. When I got back the Intel girl had gone, Jane was smiling, she had been given a message."Col Anderson is going after Saddam's sons today. New Intel had pin pointed them in Mosul. We got onto Col Anderson and booked a Black Hawk to get us there, we got all our kit together and parked up victor call sign around the side of the hanger. Any problems find me. 15 minutes later we were on the flight line, with all the kit broken down that we would need for a few days in the field. The black hawk helicopter had been specially arranged by the commander to take us to Mosul Airbase, where Col Anderson was going to personally pick us up. "All the work and Intel and good results had paid off". 20 minutes later the Black Hark touched down at Mosul Airport, Col Anderson pulled up within moments and the kit was loaded into the back of his Humvee. We were on the move and in transit to the Target house.

The Real Killer Elite, Uday and Qusay Saddam's Sons

It was shortly before 10 o'clock on the morning of Tuesday July 22, 2003 and the temperatures in central Iraq were already well above 100 degrees. Troops from 101st Airborne Division moved quietly into place to secure the area and cordon around the large three-story villa in the al-Falah district of north-east Mosul. The Activity had been running a number of Iraqi agents inside the Sunni triangle northwest of Baghdad as part of the hunt for 'Black List One' - Saddam Hussein. Now one of the former Iraqi generals they were using as go-betweens and trackers had come up trumps. A con-man who had served three years in jail for impersonating a relative of Saddam had tipped him off that the Iraqi dictator's two sons Uday and Qusay were hiding in his villa. With a $15million reward on each of their heads, it had been only a matter of time before someone sold them out.

A four-man SAS team, part of a 12-man UK detachment based in Mosul alongside the Delta and Activity operators which had proven adept at merging into the local population, had been sent in to carry out close target reconnaissance of the villa and surrounding area the previous evening.

The SAS Det commander was confident that his team could storm the building and kill the four occupants swiftly that night. It was the sort of operation that the SAS trained for routinely at their close-quarters battle training facility at Pontrilas, ten miles south of Hereford. They had a proven track record of success in such operations. The Iranian Embassy siege in London was the most famous. But the US commanders were skeptical that 12 men from the SAS would be sufficient. More to the point, it was important that if there was a major success against Saddam and the insurgency it was American soldiers who produced that public success.

The word came up from Baghdad that this operation was to be carried out by American Delta and soldiers from within the American 101st Airborne Division...

Once the US troops were in place, an Iraqi interpreter used a bullhorn to urge the brothers to surrender – to come out with their hands up. The response from inside the house was a burst of automatic gunfire, which missed the Americans and wounded an Iraqi in the leg standing outside of the Bashar Kalunder mosque across the road. As the airborne troops provided covering fire, 'shooters' from the Activity and Delta went in. They were part of Task Force 20, the special operations task force set up to capture the leading members of Saddam's regime who were designated as 'High Value Targets'. The Delta and Activity men stormed through the tall iron front gates of walled compound around the villa. Some broke down the front door and began clearing the first floor. Others entered through the basement garage where a black Mercedes was parked and climbed the stairs at the back of the building, checking possible entry and exit points. Three of the 'shooters' were halfway up the stairs to the second floor when they came under fire from behind barricades. The two brothers themselves were holed up in a bedroom at the front of the house. The 'shooters' used stun grenades to try to shock them into dropping their defences but without success and were forced back after a heavy exchange of small arms fire, the only casualty were four soldiers from Task Force 20; they were hit on their way up the stairs, and one was a 2nd BDE trooper in the street, he was felled by a round from Hussein bodyguard, who had fired from an upstairs bedroom window.One of the dogs adopted as pets by the Task Force operators, was also shot dead by one of the brothers. Despite having to make a tactical retreat, the shooters had at least discovered where the targets were. A Black Hawk med-vac chopper dusted off from a nearby field to evacuate the four men wounded in the firefight. Colonel Joe Anderson, who was commanding the operation, called in the Night Stalkers' MH-6 Little Bird attack helicopters to use their armor-piercing missiles to try to flush the defenders out and put Apache helicopter gunships and A10 Thunderbolts on stand-by. The first Little Bird mistook several Delta operators who were on the roof for the Iraqis nearly causing a blue-on-blue, but fortunately the difficult approach meant all but one of his missiles missed the building completely. A second Little Bird had no more luck so Joe Anderson ordered the troops from 101st Airborne in front of the house to open fire with Humvee-mounted TOW anti-tank rockets. One missile cut a telegraph pole outside the villa in half (Great Shot) before hitting home in the front left bedroom, blowing the window frames out onto a BMW parked in the street below.

Meanwhile, Lieutenant-General David Petraeus, the Commanding General of 101st Airborne(Future Head of the CIA) who was circling overhead in his Black Hawk helicopter spotted activity in a house 80 yards down the street from the villa in which Saddam's sons were hiding. Uday's bodyguards had been cut off by the American cordon and were preparing to fire on the US troops from behind. Petraeus swiftly ordered his men into place and the bodyguards' opening burst of fire from an AK-47 Kalashnikov assault rifle was cut short by a volley of tracer from an American .50 caliber heavy machine gun. (See Photographs)

Exclusive Photograph By Author   View from American Gunship During firefight

160

A total of 18 TOW missiles were fired into the villa where Uday and Qusay were hiding. The force of the attack on the target house was so strong that four special operations forces trying to find an entry point at the rear were wounded by shrapnel from TOW anti-tank rockets that went straight through the house and out the other side. The acrid stench of smoke and carbon enveloped the villa as its façade crumbled in the face of the battering from missiles designed to penetrate the heaviest armor. Fragments of decorative tiles added small splashes of color to the rubble dropping down in front of the building. Thousands of .50 caliber and 5.56mm tracer and amour-piecing rounds were pumped into the villa. The US troops even fired a surface-to-air missile through a window. But still the four men inside continued to respond with AK-47s on automatic. The shooters situated on the roof opposite the target house were putting down covering fire again into the house forcing the occupants to the top left hand side of the house to move to the back right, as they were doing this another little bird was lining up for a gun run. In all the confusion the little bird helicopter opened fire on the activities shooters on the roof with an bust of automatic .50 caliber armored piercing rounds. "A scream ofcheck fire, check fire, came over the military communications equipment," this was the second friendly fire incident during the firefight, simultaneously Udays two body guards started to open fire again from the balcony of the pink house, 30 meters down the road, this lasted another ten seconds, one of the belt fed .50s mounted on the top of the Humvee at the back of the target house silenced them for good. Eventually, after four hours of intensive exchanges of fire, the shooting from inside the house tailed off and the special operations 'shooters' were ordered back in, only to be engaged by automatic rifle fire from a AK-47 held by Qusay's son, who was hiding under the bed in a bedroom at the rear of the house. The 14-year-old was killed by the first burst of return fire from the Delta operators. The US troops found the battered bodies of Uday and Qusay huddled in the front bed room under a wooden table and mattresses, where they had chosen to make their last stand, (See Exclusive Photographs of Target Villa& Room Uday & Qusay were found in)

 Photographed by Author

Their internal organs quite literally battered to the point of disintegration by the shock waves from the barrage of Tow missiles. All four of the bodies and body parts were collected up, wrapped in green ponchos and carried out by members of the activity, General Petreaus, Col Anderson and placed in the back of the waiting Humvees. (See Photographs) Col Anderson got Udays blood on his combat shirt, he joked with me that he would not wash it off. "Col Anderson had called off the air strike by the A10s and circling Apache helicopter gunships. The collateral damage of an airstrike going into this built up area would have been to high".

The CIA, "The Activity's Clean Up Team"

The CIA moved in within minutes of the building being cleared, sensative sight exploration started, all information, documents and evidence was gathered and bagged and tagged, Uday's gold plated AK sniper rifle and other weapons were collected in (See Photographs) as well as large amounts of US $100 bills and Iraq dinars, $500,000 in total all stuffed into a bag, two foot by two foot in size. Another bag full of jewellery and watches was also found under the bed that Qusay had been sleeping in. Additional bags contained five assault rifles and one RPK light machine gun. Pornographic magazines were also found among Qusay's personal belongings.

British Soldiers with Uday's Gold AK-47

"The evidence that was in Uday's black brief case was staggering, both tactically and strategically, computer CD's of bank accounts and money transactions between Saddam's family and the Iraqi insurgency and prominent people outside of Iraq living in Lebanon Syria and Saudi Arabia, documents were found with bank letter heads from Lebanon, Saudi-Arabia, Lebanon... as well as Syrian, Lebanese passports for Saddam's sons."

Plans of attacks that they were planning, locations timings and counter insurgency information. "Three of the detailed plans of attacking the coalition were hiding hand grenades in ice blocks. "Uday's brother in law was running an Ice factory" and delivering them to the mess rooms of the US soldiers, the other was taping a hand grenade to the bottom of the inside of a large blue plastic petrol canister, removing the pin, filling it and delivering it to the coalition fuel depot, after 24hrs the fuel would have eaten away at the tap, releasing the hand grenade, and blowing up, the depot. There were even plans to attempt an assignation ofGeneral Petraeus, at the opening of the Olympic swimming pool later that month, as well as the first police graduation in Mosul. (See Photograph)There was also the bombshell in the case for me, files from the Bank of al-Madina, Lebanon. Adnan Abou Ayyash. My client. **"My two ongoing jobs had just become connected."** This was something I did not expect to see, not in Iraq... but there it was in front of me, in black and white. "There was alot of other data and information in the briefcase,**"something's are best left alone"**.The black Mercedes car was removed from the basement garage for forensics, as were the case of sodas on the back seat, "we toasted Udays' departure with soda".

"A little known fact regarding the intelligence that helped to pin point Saddam's sons and later Saddam himself, Kurdish intelligence assets helped... I feel that this fact should be recognised, given the way the British Government has been treating the Kurdish Government and people... Betrayal..."

Above; Exclusive the night before the worlds press was informed that Saddam's sons had been killed. Below; The next afternoon after the worlds press has been told.CNN camera crew by Author

Saddam Raid withColAndersons "Strike 6" General Petraeus, Anthony Malone

(See Photographs) As the Activity's human intelligence operators were celebrating their success, the 'knob-turners'in the electronic surveillance team, weresat outside situated on the remains of the wall next to the shot up BMW outside the target house.Suddenlyall around the green box sat on the wall became a buzz with activity, they had picked up what promised to be an even more valuable lead. I went over to see what had just come in, They intercepted a satellite telephone call from 'Black List One' himself. Spooked by the shooting but unaware of what was going on, Saddam wanted his aides to move him to a new safe house. The sat-phone's location was immediately pinpointed, but by the time the rapid response teams got there the former Iraqi dictator had just gone. Saddam had eluded the hunter killer teams again... The Activity now set out to 'take down the mountain', finding and arresting Saddam's main allies one by one as they had with Pablo Escobar, until the former Iraqi dictator had no one left to support him.

"Think Out The Box" al-Qa'dia

A term I first was told by the Senor Intelligence Officer in Iraq, "G1", in connection with understanding al-Qa'dia, and International Terrorism. Shortly after Task Force 20 killed Uday and Qusay, they were combined with Task Force 5, their counterpart in Afghanistan, to form a new hit squad, Task Force 121, a combination of Delta, DevGru, Activity, CIA, SAS and SBS commandos whose sole purpose was to capture or kill America's main enemies in the region. In Afghanistan, that meant Osama bin Laden and his ally Mullah Mohammed Omar, the Taliban leader. (I would help locate both of these HVT targets in the future). In Iraq, Task Force 121 had one role alone, a British special forces officer told me: 'pure and simple to find Number One'.

I returned to the main operations room where the demise of Saddam's sons had been conducted from, everyone was on a high, after months ofrelentless intelligence operations, all the hard work had paid off. Now anew target was in the sights of the coalition Intelligence network, and Task Force 121, Saddam himself. That night Col Anderson told me that he was going on a raid, the way he said it was strange. "he was going after Saddam", Task force, "the activity", had reports that Saddam with in a house, 600meters from where his sons had been killed, the area was swarming with US military, there was a chance he was still there (See Photographs) 101st had set an outer cordon and an inner cordon around the area, SF teams were waiting in the backs of Humvees, waiting for the order to go. It was given, the power was cut to the house, in pitch darkness theSF teams, using night vision, backed up by Rangers, stormed the house, the SF sniper teams covered them from rooftops across the street. Doors were kicked in and rooms simultaneously cleared shouts of"all clear" echoed around the house. I was stood outside the house with General Petraeusand Col Anderson when the all clear was given, they had just missed him. "There was a kettle of hot water on the stove in the kitchen". Saddam was lucky on this occasion, but his luck was fast running out. Task Force 121 carefully followed up every reported sighting of Saddam Hussein, but months went by with no sign of success. By the end of the summer, the US troops had received so many unsubstantiated sightings of the former Iraqi dictator that they had taken to referring to him as 'Elvis'. But in the background, the Activity and their CIA colleagues were working away on contact analysis, tracking the links between Saddam and his various henchmen.

I had informed 101st ABD intelligence of a location where Saddam had been staying, I accompanied Col Anderson and his men on the lighting fast raid, we had just missed him again. A branded cigarette was still alight in the ashtray... I thought we had him that day. Working in their tiny headquarters in Camp Slayer inside the 'Green Zone', the heavily defended allied stronghold in Baghdad, they used a combination of intercepts of satellite and radio telephones and human intelligence from agents on the ground and from Iraqis anxious to collect the $25m reward to narrow their search down to the area around Saddam's family stronghold of Tikrit north-west of the Iraqi capital. There were no fewer than 11 raids aimed at trying to catch Saddam during September and October alone. Task Force 121's commanders knew they had to take a fresh approach if they were going to catch the former Iraqi dictator. At the end of October, they mounted a major raid on the village of Awja, about five miles south of Tikrit, where Saddam had been brought up, arresting and questioning more than 500 Iraqis, many of whom had direct links to Saddam's family. Those interrogations added a host of new detail to the intelligence picture and formed the start point for the sustained hunt for Black List One. Delta, DevGru or SAS shooters now began to snatch relatives or henchmen of the Iraqi dictator to order, taking his inner circle apart piece by piece, ratcheting up the pressure. The intelligence experts interrogated every new prisoner, adding any new information he provided to the accumulated intelligence picture. They then worked out which of Saddam's remaining cronies was best able to provide the next missing piece of the jigsaw and sent the 'shooters' out on a 'shopping expedition' to snatch the man they needed to fill in that gap. By early December, Task Force 121 knew they were right on Saddam's tail. The shooters had brought in half-a-dozen close relatives of the former Iraqi dictator over the past few days and, while none of them had told their interrogators where he was, the accumulative effect of the detail had provided a very clear picture of Saddam's life on the run. They now knew that a reported sighting of him being driven around Baghdad in a battered orange and white

Toyota Corolla taxi was almost certainly correct and that for most of the time he had been using the taxi to move between any of several dozen safe houses, each with a secret hiding place in case American troops came knocking. Sometimes he might stay in one place for a few days, sometimes only for a few hours, often moving out only just ahead of the special operations forces tracking him down. 'They've been so close at times that they have picked up his slippers and they've been warm,' one British member of Task Force 121 said. Sooner or later, someone would get greedy for the $25m bounty and give him up or just get careless and let that key piece of the jigsaw slip.

That night was spent at Col Andersons "Strike 6" HQ, the de-briefs and the preparations for the press releases where under way. Within about six hours the worlds press would be on the door step.

 (See Authors Photographs of CNN at Target Villa doing live feed covering Saddam's sons.)

The next morning we went back to the target house, Col Anderson walked through and explained every aspect of the operation. Photographs were taken of every room, I took agood photo of one of the US boys posing inside the house,(See Photograph) he was taking notes, the inside of the house was like a building sight, rubble everywhere, there was not a wall that hadn't been hit by a bullet or rocket.

The open view of the road outside through the blown out windows was starting to fill up with the worlds press, a security cordon had been put up over the street to stop them from trying to get into the house.There were too many people here for my liking, I didn't want my face to be on international TV, "Sam a friend of mine had been watching CNN and had spotted me in the background talking to a US Colonel, on the steps of the target house" I viewed the tapemonths later, "yes it was me"", I returned with Anderson to D Main. Division HQ, Saddam's old Mosul palace. I wanted to touch base with a Col I had come across, he was in command of the engineers in Northern Iraq. His name was Col Rorex, he is a very good man. I had some time to kill. There were a lot of mass graves around Qayyarah West, women and children killedby Saddam's Hench men. Maj Flexwas the commander of Qayyarah West, and we had grown to respect each other. I had many private chats with him about certain areas of operation, I had given him multiple locations to report mass graves in, CNN were now on the ground covering one of them. The Col had given me an open invite to stay at QW whenever I needed in the future. I arrived at D- Main late afternoon, the hub had just started, "daily Intel brief" in the main HQ operations room, I grabbed a coffee and sat in on it. Jane went off to take some photographs of the palace. Saddam's sons being killed was just one off the items on the agenda, there had been a lot of activity all over Iraq and surrounding countries. After the hub I said goodbye for now to Col Anderson, "strike six" he said,"Don't be a stranger." We copied and burned the photographs onto CDs that we had taken of the target house, StrikeSix, Col Anderson and Major Sherington's promotion, and operations I had accompanied SOF on and gave them to Col Anderson and the Major for theirpersonal use. They have been used to illustrate such books as "Hunting Down Saddam, by Robin Moore", and "A Killer Elite, by Mick Smith" as well as finding their way into several other specialist publications like Combat and Survival. I hooked up with Col Rorex, we had a walk to the strike café, situated on camp, in the palace grounds. We sat outside talking about the ongoing situation in Iraq, while enjoying a Magnum ice cream.I dropped into conversation that there was a Catholic children's orphanage north of Mosul. In a place called Al Qosh, a sleepy little village, just short of the green line and Kurdistan. I said that they could do with a hand to re-build and a little help would go down well.It was set, we were to travel up there tomorrow morning. Col Rorex told me he would organise the convoy and timings would be 0900hrs ready to move. I had met Father Toma, during my time spent in Iraq and I had visited the orphanage in the past, I still hold a special place in my heart for Al Qosh and the orphanage. There was a lot of history for me in that area...I tracked down Jane in the media office, she was working on her e-mails, I told her of the plan for Al Qosh and the timings. It would be a great place to get some amazing photographs again. I sent off an e-mail to Paul D informing him off what I had found with regards to Adnan abou Ayyash and what had been found inside the black brief case of Uday, I knew that this was a significant development in his investigation into the Al Madina Bank. Major Kate arranged for us to sleep in the palace VIP area that night. He got one of the Cpl's escort us to our cots for the night. It was a private one level building located away from the main palace, it had its own AC unit and a fridge full of bottled water. A box off MREs was propping up the corner.Jane had an early night reading. The rest of my night was down time, spent next door, playing cards, smoking Cuban cigars and enjoying ice cold beers, with a Staff Sgt that I had become friends with. He was moving out the next morning to join a Special Forces unit based out of a fort on the Iraq Syrian border. Tonight was his last chance to get down time for awhile, we made the most of it.

Iraq's First Suicide Car Bomb "the beginning of the storm"

The next morning I woke up 0600hrs, all I could taste was beer and cigars, I was in desperate need of food, coffee and shower. An hour later I was good to go. I walked around the camp with a coffee in hand enjoying the morning sun, it was a beautiful day. The morning's tranquillity was shattered as a large blast erupted outside the palace grounds to my left. Col Anderson was heading out to see what had happened, I grabbed a ride. We sped off to the area of the explosion, an army check point 200m away. This was a major turning point of the insurgency attacks in Iraq on coalition forces, it was the first car suicide bomb in Iraq.The insurgent had killed himself when he detonated the explosive device inside the car, no US soldiers were killed; just a passing Iraqi taxi driver was wounded. The debris of the remains of the car lay scattered around a 100 meter radius, the engine block of the car was all that was left, burned and mangled on the side of the road. Apart from a six feet crater in the middle of the road, there were some small remnants of body parts. I looked at Col Anderson. This was not good, it reminded me too much of my time patrolling the bloody streets of Northern Ireland and the bloody attacks by the IRA. The insurgency was now playing on a different level, the coalition had to re-think its strategy on and in Iraq.Col Anderson dropped me back off at D Main, in time to catch my ride with Col Rorex.

We pulled up at 0900hrs sharp, outside the Col office, the convoy of Humvees were waiting, all fueled and ready to go. I quickly pulled a map out my combat's side pocket, laid it on the bonnet of the Humvee, showing the target location on the map to the Col, a minute later we were off. We rolled out of D-Main, it was a warm day, the sky was a clear blue and the sun was starting to get hot and high in the sky.

Al Qosh Children's Orphanage

"A ray of sunshine on a dark day

Rays of joy surround me,

The innocent faces of war come to,

My the future be there cradle" Steven Anderson

The road up to Al Qosh is pretty open and dusty, the convoy of Humvees snaked its way through the small villages along the route, Tal Kayf and passing a new Catholic Church and casino "café" that Saddam Hussien had paid to build. There are only two roads to Al Qosh, they both verge on each other just before Al Qosh. One of the roads is the only main road north from Iraq into Kurdistan, it passes though the green zone. On arrival in Al Qosh, we drove though the village, the orphanage was situated on the far side of the village with its' back to the mountains, it isdetached from the rest of the village. As we approached the tall concrete walls that enclosed and protected the orphanage, I noticed that the large wooden doors were open (they were never left open), a moment of dread set in, I feared the worst, God not another slaughter of children... it was quickly replaced with relief when I saw that some kids were playing football outside the gates. On arrival we pulled the Humvees outside the main entrance, some of the soldiers stayed with the vehicles. "Top cover". We were still in a hostile area, the rest of us walked inside. The kids swamped us as we walked in, some were calling my name in English and one jumped into my arms with a big smile, the Col looked at me, this is a welcome. Father Toma came out to see what all the commotion was over. He smiled and shook my hand (The father knew I had worked covertly in this area in the past, keeping the wolves from the door is one way of putting it... I am a good Christian, doing God's work and protecting Christian children. I had history with this orphanage and area but that's another story...) I introduced him to Col Rorex, he invited us into his office next to the chapel. Jane was dragged off by the children, to take their photographs I would jump on top of a Humvee to get a great Photograph of her later with the kids.

We all sat down and took chai. I explained to Father Toma that Col Rorex was in charge of the engineers based out of Mosul. Col Rorex said "What do you need?"This was a dear diary moment, "Some of the buildings need repairing and rebuilding" Father Toma said; not seriously with a smile"A new road from the main road to the church and village"; the dirt road was being washed away every time it rained. Col Rorex smiled. "That's do able". Father Toma looked at me, I just smiled. On top of that Col Rorex built them a computer room and kitted it out withnew computers and internet access. In one meeting that I had arranged, it had totally sorted out the orphanage "it was a feel good day all around".

Col Rorex stationed a platoon of his men there to start the work asap. Father Toma showed Col Rorex around after chai. You have to stay the night, Col Rorex wanted to but he had to attend a brief back at HQ, Father Toma looked at me, I said I would stay, he smiled, I know why...the good father had a good supply of homemade red wine he kept in a secret underground place, it was made in the mountains that surrounded Al Qosh. He had a lot of it, some very old and very good. After a good look around and being swamped by over twenty kids, Col Rorex said his goodbyes to Father Toma and promised to be back very soon. I walked the Col to his Humvee, I said thank you, he smiled at me, it's a pleasure. The rest of the day and night was spent hanging out with Father Toma and the kids. Over the coming years I would spend a lot of time at Al Qosh and the orphanage.

I also had a chat with the Major in charge of the mission to stop the black market diesel coming into Iraq from Turkey. We arranged that trucks and tankers full of diesel that had been confiscated by the coalition in the north would stop off at the orphanage and give them as much fuel as their storage tanks could cope with. Over the coming months a new large storage tanker was found and put in, a football pitch was also built, an inter village football league was set up, Major Gun kitted out all the children with football strips and boots, the children had their names put on the back of all their football tops.

Al Qosh had become a good cause. I never got refused anything from the coalition for Al Qosh. The next afternoon I arranged a Black Hawk pickup and flew back to QW to pickup my Victor Call sign, I drove my victor call sign up to Al Qosh that afternoon, after talking to Father Toma and receiving a shopping list that he needed for the kids in the orphanage, I drove over the green line, whichseparates the area of Arab Iraq and the Kurdish area. I continued on my trip into Kurdistan, to a city called,Dohuk and a little place called "Dream City", this was a western style supermarket, totally out of place in this part of the world. In prospective it would be like finding a Tesco supermarket in the middle of the African jungle. Even if it was out of place it was welcomed. I filled the jeep with supplies and headed back after about a two hour stop. I wanted to be back in Al Qosh before dark, the roads in Northern Iraq are dangerous at night. As the locals would say, "Abu Ally and the forty thieves".I pulled into Al Qosh just as the sun was setting. The locals were locking down for the night. All the vehicles were brought within the high walls of the orphanage and the large wooden gates were locked. The orphanage was a good defensive position. If the worse ever happened again a handful of men could hold off an army at this location, or if we were ever attacked by the insurgents. This never happened again, due to the relationship we had with the local people and the amount of protection I had put into place, even in the future when soldiers left the army, they returned to protect the children and orphanage from ISIS. One day I even got invited to a Arab wedding at the Catholic church to a local woman marrying a gentleman from another village which was the highlight of the week for all in the area. Everybody young and old was attending including the three young daughters dressed in white pictured below.

After a good few days break at Al Qosh, I knew that having American soldiers stationed here now meant the children were safe. I knew from experience that a small group of well-armed and trained men could hold off an enemy force for enough time to call in air support if needed. The Catholic orphanage was built like a fortress with its high mud walls, gates and ramparts, it was more like a fortress. I left it in safe hands. I planned a road tripthrough and around Kurdistan,I had been asked by a friend of mine in London to take some photographs of a certain area, on the Kurdistan, Iran border. Kurdistan was the only part of Iraq that I hadn't travelled to and around extensively at that point. I planned a two week road trip through the entire region. I had some good contacts in Kurdistan and in the KDP, which I had meet in the past during intelligence Tasks, I had fought side by side with the Pesh: short for Peshmerga; Kurdish Military against Saddam back in the day, the Kurds never forget a face. I gave them a call and set up dinner in their house in Dohukfor the next afternoon after an official visit to one of their offices. "My Detailed route taken through Kurdistan highlighted on rear map". I planned the route through Kurdistan using detailed maps and satellite images to ensure I went over and through the locations and areas I needed to photograph, Iranian border post's, isolated valleys, bridges, caves and HVT# smugglingroutes. After studying the maps and comparing them to the satelliteimagery, it was clear that a lot of the tracks and roads were not on the normal military maps. This area was one of the un-spoilt wilderness still left on this plain.I made a list of the locations and area, these would take me right over and through the snow-capped mountains and pass of Kurdistan, where few westerners had ever been.

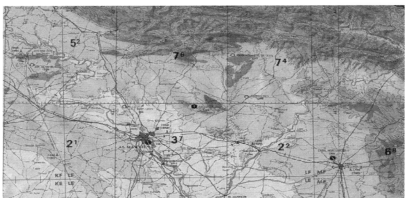

The route was to finish in Mosul. I planned to drive rounda big loop, timescales where about ten days unless I ran into trouble along the way. I briefed Jane on the trip I was going to take, I asked her if she wanted to tag along and take some photographs, she jumped at the chance. I set the timings for 0900am departure the next morning. I spent the rest of the day, checking over the GMC jeep, engine, oil, tyres, breaks, the Full Monty. I filled all the spare fuel containers, taped them and placed them in the back of the jeep with all the supplies of food and bottled water. The round trip would be covering over 1000km, through some of the most remote and staggering demanding and beautiful terrain I had ever traversed. I spent the rest of the day, planning and going over maps and personal kit, I also made sure that Jane had all her kit prepped and ready to go. I also hung out with the kids and played football.

0800am the next morning I was sat having breakfast with the children and Father Toma, enjoying my bread, cheese and coffee. I had told him about my plans, he said I would love the mountains of Kurdistan. He said goodbye and told me to come back soon and have a safe journey. I walked back to the GMC jeep, Jane was there all ready to go. The Children opened the side gate and they waved,running and shouting next to my jeep as I drove out. An hour later after driving along the notorious highway, my AK-47 was loaded and ready just in case, we passed dozens of oil tankers transporting diesel down to Baghdad via the children's orphanage. I was crossing the green line into Kurdistan, the Pesh: short for Peshmerga, the Kurdish military, "they dress in dark green uniforms", were manning the check points, after a quick look in the jeep, they waved me through the checkpoint. Next stop Dohuk Kurdistan.

Kurdistan

"The Mountains, always the mountains,
Held the old man's gaze.
There is a fascination about them that it is not necessary
to be a Kurd or a Persian to be able to acquire." "Ely Bannister Soane"

There is a saying among the Kurds: "No friends but the mountains." For, indeed, the world has scarcely noticed when century after century, conqueror after conqueror has driven these once nomadic tribes deep within their beloved mountains to preserve their culture, their language and their lives. With a population of 5 million in an area larger than Switzerland or twice the size of New Jersey, it is surprising that this region remains largely undiscovered and commercially untapped. The Kurdish people compose one of the ancient nations of the Middle East. Kurdistan, the land of the Kurds, is spread among several modern states: northwestern Iran, northern Iraq, northeastern Syria, southeastern Turkey and small parts of Armenia. There is no exact figure to the Kurdish population because each state has tended to downplay the number of Kurds within its own borders. Nevertheless, according to various estimates, the Kurdish population is estimated to range between 25 to 30 million. This makes the Kurds the fourth largest ethnic people of the Middle East.

In terms of numerical strength, Kurdish ranks fortieth among the world's five to six thousand languages. The strategic weight of Kurdistan was recognised by the U.S. Government in 1985 when Kurdish was included among its list of 169 "critical languages." However, American universities still exclude Kurdish studies from their area studies programs in spite of the fact that the Middle Eastern studies programs of the U.S. are among the most extensive of any country in the world. The persistent absence of interest in Kurdish studies among academics may be explained by their longer-standing commitment to Arabic, Turkish and Iranian studies. One shocking result is that there has been only one dissertation on the Kurds produced every decade since 1861 to every ten produced on the states the Kurds inhabit. Another result is the lack of experts on Kurdish affairs despite the growing importance of that area to the international community. The most famous Kurd in history is Saladin, who in all accounts emerges as the greatest military mind on either side of the Crusades, and the wisest and most famous Muslim ruler. Saladin was born in Tikrit (the same birthplace as Saddam Hussein) in 1137, into a prominent Kurdish family. Saladin grew up in educated circles and distinguished himself militarily in his twenties by playing a significant part in keeping Egypt out of the hands of the First Crusade. Through his own accomplishments and with the help of his powerful family, he was appointed commander of the Syrian troops and vizier of Egypt at the age of 31. He subsequently became the sole ruler of Egypt and soon set out to unite the Muslim territories of Syria, northern Mesopotamia (Iraq), Kurdistan, Palestine, and the rest of Egypt. He proved to be a wise but firm ruler, skilled in diplomacy, free of corruption and cruelty, and dedicated to the spread of Islam. In 1187, he led the re-conquest of Jerusalem and occupied it with compassion and courtesy. He died in 1193, and historians agree that he is one of the world's towering figures.

Operation Provide Comfort is the name given to the 1991 implementation by the United States and its Gulf War Allies of a safe haven for Kurds. Under the Operation Provide Comfort umbrella, allied western troops on the ground persuaded the Kurds to descend from the mountains into the plains, where camps were set up with relief supplies as an added inducement. Allied troops were also sent into Dahuk, to maintain a presence so that the Kurdish refugees who had fled that area would go back to their homes. And the area of Iraq above the 36th parallel—which includes Arbil, Mosul, Zakho, and Dahuk—was declared a no-fly zone: Any Iraqi planes flying above the parallel would be subject to reprisal. By July, the system had been established, and the western troops withdrew from Iraq to bases in Silopi, just across the Turkish border, leaving a small staff, the Military Coordination Centre in Zakho, to oversee the continuing relief effort and to act as a stabilizing force.

 The no-fly zone was regularly patrolled by aircraft from the United States, Great Britain, Franceand Turkey. Operation Provide Comfort was not the only source of help for the Kurds. There were several other relief programs supported by different countries and agencies, and a number of initiatives aimed at strengthening opposition to the Iraqi government and Saddam Hussein. "The New Kurdish".

The Kurds employed by Operation Provide Comfort are very probably typical of all the Kurds who worked for western agencies. The OPC Kurds held a variety of positions: clerks, translators, drivers, guards, cooks, and aid workers of different sorts. Those who held clerical positions are educated, sophisticated, "westernised," and able to communicate fairly well in English. Others in the group have had less education and exposure to the West. The guards, for example, speak little English, and are likely to have had about 8 to 12 years of education (many were educated as soldiers in the Iraqi army).

Each employee was allowed to bring close family members, and the accompanying parents, husbands or wives and children enlarge the first group to about 2,100. These will have a predictable range of education and experience. Service providers can assume that the grandfathers and grandmothers in the group will undoubtedly be more traditional in outlook and will have the most trouble adjusting to a new country and culture. The young to middle-aged adults will be the most anxious, as responsibility falls on their shoulders for their parents and children; it is they who will also be the most demanding of services. The children should assimilate quickly.

Dohuk

The northernmost of the three largest cities in Iraqi Kurdistan. Beneath a smudged grey sky, the road slipped through a dreamy landscape, jade kolls in the foreground and gaunt peaks in the distance. The empty old rusting oil trucks parked on the side of the road, onroute to Turkey, to refill and head down to Baghdad. Dohuk is tucked between two steep, boulder-strewn mountains, rising from the country's high plateau like crumpled hats. On the outskirts of town I passed the newly built university, still under construction, and to the left presided a ten-foot-tall, golden bust of Mulla Mustafa Barzani, father of the Kurdish Liberation movement and a row of mansions that had once belonged to Baath Party officials and now belonged to their Kurdish political counter parts. Signs for non-government relief agencies were everywhere, UNHCR, (the United Nations High Commissioner for Refugees), WHO, (World Health Organisation),WFP, (World Food Program).

I pulled over into a car park, and stopped outside offDream City, "super market", to pick up some supplies that cannot be found in Iraq; good shower gel, toothpaste and cigars, then it was off to my KDP's contacts house in town. His bodyguard had arranged to meet me outside the Jiyan, or "life" Hotel. Originally meant to become a Sheraton, the Jiyan was the hostelry of choice for foreign aid workers, journalists, BBC, SKY, CNN, politicians and businessmen passing through town. It was also the meeting place for the black market arms dealers from former soviet block countries, who were trying to get a foot hold in Iraq and were using Kurdistan as a safe base to operate from.

My guide showed up after a few moments, I recognised him from Mosul, KDP, HQ's, I followed him to the house where we were welcomed with open arms, "the Kurdish people who I stayed with or visited, always made me feel at home", always a warm welcome from K and his family, his family had cooked a lot of food, so we sat down at the table and started eating. We talked about how life was after Saddam and what their plans were for the future.It was nice to have a little normality, even if it was just for one night. We talked till the early hours of the morning, then I retired for a slept restless night of sleep. A lot of memories both good and bad were here in Kurdistan...

"At every stage of a journey you arrive somewhere,

And with every step you can discover a hidden facet of our planet,

All you have to do is look, wish, believe and love" "Omar khayyah"

My road trip through Western Kurdistan started the next morning after a breakfast of bread and coffee and warm farewell greetings. I drove away with the comfort in my mind that I would be back again in the future. I decided to use an old route "The Hamilton Road" as my template for part of my trip to maximize gathering on the ground intelligence, touching base with HUM-INT Human Intelligence contacts and photographs of interest. The Hamilton Road stretching for 180 kms between Erbil, in Kurdish northern Iraq, to the Iranian border at Haji Omaran, deep within the beautiful Zagros mountains. This wild, chasmal landscape had never been tamed by any road, just as the warlike tribes of the region had never been subjugated by any foreign power without their own consent. Between

1928 and 1932 Hamilton was the principal engineer of a British-built strategic road across Iraqi Kurdistan, which ran from Arbil, through Rawandiz, to the Iranian border near modern-day Piranshahr. The road became known as the Hamilton Road. Although Hamilton hoped the road would unite the peoples of the region, it has been fought over many times. He described the building of the road in a 1937 book entitled *Road through Kurdistan*. During the construction of the road, Hamilton became aware of the need for strong, adaptable bridges with components that could easily be transported and erected in remote and/or difficult terrain. With British Insulated Callenders Cables, now Balfour Beatty Power Networks Ltd, he designed the Callender-Hamilton bridge system, the income from which helped support his family. The parts of the bridge were bolted together like a Meccano set and it was popular with the British Army away from the battle front. The failure of the First World War Inglis bridge led to the development of the Bailey Bridge. Hamilton successfully claimed to the Royal Commission on Awards to Inventors[3] that the 'Bailey' Bridge had breached his patent. Because the 'Bailey' used a pin joining system similar to that used in a Martel design, Hamilton told the Commission the bridge should be called a 'Martel Mk2'. As I had done in the past when I had been inspired by T.E. Lawrence "Lawrence of Arabia" to spend time with the Bedu in Arabia learning their culture. In the same way Hamilton had inspired me to follow in his footsteps across Kurdistan. British and Commonwealth Gentleman had a good reputation and long history in this part of the world. Shame elements of the current British Government FCO were undoing this good reputation by their actions from 1991 onwards by their continued betrayal of the Kurdish people...

Over the coming weeks we travelled across Kurdistan stopping in some of the most beautiful and enchanting villages with the back drop of the rugged and majestic mountains. The warmth and hospitality of the Kurdish people was amazing and humbling. (See Photographs)

Towns and hamlets we visited included;

Zakho (Kurdish/Syrian border),

Batifa, Amedi,

Sheladiz, Sida.

Barzan.

Shanidar,

Soran, Choman, Harir,

Sisawa, Ranya,

Khalakan,

Dokan, Sulaymaniyah,

Penjwen, Halabja, Sangan, Bazian,

Chamchamal, Kirkuk,

Al Kuwayr,

Note; (Al-Amadiyah, petrol station, Turkish troops, tanks stationed there, town is

in Northern Iraq!)

"Travelling and reading, loving and believing, doubting and fighting and sometimes writing"

Halabja on my Reconnaissance trip across Kurdistan was an important place to get boots on the ground given its' history...

I have included a personal account by Jeffrey Goldberg of the New Yorker. It tells you all you need to know about the history and situation there and surrounding areas, what happened there is very relevant today given the political situation in Iraq and the massive influence Iran has in Iraq! This will enable the reader to understand and give them an overview of the situation and pending proxy war escalating today...

In the late morning of March 16, 1988, an Iraqi Air Force helicopter appeared over the city of Halabja, which is about fifteen miles from the border with Iran. The Iran-Iraq War was then in its eighth year, and Halabja was near the front lines. At the time, the city was home to roughly eighty thousand Kurds, who were well accustomed to the proximity of violence to ordinary life. Like most of Iraqi Kurdistan, Halabja was in perpetual revolt against the regime of Saddam Hussein, and its inhabitants were supporters of the *peshmerga*, the Kurdish fighters whose name means "those who face death."

A young woman named Nasreen Abdel Qadir Muhammad was outside her family's house, preparing food, when she saw the helicopter. The Iranians and the *peshmerga* had just attacked Iraqi military outposts around Halabja, forcing Saddam's soldiers to retreat. Iranian Revolutionary Guards then infiltrated the city, and the residents assumed that an Iraqi counterattack was imminent. Nasreen and her family expected to spend yet another day in their cellar, which was crude and dark but solid enough to withstand artillery shelling, and even napalm.

"At about ten o'clock, maybe closer to ten-thirty, I saw the helicopter," Nasreen told me. "It was not attacking, though. There were men inside it, taking pictures. One had a regular camera and the other held what looked like a video camera. They were coming very close. Then they went away."

Nasreen thought that the sight was strange, but she was preoccupied with lunch; she and her sister Rangeen were preparing rice, bread and beans for the thirty or forty relatives who were taking shelter in the cellar. Rangeen was fifteen at the time. Nasreen was just sixteen, but her father had married her off several months earlier, to a cousin, a thirty-year-old physician's assistant named Bakhtiar Abdul Aziz. Halabja is a conservative place and many more women wear the veil than in the more cosmopolitan Kurdish cities to the northwest and the Arab cities to the south.

The bombardment began shortly before eleven. The Iraqi Army, positioned on the main road from the nearby town of Sayid Sadiq, fired artillery shells into Halabja, and the Air Force began dropping what is thought to have been napalm on the town, especially the northern area. Nasreen and Rangeen rushed to the cellar. Nasreen prayed that Bakhtiar, who was then outside the city, would find shelter.

The attack had ebbed by about two o'clock, and Nasreen made her way carefully upstairs to the kitchen, to get the food for the family. "At the end of the bombing, the sound changed," she said. "It wasn't so loud. It was like pieces of metal just dropping without exploding. We didn't know why it was so quiet."

A short distance away, in a neighbourhood still called the Julakan, or Jewish quarter, even though Halabja's Jews left for Israel in the nineteen-fifties, a middle-aged man named Muhammad came up from his own cellar and saw an unusual sight: "A helicopter had come back to the town, and the soldiers were throwing white pieces of paper out the side." In retrospect, he understood that they were measuring wind speed and direction. Nearby, a man named Awat Omer, who was twenty at the time, was overwhelmed by a smell of garlic and apples.

Nasreen gathered the food quickly, but she, too, noticed a series of odd smells carried into the house by the wind. "At first, it smelled bad, like garbage," she said. "And then it was a good smell, like sweet apples. Then like eggs." Before she went downstairs, she happened to check on a caged partridge that her father kept in the house. "The bird was dying," she said. "It was on its side." She looked out the window. "It was very quiet, but the animals were dying. The sheep and goats were dying." Nasreen ran to the cellar. "I told everybody there was something wrong. There was something wrong with the air."

The people in the cellar were panicked. They had fled downstairs to escape the bombardment and it was difficult to abandon their shelter. Only splinters of light penetrated the basement, but the dark provided a strange comfort. "We wanted to stay in hiding, even though we were getting sick," Nasreen said. She felt a sharp pain in her eyes, like stabbing needles. "My sister came close to my face and said, 'Your eyes are very red.' Then the children started throwing up. They kept throwing up. They were in so much pain and crying so much. They were crying all the time. My mother was crying. Then the old people started throwing up."

Chemical weapons had been dropped on Halabja by the Iraqi Air Force, which understood that any underground shelter would become a gas chamber. "My uncle said we should go outside," Nasreen said. "We knew there were chemicals in the air. We were getting red eyes, and some of us had liquid coming out of them. We decided to run." Nasreen and her relatives stepped outside gingerly. "Our cow was lying on its side," she recalled. "It was breathing very fast, as if it had been running. The leaves were falling off the trees, even though it was spring. The partridge was dead. There were smoke clouds around, clinging to the ground. The gas was heavier than the air, and it was finding the wells and going down the wells."

The family judged the direction of the wind, and decided to run the opposite way. Running proved difficult. "The children couldn't walk, they were so sick," Nasreen said. "They were exhausted from throwing up. We carried them in our arms".

Across the city, other families were making similar decisions. Nouri Hama Ali, who lived in the northern part of town, decided to lead his family in the direction of Anab, a collective settlement on the outskirts of Halabja that housed Kurds displaced when the Iraqi Army destroyed their villages. "On the road to Anab, many of the women and children began to die," Nouri told me. "The chemical clouds were on the ground. They were heavy. We could see them." People were dying all around, he said. When a child could not go on, the parents, becoming hysterical with fear, abandoned him. "Many children were left on the ground, by the side of the road. Old people as well. They were running, then they would stop breathing and die."

Nasreen's family did not move quickly. "We wanted to wash ourselves off and find water to drink," she said. "We wanted to wash the faces of the children who were vomiting. The children were crying for water. There was powder on the ground, white. We couldn't decide whether to drink the water or not, but some people drank the water from the well they were so thirsty."

They ran in a panic through the city, Nasreen recalled, in the direction of Anab. The bombardment continued intermittently, Air Force planes circling overhead. "People were showing different symptoms. One person touched some of the powder, and her skin started bubbling."

A truck came by, driven by a neighbour. People threw themselves aboard. "We saw people lying frozen on the ground," Nasreen told me. "There was a small baby on the ground, away from her mother. I thought they were both sleeping. But she had dropped the baby and then died. And I think the baby tried to crawl away, but it died, too. It looked like everyone was sleeping."

At that moment, Nasreen believed that she and her family would make it to high ground and live. Then the truck stopped. "The driver said he couldn't go on, and he wandered away. He left his wife in the back of the truck. He told us to flee if we could. The chemicals affected his brain, because why else would someone abandon his family?"

As heavy clouds of gas smothered the city, people became sick and confused. Awat Omer was trapped in his cellar with his family; he said that his brother began laughing uncontrollably and then stripped off his clothes, and soon afterward he died. As night fell, the family's children grew sicker—too sick to move.

Nasreen's husband could not be found, and she began to think that all was lost. She led the children who were able to walk up the road.

In another neighbourhood, Muhammad Ahmed Fattah, who was twenty, was overwhelmed by an oddly sweet odour of sulphur and he too realized that he must evacuate his family; there were about a hundred and sixty people wedged into the cellar. "I saw the bomb drop," Muhammad told me. "It was about thirty metres from the house. I shut the door to the cellar. There was shouting and crying in the cellar and then people became short of breath." One of the first to be stricken by the gas was Muhammad's brother Salah. "His eyes were pink," Muhammad recalled. "There was something coming out of his eyes. He was so thirsty he was demanding water." Others in the basement began suffering tremors.

March 16th was supposed to be Muhammad's wedding day. "Every preparation was done," he said. His fiancée, a woman named Bahar Jamal, was among the first in the cellar to die. "She was crying very hard," Muhammad recalled. "I tried to calm her down. I told her it was just the usual artillery shells, but it didn't smell the usual way weapons smelled. She was smart, she knew what was happening. She died on the stairs. Her father tried to help her, but it was too late."

Death came quickly to others as well. A woman named Hamida Mahmoud tried to save her two-year-old daughter by allowing her to nurse from her breast. Hamida thought that the baby wouldn't breathe in the gas if she was nursing, Muhammad said, adding, "The baby's name was Dashneh. She nursed for a long time. Her mother died while she was nursing. But she kept nursing." By the time Muhammad decided to go outside, most of the people in the basement were unconscious; many were dead, including his parents and three of his siblings.

Nasreen said that on the road to Anab all was confusion. She and the children were running toward the hills, but they were going blind. "The children were crying, 'We can't see! My eyes are bleeding!' " In the chaos, the family got separated. Nasreen's mother and father were both lost. Nasreen and several of her cousins and siblings inadvertently led the younger children in a circle, back into the city. Someone—she doesn't know who—led them away from the city again and up a hill, to a small mosque, where they sought shelter. "But we didn't stay in the mosque, because we thought it would be a target," Nasreen said. They went to a small house nearby, and Nasreen scrambled to find food and water for the children. By then, it was night, and she was exhausted.

Bakhtiar, Nasreen's husband, was frantic. Outside the city when the attacks started, he had spent much of the day searching for his wife and the rest of his family. He had acquired from a clinic two syringes of atropine, a drug that helps to counter the effects of nerve agents. He injected himself with one of the syringes, and set out to find Nasreen. He had no hope. "My plan was to bury her," he said. "At least I should bury my new wife."

After hours of searching, Bakhtiar met some neighbors, who remembered seeing Nasreen and the children moving toward the mosque on the hill. "I called out the name Nasreen," he said. "I heard crying, and I went inside the house. When I got there, I found that Nasreen was alive but blind. Everybody was blind."

Nasreen had lost her sight about an hour or two before Bakhtiar found her. She had been searching the house for food, so that she could feed the children, when her eyesight failed. "I found some milk and I felt my way to them and then I found their mouths and gave them milk," she said.

Bakhtiar organized the children. "I wanted to bring them to the well. I washed their heads. I took them two by two and washed their heads. Some of them couldn't come. They couldn't control their muscles."

Bakhtiar still had one syringe of atropine, but he did not inject his wife; she was not the worst off in the group. "There was a woman named Asme, who was my neighbour," Bakhtiar recalled. "She was not able to breathe. She was yelling and she was running into a wall, crashing her head into a wall. I gave the atropine to this woman." Asme died soon afterward. "I could have used it for Nasreen," Bakhtiar said. "I could have."

After the Iraqi bombardment subsided, the Iranians managed to retake Halabja and they evacuated many of the sick, including Nasreen and the   others in her family, to hospitals in Tehran.

190

Nasreen was blind for twenty days. "I was thinking the whole time, Where is my family? But I was blind. I couldn't do anything. I asked my husband about my mother, but he said he didn't know anything. He was looking in hospitals, he said. He was avoiding the question."

The Iranian Red Crescent Society, the equivalent of the Red Cross, began compiling books of photographs, pictures of the dead in Halabja. "The Red Crescent has an album of the people who were buried in Iran," Nasreen said. "And we found my mother in one of the albums." Her father, she discovered, was alive but permanently blinded. Five of her siblings, including Rangeen, had died.

Nasreen would live, the doctors said, but she kept a secret from Bakhtiar: "When I was in the hospital, I started menstruating. It wouldn't stop. I kept bleeding. We don't talk about this in our society, but eventually a lot of women in the hospital confessed they were also menstruating and couldn't stop." Doctors gave her drugs that stopped the bleeding, but they told her that she would be unable to bear children.

Nasreen stayed in Iran for several months, but eventually she and Bakhtiar returned to Kurdistan. She didn't believe the doctors who told her that she would be infertile, and in 1991 she gave birth to a boy. "We named him Arazoo," she said. Arazoo means hope in Kurdish. "He was healthy at first, but he had a hole in his heart. He died at the age of three months."

I met Nasreen in Erbil, the largest city in Iraqi Kurdistan. She is thirty now, a pretty woman with brown eyes and high cheekbones, but her face is expressionless. She doesn't seek pity; she would, however, like a doctor to help her with a cough that she's had ever since the attack, fourteen years ago. Like many of Saddam Hussein's victims, she tells her story without emotion.

During my visit to Kurdistan, I talked with more than a hundred victims of Saddam's campaign against the Kurds. Saddam has been persecuting the Kurds ever since he took power, more than twenty years ago. Several old women whose husbands were killed by Saddam's security services expressed a kind of animal hatred toward him, but most people, like Nasreen, told stories of horrific cruelty with a dispassion and a precision that underscored their credibility. Credibility is important to the Kurds; after all this time, they still feel that the world does not believe their story.

A week after I met Nasreen, I visited a small village called Goktapa, situated in a green valley that is ringed by snow-covered mountains. Goktapa came under poison-gas attack six weeks after Halabja. The village consists of low mud-brick houses along dirt paths. In Goktapa, an old man named Ahmed Raza Sharif told me that on the day of the attack on Goktapa, May 3, 1988, he was in the fields outside the village. He saw the shells explode and smelled the sweet-apple odour as poison filled the air. His son, Osman Ahmed, who was sixteen at the time, was near the village mosque when he was felled by the gas. He crawled down a hill and died among the reeds on the banks of the Lesser Zab, the river that flows by the village. His father knew that he was dead, but he couldn't reach the body. As many as a hundred and fifty people died in the attack; the survivors fled before the advancing Iraqi Army, which levelled the village. Ahmed Raza Sharif did not return for three years. When he did, he said, he immediately began searching for his son's body. He found it still lying in the reeds. "I recognized his body right away," he said.

The summer sun in Iraq is blisteringly hot and a corpse would be unidentifiable three years after death. I tried to find a gentle way to express my doubts, but my translator made it clear to Sharif that I didn't believe him.

We were standing in the mud yard of another old man, Ibrahim Abdul Rahman. Twenty or thirty people, a dozen boys among them, had gathered. Some of them seemed upset that I appeared to doubt the story, but Ahmed hushed them. "It's true, he lost all the flesh on his body," he said. "He was just a skeleton. But the clothes were his, and they were still on the skeleton, a belt and a shirt. In the pocket of his shirt I found the key to our tractor. That's where he always kept the key."

Some of the men still seemed concerned that I would leave Goktapa doubting their truthfulness. Ibrahim, the man in whose yard we were standing, called out a series of orders to the boys gathered around us. They dispersed, to houses and storerooms, returning moments later holding jagged pieces of metal, the remnants of the bombs that poisoned Goktapa. Ceremoniously, the boys dropped the pieces of metal at my feet. "Here are the mercies of Uncle Saddam," Ibrahim said.

2. THE AFTERMATH

The story of Halabja did not end the night the Iraqi Air Force planes returned to their bases. The Iranians invited the foreign press to record the devastation. Photographs of the victims, supine, bleached of colour, littering the gutters and alleys of the town, horrified the world. Saddam Hussein's attacks on his own citizens mark the only time since the Holocaust that poison gas has been used to exterminate women and children.

Saddam's cousin Ali Hassan al-Majid, who led the campaigns against the Kurds in the late eighties, was heard on a tape captured by rebels, and later obtained by Human Rights Watch, addressing members of Iraq's ruling Baath Party on the subject of the Kurds. "I will kill them all with chemical weapons!" he said. "Who is going to say anything? The international community? Fuck them! The international community and those who listen to them."

Ali Hassan al-Majid, whom the Kurds have nicknamed Ali Chemical, needn't have worried about the international community, for at the time the world thought it was more important to oppose Iran, Iraq's enemy, than to interfere with Saddam. During the Iran-Iraq War, between 1980 and 1988, in which a million and a half people died, the West gave tacit support to Saddam. This support didn't end until Iraq invaded Kuwait, in August of 1990. As late as April of that year, a delegation of Americans met with Saddam in Baghdad; one of them, former Senator Alan Simpson, of Wyoming, said, "I believe your problem is with the Western media, not with the U.S. Government, because you are isolated from the media and the press." At that meeting, Saddam told Bob Dole, then the Senate Minority Leader, that his country would destroy its nonconventional weapons if Israel did the same. He also denied that Iraq was attempting to develop biological weapons.
When the Kurds dispatched a senior official named Mahmoud Othman to Washington, no one would see him. Through the manoeuvers of a sympathetic Washington *Post* correspondent named Jonathan Randal, Othman finally arranged a meeting with a low-level State Department official, but at the last moment the meeting was cancelled. "I was trying to report on the chemical bombings," Othman told me, but he was informed that the meeting "would jeopardize relations with Saddam."

Attempts by Congress in 1988 to impose sanctions on Iraq were stifled by the Reagan and Bush Administrations, and the story of Saddam's surviving victims might have vanished completely had it not been for the reporting of people like Randal and the work of a British documentary filmmaker named Gwynne Roberts, who, after hearing stories about a sudden spike in the incidence of birth defects and cancers, not only in Halabja but also in other parts of Kurdistan, had made some disturbing films on the subject. However, no Western government or United Nations agency took up the cause.

In 1998, Roberts brought an Englishwoman named Christine Gosden to Kurdistan. Gosden is a medical geneticist and a professor at the medical school of the University of Liverpool. She spent three weeks in the hospitals in Kurdistan, and came away determined to help the Kurds. To the best of my knowledge, Gosden is the only Western scientist who has even begun making a systematic study of what took place in northern Iraq.

Gosden told me that her father was a high-ranking officer in the Royal Air Force, and that as a child she lived in Germany, near Bergen-Belsen. "It's tremendously influential in your early years to live near a concentration camp," she said. In Kurdistan, she heard echoes of the German campaign to destroy the Jews. "The Iraqi government was using chemistry to reduce the population of Kurds," she said. "The Holocaust is still having its effect. The Jews are fewer in number now than they were in 1939. That's not natural. Now, if you take out two hundred thousand men and boys from Kurdistan"—an estimate of the number of Kurds who were gassed or otherwise murdered in the campaign, most of whom were men and boys—"you've affected the population structure. There are a lot of widows who are not having children."

Richard Butler, an Australian diplomat who chaired the United Nations weapons-inspection team in Iraq, describes Gosden as "a classic English, old-school-tie kind of person." Butler has tracked her research since she began studying the attacks, four years ago, and finds it credible. "Occasionally, people say that this is Christine's obsession, but obsession is not a bad thing," he added.

Before I went to Kurdistan, in January, I spent a day in London with Gosden. We gossiped a bit, and she scolded me for having visited a Washington shopping mall without appropriate protective equipment. Whenever she goes to a mall, she brings along a polyurethane bag "big enough to step into" and a bottle of bleach. "I can detoxify myself immediately," she said.

Gosden believes it is quite possible that the countries of the West will soon experience chemical- and biological-weapons attacks far more serious and of greater lasting effect than the anthrax incidents of last autumn and the nerve-agent attack on the Tokyo subway system several years ago—that what happened in Kurdistan was only the beginning. "For Saddam's scientists, the Kurds were a test population," she said. "They were the human guinea pigs. It was a way of identifying the most effective chemical agents for use on civilian populations, and the most effective means of delivery."

The charge is supported by others. An Iraqi defector, Khidhir Hamza, who is the former director of Saddam's nuclear-weapons program, told me earlier this year that before the attack on Halabja military doctors had mapped the city, and that afterward they entered it wearing protective clothing, in order to study the dispersal of the dead. "These were field tests, an experiment on a town," Hamza told me. He said that he had direct knowledge of the Army's procedures that day in Halabja. "The doctors were given sheets with grids on them, and they had to answer questions such as 'How far are the dead from the cannisters?' "

Gosden said that she cannot understand why the West has not been more eager to investigate the chemical attacks in Kurdistan. "It seems a matter of enlightened self-interest that the West would want to study the long-term effects of chemical weapons on civilians, on the DNA," she told me. "I've seen Europe's worst cancers, but, believe me, I have never seen cancers like the ones I saw in Kurdistan."

According to an ongoing survey conducted by a team of Kurdish physicians and organised by Gosden and a small advocacy group called the Washington Kurdish Institute, more than two hundred towns and villages across Kurdistan were attacked by poison gas—far more than was previously thought—in the course of seventeen months. The number of victims is unknown, but doctors I met in Kurdistan believe that up to ten per cent of the population of northern Iraq—nearly four million people—has been exposed to chemical weapons. "Saddam Hussein poisoned northern Iraq," Gosden said when I left for Halabja. "The questions, then, are what to do? And what comes next?"

3. HALABJA'S DOCTORS

The Kurdish people, it is often said, make up the largest stateless nation in the world. They have been widely despised by their neighbours for centuries. There are roughly twenty-five million Kurds, most of them spread across four countries in southwestern Asia: Turkey, Iran, Iraq and Syria. The Kurds are neither Arab, Persian, nor Turkish; they are a distinct ethnic group, with their own culture and language. Most Kurds are Muslim (the most famous Muslim hero of all, Saladin, who defeated the Crusaders, was of Kurdish origin), but there are Jewish and Christian Kurds, and also followers of the Yezidi religion, which has its roots in Sufism and Zoroastrianism. The Kurds are experienced mountain fighters, who tend toward stubbornness and have frequent bouts of destructive infighting.

After centuries of domination by foreign powers, the Kurds had their best chance at independence after the First World War, when President Woodrow Wilson promised the Kurds, along with other groups left drifting and exposed by the collapse of the Ottoman Empire, a large measure of autonomy. But the machinations of the great powers, who were becoming interested in Kurdistan's vast oil deposits, in Mosul and Kirkuk, quickly did the Kurds out of a state.

In the nineteen-seventies, the Iraqi Kurds allied themselves with the Shah of Iran in a territorial dispute with Iraq. America, the Shah's patron, once again became the Kurds' patron, too, supplying them with arms for a revolt against Baghdad. But a secret deal between the Iraqis and the Shah, arranged in 1975 by Secretary of State Henry Kissinger, cut off the Kurds and brought about their instant collapse; for the Kurds, it was an ugly betrayal.

The Kurdish safe haven, in northern Iraq, was born of another American betrayal. In 1991, after the United States helped drive Iraq out of Kuwait, President George Bush ignored an uprising that he himself had stoked, and Kurds and Shiites in Iraq were slaughtered by the thousands. Thousands more fled the country, the Kurds going to Turkey, and almost immediately creating a humanitarian disaster. The Bush Administration, faced with a televised catastrophe, declared northern Iraq a no-fly zone and thus a safe haven, a tactic that allowed the refugees to return home. And so, under the protective shield of the United States and British Air Forces, the unplanned Kurdish experiment in self-government began. Although the Kurdish safe haven is only a virtual state, it is an incipient democracy, a home of progressive Islamic thought and pro-American feeling.

Today, Iraqi Kurdistan is split between two dominant parties: the Kurdistan Democratic Party, led by Massoud Barzani, and the Patriotic Union of Kurdistan, whose General Secretary is Jalal Talabani. The two parties have had an often angry relationship, and in the mid-nineties they fought a war that left about a thousand soldiers dead. The parties, realizing that they could not rule together, decided to rule apart, dividing Kurdistan into two zones. The internal political divisions have not aided the Kurds' cause, but neighbouring states also have fomented disunity, fearing that a unified Kurdish population would agitate for independence.

Turkey, with a Kurdish population of between fifteen and twenty million, has repressed the Kurds in the eastern part of the country, politically and militarily, on and off since the founding of the modern Turkish state. In 1924, the government of Atatürk restricted the use of the Kurdish language (a law not lifted until 1991) and expressions of Kurdish culture; to this day, the Kurds are referred to in nationalist circles as "mountain Turks."

Turkey is not eager to see Kurds anywhere draw attention to themselves, which is why the authorities in Ankara refused to let me cross the border into Iraqi Kurdistan. Iran, whose Kurdish population numbers between six and eight million, was not helpful, either, and my only option for gaining entrance to Kurdistan was through its third neighbour, Syria. The Kurdistan Democratic Party arranged for me to be met in Damascus and taken to the eastern desert city of El Qamishli. From there, I was driven in a Land Cruiser to the banks of the Tigris River, where a small wooden boat, with a crew of one and an outboard motor, was waiting. The engine spluttered; when I learned that the forward lines of the Iraqi Army were two miles downstream, I began to paddle, too. On the other side of the river were representatives of the Kurdish Democratic Party and the *peshmerga*, the Kurdish guerrillas, who wore pantaloons and turbans and were armed with AK-47s.

"Welcome to Kurdistan" read a sign at the water's edge greeting visitors to a country that does not exist.

Halabja is a couple of hundred miles from the Syrian border, and I spent a week crossing northern Iraq, making stops in the cities of Dahuk and Erbil on the way. I was handed over to representatives of the Patriotic Union, which controls Halabja, at a demilitarized zone west of the town of Koysinjaq. From there, it was a two-hour drive over steep mountains to Sulaimaniya, a city of six hundred and fifty thousand, which is the cultural capital of Iraqi Kurdistan. In Sulaimaniya, I met Fouad Baban, one of Kurdistan's leading physicians, who promised to guide me through the scientific and political thickets of Halabja.

Baban, a pulmonary and cardiac specialist who has survived three terms in Iraqi prisons, is sixty years old, and a man of impish good humour. He is the Kurdistan coördinator of the Halabja Medical Institute, which was founded by Gosden, Michael Amitay, the executive director of the Washington Kurdish Institute, and a coalition of Kurdish doctors; for the doctors, it is an act of bravery to be publicly associated with a project whose scientific findings could be used as evidence if Saddam Hussein faced a war-crimes tribunal. Saddam's agents are everywhere in the Kurdish zone and his tanks sit forty miles from Baban's office.

Soon after I arrived in Sulaimaniya, Baban and I headed out in his Toyota Camry for Halabja. On a rough road, we crossed the plains of Sharazoor, a region of black earth and honey-coloured wheat ringed by jagged, snow-topped mountains. We were not travelling alone. The Mukhabarat, the Iraqi intelligence service, is widely reported to have placed a bounty on the heads of Western journalists caught in Kurdistan (either ten thousand dollars or twenty thousand dollars, depending on the source of the information). The areas around the border with Iran are filled with Tehran's spies, and members of Ansar al-Islam, an Islamist terror group, were said to be decapitating people in the Halabja area. So the Kurds had laid on a rather elaborate security detail. A Land Cruiser carrying *peshmerga* guerrillas led the way, and we were followed by another Land Cruiser, on whose bed was mounted an anti-aircraft weapon manned by six *peshmerga*, some of whom wore black balaclavas. We were just south of the American- and British-enforced no-fly zone. I had been told that, at the beginning of the safe-haven experiment, the Americans had warned Saddam's forces to stay away; a threat from the air, though unlikely, was, I deduced, not out of the question.

"It seems very important to know the immediate and long-term effects of chemical and biological weapons," Baban said, beginning my tutorial. "Here is a civilian population exposed to chemical and possibly biological weapons, and people are developing many varieties of cancers and congenital abnormalities. The Americans are vulnerable to these weapons—they are cheap, and terrorists possess them. So, after the anthrax attacks in the States, I think it is urgent for scientific research to be done here."

Experts now believe that Halabja and other places in Kurdistan were struck by a combination of mustard gas and nerve agents, including sarin (the agent used in the Tokyo subway attack) and VX, a potent nerve agent. Baban's suggestion that biological weapons may also have been used surprised me. One possible biological weapon that Baban mentioned was aflatoxin, which causes long-term liver damage.

A colleague of Baban's, a surgeon who practices in Dahuk, in northwestern Kurdistan, and who is a member of the Halabja Medical Institute team, told me more about the institute's survey, which was conducted in the Dahuk region in 1999. The surveyors began, he said, by asking elementary questions; eleven years after the attacks, they did not even know which villages had been attacked.

"The team went to almost every village," the surgeon said. "At first, we thought that the Dahuk governorate was the least affected. We knew of only two villages that were hit by the attacks. But we came up with twenty-nine in total. This is eleven years after the fact."

The surgeon is professorial in appearance, but he is deeply angry. He doubles as a pediatric surgeon, because there are no pediatric surgeons in Kurdistan. He has performed more than a hundred operations for cleft palate on children born since 1988. Most of the agents believed to have been dropped on Halabja have short half-lives, but, as Baban told me, "physicians are unsure how long these toxins will affect the population. How can we know agent half-life if we don't know the agent?" He added, "If we knew the toxins that were used, we could follow them and see actions on spermatogenesis and ovogenesis."

Increased rates of infertility, he said, are having a profound effect on Kurdish society, which places great importance on large families. "You have men divorcing their wives because they could not give birth, and then marrying again, and then their second wives can't give birth, either," he said. "Still, they don't blame their own problem with spermatogenesis."

Baban told me that the initial results of the Halabja Medical Institute-sponsored survey show abnormally high rates of many diseases. He said that he compared rates of colon cancer in Halabja with those in the city of Chamchamal, which was not attacked with chemical weapons. "We are seeing rates of colon cancer five times higher in Halabja than in Chamchamal," he said.

There are other anomalies as well, Baban said. The rate of miscarriage in Halabja, according to initial survey results, is fourteen times the rate of miscarriage in Chamchamal; rates of infertility among men and women in the affected population are many times higher than normal. "We're finding Hiroshima levels of sterility," he said.

Then, there is the suspicion about snakes. "Have you heard about the snakes?" he asked as we drove. I told him that I had heard rumours. "We don't know if a genetic mutation in the snakes has made them more toxic," Baban went on, "or if the birds that eat the snakes were killed off in the attacks, but there seem to be more snakebites, of greater toxicity, in Halabja now than before." (I asked Richard Spertzel, a scientist and a former member of the United Nations Special Commission inspections team, if this was possible. Yes, he said, but such a rise in snakebites was more likely due to "environmental imbalances" than to mutations.)

My conversation with Baban was suddenly interrupted by our guerrilla escorts, who stopped the car and asked me to join them in one of the Land Cruisers; we veered off across a wheat field, without explanation. I was later told that we had been passing a mountain area that had recently had problems with Islamic terrorists.

We arrived in Halabja half an hour later. As you enter the city, you see a small statue modelled on the most famous photographic image of the Halabja massacre: an old man, prone and lifeless, shielding his dead grandson with his body.

A torpor seems to afflict Halabja; even its bazaar is listless and somewhat empty, in marked contrast to those of other Kurdish cities, which are well stocked with imported goods (history and circumstance have made the Kurds enthusiastic smugglers) and are full of noise and activity. "Everyone here is sick," a Halabja doctor told me. "The people who aren't sick are depressed." He practices at the Martyrs' Hospital, which is situated on the outskirts of the city. The hospital has no heat and little advanced equipment; like the city itself, it is in a dilapidated state.

The doctor is a thin, jumpy man in a tweed jacket, and he smokes without pause. He and Baban took me on a tour of the hospital. Afterward, we sat in a bare office, and a woman was wheeled in. She looked seventy but said that she was fifty; doctors told me she suffers from lung scarring so serious that only a lung transplant could help, but there are no transplant centres in Kurdistan. The woman, whose name is Jayran Muhammad, lost eight relatives during the attack. Her voice was almost inaudible. "I was disturbed psychologically for a long time," she told me as Baban translated. "I believed my children were alive." Baban told me that her lungs would fail soon, that she could barely breathe. "She is waiting to die," he said. I met another woman, Chia Hammassat, who was eight at the time of the attacks and has been blind ever since. Her mother, she said, died of colon cancer several years ago, and her brother suffers from chronic shortness of breath. "There is no hope to correct my vision," she said, her voice flat. "I was married, but I couldn't fulfil the responsibilities of a wife because I'm blind. My husband left me."

Baban said that in Halabja "there are more abnormal births than normal ones," and other Kurdish doctors told me that they regularly see children born with neural-tube defects and undescended testes and without anal openings. They are seeing—and they showed me—children born with six or seven toes on each foot, children whose fingers and toes are fused, and children who suffer from leukaemia and liver cancer.

I met Sarkar, a shy and intelligent boy with a harelip, a cleft palate and a growth on his spine. Sarkar had a brother born with the same set of malformations the doctor told me, but the brother choked to death, while still a baby, on a grain of rice.

Meanwhile, more victims had gathered in the hallway; the people of Halabja do not often have a chance to tell their stories to foreigners. Some of them wanted to know if I was a surgeon, who had come to repair their children's deformities and they were disappointed to learn that I was a journalist. The doctor and I soon left the hospital for a walk through the northern neighbourhoods of Halabja, which were hardest hit in the attack. We were trailed by *peshmerga* carrying AK-47s. The doctor smoked as we talked and I teased him about his habit. "Smoking has some good effect on the lungs," he said, without irony. "In the attacks, there was less effect on smokers. Their lungs were better equipped for the mustard gas, maybe."

We walked through the alleyways of the Jewish quarter, past a former synagogue in which eighty or so Halabjans died during the attack. Underfed cows wandered the paths. The doctor showed me several cellars where clusters of people had died. We knocked on the gate of one house, and were let in by an old woman with a wide smile and few teeth. In the Kurdish tradition, she immediately invited us for lunch.

She told us the recent history of the house. "Everyone who was in this house died," she said. "The whole family. We heard there were one hundred people." She led us to the cellar which was damp and close. Rusted yellow cans of vegetable ghee littered the floor. The room seemed too small to hold a hundred people, but the doctor said that the estimate sounded accurate. I asked him if cellars like this one had ever been decontaminated. He smiled. "Nothing in Kurdistan has been decontaminated," he said.

4. AL—ANFAL

The chemical attacks on Halabja and Goktapa and perhaps two hundred other villages and towns were only a small part of the cataclysm that Saddam's cousin, the man known as Ali Chemical, arranged for the Kurds. The Kurds say that about two hundred thousand were killed. (Human Rights Watch, which in the early nineties published "Iraq's Crime of Genocide," a definitive study of the attacks, gives a figure of between fifty thousand and a hundred thousand.)

The campaign against the Kurds was dubbed al-Anfal by Saddam, after a chapter in the Koran that allows conquering Muslim armies to seize the spoils of their foes. It reads, in part, "Against them"— your enemies—"make ready your strength to the utmost of your power, including steeds of war, to strike terror into the hearts of the enemies of Allah and your enemies, and others besides, whom ye may not know, but whom Allah doth know. Whatever ye shall spend in the cause of Allah, shall be repaid unto you, and ye shall not be treated unjustly."

The Anfal campaign was not an end in itself, like the Holocaust, but a means to an end—an instance of a policy that Samantha Power, who runs the Carr Centre for Human Rights, at Harvard, calls "instrumental genocide." Power has just published " 'A Problem from Hell,' " a study of American responses to genocide. "There are regimes that set out to murder every citizen of a race," she said. "Saddam achieved what he had to do without exterminating every last Kurd." What he had to do, Power and others say, was to break the Kurds' morale and convince them that a desire for independence was foolish.

Most of the Kurds who were murdered in the Anfal were not killed by poison gas; rather, the genocide was carried out, in large part, in the traditional manner, with roundups at night, mass executions, and anonymous burials. The bodies of most of the victims of the Anfal—mainly men and boys—have never been found.

One day, I met one of the thousands of Kurdish women known as Anfal widows: Salma Aziz Baban. She lives outside Chamchamal, in a settlement made up almost entirely of displaced families, in cinder-block houses. Her house was nearly empty—no furniture, no heat, just a ragged carpet. We sat on the carpet as she told me about her family. She comes from the Kirkuk region, and in 1987 her village was uprooted by the Army, and the inhabitants, with thousands of other Kurds, were forced into a collective town. Then, one night in April of 1988, soldiers went into the village and seized the men and older boys. Baban's husband and her three oldest sons were put on trucks. The mothers of the village began to plead with the soldiers. "We were screaming, 'Do what you want to *us*, do what you want!' " Baban told me. "They were so scared, my sons. My sons were crying." She tried to bring them coats for the journey. "It was raining. I wanted them to have coats. I begged the soldiers to let me give them bread. They took them without coats." Baban remembered that a high-ranking Iraqi officer named Bareq orchestrated the separation; according to "Iraq's Crime of Genocide," the Human Rights Watch report, the man in charge of this phase was a brigadier general named Bareq Abdullah al-Haj Hunta.

After the men were taken away, the women and children were herded onto trucks. They were given little water or food, and were crammed so tightly into the vehicles that they had to defecate where they stood. Baban, her three daughters, and her six-year-old son were taken to the Topzawa Army base and then to the prison of Nugra Salman, the Pit of Salman, which Human Rights Watch in 1995 described this way: "It was an old building, dating back to the days of the Iraqi monarchy and perhaps earlier. It had been abandoned for years, used by Arab nomads to shelter their herds. The bare walls were scrawled with the diaries of political prisoners. On the door of one cell, a guard had daubed 'Khomeini eats shit.' Over the main gate, someone else had written, 'Welcome to Hell.' "

"We arrived at midnight," Baban told me. "They put us in a very big room, with more than two thousand people, women and children and they closed the door. Then the starvation started."

The prisoners were given almost nothing to eat, and a single standpipe spat out brackish water for drinking. People began to die from hunger and illness. When someone died, the Iraqi guards would demand that the body be passed through a window in the main door. "The bodies couldn't stay in the hall," Baban told me. In the first days at Nugra Salman, "thirty people died, maybe more." Her six-year-old son, Rebwar, fell ill. "He had diarrhoea," she said. "He was very sick. He knew he was dying. There was no medicine or doctor. He started to cry so much." Baban's son died on her lap. "I was screaming and crying," she said. "My daughters were crying. We gave them the body. It was passed outside, and the soldiers took it."

Soon after Baban's son died, she pulled herself up and went to the window, to see if the soldiers had taken her son to be buried. "There were twenty dogs outside the prison. A big black dog was the leader," she said. The soldiers had dumped the bodies of the dead outside the prison, in a field. "I looked outside and saw the legs and hands of my son in the mouths of the dogs. The dogs were eating my son." She stopped talking for a moment. "Then I lost my mind."

She described herself as catatonic; her daughters scraped around for food and water. They kept her alive, she said, until she could function again. "This was during Ramadan. We were kept in Nugra Salman for a few more months."

In September, when the war with Iran was over, Saddam issued a general amnesty to the Kurds, the people he believed had betrayed him by siding with Tehran. The women, children, and elderly in Nugra Salman were freed. But, in most cases, they could not go home; the Iraqi Army had bulldozed some four thousand villages, Baban's among them. She was finally resettled in the Chamchamal district.

In the days after her release, she tried to learn the fate of her husband and three older sons. But the men who disappeared in the Anfal roundups have never been found. It is said that they were killed and then buried in mass graves in the desert along the Kuwaiti border, but little is actually known. A great number of Anfal widows, I was told, still believe that their sons and husbands and brothers are locked away in Saddam's jails. "We are thinking they are alive," Baban said, referring to her husband and sons. "Twenty-four hours a day, we are thinking maybe they are alive. If they are alive, they are being tortured, I know it."

Baban said that she has not slept well since her sons were taken from her. "We are thinking, Please let us know they are dead, I will sleep in peace," she said. "My head is filled with terrible thoughts. The day I die is the day I will not remember that the dogs ate my son."

Before I left, Baban asked me to write down the names of her three older sons. They are Sherzad, who would be forty now; Rizgar, who would be thirty-one; and Muhammad, who would be thirty. She asked me to find her sons, or to ask President Bush to find them. "One would be sufficient," she said. "If just one comes back, that would be enough."

5. WHAT THE KURDS FEAR

In a conversation not long ago with Richard Butler, the former weapons inspector, I suggested a possible explanation for the world's indifference to Saddam Hussein's use of chemical weapons to commit genocide—that the people he had killed were his own citizens, not those of another sovereign state. (The main chemical-weapons treaty does not ban a country's use of such weapons against its own people, perhaps because at the time the convention was drafted no one could imagine such a thing.) Butler reminded me, however, that Iraq had used chemical weapons against another country—Iran— during the eight-year Iran-Iraq War. He offered a simpler rationale. "The problems are just too awful and too hard," he said. "History is replete with such things. Go back to the grand example of the Holocaust. It sounded too hard to do anything about it."

The Kurds have grown sanguine about the world's lack of interest. "I've learned not to be surprised by the indifference of the civilized world," Barham Salih told me one evening in Sulaimaniya. Salih is the Prime Minister of the area of Kurdistan administered by the Patriotic Union, and he spoke in such a way as to suggest that it would be best if I, too, stopped acting surprised. "Given the scale of the tragedy—we're talking about large numbers of victims—I suppose I'm surprised that the international community has not come in to help the survivors," he continued. "It's politically indecent not to help. But, as a Kurd, I live with the terrible hand history and geography have dealt my people."

Salih's home is not prime ministerial, but it has many Western comforts. He had a satellite television and a satellite telephone, yet the house was frigid; in a land of cheap oil, the Kurds, who are cut off the Iraqi electric grid by Saddam on a regular basis, survive on generator power and kerosene heat.

Over dinner one night, Salih argued that the Kurds should not be regarded with pity. "I don't think one has to tap into the Wilsonian streak in American foreign policy in order to find a rationale for helping the Kurds," he said. "Helping the Kurds would mean an opportunity to study the problems caused by weapons of mass destruction."

Salih, who is forty-one, often speaks bluntly, and is savvy about Washington's enduring interest in ending the reign of Saddam Hussein. Unwilling publicly to exhort the United States to take military action, Salih is aware that the *peshmerga* would be obvious allies of an American military strike against Iraq; other Kurds have been making that argument for years. It is not often noted in Washington policy circles, but the Kurds already hold a vast swath of territory inside the country—including two important dams whose destruction could flood Baghdad—and have at least seventy thousand men under arms. In addition, the two main Kurdish parties are members of the Iraqi opposition group, the

Iraqi National Congress, which is headed by Ahmad Chalabi, a London-based Shiite businessman; at the moment, though, relations between Chalabi and the Kurdish leaders are contentious.

Kurds I talked to throughout Kurdistan were enthusiastic about the idea of joining an American-led alliance against Saddam Hussein, and serving as the northern-Iraqi equivalent of Afghanistan's Northern Alliance. President Bush's State of the Union Message, in which he denounced Iraq as the linchpin of an "axis of evil," had had an electric effect on every Kurd I met who heard the speech. In the same speech, President Bush made reference to Iraq's murder of "thousands of its own citizens— leaving the bodies of mothers huddled over their dead children." General Simko Dizayee, the chief of staff of the *peshmerga*, told me, "Bush's speech filled our hearts with hope."

Prime Minister Salih expressed his views diplomatically. "We support democratic transformation in Iraq," he said— half smiling, because he knows that there is no chance of that occurring unless Saddam is removed. But until America commits itself to removing Saddam, he said, "we're living on the razor's edge. Before Washington even wakes up in the morning, we could have ten thousand dead." This is the Kurdish conundrum: the Iraqi military is weaker than the American military, but the Iraqis are stronger than the Kurds. Seven hundred Iraqi tanks face the Kurdish safe haven, according to *peshmerga* commanders.

General Mustafa Said Qadir, the *peshmerga* leader, put it this way: "We have a problem. If the Americans attack Saddam and don't get him, we're going to get gassed. If the Americans decided to do it, we would be thankful. This is the Kurdish dream. But it has to be done carefully."

The Kurdish leadership worries, in short, that an American mistake could cost the Kurds what they have created, however inadvertently: a nearly independent state for themselves in northern Iraq. "We would like to be our own nation," Salih told me. "But we are realists. All we want is to be partners of the Arabs of Iraq in building a secular, democratic, federal country." Later, he added, "We are proud of ourselves. We have inherited a devastated country. It's not easy what we are trying to achieve. We had no democratic institutions, we didn't have a legal culture, we did not have a strong military. From that situation, this is a remarkable success story."

The Kurdish regional government, to be sure, is not a Vermont town meeting. The leaders of the two parties, Massoud Barzani and Jalal Talabani, are safe in their jobs. But there is a free press here, and separation of mosque and state, and schools are being built and pensions are being paid. In Erbil and in Sulaimaniya, the Kurds have built playgrounds on the ruins of Iraqi Army torture centres. "If America is indeed looking for Muslims who are eager to become democratic and are eager to counter the effects of Islamic fundamentalism, then it should be looking here," Salih said.

Massoud Barzani is the son of the late Mustafa Barzani, a legendary guerrilla, who built the Democratic Party, and who entered into the ill-fated alliance with Iran and America. I met Barzani in his headquarters, above the town of Salahuddin. He is a short man, pale and quiet; he wore the red turban of the Barzani clan and a wide cummerbund across his baggy trousers—the outfit of a *peshmerga*.

Like Salih, he chooses his words carefully when talking about the possibility of helping America bring down Saddam. "It is not enough to tell us the U.S. will respond at a certain time and place of its choosing," Barzani said. "We're in artillery range. Iraq's Army is weak, but it is still strong enough to crush us. We don't make assumptions about the American response."

201

One day, I drove to the Kurdish front lines near Erbil, to see the forward positions of the Iraqi Army. The border between the Army-controlled territory and the Kurdish region is porous; Baghdad allows some Kurds—non-political Kurds—to travel back and forth between zones.

My *peshmerga* escort took me to the roof of a building overlooking the Kalak Bridge and, beyond it, the Iraqi lines. Without binoculars, we could see Iraqi tanks on the hills in front of us. A local official named Muhammad Najar joined us; he told me that the Iraqi forces arrayed there were elements of the Army's Jerusalem brigade, a reserve unit established by Saddam with the stated purpose of liberating Jerusalem from the Israelis. Other *peshmerga* joined us. It was a brilliantly sunny day, and we were enjoying the weather. A man named Aziz Khader, gazing at the plain before us, said, "When I look across here, I imagine American tanks coming down across this plain going to Baghdad." His friends smiled and said, "*Inshallah*"—God willing. Another man said, "The U.S. is the lord of the world."

6. THE PRISONERS

A week later, I was at Shinwe, a mountain range outside Halabja, with another group of *peshmerga*. My escorts and I had driven most of the way up, and then slogged through fresh snow. From one peak, we could see the village of Biyara, which sits in a valley between Halabja and a wall of mountains that mark the Iranian border. Saddam's tanks were an hour's drive away to the south, and Iran filled the vista before us. Biyara and nine other villages near it are occupied by the terrorist group Ansar al-Islam, or Supporters of Islam. Shinwe, in fact, might be called the axis of the axis of evil.

We were close enough to see trucks belonging to Ansar al-Islam making their way from village to village. The commander of the *peshmerga* forces surrounding Biyara, a veteran guerrilla named Ramadan Dekone, said that Ansar al-Islam is made up of Kurdish Islamists and an unknown number of so-called Arab Afghans—Arabs, from southern Iraq and elsewhere, who trained in the camps of Al Qaeda.

"They believe that people must be terrorized," Dekone said, shaking his head. "They believe that the Koran says this is permissible." He pointed to an abandoned village in the middle distance, a place called Kheli Hama. "That is where the massacre took place," he said. In late September, forty-two of his men were killed by Ansar al-Islam, and now Dekone and his forces seemed ready for revenge. I asked him what he would do if he captured the men responsible for the killing.

"I would take them to court," he said.

When I got to Sulaimaniya, I visited a prison run by the intelligence service of the Patriotic Union. The prison is attached to the intelligence-service headquarters. It appears to be well kept and humane; the communal cells hold twenty or so men each, and they have kerosene heat, and even satellite television. For two days, the intelligence agency permitted me to speak with any prisoner who agreed to be interviewed. I was wary; the Kurds have an obvious interest in lining up on the American side in the war against terror. But the officials did not, as far as I know, compel anyone to speak to me, and I did not get the sense that allegations made by prisoners were shaped by their captors. The stories, which I later checked with experts on the region, seemed at least worth the attention of America and other countries in the West.

The allegations include charges that Ansar al-Islam has received funds directly from Al Qaeda; that the intelligence service of Saddam Hussein has joint control, with Al Qaeda operatives, over Ansar al-Islam; that Saddam Hussein hosted a senior leader of Al Qaeda in Baghdad in 1992; that a number of

Al Qaeda members fleeing Afghanistan have been secretly brought into territory controlled by Ansar al-Islam; and that Iraqi intelligence agents smuggled conventional weapons, and possibly even chemical and biological weapons, into Afghanistan. If these charges are true, it would mean that the relationship between Saddam's regime and Al Qaeda is far closer than previously thought.

When I asked the director of the twenty-four-hundred-man Patriotic Union intelligence service why he was allowing me to interview his prisoners, he told me that he hoped I would carry this information to American intelligence officials. "The F.B.I. and the C.I.A. haven't come out yet," he told me. His deputy added, "Americans are going to Somalia, the Philippines, I don't know where else, to look for terrorists. But this is the field, here." Anya Guilsher, a spokeswoman for the C.I.A., told me last week that as a matter of policy the agency would not comment on the activities of its officers. James Woolsey, a former C.I.A. director and an advocate of overthrowing the Iraqi regime, said, "It would be a real shame if the C.I.A.'s substantial institutional hostility to Iraqi democratic resistance groups was keeping it from learning about Saddam's ties to Al Qaeda in northern Iraq."

The possibility that Saddam could supply weapons of mass destruction to anti-American terror groups is a powerful argument among advocates of "regime change," as the removal of Saddam is known in Washington. These critics of Saddam argue that his chemical and biological capabilities, his record of support for terrorist organisations, and the cruelty of his regime make him a threat that reaches far beyond the citizens of Iraq.

"He's the home address for anyone wanting to make or use chemical or biological weapons," Kanan Makiya, an Iraqi dissident, said. Makiya is the author of "Republic of Fear," a study of Saddam's regime. "He's going to be the person to worry about. He's got the labs and the know-how. He's hell-bent on trying to find a way into the fight, without announcing it."

On the surface, a marriage of Saddam's secular Baath Party regime with the fundamentalist Al Qaeda seems unlikely. His relationship with secular Palestinian groups is well known; both Abu Nidal and Abul Abbas, two prominent Palestinian terrorists, are currently believed to be in Baghdad. But about ten years ago Saddam underwent something of a battlefield conversion to a fundamentalist brand of Islam.

"It was gradual, starting the moment he decided on the invasion of Kuwait," in June of 1990, according to Amatzia Baram, an Iraq expert at the University of Haifa. "His calculation was that he needed people in Iraq and the Arab world—as well as God—to be on his side when he invaded. After he invaded, the Islamic rhetorical style became overwhelming"—so overwhelming, Baram continued, that a radical group in Jordan began calling Saddam "the New Caliph Marching from the East." This conversion, cynical though it may be, has opened doors to Saddam in the fundamentalist world. He is now a prime supporter of the Palestinian Islamic Jihad and of Hamas, paying families of suicide bombers ten thousand dollars in exchange for their sons' martyrdom. This is part of Saddam's attempt to harness the power of Islamic extremism and direct it against his enemies.

Kurdish culture, on the other hand, has traditionally been immune to religious extremism. According to Kurdish officials, Ansar al-Islam grew out of an idea spread by Ayman al-Zawahiri, the former chief of the Egyptian Islamic Jihad and now Osama bin Laden's deputy in Al Qaeda. "There are two schools of thought" in Al Qaeda, Karim Sinjari, the Interior Minister of Kurdistan's Democratic Party-controlled region, told me. "Osama bin Laden believes that the infidels should be beaten in the head, meaning the United States. Zawahiri's philosophy is that you should fight the infidel even in the smallest village, that you should try to form Islamic armies everywhere. The Kurdish fundamentalists were influenced by Zawahiri."

Kurds were among those who travelled to Afghanistan from all over the Muslim world, first to fight the Soviets, in the early nineteen-eighties, then to join Al Qaeda. The members of the groups that eventually became Ansar al-Islam spent a great deal of time in Afghanistan, according to Kurdish intelligence officials. One Kurd who went to Afghanistan was Mala Krekar, an early leader of the Islamist movement in Kurdistan; according to Sinjari, he now holds the title of "emir" of Ansar al-Islam.

In 1998, the first force of Islamist terrorists crossed the Iranian border into Kurdistan, and immediately tried to seize the town of Haj Omran. Kurdish officials said that the terrorists were helped by Iran, which also has an interest in undermining a secular Muslim government. "The terrorists blocked the road, they killed Kurdish Democratic Party cadres, they threatened the villagers," Sinjari said. "We fought them and they fled."

The terrorist groups splintered repeatedly. According to a report in the Arabic newspaper *Al-Sharq al-Awsat*, which is published in London, Ansar al-Islam came into being, on September 1st of last year, with the merger of two factions: Al Tawhid, which helped to arrange the assassination of Kurdistan's most prominent Christian politician, and whose operatives initiated an acid-throwing campaign against unveiled women; and a faction called the Second Soran Unit, which had been affiliated with one of the Kurdish Islamic parties. In a statement issued to mark the merger, the group, which originally called itself Jund al-Islam, or Soldiers of Islam, declared its intention to "undertake jihad in this region" in order to carry out "God's will." According to Kurdish officials, the group had between five hundred and six hundred members, including Arab Afghans and at least thirty Iraqi Kurds who were trained in Afghanistan.

Kurdish officials say that the merger took place in a ceremony overseen by three Arabs trained in bin Laden's camps in Afghanistan, and that these men supplied Ansar al-Islam with three hundred thousand dollars in seed money. Soon after the merger, a unit of Ansar al-Islam called the Victory Squad attacked and killed the *peshmerga* in Kheli Hama.

Among the Islamic fighters who were there that day was Rekut Hiwa Hussein, a slender, boyish twenty-year-old who was captured by the *peshmerga* after the massacre, and whom I met in the prison in Sulaimaniya. He was exceedingly shy, never looking up from his hands as he spoke. He was not handcuffed, and had no marks on the visible parts of his body. We were seated in an investigator's office inside the intelligence complex. Like most buildings in Sulaimaniya, this one was warmed by a single kerosene heater, and the room temperature seemed barely above freezing. Rekut told me how he and his comrades in Ansar al-Islam overcame the *peshmerga*.

"They thought there was a ceasefire, so we came into the village and fired on them by surprise," he said. "They didn't know what happened. We used grenades and machine guns. We killed a lot of them and then the others surrendered." The terrorists trussed their prisoners, ignoring pleas from the few civilians remaining in the town to leave them alone. "The villagers asked us not to slaughter them," Rekut said. One of the leaders of Ansar al-Islam, a man named Abdullah al-Shafi, became incensed. "He said, 'Who is saying this? Let me kill them.' "

Rekut said that the *peshmerga* were killed in ritual fashion: "We put cloths in their mouths. We then laid them down like sheep, in a line. Then we cut their throats." After the men were killed, *peshmerga*commanders say, the corpses were beheaded. Rekut denied this. "Some of their heads had been blown off by grenades, but we didn't behead them," he said.

I asked Rekut why he had joined Ansar al-Islam. "A friend of mine joined," he said quietly. "I don't have a good reason why I joined." A guard then took him by the elbow and returned him to his cell.

The Kurdish intelligence officials I spoke to were careful not to oversell their case; they said that they have no proof that Ansar al-Islam was ever involved in international terrorism or that Saddam's agents were involved in the attacks on the World Trade Centre and the Pentagon. But they do have proof, they said, that Ansar al-Islam is shielding Al Qaeda members, and that it is doing so with the approval of Saddam's agents.

Kurdish officials said that, according to their intelligence, several men associated with Al Qaeda have been smuggled over the Iranian border into an Ansar al-Islam stronghold near Halabja. The Kurds believe that two of them, who go by the names Abu Yasir and Abu Muzaham, are high-ranking Al Qaeda members. "We don't have any information about them," one official told me. "We know that they don't want anybody to see them. They are sleeping in the same room as Mala Krekar and Abdullah al-Shafi"—the nominal leaders of Ansar al-Islam.

The real leader, these officials say, is an Iraqi who goes by the name Abu Wa'el, and who, like the others, spent a great deal of time in bin Laden's training camps. But he is also, they say, a high-ranking officer of the Mukhabarat. One senior official added, "A man named Abu Agab is in charge of the northern bureau of the Mukhabarat. And he is Abu Wa'el's control officer."

Abu Agab, the official said, is based in the city of Kirkuk, which is predominantly Kurdish but is under the control of Baghdad. According to intelligence officials, Abu Agab and Abu Wa'el met last July 7th, in Germany. From there, they say, Abu Wa'el travelled to Afghanistan and then, in August, to Kurdistan, sneaking across the Iranian border.

The Kurdish officials told me that they learned a lot about Abu Wa'el's movements from one of their prisoners, an Iraqi intelligence officer named Qassem Hussein Muhammad, and they invited me to speak with him. Qassem, the Kurds said, is a Shiite from Basra, in southern Iraq, and a twenty-year veteran of Iraqi intelligence.

Qassem, shambling and bearded, was brought into the room, and he genially agreed to be interviewed. One guard stayed in the room, along with my translator. Qassem lit a cigarette, and leaned back in his chair. I started by asking him if he had been tortured by his captors. His eyes widened. "By God, no," he said. "There is nothing like torture here." Then he told me that his involvement in Islamic radicalism began in 1992 in Baghdad, when he met Ayman al-Zawahiri.

Qassem said that he was one of seventeen bodyguards assigned to protect Zawahiri, who stayed at Baghdad's Al Rashid Hotel, but who, he said, moved around surreptitiously. The guards had no idea why Zawahiri was in Baghdad, but one day Qassem escorted him to one of Saddam's palaces for what he later learned was a meeting with Saddam himself.

Qassem's capture by the Kurds grew out of his last assignment from the Mukhabarat. The Iraqi intelligence service received word that Abu Wa'el had been captured by American agents. "I was sent by the Mukhabarat to Kurdistan to find Abu Wa'el or, at least, information about him," Qassem told me. "That's when I was captured, before I reached Biyara."

I asked him if he was sure that Abu Wa'el was on Saddam's side. "He's an employee of the Mukhabarat," Qassem said. "He's the actual decision-maker in the group"—Ansar al-Islam—"but he's an employee of the Mukhabarat." According to the Kurdish intelligence officials, Abu Wa'el is not in American hands; rather, he is still with Ansar al-Islam. American officials declined to comment.

The Kurdish intelligence officials told me that they have Al Qaeda members in custody, and they introduced me to another prisoner, a young Iraqi Arab named Haqi Ismail, whom they described as a middle- to high-ranking member of Al Qaeda. He was, they said, captured by the *peshmerga* as he tried to get into Kurdistan three weeks after the start of the American attack on Afghanistan. Ismail, they said, comes from a Mosul family with deep connections to the Mukhabarat; his uncle is the top Mukhabarat official in the south of Iraq. They said they believe that Haqi Ismail is a liaison between Saddam's intelligence service and Al Qaeda.

Ismail wore slippers and a blanket around his shoulders. He was ascetic in appearance and, at the same time, ostentatiously smug. He appeared to be amused by the presence of an American. He told the investigators that he would not talk to the C.I.A. The Kurdish investigators laughed and said they wished that I were from the C.I.A.

Ismail said that he was once a student at the University of Mosul but grew tired of life in Iraq under Saddam Hussein. Luckily, he said, in 1999 he met an Afghan man who persuaded him to seek work in Afghanistan. The Kurdish investigators smiled as Ismail went on to say that he found himself in Kandahar, then in Kabul, and then somehow—here he was exceedingly vague—in an Al Qaeda camp. When I asked him how enrolment in an Al Qaeda camp squared with his wish to seek work in Afghanistan, he replied, "Being a soldier is a job." After his training, he said, he took a post in the Taliban Foreign Ministry. I asked him if he was an employee of Saddam's intelligence service. "I prefer not to talk about that," he replied.

Later, I asked the Kurdish officials if they believed that Saddam provides aid to Al Qaeda-affiliated terror groups or simply maintains channels of communication with them. It was getting late, and the room was growing even colder. "Come back tomorrow," the senior official in the room said, "and we'll introduce you to someone who will answer that question."

7. THE AL QAEDA LINK

The man they introduced me to the next afternoon was a twenty-nine-year-old Iranian Arab, a smuggler and bandit from the city of Ahvaz. The intelligence officials told me that his most recent employer was bin Laden. When they arrested him, last year, they said, they found a roll of film in his possession. They had the film developed, and the photographs, which they showed me, depicted their prisoner murdering a man with a knife, slicing his ear off and then plunging the knife into the top of the man's head.

The Iranian had a thin face, thick black hair, and a moustache; he wore an army jacket, sandals, and Western-style sweatpants. Speaking in an almost casual tone, he told me that he was born in 1973, that his real name was Muhammad Mansour Shahab, and that he had been a smuggler most of his adult life.

"I met a group of drug traffickers," he said. "They gave us drugs and we got them weapons," which they took from Iran into Afghanistan. In 1996, he met an Arab Afghan. "His name was Othman," the man went on. "He gave me drugs, and I got him a hundred and fifty Kalashnikovs. Then he said to me, 'You should come visit Afghanistan.' So we went to Afghanistan in 1996. We stayed for a while, I came back, did a lot of smuggling jobs. My brother-in-law tried to send weapons to Afghanistan, but the Iranians ambushed us. I killed some of the Iranians."

He soon returned with Othman to Afghanistan, where, he said, Othman gave him the name Muhammad Jawad to use while he was there. "Othman said to me, 'You will meet Sheikh Osama soon.' We were in Kandahar. One night, they gave me a sleeping pill. We got into a car and we drove for an hour and a half into the mountains. We went to a tent they said was Osama's tent." The man now called Jawad did not meet Osama bin Laden that night. "They said to me, 'You're the guy who killed the Iranian officer.' Then they said they needed information about me, my real name. They told Othman to take me back to Kandahar and hold me in jail for twenty-one days while they investigated me."

The Al Qaeda men completed their investigation and called him back to the mountains. "They told me that Osama said I should work with them," Jawad said. "They told me to bring my wife to Afghanistan." They made him swear on a Koran that he would never betray them. Jawad said that he became one of Al Qaeda's principal weapons smugglers. Iraqi opposition sources told me that the Baghdad regime frequently smuggled weapons to Al Qaeda by air through Dubai to Pakistan and then overland into Afghanistan. But Jawad told me that the Iraqis often used land routes through Iran as well. Othman ordered him to establish a smuggling route across the Iraq-Iran border. The smugglers would pose as shepherds to find the best routes. "We started to go into Iraq with the sheep and cows," Jawad told me, and added that they initiated this route by smuggling tape recorders from Iraq to Iran. They opened a store, a front, in Ahvaz, to sell electronics, "just to establish relationships with smugglers."

One day in 1999, Othman got a message to Jawad, who was then in Iran. He was to smuggle himself across the Iraqi border at Fao, where a car would meet him and take him to a village near Tikrit, the headquarters of Saddam Hussein's clan. Jawad was then taken to a meeting at the house of a man called Luay, whom he described as the son of Saddam's father-in-law, Khayr Allah Talfah. (Professor Baram, who has long followed Saddam's family, later told me he believes that Luay, who is about forty years old, is close to Saddam's inner circle.) At the meeting, with Othman present, Mukhabarat officials instructed Jawad to go to Baghdad, where he was to retrieve several canisters filled with explosives. Then, he said, he was to arrange to smuggle the explosives into Iran, where they would be used to kill anti-Iraqi activists. After this assignment was completed, Jawad said, he was given a thousand Kalashnikov rifles by Iraqi intelligence and told to smuggle them into Afghanistan.

A year later, there was a new development: Othman told Jawad to smuggle several dozen refrigerator motors into Afghanistan for the Iraqi Mukhabarat; a canister filled with liquid was attached to each motor. Jawad said that he asked Othman for more information. "I said, 'Othman, what does this contain?' He said, 'My life and your life.' He said they"—the Iraqi agents—"were going to kill us if we didn't do this. That's all I'll say.

"I was given a book of dollars," Jawad went on, meaning ten thousand dollars—a hundred American hundred-dollar bills. "I was told to arrange to smuggle the motors. Othman told me to kill any of the smugglers who helped us once we got there." Vehicles belonging to the Taliban were waiting at the border, and Jawad said that he turned over the liquid-filled refrigerator motors to the Taliban, and then killed the smugglers who had helped him.

Jawad said that he had no idea what liquid was inside the motors, but he assumed that it was some type of chemical or biological weapon. I asked the Kurdish officials who remained in the room if they believed that, as late as 2000, the Mukhabarat was transferring chemical or biological weapons to Al

Qaeda. They spoke carefully. "We have no idea what was in the canisters," the senior official said. "This is something that is worth an American investigation."

When I asked Jawad to tell me why he worked for Al Qaeda, he replied, "Money." He would not say how much money he had been paid, but he suggested that it was quite a bit. I had one more question: How many years has Al Qaeda maintained a relationship with Saddam Hussein's regime? "There's been a relationship between the Mukhabarat and the people of Al Qaeda since 1992," he replied.

Carole O'Leary, a Middle Eastern expert at American University, in Washington, and a specialist on the Kurds, said it is likely that Saddam would seek an alliance with Islamic terrorists to serve his own interests. "I know that there are Mukhabarat agents throughout Kurdistan," O'Leary said, and went on, "One way the Mukhabarat could destabilize the Kurdish experiment in democracy is to link up with Islamic radical groups. Their interests dovetail completely. They both have much to fear from the democratic, secular experiment of the Kurds in the safe haven, and they both obviously share a hatred for America."

8. THE PRESENT DANGER

A paradox of life in northern Iraq is that, while hundreds, perhaps thousands, of children suffer from the effects of chemical attacks, the child-mortality rate in the Kurdish zone has improved over the past ten years. Prime Minister Salih credits this to, of all things, sanctions placed on the Iraqi regime by the United Nations after the Gulf War because of Iraq's refusal to dismantle its nonconventional-weapons program. He credits in particular the program begun in 1997, known as oil-for-food, which was meant to mitigate the effects of sanctions on civilians by allowing the profits from Iraqi oil sales to buy food and medicine. Calling this program a "fantastic concept," Salih said, "For the first time in our history, Iraqi citizens—all citizens—are insured a portion of the country's oil wealth. The north is a testament to the success of the program. Oil is sold and food is bought."

I asked Salih to respond to the criticism, widely aired in the West, that the sanctions have led to the death of thousands of children. "Sanctions don't kill Iraqi children," he said. "The regime kills children."

This puzzled me. If it was true, then why were the victims of the gas attacks still suffering from a lack of health care? Across Kurdistan, in every hospital I visited, the complaints were the same: no CT scans, no MRIs, no paediatric surgery, no advanced diagnostic equipment, not even surgical gloves. I asked Salih why the money designated by the U.N. for the Kurds wasn't being used for advanced medical treatment. The oil-for-food program has one enormous flaw, he replied. When the program was introduced, the Kurds were promised thirteen per cent of the country's oil revenue, but because of the terms of the agreement between Baghdad and the U.N.—a "defect," Salih said—the government controls the flow of food, medicine, and medical equipment to the very people it slaughtered. Food does arrive, he conceded, and basic medicines as well, but at Saddam's pace.

On this question of the work of the United Nations and its agencies, the rival Kurdish parties agree. "We've been asking for a four-hundred-bed hospital for Sulaimaniya for three years," said Nerchivan Barzani, the Prime Minister of the region controlled by the Kurdish Democratic Party, and Salih's counterpart. Sulaimaniya is in Salih's territory, but in this case geography doesn't matter. "It's our money," Barzani said. "But we need the approval of the Iraqis. They get to decide. The World Health Organisation is taking its orders from the Iraqis. It's crazy."

Barzani and Salih accused the World Health Organization, in particular, of rewarding with lucrative contracts only companies favoured by Saddam."Every time I interact with the U.N.," Salih said, "I think, My God, Jesse Helms is right. If the U.N. can't help us, this poor, dispossessed Muslim nation, then who is it for?"

Many Kurds believe that Iraq's friends in the U.N. system, particularly members of the Arab bloc, have worked to keep the Kurds' cause from being addressed. The Kurds face an institutional disadvantage at the U.N., where, unlike the Palestinians, they have not even been granted official observer status. Salih grew acerbic: "Compare us to other liberation movements around the world. We are very mature. We don't engage in terror. We don't condone extremist nationalist notions that can only burden our people. Please compare what we have achieved in the Kurdistan national-authority areas to the Palestinian national authority of Mr. Arafat. We have spent the last ten years building a secular, democratic society, a civil society. What has he built?"

Last week, in New York, I met with Benon Sevan, the United Nations undersecretary-general who oversees the oil-for-food program. He quickly let me know that he was unmoved by the demands of the Kurds. "If they had a theme song, it would be 'Give Me, Give Me, Give Me,' " Sevan said. "I'm getting fed up with their complaints. You can tell them that." He said that under the oil-for-food program the "three northern governorates"—U.N. officials avoid the word "Kurdistan"—have been allocated billions of dollars in goods and services. "I don't know if they've ever had it so good," he said.

I mentioned the Kurds' complaint that they have been denied access to advanced medical equipment, and he said, "Nobody prevents them from asking. They should go ask the World Health Organisation"—which reports to Sevan on matters related to Iraq. When I told Sevan that the Kurds have repeatedly asked the W.H.O., he said, "I'm not going to pass judgment on the W.H.O." As the interview ended, I asked Sevan about the morality of allowing the Iraqi regime to control the flow of food and medicine into Kurdistan. "Nobody's innocent," he said. "Please don't talk about morals with me."

When I went to Kurdistan in January to report on the 1988 genocide of the Kurds, I did not expect to be sidetracked by a debate over U.N. sanctions. And I certainly didn't expect to be sidetracked by crimes that Saddam is committing against the Kurds now—in particular "nationality correction," the law that Saddam's security services are using to implement a campaign of ethnic cleansing. Large-scale operations against the Kurds in Kirkuk, a city southeast of Erbil, and in other parts of Iraqi Kurdistan under Saddam's control, have received scant press attention in the West; there have been few news accounts and no Security Council condemnations drafted in righteous anger.

Saddam's security services have been demanding that Kurds "correct" their nationality by signing papers to indicate that their birth records are false—that they are in fact Arab. Those who don't sign have their property seized. Many have been evicted, often to Kurdish-controlled regions, to make room for Arab families. According to both the Kurdistan Democratic Party and the Patriotic Union of Kurdistan, more than a hundred thousand Kurds have been expelled from the Kirkuk area over the past two years.

Nationality correction is one technique that the Baghdad regime is using in an over-all "Arabization" campaign, whose aim is to replace the inhabitants of Kurdish cities, especially the oil-rich Kirkuk, with Arabs from central and southern Iraq, and even, according to persistent reports, with Palestinians. Arabization is not new, Peter Galbraith, a professor at the National Defence University and a former senior adviser to the Senate Foreign Relations Committee, says. Galbraith has monitored Saddam's anti-Kurdish activities since before the Gulf War. "It's been going on for twenty years," he told me. "Maybe it's picked up speed, but it is certainly nothing new. To my mind, it's part of a larger process that has been under way for many years, and is aimed at reducing the territory occupied by the Kurds and at destroying rural Kurdistan."

"This is the apotheosis of cultural genocide," said Saedi Barzinji, the president of Salahaddin University, in Erbil, who is a human-rights lawyer and Massoud Barzani's legal adviser. Barzinji and other Kurdish leaders believe that Saddam is trying to set up a buffer zone between Arab Iraq and Kurdistan, just in case the Kurds win their independence. To help with this, Barzinji told me last month, Saddam is trying to rewrite Kirkuk's history, to give it an "Arab" past. If Kurds, Barzinji went on, "don't change their ethnic origin, they are given no food rations, no positions in government, no right to register the names of their new babies. In the last three to four weeks, hospitals have been ordered, the maternity wards ordered, not to register any Kurdish name." New parents are "obliged to choose an Arab name." Barzinji said that the nationality-correction campaign extends even to the dead. "Saddam is razing the gravestones, erasing the past, putting in new ones with Arab names," he said. "He wants to show that Kirkuk has always been Arab."

Some of the Kurds crossing the demarcation line between Saddam's forces and the Kurdish zone, it is said, are not being expelled but are fleeing for economic reasons. But in camps across Kurdistan I met refugees who told me stories of visits from the secret police in the middle of the night.

Many of the refugees from Kirkuk live in tent camps built on boggy fields. I visited one such camp at Beneslawa, not far from Erbil, where the mud was so thick that it nearly pulled off my shoes. The people at the camp—several hundred, according to two estimates I heard—are ragged and sick. A man named Howar told me that his suffering could not have been avoided even if he had agreed to change his ethnic identity.

"When you agree to change your nationality, the police write on your identity documents 'second-degree Arab,' which they know means Kurd," he told me. "So they always know you're a Kurd." (In a twist characteristic of Saddam's regime, Kurdish leaders told me, Kurds who agree to "change" their nationality are fined for having once claimed falsely to be Kurdish.)

Another refugee, Shawqat Hamid Muhammad, said that her son had gone to jail for two months for having a photograph of Mustafa Barzani in his possession. She said that she and her family had been in the Beneslawa camp for two months. "The police came and knocked on our door and told us we have to leave Kirkuk," she said. "We had to rent a truck to take our things out. We were given one day to leave. We have no idea who is in our house." Another refugee, a man named Ibrahim Jamil, wandered over to listen to the conversation. "The Arabs are winning Kirkuk," he said. "Soon the only people there will be Arabs, and Kurds who call themselves Arabs. They say we should be Arab. But I'm a Kurd. It would be easier for me to die than be an Arab. How can I not be a Kurd?"

Peter Galbraith told me that in 1987 he witnessed the destruction of Kurdish villages and cemeteries— "anything that was related to Kurdish identity," he said. "This was one of the factors that led me to conclude that it is a policy of genocide, a crime of intent, destroying a group whole or in part."

9. IRAQ'S ARMS RACE

In a series of meetings in the summer and fall of 1995, Charles Duelfer, the deputy executive chairman of the United Nations Special Commission, or *UNSCOM*—the now defunct arms-inspection team— met in Baghdad with Iraqi government delegations. The subject was the status of Iraq's nonconventional-weapons programs, and Duelfer, an American diplomat on loan to the United Nations, was close to a breakthrough.

In early August, Saddam's son-in-law Hussein Kamel had defected to Jordan, and had then spoken publicly about Iraq's offensive biological, chemical, and nuclear capabilities. (Kamel later returned to Iraq and was killed almost immediately, on his father-in-law's orders.) The regime's credibility was badly damaged by Kamel's revelations, and during these meetings the Iraqi representatives decided to tell Duelfer and his team more than they had ever revealed before. "This was the first time Iraq actually agreed to discuss the Presidential origins of these programs," Duelfer recalled. Among the most startling admissions made by the Iraqi scientists was that they had weaponized the biological agent aflatoxin.

Aflatoxin, which is produced from types of fungi that occur in mouldy grains, is the biological agent that some Kurdish physicians suspect was mixed with chemical weapons and dropped on Kurdistan. Christine Gosden, the English geneticist, told me, "There is absolutely no forensic evidence whatsoever that aflatoxins have ever been used in northern Iraq, but this may be because no systematic testing has been carried out in the region, to my knowledge."

Duelfer told me, "We kept pressing the Iraqis to discuss the concept of use for aflatoxin. We learned that the origin of the biological-weapons program is in the security services, not in the military— meaning that it really came out of the assassinations program." The Iraqis, Duelfer said, admitted something else: they had loaded aflatoxin into two Scud-ready warheads, and also mixed aflatoxin with tear gas. They wouldn't say why.

In an op-ed article that Duelfer wrote for the Los Angeles *Times* last year about Iraqi programs to develop weapons of mass destruction, he offered this hypothesis: "If a regime wished to conceal a biological attack, what better way than this? Victims would suffer the short-term effects of inhaling tear gas and would assume that this was the totality of the attack: Subsequent cancers would not be linked to the prior event."

United Nations inspectors were alarmed to learn about the aflatoxin program. Richard Spertzel, the chief biological-weapons inspector for *UNSCOM*, put it this way: "It is a devilish weapon. Iraq was quite clearly aware of the long-term carcinogenic effect of aflatoxin. Aflatoxin can only do one thing— destroy people's livers. And I suspect that children are more susceptible. From a moral standpoint, aflatoxin is the cruellest weapon—it means watching children die slowly of liver cancer."

Spertzel believes that if aflatoxin were to be used as a weapon it would not be delivered by a missile. "Aflatoxin is a little tricky," he said. "I don't know if a single dose at one point in time is going to give you the long-term effects. Continuous, repeated exposure—through food—would be more effective." When I asked Spertzel if other countries have weaponized aflatoxin, he replied, "I don't know any other country that did it. I don't know any country that would."

It is unclear what biological and chemical weapons Saddam possesses today. When he manoeuvred*UNSCOM* out of his country in 1998, weapons inspectors had found a sizable portion of his arsenal but were vexed by what they couldn't find. His scientists certainly have produced and weaponized anthrax, and they have manufactured botulinum toxin, which causes muscular paralysis and death. They've made *Clostridium perfringens*, a bacterium that causes gas gangrene, a condition in which the flesh rots. They have also made wheat-cover smut, which can be used to poison crops, and ricin, which, when absorbed into the lungs, causes haemorrhagic pneumonia.

According to Gary Milhollin, the director of the Wisconsin Project on Nuclear Arms Control, whose Iraq Watch project monitors Saddam's weapons capabilities, inspectors could not account for a great deal of weaponry believed to be in Iraq's possession, including almost four tons of the nerve agent VX; six hundred tons of ingredients for VX; as much as three thousand tons of other poison-gas agents; and at least five hundred and fifty artillery shells filled with mustard gas. Nor did the inspectors find any stores of aflatoxin.

Saddam's motives are unclear, too. For the past decade, the development of these weapons has caused nothing but trouble for him; his international isolation grows not from his past crimes but from his refusal to let weapons inspectors dismantle his nonconventional-weapons programs. When I asked the Iraqi dissident Kanan Makiya why Saddam is so committed to these programs, he said, "I think this regime developed a very specific ideology associated with power, and how to extend that power, and these weapons play a very important psychological and political part." Makiya added, "They are seen as essential to the security and longevity of the regime."

Certainly, the threat of another Halabja has kept Iraq's citizens terrorized and compliant. Amatzia Baram, the Iraq expert at the University of Haifa, told me that in 1999 Iraqi troops in white biohazard suits suddenly surrounded the Shiite holy city of Karbala, in southern Iraq, which has been the scene of frequent uprisings against Saddam. (The Shiites make up about sixty per cent of Iraq's population, and the regime is preoccupied with the threat of another rebellion.) The men in the white suits did nothing; they just stood there. "But the message was clear," Baram said. " 'What we did to the Kurds in Halabja we can do to you.' It's a very effective psychological weapon. From the information I saw, people were really panicky. They ran into their homes and shut their windows. It worked extremely well."

Saddam's weapons of mass destruction clearly are not meant solely for domestic use. Several years ago in Baghdad, Richard Butler, who was then the chairman of *UNSCOM*, fell into conversation with Tariq Aziz, Saddam's confidant and Iraq's deputy Prime Minister. Butler asked Aziz to explain the rationale for Iraq's biological-weapons project, and he recalled Aziz's answer: "He said, 'We made bioweapons in order to deal with the Persians and the Jews.' "

Iraqi dissidents agree that Iraq's programs to build weapons of mass destruction are focussed on Israel. "Israel is the whole game," Ahmad Chalabi, the leader of the Iraqi National Congress, told me. "Saddam is always saying publicly, 'Who is going to fire the fortieth missile?' "—a reference to the thirty-nine Scud missiles he fired at Israel during the Gulf War. "He thinks he can kill one hundred thousand Israelis in a day with biological weapons." Chalabi added, "This is the only way he can be Saladin"—the Muslim hero who defeated the Crusaders. Students of Iraq and its government generally agree that Saddam would like to project himself as a leader of all the Arabs, and that the one sure way to do that is by confronting Israel.

In the Gulf War, when Saddam attacked Israel, he was hoping to provoke an Israeli response, which would drive America's Arab friends out of the allied coalition. Today, the experts say, Saddam's desire is to expel the Jews from history. In October of 2000, at an Arab summit in Cairo, I heard the vice-chairman of Iraq's Revolutionary Command Council, a man named Izzat Ibrahim al-Douri, deliver a speech on Saddam's behalf, saying, "Jihad alone is capable of liberating Palestine and the rest of the Arab territories occupied by dirty Jews in their distorted Zionist entity."

Amatzia Baram said, "Saddam can absolve himself of all sins in the eyes of the Arab and Muslim worlds by bringing Israel to its knees. He not only wants to be a hero in his own press, which already recognizes him as a Saladin, but wants to make sure that a thousand years from now children in the fourth grade will know that he is the one who destroyed Israel."

It is no comfort to the Kurds that the Jews are now Saddam's main preoccupation. The Kurds I spoke with, even those who agree that Saddam is aiming his remaining Scuds at Israel, believe that he is saving some of his "special weapons"—a popular euphemism inside the Iraqi regime—for a return visit to Halabja. The day I visited the Kalak Bridge, which divides the Kurds from the Iraqi Army's Jerusalem brigade, I asked Muhammad Najar, the local official, why the brigade was not facing west, toward its target. "The road to Jerusalem," he replied, "goes through Kurdistan."

A few weeks ago, after my return from Iraq, I stopped by the Israeli Embassy in Washington to see the Ambassador, David Ivry. In 1981, Ivry, who then led Israel's Air Force, commanded Operation Opera, the strike against the Osirak nuclear reactor near Baghdad. The action was ordered by Prime Minister Menachem Begin, who believed that by hitting the reactor shortly before it went online he could stop Iraq from building an atomic bomb. After the attack, Israel was condemned for what the *Times* called "inexcusable and short-sighted aggression." Today, though, Israel's action is widely regarded as an act of muscular arms control. "In retrospect, the Israeli strike bought us a decade," Gary Milhollin, of the Wisconsin Project, said. "I think if the Israelis had not hit the reactor the Iraqis would have had bombs by 1990"—the year Iraq invaded Kuwait.

Today, a satellite photograph of the Osirak site hangs on a wall in Ivry's office. The inscription reads, "For General David Ivry—With thanks and appreciation for the outstanding job he did on the Iraqi nuclear program in 1981, which made our job much easier in Desert Storm." It is signed "Dick Cheney."

"Preëmption is always a positive," Ivry said.

Saddam Hussein never gave up his hope of turning Iraq into a nuclear power. After the Osirak attack, he rebuilt, redoubled his efforts, and dispersed his facilities. Those who have followed Saddam's progress believe that no single strike today would eradicate his nuclear program. I talked about this prospect last fall with August Hanning, the chief of the B.N.D., the German intelligence agency, in Berlin. We met in the new glass-and-steel Chancellery, overlooking the renovated Reichstag.

The Germans have a special interest in Saddam's intentions. German industry is well represented in the ranks of foreign companies that have aided Saddam's nonconventional-weapons programs, and the German government has been publicly regretful. Hanning told me that his agency had taken the lead in exposing the companies that helped Iraq build a poison-gas factory at Samarra. The Germans also feel, for the most obvious reasons, a special responsibility to Israel's security, and this, too, motivates their desire to expose Iraq's weapons-of-mass-destruction programs. Hanning is tall, thin, and almost translucently white. He is sparing with words, but he does not equivocate. "It is our estimate that Iraq will have an atomic bomb in three years," he said.

There is some debate among arms-control experts about exactly when Saddam will have nuclear capabilities. But there is no disagreement that Iraq, if unchecked, will have them soon, and a nuclear-armed Iraq would alter forever the balance of power in the Middle East. "The first thing that occurs to any military planner is force protection," Charles Duelfer told me. "If your assessment of the threat is chemical or biological, you can get individual protective equipment and warning systems. If you think he's going to use a nuclear weapon, where are you going to concentrate your forces?"

There is little doubt what Saddam might do with an atomic bomb or with his stocks of biological and chemical weapons. When I talked about Saddam's past with the medical geneticist Christine Gosden, she said, "Please understand, the Kurds were for practice." ♦

By Jeffrey Goldberg (The NewYorker)

After two weeks on the road we pulled into The City of Mosul late one afternoon.

(My Taskings through Kurdistan are sensitive and given the ongoing fight against ISIS, AQI and the proxy war and fighting going on at present with Iranian back groups and after consulting my friends within the Kurdish Government, I have decided to omit this highly detailed account. I have, however,included some of my Exclusive Photographs of the Mountains and people of Kurdistan).

Mosul

On returning to Mosul it was dark, I took a night vision image of children playing around a fire. (See Photo). I stayed at a friend's house that night, "A" was a trusted contact; the Insurgents had already tried to kill him once but had missed him during an ambush. ("A" would be ambushed outside his house a month later, insurgents would walk up to his car and open fire with AK-47s, he survived the attack and moved out of Iraq). We stayed as his guests that night, (weapon always close at hand) and talked long into the evening while enjoying good food and wine. We left the next morning with warm goodbyes.

I had received a phone call late the previous night, I had been informed about Ian from the Mine Advisory Group, he had been killed, murdered by the insurgents, his 4x4 had been ambushed by them as he was driving from Qayyarah West, to Dohuk, Kurdistan. I was shocked at the news, he was a retired senior British Military officer who was helping the Maine Advisory Group, clearing thousands off dangerous sites of UXO, "un exploded ordinance" in Iraq. This news ramped home to me the risks of driving and travelling around Iraq.I helped Jane write a good piece, out of respect for Ian and the good work he and the Mine Advisory Group were doing in Iraq. It was published that weekend in the Sunday Times. I also sent my personal respects by e-mail, to the other members of the MAG teams I had met in Iraq, Lebanon and Afghanistan. (See Photograph of Ian)

RIP Ian

After being inside a war zone for such a long period of time, it was time to get back to the world. I needed to be in Lebanon, Paul needed my help with the investigation into the al-Madina Bank, from what I had found in Iraq and all the trails leading back to the al-Madina Bank, it was only a matter of time until the lid came off all that had been going on in the bank. The money laundering for the Russian mafia, Columbian, Mexican drug cartels, Illegal arms deals to Saddam Hussien including "Surface to Air Missiles with Log Books!".

SAMs Surface to Air Missiles (With Log Book)

Senor Lebanese and Syrian Government and intelligence officials being paid off and bribed. This whole investigation was about to be blown right open...

"It was about to become an International Scandal..."

Paul was in over his head, I was one of the only people he could trust, I would not let him down. After the excursion around Kurdistan and Iraq,Jane had all the photographs she would need. "I had picked up some major shots on the way too", my Intel source would be happy with them, I also sent a few shots back to a publisher friend of mine. He later informed me that one off my shots was on the front of C & S magazine in the UK, as well as a special six page feature I had written for his personal reading. It was a compliment that he deemed it good, to put it in his magazine. I briefed Jane on my plan and route back to Lebanon. The plan was to drive down to Baghdad, Jane could catch a ride with some friendly call sign back to Lebanon, Via Jordan and Syria. I told her we could always hook up in

Lebanon when I got back there. I was not allowed back into Syria. So I made contact with Sammy, a friendly local security operative who I knew was in Amman, he had retired and was running a chain of shops. He offered to help me get back to Lebanon, he organised a safe house for me in Amman, and a plane ticket back to Lebanon;"he always looked after me".He would also look after the specialist equipment that I could not take on a plane. He also told me where to keep my victor call sign.Inturn around should take 4 days to get back to Lebanon. The rest of the day was spent preparing the jeep and kit for the long journey through the heart of Iraq.I set of at 0500am the next morning, first light was just breaking, it would be along days drive down to Baghdad.The roads were empty at this time of the morning, I drove past Mosul, Qayyarah West, Al Hatra, Takrit, Saddam Hussien's home town. As I drove past Bayji, the sky was black, over to the left the insurgents had blown up another oil pipe line, the flames were lighting up the sky, with the wind carrying the trail of mass black smoke across to the horizon.Sammara, I pulled over at one of the little cafes, a ten minuteswater stop, fiveminutes is safe, it's not enough time for the insurgents to coordinate and find you. Samara is also famous for its Mosque. After five minutes back on the road I cruised past Balad. The insurgents had removed or blacked out all the road signs, in the hope a US army convoy might get lost, so they could attack it, Iraq was the one place you never wanted to get lost.Then onto the highway into Baghdad.

Baghdad

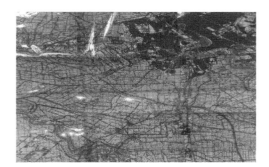

On entering Baghdad it looked old and battle worn, even more so since my last visit, a far cry from the oasis, paradise, written in the history books. The streets looked grey and bleak. I drove down unwelcoming streets until I arrived outside the Palestine Hotel, it was late afternoon.I had informed my CNN News contact that I was going to stay in Baghdad for one night on route to Jordon. CNN had located there Iraqi Officers out of the basement of the hotel. I arranged for rooms to stay the night on the top floors of the hotel. The Palestine Hoteland the Sheraton Hotel opposite, were getting attacked by RPGs and AK-47fire nightly. The safest place to be was the top three floors. Out of range of RPG fire. The hotels had become famous during the early days of the war by TV news crews reporting live from the balconies and garden during the air strikes by the coalition aircraft on Baghdad. It was now a known place where western journalists and contractors stayed, although it was not always the safest place to hang out. We dropped our gear in the rooms. I made my way down to the CNN office. Some of the lads there were expecting me, it was good to be in good company. I had a coffee with the boys from AKA security. A British private security company made up of mostly former SAS, I gave them the run down on the maps of what was going on in the north of the country and names and contacts, of safe locations and military bases to stay. I was introduced to Jane, the new head of the CNN office. We had spoken on the phone a few times when I had phoned Ibriham, who was my contact. I had helped them and their security team get out of some sticky situations. After touching base with the CNN team, I walked around the garden and phoned Sammy on my Sat-Phone my security contact in Amman, I advised him that I would be there the next night. We arranged an RV point at the border and he advised me on where to drop my jeep in the free zone close to the Syrian side of the border security. I also phoned Paul, I told him my timings and gave him an update, a time and place was set for the meeting, down town Beirut two days from now. he gave me the update on the al-Madina bank investigation. After about an hour one of the CNN camera crew came over to me and invited me up to one of their rooms, there was a farewell party about to start, one of their team was leaving the next afternoon. I told Paul to stay safe and I was looking forward to seeing him. I found Jane and told her about the party and to meet me up in the room when she was finished talking to the news crew. It was a funny night, beer and whisky, it was surreal, only when the sound of gunfire came from the open balcony did one remember where we were. The rest of the night was spent drinking and having drunken conversations, with the CNN team. It was a good wined down evening, we all needed it. The next morning Jane arranged with a bit of help from my CNN contacts to get a ride back to Lebanon. She was going to crash at her friends backpackers hotel off Monno Street, Beirut. I told her I was meeting up with some peopleand I would touch base with her when I got back to Lebanon in a few days' time. She parted with a big smile. I had breakfast with the CNN crew, "who looked worse for wear", wished them the best, I told them to drop me a line if they ever got into trouble. They liked the idea of having a guardian angel. They replied with don't be a stranger. I checked out the hotel, looking in the window of the souvenir shop, they were selling Iraqi wrist watches with the face of Saddam Hussein on them. They made me smile. I loaded up my Jeep and checked it over, I had parked it in a quiet corner of the secure car park. I quickly slipped my Arab robe over my cloths and placed my shamack on, I now looked like an Arab.

Lone drive through the Iraqi desert to Jordon.

"The sea knows no neighbours, the prince knows no friends"

I drove alone, dressed as anArab, white robe andshamackfrom Baghdad to Jordon, all westerners travel in groups or in convoys, a lone male dressed as an Arab, would not drew any attention; "risky but affective".From the Palestine Hotel Baghdad, down the Airport Road, I proceeded quite slowly, with alternating bursts of speed as I negotiated "ambush alley" AKA "IED gauntlet run", which went on for about seven miles, you never knew when you might get hit with a bust of gun fire from an insurgents A-47 or if you were unlucky, someone would shoot a "RPG", Rocket Propelled Grenade, over your vehicle's bonnet. I navigated "ambush alley" successfully and arrived on the out skirts of al Fallujah. This was hostile in every sense of the word. It was named the most dangerous place on earth by Time Magazine, I hoped my Arab dress would throw any insurgents off at a glance from trying to stop me. "It would have been very interesting if they had"; I had 12 full magazines, a lot of rounds, my rounds could move faster than any al-Qa'dia could run. Lady luck was with me, I cruised the al Fallujah highway without any trouble I past the bridge in the distance that insurgents had hung the dead and mutilated bodies of a Western, American security team after they had been ambushed and killed.

FALLUJA, Iraq, March - Four Americans working for a security company were ambushed and killed Wednesday and an enraged mob then jubilantly dragged the burned bodies through the streets of downtown Falluja, hanging at least two corpses from a bridge over the Euphrates River.

Less than 15 miles away, in the same area of the increasingly violent Sunni Triangle, five American soldiers were killed when a roadside bomb ripped through their armoured personnel carrier.

The violence was one of the most brutal outbursts of anti-American rage since the war in Iraq began more than a year ago. And the steadily deteriorating situation in the Falluja area, a centre of anti-American hostility west of Baghdad, has become so precarious that no American or Iraqi forces responded to the attack against the civilians, who worked for a North Carolina firm. American officials said the civilians were travelling in two sport utility vehicles although some witnesses in Falluja said there were four. ``Two got away; two got trapped,'' said Muhammad Furhan, a taxi driver. It is not clear what the four Americans were doing in Falluja or where they were going. But just as they were passing a strip of stationery stores and kebab shops around 10:30 a.m., masked gunmen jumped into the street and blasted their vehicles with assault rifles. Witnesses said the civilians did not shoot back.

This tragic situation was a reminder of just how dangerous being on the ground had become in Iraq...

I continued past al Habbaniyahand Ar Ramadi, before turning left passed Al Muhammadi "airfield" and on the Jordon Road. I cruised down the dusty highway. On this part of the road it is straight, you can see all around you for about 10-15km.I breathed a sigh of relief, I had ran the gauntlet and I was alive, many people had been killed on this strip of highway. I noticed H1 and H2, the airfields off in the distance. The golden sands of the open desert reflecting in the midday sun, were a welcome sight to my eyes after the dome and gloom and grey shades of Baghdad, Two hours later I was passing though al Rutbah and H3, highway strip. I pulled over of the road behind some sand dunes to stretch my legs, I was only about 100km short of the Iraqi, Jordon border.

The Bedu

The desert has a comfort of its' own; its' silence is truly golden and its environments are the most rugged, but beautiful I have ever come across. I walked to the top of one of the sand dunes, keeping my jeep in sight at all times, I sat down on the sand, my AK-47 by my side. The surface of the sand was hot from the sun, but just under the surface was cool, a slight wind was blowing the sand over the crest of the dune,I looked out over the barrenlandscape, some bedu, "nomads", were camped in the distance, I thought back to my time I had spent with the Bedu along the Saudi, Iraq border, not far from where I was now sat. Another Gentleman who inspired me was Wilfred Thesiger and his book Arabian Sands, he had spent time in southern Iraq and also Kurdistan. He had lived among the bedu for some years, and was classed as one of them. Their nomad life allowed the bedu few possessions, everything not a necessity was an encumbrance. The cloths in which they stood their weapons and saddlery, a few pots and waterskins, water containers, goat-hair shelters, were all they owned.Those and the animals whose welfare regulated their every move and for whose sake they cheerfully suffered every hardship. Arrogant, individualistic and intensely proud, they never willingly accepted any man as their master, and would rather die than to be shamed. The most democratic of people. They lived a very basic simple life and were proud of it. To be "bedu", is not an easy choice, very few from the west could even contemplate what sort of life and existence this is and even fewer could manage to live among them. The very thought of this hard, peaceful and basic life had appealed to me, I made a promise to myself, I would return and spend time with these proud people again one day. God willing. I continued my drive to the border of Jordon, I stopped close to a ravine, about 10km short of the border, it was isolated, no one around, I quickly buried the AK-47, assault rifle and the magazines, ammunition taking the bullets out and placing them in an air tight bag, this was to save the springs in the magazines and help to protect the ammunition. I took the GPS location and made a note of it. Then I made my way back onto the highway and on to the border crossing point. After the normal run-around of the border posts, "always give yourself a good two hours to cross and clear these places", I was on route to Amman.

"The land border crossing point between Jordan and Iraq"

The land border crossing point between Jordan and Iraq is a life line for trade between both countries. In the future it would be closed for many years with the rise of ISIS."Iraq's main international border crossing with Jordan and a key trade route, officially reopened Wednesday after being officially closed for three years due to ISIS. Privately-owned U.S. security firms, along with Iraqi ground and air forces, will be responsible for safety along the 500-kilometer route from Baghdad to Amman, which goes through Iraq's Anbar province".Iraq and Saudi Arabia would also reopen their land border, which had been closed since 1990.

There is only one main road from the Jordan/Iraqi (**Highway 10** is the northernmost East-West highway in Jordan. It starts at Karameh Border Crossing, from Freeway 1 on Iraq's border in the east and ends at Shuna al-Shomaliya with a junction with Highway 65 in the west after passing through Mafraq and Irbid.) It's long and straight, good for travelling, I made up alot of time even with all the military and police check points. Driving along this highway has always beena lot safer that driving across Iraq, but even so, you have to still be switched on at all times. The reality is that there is nowhere safe for a Westerner in the Middle-East, anyone who states anything else is both a fool and naive, or works for the British FCO! I was heading for the Jordan Syria border crossing point and a safe place to store my jeep. No one would ever think of looking there for me given my history with the Syrian Government and their Head of Intelligence...

Dusk and the night was closing in fast when I pulled into the Free Zone on the Jordan, Syrian border. The Free Zone is just past the Jordan check point and border crossing, it's a no man's land between the two countries. A very unlikely place for anyone to place a jeep. With Arabic plates it would just blend in with the other cars. I dropped the jeep off, one of my Lebanese contacts could pick it up at a later date. I started to walk back to the Jordan side of the border area. Sammy had been observing me from the cover of a Jordan military building, he pulled out at speed towards me in his BMW M5 with diplomatic plates. In a cloud of dust, Sammy skidded sideways towards me stopping a couple of feet away and opened the door with perfect timing... Hello my friend, I just smiled at him, Sammy always knew how to make an entrance... I quickly threw my day sack into the back seat and sat in the front. In a cloud of dust we were off, driving past the border guards with a wave and smile, one happed to be his brother! Sammy flicked open the glove box, a Glock 19 and two loaded mags were ready for me, Sammy said I thought you would like that. Sammy knew I never liked being unarmed anywhere in the Middle-East. I knew Sammy from the old days, Jordanian Intelligence and we had worked closely with Israel Intelligence.**(The Israeli Intelligence Community is made up of Aman (military intelligence), Mossad (overseas intelligence) and Shin Bet (internal security)**back in the day against Hezbollah in

Lebanon. We had worked on sensitive Tasks together so I trusted him with my life. He was forever trying to recruit me... but I was happy always helping him out as a friend. Anyway the door swings both ways. Sammy had an urgent Task for me to complete for him, it was a favour, "One photograph". How Dangerous or difficult could one Photograph be... In true Anth Style it would turn out to be epic... Sammy drove into Amman and to his home. We spent that night drinking Arabic coffee and eating kebabs. We talked for hours catching up and laughing at some of the situations we had found ourselves in during past adventures... Sammy was a lot older than me but an old dog when it came to operating across the Middle-East, even so his beautiful wife always told me to keep him out of trouble and bring him home safe! I slept well that night in the company and safety of friends. The next morning over breakfast Sammy gave me an airplane ticket to Lebanon. The flight left in two hours Sammy knew I wanted to get back ASAP. He drove me to the airport and escorted me through security. We said our goodbyes and with a handshake I boarded the plane.

Return to Lebanon

It was a bright sunny Saturday morning in Beirut, I walked alone the streets of downtown and along Hamra Street, "before the devastating civil war in Lebanon, Hamra Street was the shopping street to be seen in, all the rich and famous shopped there. Stars had been fitted into the walkways Hollywood style. Beirut was back then the Las Vegas of the Middle East". Now it is a shadow of its former self. I was making my way to the Meridian Commodore Hotel to meet Paul D for our morning coffee and update. The journalists bar in the Meridian Commodore is famous for being the journalists hang out place in Beirut, Lebanon, during the Lebanese civil war. It still holds a lot of prestige to this day. The manager was a friend of mine, I often held meetings there. I was enjoying my coffee when my sat-phone rang, a friend of mine and intelligence contact in the US Military was on the other end, he asked where I was, I said Lebanon. "Unlucky", we got Saddam, I've sent you an e-mail. I walked over to the business suite and logged on. I opened the e-mail report.

Saddam Hussien Captured by Task Force 121, (the activity)

At ten minutes to 11 on the morning of Saturday 13 December 2003, "The Activity" got the tip-off they were waiting for. A new detainee, a member of Saddam's family, said he was hiding up in a farm in the village of al-Dawr, ten miles south of Tikrit. The farm was owned by one of the Iraqi dictator's former servants, a man called Qais al-Nameq. The Activity intelligence specialists downloaded satellite imagery of the area. There appeared to be two sets of buildings in the area indicated by the tip-off. Task force commanders codenamed them Wolverine 1 and Wolverine 2 and put together a plan to close down the whole area. At 2000 hours, all electricity supplies to the two farms were cut off plunging the area into darkness and 600 troops from the Raider Brigade of the 4th Infantry Division's 1st Brigade Combat Team moved in to seal it off. Once a tight outer perimeter was established, quarantining the two farms and any possible escape routes, around 40 shooters and intelligence operators from Delta and the Activity moved in. This time there were going to be no members of the SAS involved. The decree had come down from on high. The capture of Saddam Hussein had to be 100 per cent 'made in the USA'. As the US special operations troops combed the two farms, a CIA Predator loitered overhead, relaying back live infra-red video images to Task Force commanders watching back in CampSlayer. But there was no trace of 'Black List One'. Perhaps this was yet another false trail. The Activity interrogators went back to their man. Saddam was definitely there, he said. If they couldn't find him, they should look for an underground bunker, 'that's where he'll be'. The US special operations forces began a thorough search of the whole of the area. It led them to a small mud-brick building, little more than a hut, sandwiched between Wolverine 1 and Wolverine 2. Parked outside was a battered orange and white Toyota Corolla taxi. One man, armed with an AK-47 Kalashnikov rifle, tried to make a run for it and was detained. Another man was arrested inside the mud-brick house. It had just two rooms, a makeshift kitchen and a bedroom with new clothes, some of them still in their packaging, lying on the bed and underneath the bed, a green metal ammo box containing $750,000 in $100 bills. But there was no sign of Black List One. Then one of the US soldiers noticed a crack in the ground, alongside a dirty rug. He pulled the rug aside to expose a muddy piece of Styrofoam that appeared to be covering a hole in the ground. A Delta shooter readied a hand grenade, in case anyone in the hole started shooting at them. Another carefully lifted the Styrofoam lid and there underneath was a 6ft deep hole, its walls braced with pieces of wood. At the bottom it opened out into a wider cavity, barely high enough to crawl in but just long enough to let a man lie down, and there, flat out with a pistol stuck in his belt, was the unmistakable figure of the self-styled Lion of Babylon, aka Elvis. He was 'caught like a rat' in a trap, one US commander said. Wearing an unkempt white beard, Saddam looked shattered, almost as if he was too tired to carry on any more and was just glad that his nine months on the run were over. The former Iraqi dictator raised both hands in surrender and said: 'I am Saddam Hussein, I am the president of Iraq and I'm willing to negotiate.' One of the Delta operators looked down at him, trying to work out how this tired, shaken old man had imposed a reign of terror on the Iraqi people, and said, dismissively: 'President Bush sends his regards.' The capture of Saddam echoed around the world, on all news channels. It marked an important turning point, the insurgency in Iraqincrease in size tenfold, by this point the US and coalition forces where losing men every day and the numbers were increasing rapidly. IEDs, "improvised explosive device", car bombs, and suicide attacks where fast becoming a part of daily life in Iraq. The CIA had sent their best Saddam experts up from Baghdad and Balad (JSOC). One man above all would be assigned to ID and confirm that they really did have Saddam. This CIA agent had spent time at 101st D-Main and had compiled a list of highly detailed questions and answers that only the real Saddam would know. After questioning it was confirmed, Saddam had been captured. (See Photographs). I was gutted that I had not been there for the Capture of Saddam, I had come so close so many times...

Paul had arrived and was taking coffee by the time I got back to the journalist bar, he was contemplating about the news that Saddam had been caught, sipping on his coffee and lost in thought. We had a few days to put together a plan of action and arrange a detailed report for Adnan Abou Ayyash. Paul had been working hard on the meetings while I had been in Iraq, it was one of the longest investigations he had carried out and the most high profile and dangerous. People had been killed by the Syrian Secret Police in Lebanon trying to silence an investigation into the bank and any witnesses. After talking in length for afew hours, we arranged to meet up the next afternoon. I drove back to my sea front apartment in Biblus. I needed some quiet time to go through the notes and reports that Paul had compiled and I had a meeting with one of my trusted contacts in the Baka valley "the strong hold of the terrorist group Hezbollah" later that afternoon; he had something to show me.Jane called me, she was in Beirut, just round the corner from me. I thought there was time for a quick coffee. I told her to meet me at a coffee shop 5mins away.

I walked into the coffee shop and she was already there, she smiled and I gave her a big hug, we had made it out of Iraq in one piece and alive. She told me of her plans to head off and fly over State Side for a visit. I said great, she asked what my plans were, Jane always wanted to know what my plans were, "I never told her much", she could be trusted, but not with everything. "It was better she did not know everything, this was to protect her". I told her I was just hanging out, might take some time off. If she knew I was about to take over the Al Madina Bank investigation, for Adnan Abou Ayyash, this subject was all over the news in Lebanon and was the talking point over coffee all over the country, there was a chance she would stay if she was aware of the Task, as well as all the connections the Al-Madina Bank had tooand in Iraq.I told her to enjoy her time off and have a good time. I told her I hoped her photographs worked out ok for her in America. With a hand shake and a Stay Safe I wished her the best and a good journey. We parted with me saying "you never know our paths might meet again".

"Emotion after seeing so much death and destruction"

After my one hour car journey north I was outside my little one bedroom split level apartment, I had chosen the area to the north of Beirut because it was quiet and tranquil. I had decided to set up home here some time before, it was a bit rough but I liked it. The idea was to use it as anoccasional base to work out of. I had grown to like its location, I had flown here from Cyprus many times in the past, I had made it a home from home. My own personal space, that no one else knew about. It was furnished with all the trimmings of my travels in the Middle East and Africa. Persian rugs laid on the tiled floor, colourful embroiled blankets laid over the back of the chairs, enlarged photographs of some of the places I had travalled were hung on the walls, there was an old wooden sea chest in the corner of the lounge area with a selection of water pipes, from Turkey,Syria, Saudi Arabia. A large array of books were piled up between two old wooden book ends. I had collected on route many books from every walk of life, History, Politics and Lebanese Cookery. Red silk was draped and hanged over the patio doors, which lead to the large balcony, the ocean was only 25meters away and the sunset view that filled the sky from the balcony was breath taking. "I had spent many a night sat there", enjoying the red wine of Lebanon, it was strange, this was one of the only places that I could be at peace with myself. The relentless high tempo of operations in Iraq had taken its toll on me, I had witnessed too much death and destruction, no one person should see so much! The bodies of the children in the slaughter house in Mosul still haunted me. Everyone who knows me thinks I am just ice cold with little emotion, even mercenary at times. That is so wrong, I lock away my emotions so no one can see them, I see it as a sign of weakness if people see me as being soft, as a team leader people follow strength. At the end of the day I am human and just a man... **That night I put on a CD Shakira, Estoy Aqui and left the music playing in the background...**

I opened a bottle of red wine and sat watching the beautiful sunset from my balcony overlooking the ocean. The tears rolled down my face as I remembered all the people I had met and known that had been killed in Iraq, the number was growing weekly. Another friend had been killed that day in Northern Iraq. The children I had seen slaughtered by the Iraqi insurgents were a major sore point for me, why kill young children... I drank my wine contemplating life... Sometimes a person needs to let out their emotions to find a balance and be able to move forward...

I poured another glass of wine and moved back to the balcony, I started to read over the files of the Al Madina Bank. Adnan Abou Ayyash has written a document stating all that had happened, from his side of this and point of view. Paul had complied with my contacts an comprehensive report, with files of documents and information. The files also included a list of all the details of the luxury yachts that had been brought by the al-Madina bank, as well as a comprehensive, list of other assets. (See Email) This list cover several countries, giving locations of HVT#, assets, black bank accounts. There was also a colourcopy of Adnan Abou Ayyash's passport. Along with other personal information there was a file marked banks. Within this file was data and documents. Bankchecksfrom banks included, The British, "RBS", The Royal Bank of Scotland, HSBC, Midland Bank, and Barclays Bank, off shore, division.There was also the letter that I requested from Adnan, giving me total power over the investigation. The latter stated that I was the sole liaison between all governments and intelligence, with regard to Adnan Abou Ayyash, and the Bank of al-Madina, investigation. (See Document) All contact were to go through me. I also had the power to appoint other agencies and companies during the international investigation.Correspondence from the Arms companies in former Soviet bloc countries were also listed, as well as the Intel about the arms deals to Iraq that had gone through the bank.Names of informers in the Lebanese government and security services were also listed under sources.Warning bells were going off, if I was not careful I would find myself right in the middle of a political cover up by the Lebanon and Syrian government. They both had too much to lose if this was all to be made public.I contacted Paul, "who else has got copies of this information, there was a silence, only Paul and me, Adnan Abou Ayyash had been given some of the data but not all... Paul thought it best that I look and read through it before it went out to anyone else. We need to keep it that way, it would be dangerous to let these documents out at this stage.I anticipated that it would be along meeting with Paul that next afternoon and evening.The conversation ended with Paul and I went back to study the files on the al-Madina Bank.My phone rang again. It was my Hezbollah contact who wanted to show me something of interest in the Beeka valley (This was the little favour that Sammy in Jordan had asked me to do...) we arranged to meet in an hour on the main northern highway, at a prearranged meeting point. Curiosity was getting the better of me. I wondered what my source had.I splashed some water on my face then put the files and reports into my hidden safe, slipped my Glock 19 (with the serial number removed) into my shoulder holster, jacket on and spare mags in the pockets. I threw some kit including Nikon camera D100 with 300m VR lens and some night vision into my day sackand I headed out.

The Beeka valley. TerroristTraining Camps

An hour later I picked him up from the meeting point and he directed me to the beeka valley and up some dirt tracks. On route he briefed me on what and where we were going. "this did surprise me", he was taking me to an Iran backed military training camp, known international terrorist had spent time there, refreshing on their skills, IED's improvised explosive devises, car bombs, homemade mortars, the planning of many terrorist acts werebeing planned from this camp located in the east side of the valley. Everyone in the International Intelligence community knew that Iran was supporting and financingterrorist camps in Lebanon, this would be quite a substantial piece off Intel if I had the location of one of them. what got me thinking was that my Hezbollah contact was very reliable and had never let me down, when his young daughter had been very ill I had paid her hospital expenses, I always cultivated my Intelligence assets and contacts well, with this my trusted Grade "A" intelligence network had expanded across the Middle-East. I parked the car up by some deserted buildings and we walked for about 60 minutes. Then we slowly and carefully moved through some dense wood land, we sat just back in the dark tree line, observing through some laser range finders and American night visiona compound 100 feet below us. It was definitely a Military compound, some of the troops moving around were in Iranianclothing, from the look of the 30 or so men walking around the area, there were from Syria, Iraq, Iran, Saudi Arabia. I noticed a man in a western style suit, he was looking and holding a new AKS, machine gun that he had picked out of one of the green creates. This got my attention, he looked out of place, what caught my eye was that he look like he was Western European, I had heard that former KGB and former Russian Spetsnaz, "Russian's old counter part of the British SAS", had set up shop and were supplying arms to Hezbollah and other terrorist groups operating out of Lebanon. This just seem to back this Intel up. Some of the men in a group of eight sat outside a building being taught and instructed on how to use a heavy machinegun, of Russian origin. Some others were being shown around an RPG,"rocket Propelled Grenade". The preferred and weapon of choice of terrorists organisations of the Middle East.

Unbeknown to me at that time, I had just witnessesed the location of just one of the Hezbollah underground bunkers, that was full of American Money $, Iraqi Gold and containers containing Some of the Iraqi Battlefield Chemical Weapons that Russian Special Forces had smuggled out of Iraq just before the war, these were spred across several underground bunkers in Lebanon controled by Hezbollah!

I had seen enough, I did not what to be caught up in this area., people disappeared up here in these areas all the time. I quickly took some photographs, I always taped the flash down on my Cameras, just in case the flash went off at a bad times... I recorded the GPS location and we moved back through the woods slowly and quietly. On exiting the woods, we followed a dirt track down the valley and onto where I had parked the car. We talked when we were clear of the area, "is it good, is it what you have been looking for? Yes.There are more camps to the north...I thanked him and dropped him off 400m from the pickup point. I had looked after this contact and his family in the past, when they were in trouble I always helped them, when many others did not, this was his way of saying thank you. When I got back to my apartment it was late, I put all I had seen into a report adding a few photographs and sent it off to Sammy in Jordan and my CIA contact. I knew that there would be some people very interested in this. If Israel did not send in an airstrike I would be very surprised. They sent fast jets at low level across Lebanon all the time taking out targets... I spent the rest of the night going through and reading all the files of the Madina Bank, the more I read the deeper the scandal went. The heads of the Lebanese and Syrian intelligence agencies where implicated. As well as several prominent people from other countries. Even British high street banks where named. I woke up at 10.00am the next morning, it was the latest I had slept in in along time, my time in Iraq had taken it out of me, my body was starting to recover now. After a quick 45min run alone the sea front, showered and booted and suited, I was on my way to Beirut, the drive in is between 45mins and an hour. "if you can drive in and around Beirut you can drive anywhere in the world". It's a cross between "bumper cars, and dodgems", it's that bad...I made it to the meeting place with time to spare, I parked up outside the coffee shop, which was situated on Mono Street. Mono Street is the main night life street in Beirut, it has over thirty bars clubs and restaurants, it is the major hub of where the young people come to enjoy the night life and discos western style with the Middle East influence. On a hot bright star lit night, there's nowhere that can compare to it. The craziness of the night is replaced by the calm slow movement of little coffee shops during the day. I was taking coffee and smoking water pipe when Paul turned up. He smiled at me and commented "You're more Arab then Western now", I laughed, he was not the first person I knew, that had commented on my ability to blend in, go native, my fondness of the Arab culture and way of life was no secret. I always said you have to live amongst your enemy's people in their towns, lands and cities to get to know how your enemy thinks and only then... will you be able to anticipate your enemy's actions and moves! We sat down outside at one of the tables overlooking the street, I asked Paul what his plans were, personal and business, he told me that he was focused on the Bank of Madina project. I commented, you do know what you're getting into, he nodded his head, ok, I will back your play, what do you need?He told me his plan. It was good and well thought out and put together, he had been spending a lot of time on it while I had been in Iraq. He asked what I thought, I asked one simple question. "Did or was Adnan abou Ayyash involved in all the illegal activity in the bank and was he guilty of being involved in the arms deals to Saddam and Iraq, breaking UN sanctions?" I was told no. "Ok", so you think he is innocent. "yes". Set up a meet I want to meet and speak to Adnan face to face, I want to look him in the eyes when I ask him questions, ok, Paul said, making a note to book flights and update Adnan on my plans and dates to see him in person. We started going through the list of assets of the bank, over 40 new top of the range luxury cars, BMW, Mercedes. Houses, villas and penthouse apartments, ten luxury yachts, the list went on...Paul was now putting me in charge of finding and retrieving the assets. Another area was bank accounts, there were a lot of them, in several countries, including Britain, France, and the US. Some big named banks were named. I had some experience in tracing data and information and my contact base and intelligence network was strong in this subject area, I made the phone call and my contacts started to move on the data I required. They asked me to give them a few days to put together a file for me on the different areas I needed data on. Paul had to go and meet another contact, who was handing information over to us, his contacts name was "Akram", he had been a financial controller at the bank of Madina, he had important documents that proved where a lot of the money had gone to from the Madina bank. He also had documents that incriminated senor members of the Lebanese government. I told Paul that I would be back at my hotel and he should come and see me later after his meeting. Paul was happy in going to the meeting alone he and Akram had been in contact for some time. I finished my water pipe, rapping the pipe around the glass stem, took my last mouthful of Arabic coffee and made my way to the hotel I had booked in down town Beirut. It was 1400hrs, when there was a knock at my door. No one but Paul knew I was staying there, it seemed strange. I checked the windows all seemed ok outside, I looked through the peep hole, there was a well-dressed lone Lebanese man standing in the hallway, his hands were empty. I opened the door, He spoke in good English, I had been summoned to the security general's office. The man was a Lebanese secret service agent. There was a car waiting for me down stars. I though what the hell did these people want, there was nothing wrong that I was aware of. I phoned Paul, his phone did not have a signal, I left a message of my sit-rep, "situation report", with him. You never go away with any security services or secret police without telling someone. "People are killed and disappear without trace while in custody" in Lebanon.

Caught up in the al-Madina Bank Investigation

At this time the political situation in Lebanon had gone totally pear shaped, all involved in the Al Madina bank investigation were being taken away and questioned, if not arrested. The security forces had searched my apartment, and found maps, these were civilian maps, along with some note books, I always kept all my sensitive material in a safe place. The Lebanese security service wanted my lap-top, they were not impressed when I told then no I do not have one. Remember in Lebanon there are no human rights, they can hold you for months without a court case or answers.

I was arrested and put into a holding cell. I was lucky, when Paul got back to his hotel he was woken up by 20 armed men with AK-47s breaking down his door and dragging him away to a dark cell. Three days later I arranged to smuggle out a message to the British Embassy, to inform them that I was being held without charge. Within a day an Embassy representative, Nicole, came to see me. I knew Nicole from the meetings I had at the British Embassy and meeting up after work for drinks at the bars down town. This was a serious turn for the worst. The embassy had been informed that I had upset the manager of a hotel, "total crap". I found out later that the person pulling the strings on my arrest was The Head of Syrian intelligence... bugger me, it was his payback time...

I was to be moved to the notorious Roamey Jail situated in the mountains overlooking Beirut. Which was also surrounded by the Lebanese Special Forces HQs. I was held without trial for three months, and then to be held for another four months on top of that, only bribery and corruption got me out, just in the nick of time. I called on my Hezbollah contact to help me and find out what the hell was going on, I ask him to clear out my secret large floor safe and keep all the contents secure (luckily all my files, expensive kit, military maps and weapons had been in my safe when my place had been searched). As they tried to keep me locked up for another 12 months. The Bomb shell. The mighty British consulate, cannot get involved to get me released, **Britain was breaking human rights of Lebanon's nations in the UK...So the powers at "B" could not put political pressure on the Lebanese government, or should I say the Syrian government, these were and still are the governing force in Lebanon, the Lebanese Government are just puppets of the Syrian government.** They do what they are told to by their Syrian masters...

My gut instinct was telling me that I was proper fucked, when I was being transported by escorts armed with AK-47s, from the holding block up the short drive "20min" to Roamey prison. The lack of power over anything and everything was bewildering, it was the first time I had been handcuffed in my life. I tried to stay calm, I needed to be sharp and switched on at all time here, I could not afford for my emotions to get the better of me. I was minutes away from one of the most dangerous prisons in the world, people died here on a daily basis. And the torturestories of Roamey made Saddam look like a pussy cat.The van stopped, the inside of the van was dark, I was handcuffed to a railing inside with five other men.I had seen all the prison movies when I was a kid, now I was in the heart of one. The movie that kept in my mind was "midnight express", but this was no movie.

The Notorious Roamy Prison Beirut

"My home is dark, the heart of my garden and the desert is dark,

….every corner of this ruined city is black.

The sky is tired; the sun has given up.

Like a prison cell, the travelling moon is dark." Quhar Ausi, Darkness (Tareeq), 1990

Unbeknown to anyone else, I had several intelligence contacts/assets already in this prison and other prisons around Lebanon. I had found that keeping tabs on who was in the prisons had led to some good intelligence. These contacts had helped and would help again in the future to stop terrorist attacks on British and American off duty soldiers in Cyprus. One thing was for sure, this next part of my life was going to be emotional... This was going to be a bit of first hand intelligence collection. The van suddenly stopped and the heavy metal doors swung open. A rough group of guards in blue military uniforms holding AK-47s came forward and dragged the first man out of the van, they throw him onto the ground and started to laugh, the rest of us walked out and lined up against a grey bullet riddled wall. Our hands were still handcuffed. The bright sun was beating down on us. From being in the confines of the dark van to suddenly being in bright sunlight it took a few minutes to be able to focus properly. I stepped off to one side, taking a moment for my eyes to adjust, observing my surroundings.

I was stood in a small compound, with high walls covered in rusty razor wire and groups of armed guards all around, a watch tower with a search light and a heavy belt feed machine gun was to my left. "I had entered the lion's den".The block to my left was littered with cloths and towels hanging out of the cell windows. The prisoners were banging and shouting, from within, "fresh meat", we were made to strip naked. (Thank fuck, I did not have a British Parachute Regiment Tattoo, that would have gotten me killed in a heartbeat in this lawless place...) the guards searched all the clothes and personal belongings, they ripped and cut apart all the shoes, taking the heals from all of them, all belts where removed, watches and rings, went into the guards pockets, wallets were put into a bag and sealed, the guards opened them later.Clothing and jackets where cut and inner liners checked. My clothes looked like I had just be attacked by a wild animal. The man next to me turned his back on me, his back was covered with whip marks and lacerations. The guards had whipped and tortured him with a metal whip, I looked down the line of naked bodies; all of them had serious bruising and marks of torture. A guard came over to me and handed me my cloths. "You Britannia", I answered "yes." He walked off. There was a chair next to a door. One at a time the guards took one of the men over and an inmate, barber, "butcher" gave them a shaved head. When it came to my turn I said no, for some reason they never gave me a second look, just moved onto the next one. Next we were all made to write our names and put a thumb print into a book. Then we were taken to a holding cell, I was there for three days without seeing day light, it was a small room with 15 of us in there, it would have been made to house maybe five. It had a hole in the ground in the corner, that was the toilet. There was no running water and nowhere to wash. There was three old rotten bug infested mattresses stood up against the yellow dirty walls. We all just sat there not knowing what was going to happen next. Food for three days was old bread and a small tub of nasty yogurt. Three days later we were taken outside and hose piped down, "washed", with ice cold water. Then we were put into small groups and taken into the main prison blocks, the smell of disinfectant was over powering. I was taken into the "big room" 120 men were located here. It had been built for 20 men, it was small, not an inch of space, there was no furniture, just a pile of old green army mattresses in the corner and plastic bags hanging from string around the outside of the room, these contained the men's worldly possessions. A large Syrian man stood up, punching a man next to him in the head as he rose, he was "Abou Salam", the leader of the room, he was an animal. The men were huddled in their little groups talking amongst themselves, I was one of three that had been put in this room. Abou Salam, pointed to the other two men I was with, both of who were from Sudan, he motioned them over to him, when they were in range he slapped both of them hard around the head "so they knew their place". They were then moved and told to sit down and be quiet at the back of the room. Abou Salam looked at me, rubbing his chin, he looked me up and down, I moved over to him slowly, putting my hand out and greeting him in Classic Arabic "As-salamu alaykum", he shook my hand, he smiled, then kicked one of the other men out the way and asked me to sit down. John came into the room from the corridor, John was an old Lebanese man whose English was good. He sat with us, he asked what I was in for, I answered I am not quite sure, you don't need a reason for being in here, the Lebanese and Syrian government put people in jail without just cause, they don't need a reason. John asked if I was English, I said no, I'mScottish, "ah like the whisky", John smiled, I thought it better that the word got out that I was Scottish, not English, I know that there were members of Al Q in this jail, I found out later that there were over 50 terrorists here, even the terrorist who blew up the US embassy. I was the only westerner that they had seen. I had to try and cover my ass. If Al Q found out who I was, I would be killed in a heart beat. Britain and the US were not well liked in this part of the world. "Given the chance a lot of people would kill a westerner if they thought that they would get away with it". We sat around talking for awhile with John, he told me what the score was in side. It's like anywhere, there are unwritten rules, the difference in here was if you don't follow them you will end up with a home-made "blade" in you as you slept. After afew hours Samone called out, it was rolecall the guards came into the room, everyone was lined up and counted in view of the guards. As soon as they were finished and happy that no one had tried to escape, food was brought out. Some of the families had managed to get some food to the men inside the prison. 30min later, Abou Salam shouted to the group of men in the corner of the room it was obvious that he was the Alpha male in this grouping, best to keep him on side, he could come in handy in the future as an asset. The other prisoners started to pass out the green mattress, they covered the floor space. If someone wanted the toilet, they had to ask permission. Most the men in the room were living in fear of getting a beating. If they made too much noise they would also receive a beating. It was a very violentenvironment where only the strong would survive! It was obvious that only people who had money or could fight could do what they wanted in here. I was just trying to keep my head down, I had not eaten anything but bread for three days, John brought me an apple and some bottled water, it was a gift. I ate it and sat in the corner watching and observing everyone in the room and the way they moved around, profiling in my head everyone in this room. There was a pecking order, a chain of command. The first night I was with the minions, we all slept top to toe on our sides, there was not even any spare room to lay on your back. The smell of 120 sweating bodies was unreal, not the most pleasant of nights. The next morning about 0600am Abou Salam, woke everyone up by kicking and shouting at them. I stoodup and moved to a corner, while the rest of the men put the mattresses in a pile in the corner. I walked out into the corridor, which ran down the side of the block, the main door entrance, the only entrance/exit, "way out" of our room, was still locked. John was sitting on his bed, the senior men in the room slept in the corridor. Samon was the gate keeper, he held the key to the room. John called me over, "do you take coffee?"I answered "That would be great".He pulled out a plastic cup and an electric element, with two wires at the end. John stuck the two wires into a very old electric socket and placed the element into the plastic cup, holding the element as so not to melt the plastic. John smiled, this is the only, electric in this place. "We don't have access to a kitchen or anything like that, we are only allowed to have a handful of these elements in each room". John added some Lebanese coffee to the water, he said this is coffee roomy style. We sat on a rolled up mattress, he asked me "How was my first night?" I answered "Interesting". I sat talking to john for a few hours, the only clock was an old clock on the wall opposite the main door to our room, I could see it through the bars of the door. Abou Salam came into the corridor, he came over and sat next to us, he smiled, Johnsaid you meet Abou

Salam, ya, Abou Salam could not speak much English, I shook his hair on his head, just to break the ice. He laughed and did the same to me. He walk off back into the room.Johntold me I was ok. Abou Salam classed you as an equal. That's quite rare. He likes you. He's trying to figure you out. John smiled and said I was doing the right thing, keeping my head down and assessing my new environment. I told Johnyou can tell a lot about a person from their eyes, he agreed, John is an old wise Lebanese man who is respected by all the inmates, even the guards. He would be a good person to tell me how things worked around here. An old man with his hair combed back came out of a side door into the corridor, everyone stood up as he passed, he looked at me as he passed, John said good morning to him, Samon unlocked the door, and let him out. When he was out of ear shot John told me that was Evon. He is the head prisoner and he runs the inside of the prison. He has that small side room, it's like the VIP room for inmates.It was a Wednesday, lock down day, no one was allowed out of the room. John explained to me, that the room was allowed out two times a week for an hour a time. They keep us caged up in here like animals. The big thing in the room and though the prison was routine. The entire place had a routine set in stone. This was the perfect place to put someone to keep them quiet for a period of time.There was absolutely no way to communicate with the outside world, I asked John what people did in here, there's nothing to do, boredom can kill you as much as torture or a knife. Privileged people used to have access to a gym and library, "not many books init though".

"All was stopped when the terrorists "Al Q" rioted last year. "They took over large areas of the prison for awhile, mobile phones were found and explosives, knifes and a list of all the Catholics in the prison, their plan was to kill all the Catholics and escape".

Now only they have access to things like the gym and library.The prison General is scared of them, prison guards have been killed outside the prison because they upset them in here. John looked at me, keep away from them, you're the only westerner in here and they are very dangerous. I nodded to John, thanks for the warning. It was just after 1400hrs in the afternoon, when a guard came to the door and shouted my name, John looked at me, you must have a visitor. Samon opened the door and I was shown to a long room with wire mesh and reinforced glass down one side of it, I walked down towards the bottom of the long room, it was the Embassy people, Nicole Smith the British vice consultant, she did not look pleased. She pointed at a telephone at the side, I picked it up, she asked if I was ok, I said I'm alright, what was going on, she told me that she had been given the run around of where I was and where I had been taken.OK so why am I here, we are working on that one, they're saying it's got something to do with a hotel.Ok , what. We don't know yet, we're working on it. The Lebanese are being very secretive about a lot of things to do with you.. (I toyed with the idea of dropping the fact I was tired up in the Bank of Madian investigation but I decided against telling her, 60 other people had been arrested and the senior level of my real involvement was not well known at that point). I asked why can't the British government pull some strings and get me out. They can't get directly involved, why not I'm British. It'sdangerous for me in here, there's Al Q cells and known terrorists in here. Nicole was shocked when I told her this, I looked in disbelief, she did not have any idea what this place was like or what was going on inside. I told her my situation, she asked about food, I said what food, the only food is the pot of slop that comes in ona daily bases, it has cockroaches in it. And I'm in a room of over 120 men, with two toilets, four cold water tapes, with running water two hours a day, if we're lucky. I also told her that there where maggots in the drinking water, so you could not drink it. She looked at me again in disbelief. I shook my head at her, the British government had no idea what was going on in here. I told her that there was a lot I have seen, I can't tell you in here, it would cause me problems. She said she would get back to me as soon as she found something out, that might be in a week's time, Lebanon's legal system was slow. Ok, I said, can you get me some food. She said yes, she said she would get to a shop and send me in some suppliers, I told her to go to the little market stall outside the main entrance to the prison, John had told me about it. I thanked her for coming. She put the phone down, and walked out. It must have been a doubtingexperience for her, I could tell that she had never experienced anything like the lion's den before. As she walked out into the court yard I could hear the inmates upstairs banging and shouting abuse out the windows to Nicole. "I thought she won't be back in a hurry". I had to keep the fact I was involved with the bank of Madina investigation a secret in here. The whole prison was awash with people talking about it... I had to sit tight and wait for the Saudi's to start pulling some strings behind the scenes - that was also a fact I had to keep from the British Embassy due to the fact the Brits would be pissed that a British guy was heading up an investigation that would implicate British banks... Were the Brits responsible for putting me in here? I had heard of the way the Brits, MI6 had put people in the fridge/prison in the past to keep them quiet. I knew a list of names that this had happened to, even members of the SAS had been disowned by the British Government and left to rot in a Saudi prison when a covert operation had gone wrong... (The Saudi Government would give me the run down on this at a later date, I would just act shocked when I was told). I walked out of the visitor's room, Samon opened the gate, I went back in to the corridor and sat next to John, he looked at me, any news, I looked at him no, the British Embassy has no idea what is going on. John said don't worry, they know where you are now, all will be well, god willing. Samon lifted a piece of black material of a plastic stool, I had to double take, an old colour TV, Johnsaid the reception is bad, but at night its watch able. He smiled, "god bless small mercies". He cheered me up alittle. There was a bang on the gate, Samon opened it up to speak to one of the guards, he cameback in with a plastic bag full of food, a cooked skinny chicken, garlic, "tome", bottled water, "mi" and some tomatoes, "panadora". The Embassy staff had kept to her word and somehow got some food and water in to me, I looked at John tonight we eat like kings, I gave the food to John to store, he had acquired some containers. I got into a routine with John and Samon, every day at 1700hrs we would eat our dinner, sometimes we did not even have a lot just tomatoes, "panadora" and a glass of bottled water, but it helped break up the monotony and the boredom. Sometimes when one of us was lucky and someone brought us food in from outside we ate like kings on salad and a little chicken. Coffee was kept for the mornings and if we had a little extra we would treat ourselves on a night time. I treaded water for three days, just blending in to this new hell I found myself in, when I got a surprise. I was sat in the room talking to the boys from Sudan, when a familiar face walked in. I was stunned, it was Paul. What a bomb shell. He did not see me. He was greeted by Abou Salam and told to put his bag into the corner. He looked like hell, lost and bewildered. I stood up and went over to him. He turned around, "fuck me", he had never seemed so pleased to see me, we sat down and he told me what had happened to him. He had been arrested on the same day as me, the only difference was 20 guys with AK-47s kicked down his hotel door and dragged him away. They had held him in an holding cell somewhere in Beirut. He told me that the rats were massive in the cells he had been in. All he was asked was what is your involvement with the Al-Madina Bank and Adnan Abou Ayyash. Paul informed me that an arrest warrant had been issued for Adnan Abou Ayyash by the Lebanese court. The lid was about to come off the case and we were caught right in the middle of it. John came in, he sat with us, I introduced Paul to him, I spent the next few hours briefing Paul on how things were ran in here. He asked had I been in touch with the British Embassy, I told him what had happened when Nicole had come that afternoon, I told Paul that The Embassy might not even know that he was here. Paul shook his head. I warned him that this Task he was doing with the Madina Bank was very sensitive and political. He agreed, well no point in crying over spilled milk, let's just focus on staying alive right now, we arranged that we slept next to each other at the side of the room, in our own little space,(We could watch each other's back) it cost me a chicken leg for Abou Salam. We were getting by one day at atime. If we had not been former military and able to adapt to any environment and situation we would have been totally fucked. I had slept in worse places. A normal person from the west would not have lasted two minutes in this barbaric hell hole. Paul told me alittle of the situation that had transpired when he had been first arrested.

Paul had been thrown into Jounieh police station cell (8th Feb) a rat infested, 4metrs x 3mtrs cell with an old dirty mattress on concrete floor. No windows solid metal door small 6inch x 8 inch opening in door.

Large fan with a single light bulb ventilates the room making it very cold. That afternoon the power was cut for about one hour, so dark you cannot see your hand in front of your face. (This was the start of constant power stoppages for several hours at a time making it impossible to know the time of day). My watch had been taken away together with my passport and backup wallet.... Id been given the heads up by a contact they were coming for me, so I hid my hardware, information, wallet & ID in a safe place. My heart rate started to rise and claustrophobia (my biggest fear) started to engulf me, but I knew this was not going to be a short term problem so I slowly got my composure and very slowly managed my claustrophobic fear.

The toilet was a hole in the floor, piss and shit scattered all around it and the stench was very strong it almost made me puke. (This was the only type of toilet I would use for the next 152 days). I soon learnt to take of my shoes one at a time take off my trousers one leg after each shoe, put one shoe back on then repeat for the second shoe and trouser leg. Take off trousers and sling around neck and shoulders while squatting to shit. If this ritual wasn't done then your trousers got covered in whatever was dumped on the floor..... but no water to clean so the undies are sacrificed as dunny paper.

Several hours passed and I was taken out of the cell and interviewed by the police colonel. It was made clear to me the brother of Rana Koleilat, Basil and several others who I was familiar with were handing big rolls of Lebanese cash to the guards..... so it looks like this is going to take some big money to play this game! The whole bloody situation was all about Goverment curruption and dirty money!

The colonel was smoking a big fat cigar and sat in a big chair looking down at me on the other side of his desk.... He said "take your hands out of your pockets when I'm taking to you" I was not afraid and said "well now you're talking to me I'll take my hands out "he said "do you believe in God", I answered "Yes", he said "In Gods name trust me and it will be alright".

Like fuck I was about to trust this man....

He asked if I had met with Dr Adnan, I answered Yes, he then asked how much money I had been paid by the Dr ! I told him the truth I had not received any money from the Dr or anyone associated with him.

He asked me if I had ever threatened Basil Koleilat, I told the truth 'No I had not' and thought what a very odd question. I had met with him at the rouge café they owned and had only said hello and goodbye, he didn't speak English and I didn't speak Arabic well enough to hold a conversation.

He then asked if I speak Arabic I said "NO apart from Hello, thank you, how are you and a few numbers" He asked me to speak Arabic so I did these basic words an numbers, He said it was quite good and then asked "if I knew any important people in Lebanon" ..... although I did I said "NO"

This routine of being locked in the cell with constant power cuts (some lasting many long hours in total darkness where you can't see your hand in front of your face) and interviews (interrogation) with the colonel continued for four days , but my answers were consistent despite feeling the effects of a scramble brain from the sleep manipulation of not knowing the time or day.

Food and water was sent by some Lebanese friends, but it was scarce so I was very hungry and thirsty.

Suddenly I was taken from this cell hand cuffed and loaded into a police car. This took me to Beirut court house prison; it was raining and very cold. One Guard in the car said he had my phone and wallet and for twenty dollars he would let me use my phone to send text a message. I paid and got my phone, quickly I sent out text messages to contacts (coded of course) help request would be activated. I had to hand my phone back he was scared of being caught.

Arrived Beirut and put into a reasonably clean cell 3 metres x 4 metres with thirteen men. No mattress to sleep on, it was a long uncomfortable night.

Next day (day 7) transferred to Baabda prison, hand cuffed I arrived and was led down two steep sets of stairs underground to the cells, the stench was horrific actually sickening….. Very vile and putrid as I got closer to the cells. Put into a cell with 38 men, a room 5 metres by 4 metres. A half meter open window the length of the cell covered with steel mesh at the top of the room, where you can see the feet of people walking past on the street above. Two holes in the floor with doors for the toilets.

All those eyes focus on me as the cuffs are removed I am thrown in the Lions den! Its very crowded but I'm thrown a foam matrass, so I find a small spot and squeeze between bodies and get my head down for a much needed sleep.

Next day had a visit from embassy (the text message had done its work people knew where I was) but the lady explained for now their hands were tied and they couldn't interfere. Interfere with! I haven't committed any crime! I should be released immediately. Its Guilty here in Lebanon until proven innocent, that's if you get the chance to get to court or what I'd learnt from many in this cell especially those French Embassy workers accused of issuing visas for $1000 each….. just pay/bribe your way out of jail. She said she would have a lawyer contact me. It would be weeks before I was allowed to speak with a lawyer.

This was camp for 4 days…. It was disgusting conditions; the smell disappeared because my nostrils had become accustom to the stench. The room filled with cigarette smoke from early hours of the morning as soon as people woke up and only cleared when the exhaust fan was turned on for a few minutes every few hours. I don't smoke so it was hard to breath with the air thick with smoke. At least there was a water tap to fill small buckets (like little buckets kids take to the beach) and take them in to have a wash after the visit to the toilet hole…. There's no toilet paper, it would block up the hole in the floor anyway. Problem was the tap dripped 24 hours day, it was torcher and hard to sleep.

Food was served from large 1.0 metre diameter aluminium pots scooped up in plastic buckets onto plastic bags on the cell floor. Lebanese flat bread then used to scoop a serving from the plastic bag.

Today its green beans & rice, in the process of serving one plastic bucket is dropped onto the cell floor…. The rice is scooped up by hands and put onto the plastic bag. I will not be eating again today.

It's the lack of water I'm concerned about; I cannot drink the tap water like the others do. I will get sick. I had asked the Embassy for water and food, but nothing has eventuated.

I'm told many more stories by the men there being held in here for weeks, some even months for minor crimes without seeing lawyers or a judge. … and they don't have any money to pay for help.!

A group of Egyptian men held here because they had no valid visa find comfort in playing drums on cardboard boxes and tin cans the really get a good rhythm of Arabic music and singing happening every evening long into the night, until the guards shout and make them stop.

I was taken out of the cell up to a room with a man dressed in a suit, this is judge Fauzzi Adnan a hard faced man, but gently spoken and made me feel comfortable. At his side sat a young lady she introduced herself as a court reporter.

I was asked questions by the judge similar to the previous questions by the colonel in Jounieh. They really wanted to know if I'd been paid money by 'The Dr'. I could only answer the truth… I had not.

She spoke and said this man is a fair and honest judge and I have nothing to fear, the judge offered me a chocolate which I took and he asked if there was anything I could do for me, I asked him to contact my lawyer, he looked into my eyes and said I can see your upset, I'm sure a tear came into my eyes and he offered me a tissue and said I was a strong brave man not to cry under such conditions.

When the questions finished the lady asked how I was being treated, when I told her of the conditions she was shocked. They both said they would try and get me transferred to Roumieh prison the main jail with some better amenities…. Little did I know they weren't much better.

The judge left the room and she told me she was shocked when I had told her of the conditions I was enduring. She said she would try and get me transferred and she would send me some toiletries.

Maybe our contacts were working behind the scenes!

As I returned to the cell I saw a woman in handcuffs, the last two cells were full of women. I would have preferred to watch them dancing to the musical drums, but I'm in for another night of drums and singing with men dancing in the men's quarters !….. as I descended into the dungeons of hell I noticed the smell and stench had returned, I must have smelled just as bad !

The next day she kept her word and a package arrived in the cell, in it was a bar of soap, shampoo, tooth brush, tooth paste, a comb and a towel in a bag. I was very grateful, but there wasn't any room or running water to wash my body.

I had been at this place for three days, the next day I'm transferred to Roumieh prison.

I'm loaded into a prison van with my bags. Waiting to be transported several prisoners are beaten by the police for not obeying their orders and staying in a straight line.

Being processed at Roumieh was very unpleasant. All the men were strip searched! Naked with all holes and cavities checked in front of me. Everyone had their hair shaved off, when they came for me, I protested and refused to allow my head to be shaved or stripped naked. A friendly English voice, actually Australian asked the guards to not shave my head and let me through without stripping. CGG was an Australian inmate and became a major rock of support and help…. A few others tried to object and protest, but were just pushed forward, stripped and shaved. I guess I'm already known for something in here!

My shoe laces had already been taken in Jounieh, but I had chewed them in half hidden half of the laces in my jacket hood lining. I hope they don't confiscate them. The soles of my shoes were taken apart and a metal bar taken out…. obviously been shivs made this way before.

My laces were not discovered so I put them into my shoes the first chance I got. I had lost weight and my trousers were falling off as my belt had been taken, so I rolled the top of my trousers to make them tighter.

Roumieh prison east of Beirut is second to none when it comes to the sheer horror it invokes in every Lebanese person's heart, guilty or not. This sprawling prison complex housed behind a thick, stone, barbed wire topped wall just north of Beirut is one of the biggest in the Middle East. It was holding 4500 inmates. On average Roumieh holds more than 5500 prisoners at a time, but has a capacity of only 1,500. With rumours/reports of Lebanese prison guards beating prisoners, burning the genitals of an inmate, major drug use and prisoners governing themselves, not out of an inherent fear of authority and punishment, but due to the fact state and security control ends at the door.

In Roumieh the stronger prisoners have the power and are in control. The rules and norms are governed by the prisoners themselves. These 'Boss' prisoners are in full control of the prison. A group of prisoners (selected thugs) who are appointed by the security administration. Most of the time they are the ones who create problems.

What happens inside is not under surveillance. This allows the flourishing of black market industries like the drug trade, everything is denied in the prison, but that does not stop the underground market from booming. Money, unsurprisingly, provides a potent tool of power. A financially well-off prisoner has more wiggle room, and can buy whatever he needs in a world where the main currency is cigarettes.

The weaker prisoners can be sexually exploited, and are dubbed aranib (rabbits) by the other prisoners. Others are known as khadam (servants), who clean the rooms and clothes of stronger prisoners, prepare and bring food to them, and generally do their bidding. The servants are sometimes paid in cigarettes, or are provided cover by their masters.

Generally, building A is for those who are formally convicted and are serving out the last of their prison sentences. Building C known colloquially as the "Building of the Poor" holds minors and the weakest prison population, while building B holds the main prison population. It is famed for being the location in which prisoners linked to external forces have the most control, and thus the best infrastructure, but a corrupt, brutal hard place.

I was herded into the exercise yard and immediately saw the horrific sight of four levels of steel bared windows with clothing hanging from every possible opening, hundreds of eyes looking at the new arrivals. Huge high walls on all sides patrolled by guards on the top holding AK47 guns.

I can see life in this prison is going to be like being in a real jungle and I would soon learn the sharawishe are the strongmen who govern the prison halls. They are selected based on how long they have been serving time inside, or on their ability to garner respect either through violence or fear. Most of the sharawishe naturally exploit other prisoners to further their own interests, and only a few attempt to protect the weak.

In places like these "Knowledge is power". If you know nothing when you come in, you are in trouble. If the prisoner has been there a long time or is simply returning, they've got an advantage.

I was a newbie to this, but I had to show no weakness or I would be a target.

I was taken up steel stairs and put into a cell one old prisoner directing the guards where we are to go, they spoke Arabic and I heard the conversation and the name Brahim Abou Ayyash…. I recognised the similarity, he looked like the Dr….Yes it was Dr Adnans brother. I looked at him and he said in English "do you know who I am" I said "No never seen you before" he said "good you don't want to fucking know me" I replied "fuck you" (show no weakness) and continued walking.

I was put into a cigarette smoke filled cell 4 metres x 3 metres with 10 men inside, a couple I recognised from Beirut jail. I grabbed a mattress and grabbed a spot next to the open window to breathe some air. Suddenly the door opened and a fat man in a black beanie hat shouts in English "so you don't recognise me hey", he pulled of the beanie hat and said "I'm Brahim Abou Ayyash, why are you getting my brother into trouble, those bastard Koleilats stole his money and him and his son stole mine" I said "I'm please to meet you, I'm sorry for your money problems, but I know fuck all about them. I've met your brother and I had agreed to help him by getting qualified people to manage some of his business. Now…. I'm a friend of your brother and trying to help him " I don't know anything about causing him problems, and I haven't received any money from him, which is the question everyone seems to keep asking me."

With that he said "hmmm ok, is there anything you need" I replied no not for now thanks, I'm fine".

Maybe I should have been scared, but I wasn't .

Suddenly my name is called through a hole in the door, it's a fresh faced young man who gave me the phone number of the Embassy and said call them tomorrow. Suddenly the door opened and the

guards gave me a bag containing 4 toilet roles, a thermal T shirt and long johns and a pair of socks. The guard said these are from Brahim Abou Ayyash anything else you need just ask.

I said "tell Brahim thank you very much".

I put on the clothes and bunked down for a sleep.

Next morning I'm moved through the jail down a huge 20 metre diameter spiral stair case.

Moved into another crowded room with disgusting toilet holes, this had a black and white TV with 95 % Arabic programs, but it's better than the Egyptian drummers. I saw the guard who brought the clothes from Brahim , so I asked if he could ask Brahim for some food and water. Soon after he delivered two tins of sardines and a tin of tuna and a bottle of water. Paid my tax of one tin to the room bosses Samir who is very dirty with rotting teeth and Rodger (a Christian) who turns out to be a good guy, they gave me some bread to make sandwiches.

My letter which was smuggled out had hit its mark, got some money, regular supplies of food and water and new clothes.

Chicken, ham, cheese, tomatoes, fruit and now buying full boxes of Mars bars and Twix from the buy up shop. Mars bars are good currency for getting favours and special treatment. Although I don't smoke I would also buy cigarettes, they were good currency for trading favours.

Still no sign of my medication I had ordered.! I go on a mission to get it. Trying to get to the doctor without an appointment is difficult, I spent a couple of hours locked in overcrowded rooms of sick people. Some screaming in pain and being transported on hospital beds from room to room.

Eventually I had to start shouting and demanding to see the doctor and demanding my medication that I had paid for! I didn't get to see the doctor, but they relayed the message to him.

I made my way back to Anth in the room, I'd been there for a short time when they handed me some of my medication. It had been taxed ! half the bottle of cough syrup had been taken. I gave it to Anth, but there was no anti-biotic which I had ordered with a script from the prison doctor.

I had requested a pen/pencil and paper to be brought in as I wanted to start to draw things, an old hobby of mine, but these are not allowed. We are only given enough paper to write a letter on and they count every page and take the pen back when it's finished. The letters have to go to be approved before they are sent out. I write several letters to friends and family and send them for approval, hoping they get sent.

Day 37. Its Terrorist Tuesday ! we aren't allowed outside until 3pm they get to use the yard all day and we watch them though the room windows.

We receive two BBQ chickens, Lebanese bread and other supplies. I strip the chicken clean down to the bones and go to throw the bones in the garbage bin, but I'm stoped by young guy Samir from the bosses room and asked if I would give them to him to make soup from the bones. I did this and it became a regular thing whenever we got BBQ chicken.

Watched TV, a very small screen and mainly Arabic shows, but tonight we got to watch … soccer! Lebanon got beaten by Japan….. yes! we supported japan, all the other foreign nationals supported Lebanon, maybe they were to afraid not to! The long term prisoners and guards find it hard to work us out, we are taking liberties, pushing boundaries and getting away with breaking lots of rules and regulations.

Day 45. We have been trying to spend as much time out side as possible and we are finding a lot of co-operation from inmates and guards obtaining information about the jail system and ways to make things better for us. Many Guards & police are asking to help them get out of Lebanon and give them work opportunities in the UK. Prison guards from the Internal Security Forces who are assigned Roumieh feel that they are sent there as a form of punishment, they see us as a way out and they are saying we are very important people in here because we get special treatment. We are given lots of information on the Terrorists up stairs; we start to look deeper into this!

Getting back to the room a young man from the boss's room starts to celebrate because he is being released the next day. He says the first thing he will do is have a fuck, he starts thrusting his pelvis and makes a hand gesture to move a long tail (some kind of animal tail) up and to the side so he can thrust his pelvis further in. It was funny and I said " looks like you've done that a few times before" suddenly the room boss got offended and stood in front of my face with his two fists in the boxing position and said "You are an English sharmuta (slut) and a goat fucker"…….. This man had been getting more and more aggressive with me, I think it was because we were starting to get too many privileges and becoming too important and he saw this as a threat to his position. I couldn't let this pass making me look week, so I gave him two quick left jabs slaps with my flat hand to his right cheek and followed with a right hook slap to the left side of his head and this pushed him to the ground. I stood ready in a boxing stance ready for him to get up and have a go at me, he looked up at me and said   " looks like you've done that a few times before, I was only joking" and with that he stood up held his hand out to shake my hand. We shook hands he said "so every things ok no need for any more fighting". We've witnessed a couple of arguments turn into a group fight and they all fight by wild slapping and pushing, nobody seems to know how to fight or do any kind of boxing or martial arts.

 I return to the big room and have a lie down on my mattress and read my book Vince Flynn 'Memorial Day', a couple of minutes later the young guy who's leaving tomorrow tells me he took no offence from what I said and he found it funny. He handed me a green diary and a pen and said he knows I had been asking for paper and pencil to draw pictures, it was his diary he had been given as a privilege because he had been in prison for 3 years.

He gave me his details and asks could I contact him when I got out… It seemed everyone wanted to get out of Lebanon.   I started to make drawings from some of the old magazines and books we were allowed to read and some pictures from my memory…. And some wish full thinking, but the drawings were all in ink pen as I did not have a pencil. I had drawn a picture of Jesus and when Samone saw it he asked me to draw one for him, I did and he hung it on the wall above his head. Samone was a long term prisoner who was one of the privileged he slept in the hallway at the entrance first spot at the steel bared gates and had the responsibility of letting people in or out of the cell.

I started to get prisoners bring paper and ask me to draw pictures of their loved ones (from pictures they had), some asked for portraits, some asked me to use these pictures and add them into the portrait, so I obliged. I found these people opened up with lots of information about the activities going on in this jail. I started to draw portraits of men just going about their business, and this gave me the opportunity to draw people who were outside in the yard, even on Tuesdays!. I would make sketches and sometimes I would get others to write their names and information on the sketch. Some of my sketches. Shown Below. I could also record other information in this book, I kept a diary of events and hid information in the daily details, being careful to word things discreetly so as not record anything to get me in trouble…… getting these drawings and book out with me would be difficult.

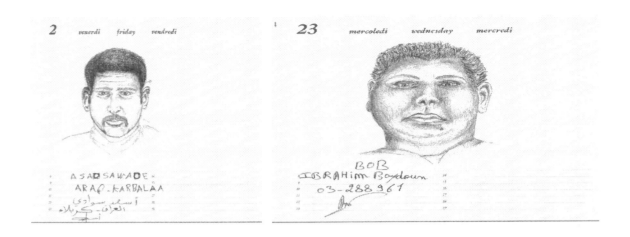

Started to piece together a disturbing picture of what's really happening in this jail especially with the Muslims on level three. Evidence of mobile phones, computers, internet connections were operating in this Islamist block and they are fully in control things, the third floor Islamist quarters are off limits and they enforced the rules of Islam with an iron fist…… however people were still willing to give information about this place, especially with the hope of getting our help and a few mars bars or cigarettes.

They seemed to have been left to run their own agenda and sometimes had visits daily for up to several hours at a time. It was rumoured they were controlling and directing business activities from inside this prison. In addition to the mobile phones and computers, there were flat-screen TVs, fridges, cookers, hot water units and these inmates received regular un checked food deliveries from the outside.

Day 155. After establishing our privileged status in the jail and getting to know the inside running of this place I finally got released, and I'm told there are no charges ! the jails General and head police

officer say they are sorry for what I have been put through….. There's are no amount of sorry that can compensate for being banged up for five months of incarceration in a living hell hole and enduring sub human conditions, but I accept the apology. Those guys are doing a job where they enforce conditions on inmates governed by a system of a corrupt government. They really don't want to be there!

Normally foreign prisoners are immediately deported after any prison sentence in Lebanon, I was not deported and in fact returned to Lebanon for several visits after this… yes I'm crazy, or was! don't ask me to go back there again the answer is NO.

Some prison inmates were moved from block B which allowed them to be dealt with but, the political situation in Lebanon, Syria and Israel restricted any direct movement on the activities being directed by Fatah al-Islam prisoners in Building B and they appeared to be untouchable.

Ten years would pass before all the Fatah al-Islam prisoners in Building B would be dealt with.

Lebanon's interior minister Nohad al-Machnouk confirmed Roumieh prison was an operations room for ISIS, the jail from which terror attacks have been directed. A suicide operation in the city of Tripoli was directed from inside the jail …..DIRECTLY from the third floor of Block B of Roumieh.

Although a politically sensitive issue, a plan to clean up the prison started in 2014. Only in January 2015 did security and the political establishment with the military and technical resources converge to tackle block B. General Zikra said it required a Special Forces team to do it with a raid later in March 2015 that exposed hundreds of mobile phones, computers, multiple Internet connections, video conferencing capabilities. Even satellite phones were found in Block B the 'Islamist block'. The block then housed 865 prisoners who were incarcerated on terrorism charges.

One of the evil serpent's terrorist main cells had been cut off at the head.

The Lebanese Government have no form of human rights, The Syrian Government, more to the point the Syrian security services have a hold of fear over the people, just the name of their HQ in Beirut makes the blood run cold in so many Lebanese people... The brutal stories of people being tortured are whispered in the backstreet coffee shops of down town. I thought a lot of this was just talk, I was very wrong, the amount of people that had been interrogated and tortured was very close to absolute. The cuts and burn marks that I personally witnessedon their bodies were horrific. Some of the worse were the burn marks after someone had been put through electric shock treatment. When one young boy came in I helped to tend his wounds, his back had 27 lacerations, each one cutting deep into his flesh and over 10inches long, he also had been whipped, with the guards metal whip. The so call Dr in the prison was off the scales, he had qualified, as a vet, he could work on animals, so the Lebanese government gave him a job as the prison Dr.... could only happen in Lebanon, he must have been the son of someone. Men died in the prison every week from conditions and diseases that in the west would not exist. Dehydration and malnutrition were common place.There was no segregation for crimes, killers, rapists, paedophiles, terrorists, drug lords, all were thrown in together. There where groups and gangs within the prison, some were Catholic, some were Muslim. Most groups had their own rooms and floors (including Hezbollah and Al-Qaeda). In here, life was cheapand compared to the west, there were no rules. I had just been through the nightmare of Iraq, with all the killing and bloodshed.I would be dammed if I was going to let a bunch of animals, "the Lebanese and Syria Security services,", get the better of me.That afternoon there was a voice through the bars of the window, he spoke in English, "how are you", I went over, it was a man called Abou, "little Bro", he asked were we ok, "ya", room service sucked. Have you settled in. The conversation went on for about an hour. He had been put in prison because someone had paid the police to put him in jail, just another example of how backwards and corrupt the Lebanese Government is. He was trying to get out, it was just a case of money, if he family could raise $50.000 he would be released. Abou had been here four years, he was one of the old hands around the place, he was also Hezbollah. Everyone respected him or, feared him, he always hit first and asked questions later, right from the first meet, I know we were going to get on well. To survive in a place, you have to have a certain kind of mentality, basically you need to be an animal, the rules and standards in the outside world did not mean anything in here.

Abou, told me he would get us a blue card, this would enable us to go out for an hour every morning, and afternoon. Abou had been here so long he was free to walk around the prison block as much as he wanted on any floor, the guards ran the outside of the prison, the cons ran the inside. Abou asked did we have food, not the slop "prison food", but real food. "I will send you some down". I put my hand through the bars of the window and said thank you. **"Our Hezbollah contacts had really came**

through for me, I felt bad that Israel had just air-striked the Hezbollah Terrorist training camp that I had given them the GSP location for... But thats life, Terrorist Attacks had been stopped!".

If you're going to survive in here you have to work as a team, what you have you share. Always look after the head of the room. Give him a little food, and joke with him, even if you don't want to. And always stand your ground, work as a team, a team is stronger together than any one man, regardless of the man. If you fight you all fight. If someone has ago, you all have ago back.You had to appear not to give a dame, even if you did. You had to appear strong at all times and in control, if you appeared weak, it was game over. I managed to borrow a book from one of the boys in the room, "Samarkand", I had already read it, it helped to pass the time, I told Paul to do the same.Today was Thursday, visitors day for the locals. Most of the people in the prison did not get visitors, but some did like clockwork, Paul had arranged for a contact to bring food up at regular intervals. We had no choice, we could not survive on the prison food, within the first week I had lost over a stone. And my health was going downhill. There was nothing I could do to stop it. Johns family had also visited him, he was happy, he had food. Pauls contact brought foodand news, the Al Madina bank scandal was totally up in the air, another thirty people had been arrested who were in any way connected to it. Paul told him to keep us informed and to double the amountsof food from now on,we gave him a list of things to buy and food was arranged to be dropped to us on Saturday, on the next visitors day.Paul had left a message with people to find me so I could get him out, he had found me alright, I was in with him. We had hired a top lawyer to work on getting us released, it was going to cost 10s of thousands to secure our release but what the hell, you cannot put a price on a man's freedom. Unbeknown to us at that time no amount of money could have got us released, the Madina Bank scandal was too incendiary and sensitive, it was also now implicating the Head of Syrian Intelligence...When food is left by visitors, there is a search team that go through the food, they rip and cut open everything, bread buns get to you after being searched in four or five pieces. Chickens are massacred with a knife. By this time the food gets to you, there's not much left and then there's the tax, food is taken by the people who search it. "I thought tax was bad in England".After visitor time me and Paul sat down and looked over our food, we didn't have enough for two of us for 2-3 days, we rationed it per day each, one mars bar, a piece of round Lebanese bread, a tomato, a very small cucumberand 1LT of bottled water. We had one very small skinny chicken, we ate this sharing some out, it was hot and we had nowhere to store food. We had three mars bars spare.We gave one to Abou Salam, John and Samom. Chocolate was a major luxury and it was worth its weight in gold.A small gift like that would go a long way. The mood in the room was ok, people were happy to get some food and contact from the outside world.Abou, Hezbollah, came down to see us at the window again, he had organised the blue cards for us they would be with us later on in the day. I offered him some food, he refused, telling me thank you but he did not expect anything. He said it was great to help a friend of a friend and was just nice to speak to people who were English. It was time for lock down, he said he would come and see us in the morning, if we had our cards by them, we could go for a walk in the yard. Samon came into the room and call my name, he waved two blue cards in the air, "you have powerful friends"... we had our passes to walk two hours a day. This was like gold dust, even Abou Salam, did not have one of these. The fact that we had these earned us 100 cool points all round, it put us right up there in the pecking order. And the fact that we had food and had passed it around, also meant a lot in certain people's eyes. I went out into the corridor to talk to John, he was sat trying to make out a program on the TV. I patted him on the back, you ok, he looked at me, as good as one can be in here. He was coming down after the day's high of having visitors. Everyone gets down when you're in a situation like this, it's up to the other people around you to pull you through. I asked John about the history of where he was from, I wanted to get his mind off the situation. It worked well, after 45 minutes, John jumped up, do you want coffee, "yes why not, it would be rude not to". He laughed, he poured the coffee, I cut a mars bar up into small pieces, using a plastic knife and offered it around people sitting around us. "chocolate and coffee" and good conversation, I could think of worse ways to spend the afternoon.I walked back into the room to find Paul asleep in the corner. I left him till 1700hrs when the guards came in to do the head count. After that the mattresses were laid down in routine and the lights went out at 1900hrs. The room was dead silent after that time, we could talk but only quietly. It was closing in dark outside, it was a bright starlit night, I could make the constellations of the stars out through the bars on the windows. The silence was shattered by piercing screams from within the prison. This was to become a nightly occurrence, "I found out the next morning that someone had been slashed with a razor across his face", I drifted off into a deep haunted sleep.The next morning I woke early, I walked through to the bath room, there was no one there yet, it smeltreally bad from people using it during the night, there was running water, quickly I washed, "haman" all over, I poured containers of ice cold water over me, it was cold but great to feel clean. I walked out the wash room, John was making the morning coffee, we grabbed a plastic cup full, I gave Paul a kick, and we used out blue cards to get outside into the yard, it was quiet, only a handful of people were in the yard. The sun was shining bright in the clear blue sky. We walked up and down the yard, my legs felt weak form the lack of exercise. I would grow accustomed to the yard, it was the only little bit of freedom we could have. The sun warmed my body, the heat of the sun on my face felt great and welcome.I looked for Abou, he was not here, I found out later that he had been up most the night playing cards. A lot of the old timers slept most of the dayand were up all the night. It helped them deal with the situation and environment that they were in.The Yard was about 50 meters by 50 meters, it was totally enclosed, by a 30 foot wall at one side anda 80 feet wall at the other, guards with machine guns on all sides, it was that tall it looked like a climbing wall, columns of rusting razor wire were covering every inch of the top of the walls. A watch tower was overlooking the yard, a guard was observing us below through the sight of his AK-47. We walked for an hour and then were called in. The room was very dark, gloomy and depressing, after being out in the sun light. "I never thought I would take the freedom of being able to walk out in the sun light for granted ever again".Being locked up is bad at any time, but it's your freedom and liberty that hits you the most. Not being able to pop out for coffee, or buy a newspaper. Or eat when you are hungry. The big thing for me was not being able to have a hot shower, with clean water. It's all the things you take for granted that you suddenly miss. The absolute lack of contact and communication with the outside world is the absolute killer. The feeling of being isolatedand alone, it can break a man down very quickly. (Unbeknown to me but this little situation was going to prepare me for something much worse and dangerous in the future). The most important thing to have in prison is a sense of humour and you need to keep your mind occupied, "reading, chess, talking about politics", anything, you need to keep you mind off where you are, when you start to think about where you are and the situation you are in, you go into bad depression". If you do this you are totally fucked, you lose your motivation and your health, mentally "physiology" and physically, spirals downhill very fast. When you lose the will to fight and you lose hope, the soul dies, I have seen men who lay down and died because they just lost hope... I swear I would never be one of those men. They would never break me no matter what they did to me. "soldier on no matter how bad it may seem". The Wilson and Phillips song, "hold on for one more day", came into my thoughts often.Time in prison has no meaning, only the Hezbollah and Al-Qaeda, terrorists are allowed to wear a watch, funny story... I was given a watch to wear by one of my contacts in the prison, they had cleared it with other people, that made a statement and also helped to protect me... Mornings and afternoons blend into one, only when it gets dark do you realise that another day has gone buy. Three days went by, when a prison guard came to see me. I had a visitor, I was escorted into the visiting area. Two female British Embassy staff were standing on the other side of the wire mesh fence, it wasNicole and her understudy. I picked up the intercom phone. She asked if I was alright, ya I'm ok, getting by, it's the usual question that visitors always ask, sometimes you want to tell them the truth. "which would be this is hell in here, get me the fuck out of here". But you can't, everyone tries to put on a brave face, you get the odd person who breaks down and cries when he has a visit, this is not a bad thing but it is a sign of weakness in the eyes of the Arabs. The Arabs like men to be men. Women are second class citizens to them. Nicole told me that I was being investigated, "in Lebanon this means, someone is paying to keep you inside". This situation is very political, it will take time to sort it out. There was no other news. She wanted to know if there was any family I wanted notified of my arrest. I said no, there was no point, I did not want to put them in the firing line, which they would have been if they had tried to help me. I thought it best to keep a low profile. I almost had a heart attack next, Nicole asked if I wanted to inform the British press to put pressure on the Lebanese Government to release me. I looked at her, no way, ever, if Al Q, found out who I was, former British military, I would be dead by morning. I told her this. Her face went white, she really had no idea of the dangers involved in this situation. I had no choice, but to sit tight and keep my head down. I had faith that my contacts would get me out quietly. Nicole had brought me some more food, one cooked chicken, tomatoes and two mars bars. She even thought that I was given three good meals a day by the prison! She was shocked when I put her right on this. She asked to see the cell where I was being kept, she was told "no", she was told to get a letter from the government and that would take time, many weeks. Even then it would have been blocked. Paul had a visit for a lawyer, intelligence friend, he had brought some food up for us both, the news was not good, he informed us that we had been caught up in the politics of the Al Madina bank and that he was trying all avenues to get us out. The lawyer had dealt with some high profile cases in the past and had even meet "Carlos the Jackal" on one off his trips to Beirut. Paul said we were in good hands. The fact that Adnan had lost 1.4 billion dollars was hard to comprehend. The fall out over this was global. The situation that we were in was not good, someone was pulling strings to keep us in jail... (I would find out the real name of the person responsible in the future). We had not even been charged with anything. There was not even any documents we could see to answer any of the many questions that we had. We were under investigation and that was it as far as the Lebanon/Syrian government was concerned. We started to get into a routine, there was nothing else to do, I used to have my afternoon walks with Abou, he filled me in on all the talk going around the prison. The Al Q, terrorists had taken an interest in me. "Not the best news I have ever had". The terrorist played football in the yard every afternoon, they had the run of the prison, even the prison guards were scared of them. I started to make contact with them, at first just greeting them in their own language and then talking about football. It's strange that theextremistswho would kill anyone from the West would like football. I needed an angle into them, something to break the ice. Football would be the way in, my thoughts were: if I'm not a stranger to them, I might survive in here. I remembered British history, the Scottish were fighting the English for many years. I had old Scottish heritage. I had to some way make sure everyone knew that I was Scotland not English. I had to time this right, it had to be subtle, I knew that the right time would come. The time fell into place when anquittance of the Al Q crew started having a go at me when I was sat alone in the yard one afternoon, he spat on me and called me an English dog, he tried to make himself look like the big man, there was only one answer to this, "within a second", a Glasgow kiss landed on his face and a well-placed upper cut under his jaw. He fell to the floor screaming, I had given him a broken nose and a bad jaw. I stood over him as he wailed in Arabic,his head in his hands covered in blood, in a pile at my feet. I kicked him so he rolled against the wall, I shouted Scottish, not English you infidel, my family had fought the English, "that's like saying whisky comes from England", switch on you Muppet, with a parting slap across the back of his head, I walked back into the block and my room. One of the Al Q group was sitting reading, outside, observing my actions. I found out later that he was a teacher of history, he was aware that the Scottish had fought the English, he passed what he had seen on to the rest of the Al Q cell. Abou told me later that I was ok, the word around the prison was that I was crazy. I never got called English again by anyone. I felt bad for having to make an example of him but I had no choice; it was the only way the Arabs in prison would accept me. "It's their mentality", they respect strength and at the end of the day he was a convicted terrorist so in my mind that was payback for a lot of my friends being killed by Al-Qaeda and insurgents in Iraq!John and Samone had their little routine going on, they lived for it, like everyone else in the prison, their every moment was organised around routine.The next morning after everyone had been kicked and slapped out of bed by Abou Salam, in groups of four they were sent into the toilets to wash, he gave a squirt of shaving foam, into the men's hand in turn and the razors being used to shave were the orange bic, one razor between 10+ men, the idea of shearing a razor between ten other men was not an option for me, HIV and other blood infections were rife in the prison. I answered to Abou Salam, "no way, me and Paul would use the razors" . It would be like hacking your face off with a blunt razor and a splash of cold water. No way.This was the first time I really upset the apple cart in the prison. The rule was that everyone shaved twice a week. "everyone", I said give me a new razor and I would do it. I got called into the guards office, after much shouting and fist banging on the table, it was agreed that twice a week I could use the barbers office to shave, the guard office also guaranteed me a new razor every time. This was a luxury, but a necessaryone, the thought of getting HIV did not appeal to me. I knew that the guard shouting at me was Hezbollah so after him shouting to save face with the other guards, I knew that it would be sorted. It also cost me afew packs of cigarettes each week but it was worth it, I got Paul in on it to. The little barber office was a very small room off the yard, it had one chair and a mirror, it had a sink, but no running water, to shave I had to take a bottle of water in with me. It was a meeting place where the prisoners who were running things would meet on a morning and take coffee and talk about what was going on. I would use this place to meet my contacts in the future, there was a rumour that Al-Qaeda was planning attacks on American and British off duty personnel in Cyprus, I was perfectly placed to find out details and relay them back to my contacts outside and help stop the attacks and save lives, the attacks were being

250

planned from inside this prison! I was sat reading in my room, I had my own little area within the room now, we were even allowed to have a mattress down on the floor during the day, this cost me food to Abou Salam every week. In prison the only money and currency is food and cigarettes, if you need anything it has to be traded with these. There was a knock at the window, Abou had come down, he had heard that I had thrown my "toys out of the cot" when they had tried to make me shave in the morning, he laughed. It was not a bad thing, the guards understood that I would not take any crap from them. He arranged for me and Paul to come out into the yard for a walk, you never talk too much in the room. Too many ears and it's known that the prison guards bully other prisoners into telling them what's going on the inside of the prison. As I walked out I recognised a young boy sat with his top off outside with his back to the sun. He was silent, we went over to him, he looked up at me-his eyes were eyes of pain, tears rolled down his cheeks. I looked at his back, it was red raw from being whipped, there were over twenty inch long lacerations all over his back, the wounds were still fresh and bleeding every time he moved, he had been whipped with the metal whip. He was trying to dry up the wounds by sitting in the sun. I put my hand carefully on his shoulder even Abou was moved by the sight of this young boy in so much pain. The Security Services "Syrian", had come last night and taken him away for interrogation. I thought what animals could have done this. This was not an uncommon event, if it was not the whip it was the chicken, "they put a piece of wood under your arms and then hang you up off the floor; this is painful on the joints. They would throw in a beating for good measure. Their other party trick was hand cuffing your hands behind your back and tying your feet to a chair, beating the soils of your feet until they bleed. You could always tell who this had happened to, they could not walk for over a week. People had to carry them around. I saw burn marks from electric cattle prods on a lot of the prisoner's bodies, I had seen these kinds of torture used by terrorists and Governments in Africa many times. When the world comes around to realising that Lebanon and Syria have no human rights then things might change, until then people are being tortured on a daily bases in these countries. The British Government in the words of the Vice consulate, "cannot get involved, Britain is breaking the human rights of Lebanese nationals in the UK... so they cannot interfere in their human rights in Lebanon". This was news to me, there had been no reports of Lebanese being mistreated in the UK, or was the British Government doing things behind the scenes again... I had this confirmed at a later date by my MI6 contact! I got called inside by one of the guards, the British Embassy was here to see me again. I was taken into the visitors room. It was Nicole Smith, the vice consulate again with herfriend. I picked up theintercom. "How's it going, are you ok?""I'm hanging in there. Any news?" She informed me that her contacts within the Lebanese government had informed her off the record that I was being held because there was a hotel bill that needed to be cleared, it was the one I had been picked up from, so no time at that time to pay that small amount. ok I said, I will get someone to call in and deal with that today, but why did they pick me up in the first place...there also trying to press charges on you for treason, "what" where the fuck did that come from. "Your name has come up within political circles, the al-Madina bank". Nicole asked what I was doing in Iraq and Syria, "Travelling" I said. It was not her place to know.She said whoever it is keeping you in here is very powerful, they must have Syrian connections... She said that she had been given the run around, by the Lebanese Government. And no one was giving her straight answers. In these situations the official line from the British Embassy is that they cannot get involved in the legal system in a country which they are guest in, especially one like Lebanon under Syrian influence in which the tit for tat childish games between the two countries had been on the boil for some time. Every time Lebanon was upset with the way the BritishGovernment representatives had complained to them about something, they would change the visa requirements and regulations for British people coming into Lebanon, this was done quietlyover 24hrs as to cause maximum disruption. It worked very well. On just one occasion three plane loads of British citizens had flown into Beirut from London on a BA, British Airways scheduled flight. They were not allowed into the country without obtaining a visa first from the Lebanese Embassy in London. For the past six months visas could be obtained at the Airport on arrival. This incident caused chaos, over 180 people had to be flown back to the UK. It was obvious that the Lebanese Government did not respect or follow a high degree of professionalism. This was to become even more apparent when the Government and heads of the Lebanese Intelligence were implicated and named in the al-Madina bank scandal. I went back to the room. I briefed Paul up on what I had just been told. He looked shocked, he ask so what are the British government doing, I looked at him, from the sounds of it nothing. Paul was in the same predicament thatI was, nothing either of us could do. What would normally take a day to do in the real world, when you're locked up with no secure means of getting out takes forever. We needed a plan. The people who were scared of us blowing the whole al-Madina bank scandal open had managed to get us all out of the way for the time being - over 100 in prison. Adnan Abou Ayyash was also being summoned to Lebanon, they wanted to put him in jail as well, they had already issued an arrest warrant for him. He was safe though, the Saudi Royal family would not let anything happen to him.Paul had been told by the lawyer that he was being investigated and they was no way of him being released. They can hold you for 6-12 months while they investigate. Paul had a sense of melt down and brain failure when he was told this, whatever happened to evidence, just process, justice. The answer to that was easy, "you're in Lebanon now". There are no real laws or justice. At this point key people who were involved in the al-Madina bank were being killed in mysterious car bombs and accidents. Others had just gone missing never to be seen again. The Lebanese government was not doing anything about these topics and disappearances and were not even investigating who was behind them..? It was clear that I and Paul were a threat to the people trying to cover up the illegal dealings of the bank. That was why we were in here, regardless of what excuses they might come out with. Good bloody job no one has gotten a copy of the letter from the chairman of the Bank naming me as the Head of the Investigation. If they had I would have just been marched straight outside and shot by Syrian firing squad. When you're locked up and have no control over any part of your life, it slowly grinds you down. The room, no privacy at all, having to ration food and drinking water. Watching your back all the time. It's like living on the edge of a knife 24/7. There was a loud banging on the gate the prison food had just arrived. Some of the inmates from Sudan and the poorer countries had no choice but to eat the prison food, many were ill after eating it. They had no plates, cups or utensils; they had to put the food in plastic bags and use their hands eat to what they could. It was like watching animals eat. After the first few weeks I managed to obtain a few paper plates and a piece of card two feet by two feet, "table". We even managed to get hold of plastic cups, the only way of staying sane in a place like this was to keep as civilised as possible. From the sound of it we might be in here for awhile... I decided to make the most of it, I put together a routine with set timings, for training, Arabic lessons, reading, journal time, one of the terrorists had acquired a chess set. I even arranged to watch or hear the television so I could keep up to speed on current events and world news. My basic day was as below. If I didn't rock the boat and get put into solitary confinement, "the cooler" or the hole (this was a room three foot by three foot, no window and no light, this was hell itself. Only prison food allowed and no visitors). I was determined to use my time in here constructively.

Prison Routine

0600   Room wakes up

0700   Training outside, 500 press-ups and 400 sit-ups, walking and running for 30min

0800   Wash with bowl of water, training shorts washed at same time

0830   Coffee with John, listen to news on Arabic news channels

1000   Arabic lesson with my Armenian school teacher

1200   Lunch, an apple and cup of water

1300   Reading, Arab history and politics

1500   Walk in the yard with Abou, get updates, play chess with Al-Qaeda members

1600   Dinner, rice, fruit, dates etc.

1700   Prison guards count all prisoners, lock down

1800   Reading books

1900   Light out, any noise after lights out resulted in a bad beating or whipping.

This was my normal day and routine, visitors, lawyers, Embassy staff, slipped in whenever they came. There where fights every day in the room and prison, some were quite bad, bodies being carried out in body bags with blood dripping from them...Others were funny. Arabs cannot fight or box properly, they slap, "handbags at ten passes". A good right, they go down, every time. The big fights with ten or more were normally in the yard, these ended in blood and snot everywhere, old scores, grudges and blood feuds were settled in public. It was either a razor blade across the face or throat, or a cup of scolding water in the face. I would class this as a hostile environment. After a big fight the whole prison would be locked down for a few days, visiting days were cancelled.

Because I had flexed my arms in giving an inmate a battering, he tried bullying a young defenceless boy. The inmateI found out later was a paedophile.People knew better then to play around with me or Paul, being known as a little crazy would not hurt in here. The rules I had been brought up with did not apply in here - this place was survival of the fittest. When someone in the room died, they were just carried out and put on the floor outside the gated entrance to the room. We had bets who was going to die next, you could always tell, it was the men who had lost hope, some people had been in here for years without being to court, some of the African men had been waiting to be deported back to their country after serving their time.It was not uncommon for a person to be put in here and his paper work had been lost; "if you're in here for 12 months and you have not been charged or been to court, and they lose your paper work and you don't have a lot of money to get a good lawyer", now that is a mind fuck. The hygiene conditions within the prison were horrendous, pretty much everyone had "bugs" little animals in their clothing, they bit you all over; these were very painful. Trying to keep your clothes clean with nothing to wash them with was an impossible task. On a hot day the smell of "BO", from some prisoners made you want to throw up.

I had started to influence the politics of the room, it was more relaxed, I was joking around a lot with Abou Salam and keeping him in agood mood most the time, the beatings of the younger men in the room had reduced a lot, disciplinehad started to set in. The men in the room could see it was better for them, they were treated like men not animals, John commented on this. We even had a vote on a Thursday night, film night, we could not hear it but we could watch a film, sometimes even in English or Arabic. A show of hands would indicate which film was shown that night. Abou Salam was also well looked after by the men who had Lebanese family visiting, they would give him a chocolate bar, they were leaning how to work the environment to theiradvantage. It was all about making life liveable in this hell of an environment.I even got given some food from the young ones in the room for sticking up for them. I felt sorry for some of them they couldn't even stick up for themselves, never mind stand up for themselves. Abou had arranged for an Ice box, "plastic cooler box" to be sent down to the room, a contact in the prison could get fresh ice every other day. This was the only way to store food because of the heat of the days.Somehow he also managed to get hold of some books in English to read, these were like gold dust.What a result. This wouldn't mean anything to anyone back in the real world, but in here, they meant everything. After afew more days I was able to walk onto different floors Abou had arranged it. I had started to move around and be seen with the group of prisoners who ran the inside of the prison.All it took was a nod of the head and a gate to another floor was opened.Abou had arranged for me to walk different floors, this was the first time I had seen the rest of the prisoners, in the block. The terrorists from Al Qaeda and Hezbollah had the run of the place, they even had metal beds and mattresses. I took coffee with Abou in his room, we talked about afull range of things, from politics to the al-Madina bank. He gave me the run down on who was in the prison and who to look out for. After two hours it was time to move back to my room, on the way down I stopped at the window, Abou was on the top floor, you could see trees from here, it was the first time I had seen greenery since my arrest, the trees seemed a life time away. **A Lebanese man stood next to be. I know who he was, he was one of the leaders of the group that had blown up the US Embassy, in Beirut. He was in bits metal plates and polls running down the outside of his legs, he had been caught by the Lebanese security services and they had interrogated the hell out of him, smashing his legs and arms with iron bars, his body was badly scarred. We stood there chatting for awhile. I joked with him, light hearted conversation, when really inside I wanted to rip this guy's head off. This was a terrorist an extremist, a very dangerous man. I was called by one of the guards, "time". I parted with, look after yourself and we can talk some other time.**

Site of the former American Embassy in Beruit Lebanon blowen up by Terrorists

It was hard to understand these people, they looked normal, just like anyone else in the Middle East, but this was also hiding the monsters that lay beneath the surface. Regardless what anyone might say, any westerner, regardless of who he was or what training he may have had would find time in the lion's den, a living hell. You have to literally turn into an animal to survive. How there had not been an outbreak of plague or some other fatal diseases was unknown or it could be that the guards keep things like that quiet and covered it up.I went back to my room, I was getting bitten by mosquito's and bugs badly again, the ones that were flying around the room were fat and full of blood, they had been feeding on the men in the room again, I clapped my hands killing one, it splattered in the palms of my hands, it was full of blood. I put on some antiseptic, it was the only thing that kept the little fuckers from biting you to death and spreading disease. After a few hours I could walk in the yard for an hour, the blue pass Abou had arranged for me to have access was a god send, it stopped me from going mad, from being caged up all day. I would never take for granted all the things in the west and back home people take for granted, clean drinking water, food, being able to walk outside to get a newspaper. Even the British Embassy could not arrange such a simple thing as getting me permission to have an hour outside aday. I walk up and down the yard alone thinking things through, I was counting the bullet holes in the wall, I lost count, this was where the firing squad executed the prisoners. The wooden post was standing alone, full of holes and blood stained, the surrounding area on the floor was also stained deep red.The guards would bring the prisoners out that had been sentenced to death, tie them to the post and shoot them. Because they used high powered rifles the bullets would rip through the man's flesh and hit the wall behind. All the barred windows on the east side of the block overlooked this part of the inner yard. It was an eerie and chilling place. It made me think of what the conditions would have been like in the Nazi concentration camps of the second world war. Roamy had that smell of death and loss of hope coming from it. I thought of how the hell could I of ended up in here. "I swear a blood oath on payback to the person responsible".

I went back inside, Paul was feeling down, I joked around with him to pick him up a little, I told him don't let the bastards get you down. I gave him half of my last apple, he smiled. "When we get out of here, we will eat and drink for England". I spend the rest of the afternoon reading, trying to take my mind off where I was. My name was called that night over the loud speaker system on the inside of the prison.

My name had been called out with ten other people, I was being taken to court in the morning, this seemed to be good, at least I would find out what was going on. Paul was still up in the air, we made a promise to each other, the first one out fights till the other is out. A hand shake and oath was given. Next morning 0600hrs, I was up. I had no decent clean clothes to wear, I put a T-shirt on and a pair of black trousers, that were now grey. I washed the best I could and went out to the yard to walk until I was called. Paul was up and wishing me luck in court. I thought that the British Embassy would be there in court, the Embassy had to be good for something... I was called with the other men, and we were striped and searched, chained and cuffed to each other. The man in front of me had the handcuffs on him reallytight, his hand where going blue, he must of upset the guard. The guard looked at me, Abou was there and nodded to the guard, my handcuffs were put on loose. I nodded at Abou, "thanks". The line of men were marched outside and put into the back of the waiting van, one of the men fell over, the guard gave him a hard slap and was dragged to his feet. The inside of the van was dark, it was just a metal box, with some air holes. It was a sweat box under the heat of mornings sun, it took about 45min to get from the prison to the main court house. When we got out the other end we were blinded by the light of the day, we were all dripping with sweat from the heat within the van. We were herded down some steps into a dimly lit set of old cells. It was old and smelled of damp, it resembled a dungeon, with the bars and chains hanging off the walls, this was where the holding cells for the courts were. The first two men were thrown into the cell, the rest of us quicklyshuffled in still all chained together. Once inside the cell one at a time we were taken out the chains and handcuffed separately. I crouched down, lent against the wall, the paint was flaking off, and dirty street water from above was dripping from the ceiling. A rat ran across the floor. This place was bad.My name was called, I was taken up stars to a closed court room, there was no one there, no one from the British Embassy... only two men behind a desk; they were the judges. One of them called me over, he asked what my name was and I gave him my name. He asked what I was doing in Lebanon, I said I lived here for afew months of the year, the immigration records could confirm that I had spent a lot of time in Lebanon over the past few years. The judge asked what was I doing in Syria, I answered on holiday. He informed me that I was under investigation by the Lebanese/Syrian security services. But he could not tell me over what matter. He also asked what was my association with Adnan Abou Ayyash... I answered, he is a friend. The judge looked at me. Why haven'tyou got a lawyer and where isyour Embassy representatives. I answered I had no idea. There was five minutes of silence whilst the judges talked quietly between themselves. A court clerk walked over and said something to the judges. The judges called me over to them. Your Embassy does not even know that you are in court, no one has told them and some of your paperwork official file has disappeared... The judge motioned me forward with his hand and leaning forward so on one else could hear said "Who have you upset in Lebanon...". I looked at him, I don't know. He looked at me with a worried face, this did not make me feel good at all. The judge said in hush tones... Get out of Lebanon as soon as you can, it's dangerous here, your Embassy should pull you out... The security services under the control of the Syrians could hold me indefinitely, without charges. The judge sat back in his chair and said you will be informed about the outcome of this court and the investigation over time. And that was it... I was taken back to the holding cell. My head was spinning, I had no idea or answers to the many questions that I had. I was no closer to finding out what was going on. After five hours in the holding cell, all the men were chained together again and frog marched up the steps and into the back of the waiting van. 45min later I was back in the Lions Den.. When I eventually got back to the room I briefed Paul up on what was going on, "he was lost for words", his name had been called over the speaker; he was to attend court the next day. Abou came down to the barred window, we talked for awhile I told him what was happening.He told me that the court would give a judgment on the investigation over the next week, he said everything in Lebanon takes time, Paul's in court tomorrow, he might find something else out to shed light on the situation. It was 1700hrs there was a shout by Samon, the prison guards were doing their rounds again, counting the inmates. After counting we settled down to a dinner of three tomatoes between four of us, afew cucumbers with saltand some rice. We should be getting a re-supply of food in two days' time. They had been many times that the guards had refused to let food in from outside for us, the guards would just take it home. We hoped the next set of food was allowed in. I had a restless night sleep that night.I woke up early, Paul had his brown cord trousers on they looked really old, they had been hand washed in the dirty water the day before. I walked outside with him and we took coffee from John. I told Paul to relax, it would all come right in the end. His name was called over the loud speaker, I shook his hand and wished him luck. He was chained and put into the back of the van.I spent the day walking around the prison block talking to people and having coffee with Abou and members of the Al Qaeda cell. One of the Al Qaeda boys had a **"photograph of him with Bin Laden"** at a terrorist training camp in Afghanistan, this was a dear diary moment for me... They talked openly about the US soldiers that they had killed during their time fighting. They asked me about the lock-ness monster and Scottish Whiskey, they liked the Blue Label.Like clockwork they would pray five time a day. And other times they would read and study the Quran. They wore mostly Arabic clothing, but western sports kit while playing football.

They all had and wore watches, this was not allowed for the rest of the prisoners.I was told later that they had a cell-phone in the room, they hid it behind the tiles of their bath room. They only used it to contact their commanders outside the prison.They were all well-educated, some of them had been educated in Britain and America. The teacher as he was referred to had university degrees in chemistry and computers. He had been using the office computer in the office to access information on the prison, including plans and the layout of the prison. He had also been corresponding with other senior members of al-Qaeda via the internet connection. Only the guards had access to this office, Al Qaeda had paid them to use it. The guards who could not be brought off or bribed were threatened and blackmailed, them and their families. If this did not work they would just be killed by Al-Qaeda outside. Some of the guards' families had even been attacked while shopping downtown. This explained why the guards did as they were told. If the Lebanese government stopped playing with Al Qaeda and stop being scared of them and managed to get rid of some of the corruption within the Government ranks, Judges, police officers, secret service etc., Lebanon could be a good place. The computer hard drives within the prison could open the box to a lot of the terrorist activity in and around Lebanon. This place I had found myself was an Intelligence gold mine, why the hell hadn't the Americans hit this place...Did they even know who was in here. I got a shout from one of the guards, Paul was back. He walked into the room. He looked full of hell, he had been given the run around, all he was told was that he was being investigated by the Syrian Security Services. That was it, nothing else. He could not understand the mentality of these people. He was slowly understanding the way it worked in Lebanon. "There are no rules here". We have no rights at all. Even POWs, "Prisoners of war", are treated better than we are, at least POWs, have the Geneva convention to protect them. What do we have, nothing.

I talked to Paul, trying to calm him down, "they can't keep us in here forever and they can't kill us". We were too high profile. That was one good thing we had going for us.I gave Paul one of the books to read I had borrowed from one of the Arab men up stairs, Paul read "wise guy" by Nicholas Pileggi. The book the film is based upon, I had started to read "The Assassins" by Elia Kazan. We were getting very low on food, we ate half a mars bar, with bread and water for our dinner that night. The next day our contact brought us food, it would feed us for four-days.

During my time playing chess with one of the Al-Qaeda Commanders, I was given a t-shirt from one of the Al-Qaeda, it was a Black T-Shirt he had brought back from Pakistan during his time in one of the Al-Qaeda training camps there. It had a picture on the front, the Twin Towers Sept 11. I was stunned at this, he gave it to me as a gift. Joking I said could him and his friends sign it... they did. (I now had a sample of their handwriting...)

Freedom

"Sensitize yourself to the beauty and variety and excitement of living, don't just take it all for granted, are you ever fascinated by the infinite variety of form and colour, light and shadow that surrounds you, do you ever walk out at night just to feel the charm and mystery of the stars, are you thrilled when you see a crescent moon appearing through the branches of a tree or over a shadowy rooftop. Do you get excited about the wonderful discoveries and happenings going on in

the world, do you reach out for new books as they come off the press, searching for the thoughts and wisdom of the leaders of our generation, do you follow with keen interest the political, international, and sociological movements of today. Are you alive."

(Omar Khayyam)

Over time the Syrians had eased their hold on me in Lebanon and Paul had paid to bribe Government officials and judges. Luckily for me the Lebanon Justice system is one of the most corrupt systems in the world, almost as bad as Afghanistan... Bribes and murder are not uncommon, a man can be imprisoned for years on a rumour and it takes more than six months for some cases to even get to court. Not to mention that Lebanon has no human rights, the screams of people being tortured at night will stay with me for a long time...

Suddenly, unexpectedly and quickly,I was released from the hell of the prison in Lebanon, it had only been 6 months but seemed like a life time. Payback time for me on the Syrian Intelligence and Al Qaeda...

"Little did I realise at that time, but events outside my control had forced me to spend time in a Lebanese prison with Senior members of Hezbollah and Al-Qaeda. This fact would save my life in the future in Afghanistan when I was Tasked by American Military Intelligence "WD" with official "Top-Cover" to covertly infiltrate the Afghan Taliban, Al-Qaeda leadership inner circle and the fearsomeHaqqani network, (in the 1980s Jalaluddin Haqqani was cultivated as a "unilateral" asset of the CIA and received tens of thousands of dollars in cash and American stinger surface to air missiles and other weaponry).While in Max-Security Prison, Afghanistan I would become close to Saladin and Talib Jan, two of their top International Commanders with a $10 Million FBI Bounty on their heads". I had a "Rendezvous with Destiny". American, British and Coalition lives had to be saved! This epic future mission and situation is covered in my first book;

Honour Bound Rogue Warrior Part 1.

"The Crusades and the age of the Assassins, Saladin and Richard the Lion Heart"

The other very important fact when assessing and understanding international terrorist networks is most networks are in some way interconnected. The connections sometimes are not the obvious ones, but if you look hard enough there are always links and cross-overs. International terrorism comes in many different layers, terrorist ideology and extremism is always at the core. Prime example is Project Cassandra which is a joint DEA, CIA, DoD and FBI Task Force which I had the pleasure of working with in the past. Century old blood feuds and disagreements can also be found, and in many cases, manipulated. Within the Islamic culture, old feuds are as relevant today as there were 200 years ago. In some Islamic countries the locals speak of the Crusades, the age of the Assassins, Saladin, Richard the Lion Heart and Alexander the Great, as if these historical figures and events existed just yesterday. Some of the villages I have visited in the middle of the desert and up in the snow-capped mountains of the 'Hindu Kush' would tell their children stories around the campfire on cold winter nights. The stories about Alexander the Great were retold from one generation to the next, some of these isolated villages were truly living in the dark ages.

"Al-Qaeda International Terrorist Network"

The Al-Qaeda intelligence network is vast and far reaching, from Afghanistan NDS (security services) to the Afghan Army 'ANA' to the Pakistan ISI and their military. Al-Qaeda has even infiltrated the police in 'UAE' in places like Dubai. Even some airport staff at Dubai International Airport are on the Al-Qaeda payroll. This would explain how Afghan illegal narcotics are sometimes shipped through Dubai International Airport freight. Even a small number of baggage staff in European airports were supporting the Al-Qaeda and Pakistan Taliban cause. This was confirmed by Al-Qaeda Commanders with whom I personally spoke. Major Bevan Campbell and I also learned from an international drug dealer, Marius Venter,that some DHL staff in Afghanistan were involved in, and facilitated, the transportation of Afghan heroin from Afghanistan, via Dubai and on to European and West African countries. Al-Qaeda, the Afghan and Pakistan Taliban have utilised all their international contacts to the maximum, on every level. Many of their weapons, foreign fighters and narcotics smuggling networks would overlap when required. It is fact that a lot of the Al-Qaeda and Pakistan Taliban terrorist operations are funded through the Afghan narcotics trade. The money markets of the Middle-East, Europe (Italy) and Asia including Singapore, are used to launder terrorist money. The Government owned Casino in Lebanon is also one of the places where large sums of money is laundered (American military intelligence 'J2' confirmed my findings on this point during future meeting in Basra, Southern Iraq). Exclusive hotels in Lebanon are used to launder large amounts of money. The hotels have been brought by terrorist front companies. These hotels, on paper, are kept at full occupancy all year round? In reality the hotels are empty most of the time. This is pretty obvious to see, big flash hotels built in the middle of nowhere, north of the Lebanese Capital Beirut. The Russian Mafia have got a big foothold within many of these hotels. Many Middle-Eastern black market arms deals are carried out at these hotels located in Jounieh, Byblos and Tripoli. Another interesting point is that Hezbollah are involved in the Afghan smuggling operations, both of narcotics and weapons, it's a two-way street flowing through the networks, drugs go out and weapons and foreign fighters come in. Large amounts of money, weapons and drugs make for a potent mix, add international terrorism into the melting pot and I would say we have a major problem on the door step of Europe. 'It only takes 45 minutes in a speed boat from Western Lebanon and Syria to Northern and Southern Cyprus'.

"Al-Qaeda and Terrorist Funding"

An American report which was leaked to the New York Times in November 2006, estimated that the Iraq insurgency was financially self-sustaining. It was reported that between $70-$200 million a year was being raised from illegal activities, including oil smuggling, ransom from kidnaps, counterfeiting and the connivance of corrupt religious charities. The total included up to $100 million in smuggling and other criminal activity involving the oil industry, helped by corrupt and compliant officials, other estimates of the income of insurgents were even higher. Fast forward to 2011, Al-Qaeda and their Iraq, Afghan networks have joined forces. The Pakistan, Afghan Taliban and Al-Qaeda are running their illegal narcotics trade out of Afghanistan. 'AQI' (Al-Qaeda in Iraq) are now running a $200 million a year operation; they have combined their smuggling routes, safe houses, foreign fighters and resources. (See glossary Dubai money laundering and Haqqani network) Al-Qaeda and international terrorism is now self-sustained. This is made possible by Government corruption. The latest corruption perceptions index released lists Afghanistan, Iraq, Somalia, Yemen, Democratic Republic of Congo and Zimbabwe as being the most corrupt countries in the world. Al-Qaeda and radical Islam are well established in most of these countries, the Al-Qaeda foot print is clearly stamped in many corrupt Middle-East Governments. Corruption and terrorism go hand in hand in countries like Afghanistan, Iraq and Syria. Where there is no real 'rule of law', terrorism and corruption will flourish. Afghanistan is a perfect example of this fact. This example does not bode well for the British Embassy in Kabul which was responsible for the mentorship program of the Afghan Justice system. This could very well go some way in explaining why senior staff from the British Embassy Kabul covered up the level of corruption within the Afghan Justice system and the reported miscarriages of justice and ill-treatment from British and Commonwealth nationals. Afghanistan is very close to becoming a failed state as of 2014. The fact that the corrupt Afghan Government is now blaming the West, including America and Britain, for the high level of corruption within the Afghan Government is an example of how dysfunctional the Afghan Government really is. The power sharing agreement that the Afghan Government is signing with the Taliban is another example of how dysfunctional Afghanistan is. The question has got to be asked by Western Governments, what has the Afghan war achieved, when the very people who were removed from power over 12 years ago, the Taliban, are now coming back into power? What has changed and what have Western Governments achieved, were the 2000+ American and 450+ British ISAF soldier's lives, which have been killed fighting in Afghanistan, worth the cost? My personal view is that not one American, British or ISAF soldier's life should have been sacrificed. Western cities and streets are not safer from terrorists now following Afghan and Iraqi wars. The fact is that the threat from terrorism, the bleed out effect from Afghanistan and Iraq is worse now than it has ever been. Poverty in Afghanistan is also playing its part in the instability; another cause for the increasing poverty is that women are no longer as economically active as they were, due to security and religious reasons. Unemployment has also soared outside the cities, making the poverty stricken and lawless lands ripe recruiting grounds for the terrorist's networks. The old saying 'a man has to feed his family' is very true. The situation is exploited by extremists. Al-Qaeda and the Pakistan, Afghan Taliban are able to infiltrate Afghanistan and Pakistan at will, in order to inflict casualties on American and British ISAF forces and the civilian population. The Al-Qaeda and other terrorist networks enable its foreign fighters to come into their 'AO' Area of Operations from any angle, whether manipulating safe houses and passage through Iran, Iraq, Syria, or through several other routes via Pakistan, Tajikistan and Uzbekistan. Multiple routes into the country and multiple escape routes with protection and safe passage from within elements of corrupt Governments like the Pakistan ISI give terrorists the advantage to move almost at will, wherever they want. Al-Qaeda is growing in strength and cunning, this is contrary to what politicians will have the general public believe. The prospect of a strong, prosperous and unified Afghanistan is further away now than at any time before. The problem is when Western military forces pull out, will the infighting start and will that lead to another bloody civil war. The fact that this is a concern to Western Governments speaks volumes; the truth is that Western Governments just want to get out of Afghanistan as quickly as possible. It will not be admitted to, but Afghan is looking more like a lost cause with every month that goes by. Terrorist networks are taking full advantage of the situation. It is now just a case of when, not if, there is another major terrorist attack on a Western city that has been ordered and planned from Afghanistan, Pakistan or the Levant. I hope that I will be proved wrong but the facts speak for themselves. Western governments cannot afford to overlook or ignore the lessons of history, a short term fix will only lead to more 'Blow Back' on the Western countries and more 'bleed out' of radical Islam. When the former British Defense Minister Fox, publicly called Afghanistan a 13th century broken country, the Afghan Government were not happy. 'Sometimes the truth hurts'. British politicians need to save face and will publicly say that things have improved in Afghanistan and Iraq and that Iraq and Afghanistan are not safe havens for Al-Qaeda. From my perspective, after sitting within the heart of Al-Qaeda and terrorist's international operations, the Western politicians are very wrong on both counts. The sands of time will tell.

"A lot of Terrorist weapons in the Middle-East come from Russia and China"

A lot of the terrorist weapons in the Middle-East come from Russia and China. Ships are the chosen means and method of transportation. The shipments are broken down at sea and moved to small boats that then make their way to locations in Pakistan, Syria, Yemen and Somalia. Other large shipments are split up and broken down, then moved over-land into Iran, Iraq and Afghanistan, then dispersed amongst terrorist groups and their safe houses. During my time, several years in Saddam's Iraq from 2002 onwards, I had found and photographed many weapons, including; Chinese land mines, Russian Rockets and French 'TOW' anti-tank missiles. French jet aircraft engines were also found. An endless supply of small arms from Russia and China littered Iraq, before, during and after the 2003 war. Al-Qaeda and other terrorist groups had acquired large amounts of these weapons from Iraq and stockpiled them at key secret locations in Eastern Syria along the Syrian and Iraqi border. I had provided American military intelligence with several such locations. Some of these weapons that came out of Iraq in 2003 are now being used against American and British forces in Afghanistan 2014. A small number of Surface-to-Air missiles were also taken out of Iraq by the Iraqi insurgency and other terrorist groups, these have not all re-surfaced yet.

"Terrorist Afghan narcotic shipments are processed in drug refineries, hidden in the Mountains of Lebanon and Black market arms deals in Beirut and Damascus"

One of the main smuggling routes used overland is from Afghanistan, through Iran, Iraq and Syria and into Lebanon. Narcotic shipments are then processed in drug refineries hidden in the Mountains of

Lebanon. The narcotics are cut and processed; this quadruples the street value. They are then packed and moved down to the coast, close to the port of Tripoli, picked up by speed boats and taken to larger ships in international waters, which then disrupts the illegal narcotics worldwide? Confirmed end users are drug gangs in South America and across Europe. Marina communication equipment is used by the terrorist groups whilst they carry out their illegal activities. The Marina communication radios are the same equipment as those used by the big oil tankers moving around the shipping routes. America will not interfere with this marina communication network as it could compromise the safety of other vessels in the same area. Al-Qaeda had cottoned on to this and used it to their advantage, using this equipment on their operations and across their smuggling routes and international networks. I had used the Marina communications setup in 2003 and 2006 in Syria and Iraq, it is very affective. It's a system that was designed for ships at sea, but also works extremely well on land. My exceptional operations manager 'Sharpy' was able, in a coms test, to reach a call sign in Brazil, Southern America. The test was carried out from our operational base located in Cyprus. It was just one example of how effective the Marina coms set-up can be. Within a short time Al-Qaeda and the Pakistan Taliban had realised just how effective Marina coms could be so it was rolled out to their terrorist operations in Africa and Yemen. Al-Qaeda suppliers would meet every few months to negotiate further deals and confirm orders for future supplies of equipment. The 'Phoenicia Hotel' in down town Beirut in Lebanon was a regular meeting location. Other smaller more discreet hotels were also used along 'Hamra Street', but the Phoenicia location was one of their favourites. The excellent wine bar and restaurant on the top floor may have had something to do with their choice of venue. This restaurant has the biggest wine list in the whole of the Middle-East. I have spent many a night sampling its vast array of wines, whilst witnessing Al-Qaeda and Hezbollah black market arms negotiations and deals. The view is splendid from the top floor, out across the bay of Beirut towards Jounieh and the rugged dark backdrop of the Lebanese Mountains. The city lights dance in the sea at night, it was quite enchanting. It is very easy to forget that there were wars being fought on the other side of the mountains. I had lived in Lebanon prior to my time in Afghanistan, so I knew it well. The Al-Qaeda and Pakistan Taliban were taken aback by how much I did actually know.

"Freedom"

Over the next two days I wasback in London, as if the whole Lebanon hell had never happened, but it had... My contacts and Paul had worked some magic and everything had been quickly and quietly sorted out. We had used every contact we had working on sorting this out...(It was just a case of time). Everything had been prepped, location to stay in London, expense money, new passport, clothes, new mobile phone, all was waiting for me. I had been planning this for six months. My apartment in Lebanon had been ran-sacked by the Syrian intelligence service and all my personal belongings hadbeen confiscated, with no chance of getting any of them back, one of my sources had told me that all of it had been lost or misplaced by the Lebanese/Syrian security services. (But the contents of my hidden floor safe were safe). It did not matter, they were only material things, that I could get back over time.

On the first morning back in London I woke to the hustle and bustle of the streets of London, I put my new sports kit on and went for a run along the embankment, the sense of freedom was amazing, past London Bridge, Westminster Bridge, the Houses of Parliament, MI5 HQ along Milbank, over the bridge and past Vauxhall MI6 HQ. I stopped off for a rest at the bandstand at the back of MI6 HQ then after 5 min I continued on my run back to waterloo and the hotel. Rox phoned me as I got back to say hello and gave me an update, he had been kept up to speed when I was away by friendly call signs and all was moving very well and fast. I had contacted my senior friendly call sign at MI6, a meeting was set up again to be held the next day at the Union Jack Club, Waterloo where I was staying as a member, a quiet location, with good tight security. Paul was flying into London within 24hrs, I had made a phone call and a full set of operational equipment for two people was on its way to where I was staying. My plan had been back to London, get briefed from British Intelligence, hand over all the files and documents on the Al Q operatives and cells operating in the UK and Europe. Get kitted out with operation Equipment and take Paul back into Iraq and the Military intelligence HQ, this was the only place on the planet I could access all the falcon view satellite imagery "the US Pentagon would not let me use theirs". Top secret mapping and surveillance imagery equipment, satellite photography in real timeand a direct link to Washington DC and Langley Virginia, (CIA) HQ. I had a plan of action and I was moving on it. Adnan Abou Ayyash, had also made contact with me, via Paul, he was flapping about what I had uncovered in Iraq about his Bank... I had a bomb shell to drop on him, He was sending his No 2, Jamil, to meet me in London, I had a CD disk to give him. Jamil would be with me in two days, he had a stop off in Jordon to see the Prime Minister, he also had some business to tie up with the Jordanian Royal family there. I was prepped for his arrival. That night I slept in a bed for the first time in six months, clean sheets, a hot shower, good food, I was in heaven. "I think that was the best most content night's sleep I have ever had".Next day, up early, I went for a run along the river Thames embankment again, I was good to be back in the UK, I had come though the past two years, alive. I would be lying if I said there were not times that I thought I would make it, there were many times, but I never gave up, did it and it was character building. I was a credit to the way my family had raised me and to the way the British Government/military had trained me.

MI6 British Intelligence

"... waving our red weapons o'er our heads,

Let's all cry, 'Peace, Freedom, and liberty.' Shakespeare, Julius Caesar, III i 110-11

I met my MI6 contact the next day, he was escorted by security to where I was sat in the Bar area, he said "Good to see you again." We talked about what I had been doing with Adnan Abou Ayyash, Iraq, and Al Q. and my time in Lebanon. I was informed that the British government had no problem with anything I had done or the way I did it. He gave me a pat on the back, the problem in Lebanon was I was caught in international politics and me being arrested had given the west an opportunity to have someone on the inside close to Al Q, active operatives and Insurgents. They had tried many times to do this, most people sent were killed. "I was relieved when I was told that there had been a big meeting with all the heads of the departments of MI6 about me. At one point some people thought I had turned, and now was one of Al Q. People who knew me stood their ground, they said no way". Theirsources had said that I had been seen spending hours with Al Q operatives, even playing chess, with one of their head boys, this boy even had a photo of him and Bin Laden on the wall of his prison cell which freaked a lot of people out... This was the same terrorist Commander that had given me a signed twin towers t-shirt when I left, I wanted to ram it down his throat and kill him at the time; I just smiled and thanked him in Arabic. My Contact from MI6 just sat in his chair, staring at the file I had given him in disbelief, he was looking at a list of over twenty names, alias, personal data, passport information, where they had been educated, "Oxford and Hull". What their skills were within Al Q framework, explosives, bomb maker, (IED's), computers, chemicals, electronic counter measures. Which terroristtraining camps and locations they had trained in. Who theircontacts were, the names of the Banks being used to launder their money "The Lebanese Bank of Al Madina", the front engineering companies they used to get visa's for travelling around Europe and Britain. The file was substantial, he looked at me. There was a moment of silence. "This is even better then what you handed to us just before the Syrians picked you up and imprisoned you in Lebanon". "Well done". Remember this time was before the 7th of July attacks on the London underground, Al Q was a far off name to most people in the UK. Only the British intelligence knew that it was only a matter of time until the UK main land was hit by Al Q. The clock was ticking..."The Madina Bank, is that Adnan Abou Ayyash's bank?" I answered "Yes".This was like a bolt out the blue, I had mysuspicions Adnan had lied to me, but I needed to look him in the face to be sure.My MI6 contact looked lost in thought, I better get this back to HQ, my MI6 contact shook my hand, said we will be in touch and thank you.

I sat enjoying my coffee, when the hotel manager, a friend of mine came over to me, "there seems to be three very large plain brown boxes that have arrived for you, Anth", I knew it was the equipment I had ordered in. I went down signed for it and had it moved up to my large double room, I spent the rest of the day checking it over and booking flights to Kuwait and Saudi Arabia and getting intelligence updates from Rox.

Paul arrived the next morning, he flew into Heathrow and arrived at Waterloo about 0800am, just in time for breakfast. We talked for over four hrs, through breakfast and into lunch, it was good to see him again. Paul met Jamil that afternoon as he arrived by Euro Star from Paris. He escorted him to the Union Jack Club, where I had the elegant old private library room set up for the private meeting with tea and coffee. My trusted friend the manager was the only other person allowed into the room during the meeting. Paul showed Jamil into the room. We shook hands and I motioned him to sit down, Jamil is a close friend, confident and senior adviser to Adnan Abou Ayyash and the Saudi Royal family, he is also a very influential man behind the scenes. Over time Jamil, would become a close trusted friend of mine as our investigation took us across Europe.

Adnan Abou Ayyash, al-Madina Bank

Over the next few hours, we discussed Adnan Abou Ayyash, his Bank of al-Madina and his position and situation in great detail. I laid out my advice and plan for resolving several areas of the situation.I informed Jamil that there were several different country's intelligence agencies running their own independent investigations into the activity of the Madina bank, Adnan himself and the employees of the bank. There was a large court case in France against Adnan, for bouncing bank cheques worth over five million, the French authorities had taken a keen interest in him; as a result his accounts had been, frozen in the Arab bank in Paris.Several other topics were discussed, including Adnan's personal safety. My sources had heard, that there was a contract out on Adnan, a professional team had been put into place by persons unknown to kill him. I had a conference call and meeting organised in St Petersburg a few days later to confirm this, as well as the data on the illegal arms deals that went through the Madina bank. These deals were and are of significant interest to the UN because they were in the time of Saddam Hussan and his torturous regime, which were in clear breach of UN sanctions. Some of the items that were part of the illegal arms deals were: SA7 Surface to Air Missiles, Semtex explosives, military communications equipment, NBC (Nuclear Biological and Chemical Warfare), equipment and training aids, G4 assault rifles, the list was extensive, as well as the massive quantities involved... This subject was to become very politicalover the coming months and years. I told Jamil I would keep him up to speed on what was going on.I asked him if he thought Adnan was part of this or if he was innocent, he answered that his friend Adnan was innocent and that he knew nothing about what had been going on in the bank. I was happy with this answer. Jamil continued to update me on all that was going on with the ongoing situation with Adnan. Hours later, I called the meeting to an end, Jamil had to catch the 1800hrs Eurostar back to Paris due to meetings that evening at Prince de gale. We shook hands and Paul escorted him out. I sat for a few moments in silence, my gut was telling me that something did not seem to fit. I needed answers to a few questions, all would reveal itself in due time. When Paul arrived back to the hotel, we went through our itinerary for the coming weeks and firmed up on timings, flights to Kuwait and Iraq. That night I went for a walk along the embankment, towards Vauxhall Cross, my conference call came in, my St Petersburg source confirmed the contract out on Adnan, to kill him and that the arms deals were real and with a word of warning to watch my back. I was informed that there was some major international players involved and the whole subject was very political. I said can the contract out on Adnan be lifted or arranged to be put on hold, the answer was, it might be, ok by me two weeks I said, I will get back to you, I will be in Saudi by that time. "I had just used up a very big ace card" from an old Russian friend.

I made my way back to the hoteland met up with Paul in the Bar. We had a few drinks, the flights to Kuwait had been confirmed from London Heathrow late the next afternoon, all was going well, my contacts in Iraq and Lebanon had agreed to hand over important information, documents to me with regards to the Al Madina bank and its' illegal activities.This was to include, people's names, dates, European banks used to lauder Iraq money, as well as information on UK banks, front companies set up by the banks and large money deposits made to the banks by Uday, Saddam's son. My Arab contacts also had information on Al Q, there were too scared to take it to the authorities, they said (some of the people in the authorities were Al Q). These people trusted me because they had passed me fruitful information in the past and I had always looked after them and protected them and their family's identity. We spent the rest of the night relaxing in the club bar, talking about different areas of our tasks.The rest of the night pasted without incident.The next morning I was up bright eyed and bushy tailed, morning run along the river Thames and then breakfast. Paul joined me at breakfast, all was in place. The phone rang, it was my MI6 contact Jay, wanting a meet. I informed him I was flying out that afternoon. The meet was set for midday, again at the Union Jack Club. I was receiving an update from Rox my intelligence officer when Jay walked into the bar area. I motioned over to him to come over, coffee was ordered and we started chatting. I outlined for him my plans for the coming weeks, just so he was aware of what I was doing and I didn't want to get cross swords with any other operations going on at that time, official or non-official. He went on to explain to me what I should do with tactical, (24) hr response and strategic and (48)hrs response, information and data. Tactical is to be handed into the closes military operations room (American), strategic is to be sent back to HQ for analysis. My MI6 contact knew that I was close to American Intelligence and did not have a problem with that, obviously other elements in FCO and MI6 did... As far as I was concerned we were all on the same side...

He informed me that the file I had given him the meeting before was baring fruit, they had already picked up one of the names on the list and he was in custody, being questioned, "He was a strategic player in the ranks of al-Qa'dia". It was a good result all-round. We finished our coffee and stood up, I walked him to the door, we shook hands, he said "look after yourself, Stay Safe", I answered "I will". This was now a two prong task, The Adnan Abou Ayyash investigation and Hunting al Qaeda and their international cells. They were fast becoming one of the same task...

Kuwait, al-Qa'dia, and Adnan Abou Ayyash Tasks

We flew out of Heathrow that afternoon on a British Airways flight to Kuwait, I was going to trade the rain of the UK for the glaring sun and deserts of Kuwait and Iraq.The wheels of the BA flight touched down on the tarmac at Kuwait International Airport, the overwhelming heat rushed in as the doors of the plane opened. After the obligatory waiting at the airport for our baggage and equipment and passport control, we were in a local taxi heading towards the Crown Plaza Hotel, Kuwait city. After checking in and dropping the kit into the room and touching base with the **RSO Regional Security Officer by phone, (CIA), at the US embassy** setting up a meet there the next morning, I sat down with Paul and we went through our plan of action. Paul was to deal with the documents of introduction and the Saudi Embassy, because of who Adnan Abou Ayyash is, our visas were ready within 24hrs, for our trip at the end of the week to Saudi Arabia, (Ryahiad).This gave us one week to get in and out of Iraq and catch our flight to Saudi Arabia. It was tight but, "do-able". I organised a car to drop us off the next afternoon at the military check point on the Kuwait Iraq border, this was where our military ride would be waiting for us, to take usinto Country Basra military Air base. I chose to go into Iraq by land this time so I would not red flag myself, going into country by land is a lot more low-key then organising a flight on a military helicopter, I wanted to be the "grey man".That afternoon I also contacted a friend of mine in the "CPA" (Coalition Provisional Authority), based out of Saddam's old Basra palace, now known as Palace Camp. I had meet "B" back in Lebanon, he was now head of the CPA in the South off Iraq. He was also former US, Airborne and WestPoint officer and was proud of it. He wore the WestPoint ring with absolute pride. He had told me on our last meeting in Beirut, Lebanon to touch base and have a brew when I was back in country. So I fired him off an e-mail giving him my sit-rep and ETA in country, e-mail is sometimes the best way to contact people in countries like Iraq, and Afghanistan. Their internal communications network sometimes is not good.

I was sat in the Lebanese restaurant on the first floor of the Crown Plaza, chilling out with some waterpipe and chai, when my sat-phone rang,

A familiar voice in Arabic" one of my sources" told me to check a secret e-mail account, that I use as a drop box for important or urgent information. I went up to the club lounge, where the business suite is situated and checked my e-mail. **My source HUM-INT was good, he had given me the Location of a UN camp, on the Syrian border, which was being used by insurgents to launch attacks against the coalition troops on the ground. There was also information on a helicopter being used by insurgents, to transport and assist in movement from Iran to Iraq, type of helicopter and areas of operation and log and register numbers.** This was the Intel. I had heard rumours about of the insurgency using helicopters, but it was just vibes going around the intelligence community. Now I was looking at accurate Intel, from a very reliable source to back it all up. I would hand this over to my US Embassy contact in the morning. I called Paul who was in his room going over Maps and taking care of personal admin, to come down and meet me for a cigar in the lobby of the hotel. Paul came down, I smiled, "let's go for a walk". We walked out the hotel and had a wonder down the road. I always wore long trousers or bottoms and a long sleeve shirt; it does not upset the locals and protects your skin from the sun; a cap or hat can be a good asset to have as well. It was the middle of the afternoon now, the hottest part of the day, I knew from my past visits to Kuwait that there was a small local market about 20min walk from the hotel, I wanted to pick up some kids toys and clothes to take into Iraq, I always did this, children in the villages in Iraq did not have a lot of things and for them to get new cloths or even a toy was a big deal. I filled Paul in on the new Intel that I had received, from my source, he said "You never fail to surprise me, where the hell do you get this information from?"He could not understand why people trusted me. I told him that I had known these people for some time and that I had helped them get through some bad times over the years. I never divulged to anyone who my sources were or their real identities (even when I was pressured in the future by elements within the British Government I never divulged anything - what kind of Team Leader would I be if I ever did, hence why my personal Team members stated on video interview that they would follow me into hell and back. Absolute trust.). We walked on and passed a pizza restaurant, it was closed, but got our attention. It had an aeroplane tailgate, "back half of a plane", sticking out of the front of the restaurant, it was a gimmick "we both laughed". I commented, it should have been called "UBL", "bin Laden restaurant". Paul took a photo as a keep sake. We followed the road around to the market, it was situated on a busy street, one side of the street was the money changers, twenty different ones in all, on the other were stalls selling everything from CDs to household goods, a young boy was stood on the corner with his little stall selling, "fawofal" and kebab. Even though it always smells good, only eat from these places if you have a strong stomach. I made my way to a little stall that had grabbed my attention, it was a girls' make up stall. I picked up some bracelets and hair bands/bangles, from my experience, kids love these. It puts a smile on their face. I have two little girls of my own so anything pink works! Paul was mulling over having a kebab, he gave in and walked over and had one. We both had got what we wanted from the market, we made our way back to the hotel. We spent the rest of the afternoon catching some rays and reading by the hotel's swimming pool. I grabbed an early night. I was reading Robert Fisk "Pity the nation", a very good book about the Lebanese civil war, it gives the reader an over view of the Internal complexities of Lebanon, then and now. The sun is bearable most late afternoons, but the midday sun is too hot, you cannot stand in it for too long or you will burn. Water is a must; carry a small bottle around with you if you are out walking, it's very easy to get dehydrated, in these environments and hot climates. Also always carry the card of where you are staying, you can always show it to a taxi driver if you get disorientated.

US Embassy Kuwait, CIA Contact

The bright beams of golden sun shone though the thin blinds and woke me early the next morning, it was 0600hrs, up bright and early, "Bright eyed and bushy tailed". Hit the gym for an hour before breakfast, then was enjoying my first morning Arabic coffee, the smell of the coffee was wakening up my senses, I was reading though the mornings Kuwait daily newspapers when Paul joined me.It was 0730hrs, Paul never was a morning person. After a hearty breakfast, Paul was back to his larger than life self, note books were out, things on the agenda today, first port of call, US Embassy. I had Tactical Intelligence to hand on to the "RSO", Regional Security Officer CIA, it was meant to be a meet and greet, but operational requirements and the fast changing situation on the ground had changed this to a Brief. The transport had been arranged for 1500hrs, to take us to the border, to hook up with the military to transport us to Basra Air Base, HQ. Paul had coordinated with Adnan Abou Ayyash and Jamil, so our visas and travel arrangements from Kuwait to Saudi Arabia were in place and confirmed for one week to the day. I had been given intelligence from Rox and London, my e-mail accounts had been read, downloaded and cleared. One night stay in the hotel had been arranged and booked for our return to Kuwait, one night stop over. Before we were to fly to Saudi. I phoned reception, a car was organised for 15min to take us to the US Embassy.

Friday day is a day of prayer in the Middle East for Muslims, it's like a Sunday in the UK. Everything is closed. Only foreign Embassies are open. We arrived outside the US Embassy, I told the driver to wait over in an area marked visitors parking. We exited the car, I walked over to "Post 1", I gave a name and I was escorted through security and greeted by the RSO, we shook hands. "We have been expecting you". I asked can we talk in private, he walked me through all the internal security, grabbed a coffee and we entered a secure room. "What's new", I gave him the Intel my source had given me, he looked at it, good skills, we were aware of a staging post, we'd never thought of the UN camps being used as cover in Syria...

He read on, The UN refugee camps were being used as the staging/storage and safe location points for insurgents, attacking and killing US and British Forces in Iraq. The GPS locations of the camps were there, as well as other data. "I will pass this up the chain to Intel straight away". "What's your plans?" I told him we were heading up to Basra area, "sounds like a plan" he told me to give a copy of the Intel to the US J2 Intel officer stationed there, he's a good man, I will give him heads up that you are coming, you might be able to help each other out. Intelligence decisions outside a combat zone work very slowly, too much red tape. On the ground intelligence in country gets moved on straight away. He said;"You know how it works, you have been in the game as long as me". Surveillance assists are in place on the runway in Basra to take images of any areas of interest in and around our AO, area of operations. Work with our Intel people and put target packages together, give us some targets to hit...

He said; as we were leaving, give me a shout when you're back in the week, we can meet up for a beer, he gave me his personal contact details, then walked us out to where our car was waiting.

Time to head back to the hotel, our transport to the Iraq border would be there in a few hours.

I loaded the car and checked over our kit, all ok. Right, time to get on the road. The driver was a friendly call/sign, he was aware of exactly where I wanted to go. It's a three hour journey from Kuwait Airport to the Military crossing points into Iraq, I had arranged that we got escorted into Iraq Basra, from the Kuwaiti border by a British military convoy, this would give us some good protection against insurgent attacks, IEDs. We drove up along the dusty highway out of KuwaitCity and north towards the Iraqborder, there was a lot of activity on the main highway, it was the only road to Iraq. Military convoys, loaded with heavy equipment were passing us on the other side of the road heading into Kuwait. It was just after midday when we got to the infamousIraqi border area.

Iraq

I noticed the black flag flickering in the wind, 101st Airborne had located on the border area, most of their boys were on R & R, "rest and recuperation". We pulled up outside the REME transport office, Paul unloaded the car. I walked over and stood under the raised flag of 101st for a silent moment, many of my friends had been killed serving with 101st ABD during my last time in country.A Colonel from 101st walked past and gave me a node of recognition... After a moment I turned around and walked slowly into the office to sort out the paperwork and timings of the military escort. Ten minutes later, I came outside to see how Paul and our kit was, I had a piece of paper, authorising"2 X Packs" me and Paul, into Iraq, there's even red tape in war zone. In a cloud of dust, two white SUVs pulled up, eight British soldiers debussed, this was our ride. I thanked the driver and we packed the kit into the back of the SUVs. I briefed Paul, he was in the second SUV, I jumped in the lead one. We head off straight into Iraq via the military crossing point. Red flags in the sand marked the route, outside of the markers were land mines. There was no road, just a sandy track. After about a mile off road, we joined the main highway again.

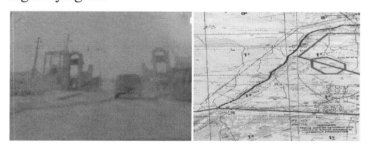

We kept having to go off road around the bridges, they had not been repaired yet from the US blowing them up at the start of the war. IEDs were a risk so we drove on the wrong side of the road as much as possible. Black Hawks with door gunners at the ready flow low level overhead on patrols looking for IEDs and insurgents/bad guys, ambushes and attacks on military convoys were on the increase.We pulled into Basra Airbase at last light, the security on the base was tight. I was hoping to get to the Palace in Basra to hook up with my US CPA contact, it was too dark to move into town now. The rule is in Iraq, no travel at night unless there's three or more heavily armoured Humvees, or Land Roverseven then it's not advisable. I phoned my US CPA contact from inside the camp HQ, there had been a security clamp down, no movement tonight at all. They were expecting an attack by the insurgents. I arranged with the British QM of the Base for us to bunk and be located in the transit accommodation. He drove us over to the cabins and showed us around, mess hall, accommodation etc.

It was dark now. I told Paul to chill out and have a wonder around, I went off to have a chat with the QM.I came back about an hour later, I had found out that there was a US J2 intelligence officer based on camp and that there was Falcon View here. This just made our job a lot easier. After a quick beer and banter with the soldiers in the "buss bar", a bar made by members of the army. It was so out of place, it was like a tropical open beach bar, with the neon lights and colourful banners and flags. The one thing that was not in short supply was sand, we were in the middle of the Iraq desert.I went back to the accommodation. I started going through all the Intel, I was going to hand over and the bombshell I had to drop on the American J2 Intelligence officer...

British Military Intelligence Headquarters Basra Airfield "The Hotel" Iraq

The next morning up bright and early after breakfast and a quick run through our basic movements over coffee in the cook house (See above Photo) we went over to the "Hotel", this was the nickname for the HQ for British military intelligence in Iraq, it was also the location of their main operations room, the US J2, also had an office there. On entering I handed my passport in to the front desk and asked to speak to the Major in charge of Intelligence, the CSM had given me his name and details the night before. After a short wait he came down and took us up to his office, the "CO" Commanding Officer of the base, was in the officewhen we arrived, we sat down. I opened my brief case and handed the Major a file marked data, he looked through it and handed it to the CO, part of the file was a list of over20 names of members of al Qaeda and Iraqi insurgentsand HVTs#who were operating inside and around Iraq at that time. It also contained other valuable information. I explained what was of tactical and strategic importance, there was a lot of information held within the file. I told him I had arranged to hand this over to the US J2 intelligence officer based here as a professional courtesy and with this base being British, I had made a second copy of the information for the British, and personally wanted to give him a copy. He looked at me, he asked if we wanted coffee, "yes" he left to organise the coffee and make a phone call, he came back ten minutes later, with the coffee. He asked how can we help you, I explained about what I had been tasked with and that I had afew meetings set up here in Basra. I asked him; I needed access to a secure line and satellite imagery, he answered no problem. He had a look through the data, he looked at me again, we have been looking for the staging posts for the insurgents, they always seem to be one step ahead of us. This Intel should even the score. He walked over to the office phone, he organised a meeting with his Intel coordinators, the "CO" came back over and sat down, "I've got surveillance assets just sitting on the runway collecting dust, they will be up in the air by close of play today". It was nice to see people acting on good Intel. One of the key areas of staying alive in this line of work is not telling many people what you're up to and don't tell many people of your planned movements. The look on the "CO", face when he opened the file I had given him was total surprise. "They never seen me coming", always be the grey man. The CO asked "Are you staying on camp?""Yes, at the moment." "Are you being looked after?" "Yes, your boys and the CSM, are taking good care of us." "Good. Is there anything else you need from my side?" I asked to be introduced to the US, J2, not a problem, the "CO" looked at the Major, I will let you handle that.We stood up and shook hands, the Major walked us out and down to the US J2 office.The British Major knocked on the door of the J2s office and walked in. He introduced us, I dropped the US RSO, CIA name back in Kuwait and the J2 knew who I was, I thanked the British Major for his time and I would call up and see him afterwards. The British Major left the room, closing the door on the way out. The J2, asked how much time do we have, I can stay for 48hrs on the base if needed. I presented him with a copy of the file I had given the CO and also gave him another file. This containednew crossing points from Southern Syria to Iraq and Saudi to Iraq these where in the Americans area of operation not the British. He called his No 2, over to the table and told him to compare my locations to the locations US Intel had come up with. "Falcon View" was brought up on the large screens on the walls and on my operational laptop.

One of Malone's Laptops with American Military Falcon View Imagery

The locations were nearly the same, my Intel had pin pointed three that were not on the screen. I also zoomed in using the satellite imagery, and located the camp in Syria, on the border being used as a safe haven by the insurgents, it was the UN refugee camp. I asked if they had tracked down the insurgents helicopter in the south. They both looked at me, they had been trying to find this for some time, it had popped up on their radar out east a few times, but they were not able to get a fix on its location. I showed then the area deep inside Iran on the tactical pilot chart, "Have alook there, you will get a heat source, that's where it is kept". They asked how did I know this, I clickedthe mouse pad on my laptop, the helicopter file came up, photographs of the helicopter, costumed specs and serial ID numbers. One of my sources had sent it to me. The helicopter was a formerRussia military gunship, it had been brought from a private company in Southern Turkey. I burned and gave them a CD with all the information on.

Target Packages Sent to Washington DC for Urgent Approval

Cover Page TS Doc Example

Paul had been working on one of the computers checking e-mails and corresponding with Dr Adnan. I went over to him, lets grab some food, it was 1800hrs. We all called it a night and agreed to meet at 0900hrs back in the operations room the next morning. On leaving the J2 said that there's a Pizza Hut up the road, next to the motor pool. Sounds good to me, I looked at Paul, pizza it is, we walked up the road towards the motor pool past the terminal buildings and there it was, a trailer with Pizza Hunt on the side in the middle of an open space. There were green plastic tables and chairs scattered outside. We ordered a large meat feast each, the Iraqi boys working there told us to have a seat and they would bring it over. I paid in US dollars "$5" and moved over to the green chairs. The sun was just starting to set in the sky. It seemed quite peaceful just sat there, the Iraqi boy brought our pizzas over.

A group of British Army Landroverspulled in next to the Pizza Hut, they were a snatch team that had just finished patrolling Basra looking for bad guys. They all grabbed a pizza, they must have pre-ordered them. We went over and had a banter with them, as soon as they found out I was former British Airborne, all was sweet, I got a good photo of Paul with the snatch team.

Paul /SA/

After Pizza and a good chat with the British boys about what was happening on the ground, we walked back around the camp, enjoying the fresh night air.

Basra (British Base)

The distant sound of AK-47 gunfire could be heard in the distance. We were talking about our scheduled meeting with Adnan. My contacts had been working round the clock on multiple tasks for him. It seemed that we were getting close to the truth of what had been going on at the Al-Madina Bank.The next morning we woke bright and early, there was an operation going on up in the north of the country. Waves of helicopters were coming in landing and refuelling on the runway. "fast turnaround", I made my way to the mess room, it was buzzing with activity, there was a lot of troops collecting breakfast. I grabbed some fruit and filled my thermos cup with fresh coffee, then moved over

277

to a table, Paul grabbed the full works, a hearty English breakfast. The buzz around camp was that the insurgents were moving in the area to the east of Basra, an Iraqi source "human resources", had given the location of a meeting point of the local insurgency. The British military were going in for the kill.Paul had a lot of e-mails to send, we agreed that he should deal with the e-mail communications and I would finish off the work with the J2 at intelligence headquarters. We agreed to meet back at the accommodation at 1400hrs. He had my sat-phone number if he needed me.

"I chose to walk with men, not vermin"

" Target Packagers to Washington DC, had come back as a Green Light, Mission was a Go..."

When I arrived at the J2's office, they were hard at work, **Washington has given the green light to the target package and the birds had been up overnight taken photographs of locations over Iraq and inside Syria. The Photographs were sitting on a table in a folder market top secret,** "if Syria knew that the US was taking spy pictures of locations in their land, they would be a little upset". The J2 had already had some good comeback, from the US internal intelligence sources. My target package had caused quite a steer in Intel circles. All was a go... we looked over all the aerial images and pinpointed all the locations that we were looking for. All data was sent off simultaneously. The J2 sat back in his chair, it had been a hell of an 24hrs **(We had located and sent off target packages of HVTs and sites in Syria and Lebanon where Battlefield Chemical Weapons had been hidden by Russia Special Forces, these weapons had been smuggled out of Iraq in the weeks before the Iraq war had started)...**

I looked at him and said do you want to go for a walk he looked at me I nodded, he knew I wanted to talk in private, one on one. We went to a quiet area to the back of the main operations' room. We sat in the enclosed briefing area, this was a secure area used for top secret briefings. What's on your mind. I gave him a sealed envelope, he opened it and looked down as he read it. Enclosed were the details of a US Military officer whose brother inlaw though marriage was senor al-Qa'ida, he looked at me. All the information was there in black and white... American intelligence had somehowmissed this... He understood why I wanted this dealt with quietly, there was a small chance that the US officer did not know, the fact that military books and US Government military aid memoirs on US military tactics and NBC "nuclear biological and chemical warfare", with his name on them had found their way into al-Qa'dia training camps and with active terrorist cells, was a major security breach. It could be a lot worse and deeper than what I had uncovered. He looked at he again, "if all the Intel you had given us wasnot first rate, I would not believe this", I'll have to take this to Baghdad personally. It's always hard to contemplate that a member of you own could be working with the enemy. He might not be, my Intel source had told me that he was just being used... I'll give this to my commander, he will deal with it. Wewalked back through the op's room which was active with ongoing operations east of Basra. His office was still a hive of activity, he made arrangements to fly up to Baghdad"camp victory", HQ that afternoon. It was getting on to 1400hrs, I was meeting Paul back at the accommodation. I said my goodbyes and exchanged personal e-mail address with the J2, wished him luck and Stay Safe. I left and had a slow walk back to meet Paul, with a quick stop off at the map store. I wanted high detailed maps of Iraq, Iran, Saudi, Syria and Lebanon. The officer who was running the map section had been briefed by the J2 and was expecting me. After introducing myself he just asked what I needed, within 15minuits I had all the detailed maps and satellite photographs (Falcon View) I needed on all the countries that were of interest to me on any and all Tasks. The map officer put a few other things into my day sack that he thought I might find useful. I thanked him with a handshake and left. I made my way back to the accommodation (See Photographs of Elite Team Members in Iraq).

Where and how the insurgency was obtaining their large amount of weapons had came into the brief to the American J2 at Basra. This subject was deeply worrying even then. The terrorist groups operating across Iraq, Syria, Lebanon at that time were getting even more weapons, range from small arms to anti-tank rockets. This factor would reach epidemic levels when in the future AQI and ISIS would take over large areas of both Iraq and Syria. when ISIS entered Mosul in Iraq, the entire Iraqi army ran away to Baghdad... Not one Iraqi unit stood its ground against ISIS in Mosul. All the military hardware and American military equipment given to the Iraqi army in Mosul City fell into ISIS and AQI hands. This included 100 of Armoured Humvees, Armoured

Personnel Carriers.1000 AK-47s and heavy machine guns, 1000 of boxes of ammunition, 1000 of RPG Anti-Tank rockets.

This was enough to arm an army but add to that fact that Surface to Air Missiles are now in ISIS and AQI hands that is a real game changer. When the Pesh, Kurdish Military was advancing on ISIS positions you can imagine how surprised they were when they came under fire from an American Abraham main battle tank that had somehow fallen into the hands of ISIS... The Pesh destroyed the tank with an "Advanced Anti-Tank Missile" but some things are best left not written about... Another important fact is when in the future the American Government cleared airdrops by USAF, who were dropping a re-supply of weapons, ammunition and rockets to an Kurdish element in Northern Syria fighting ISIS. The airdrop was put in the wrong place and fell into ISIS and International Terrorist hands...

Another important futurediscovery: ISIS/AQI are in possession of powerful anti-tank rockets manufactured in the former Yugoslavia. Such rockets had reportedly been provided to U.S.-aligned Syrian rebels in 2013 by Saudi Arabia, a main backer of the rebellion and a U.S. ally. In refusing to allow moderate rebels to receive significant military support in the form of heavy weapons as the war has raged on, the U.S. has often cited concerns that these weapons might fall into the hands of extremists.

The photos that follow show the U.S. weapons — as well as the anti-tank rockets — found in stockpiles captured from ISIS/AQI/Hezbollah in Syria and Iraq.

The appearance of the weapons in Syria, shows the "logistical fluidity" across ISIS' battlefields in Syria and Iraq. Courtesy of Conflict Armament Research

Back to Basra Iraq

I found Paul still on the internet, he was dealing with one of our Lebanese sources that had contacted us to hand over original documents, from the al-Madina bank. I briefed Paul on all the day's activities and he briefed me on the updates with the al-Madina bank. My US CPA contact had contacted me, "Heads Up" and was out of country on Government business for a few days. "looks like that drink will have to wait till next time". I talked through the time scales with Paul and a command decision was made...

 Basra Iraq

The British Ambassador Iraq

The British Ambassador in Iraq had been contacted by the military intelligence "CO" and he had cleared and organised a ride the next morning with the RAF. "There's a lot of red tape with the British Army". There was a RAF helicopter doing a VIP run to Kuwait "camp wolf", in the morning at

0700hrs. Sounded good to me, two seats were reserved for us. This was the safest and quickest way for us to keep on track and on time with the time scales I had planned.

The rest of the day spend as down time, the past few days had been very intense, after dinning in the mess room, I retired to the accommodation for the night. I smoked agood Cuban with the CSM out on his front porch, the conversation was of different places and times. I bid my good nightsto all the gentlemen that had gathered around, then I got my head down. 0530hrs the next morning, the sun was bright and the camp was just wakening as we had our coffee from the cook house and made our way over to the British flight line. There was no one around... After tracking down a RAF officer in one of the hangers, I was informed that the ride we were getting on was not logged in. All VIP flights are not due to security... ETA 5min...

RAF Puma helicopter, To Camp Wolf

The RAF Puma helicopter came in fast over the hangers and landed just 100 meters to my front, the RAF officer smiled and pointed, that's your ride. I grabbed my kit and we made our way towards the waiting chopper, you always approach a helicopter from the sides, it's the safest route to board a helicopter. Within a couple of momentsof boarding the puma, it quickly lifted straight up and with speed banked left and continued to gain altitude. We were at 2000 feet when it levelled off, the sound of the rotors were deafening.We flew over Basra city then banked over camp palace, Saddam's old presidential palace. The views out the door were clear for miles around. With a sudden bank to the left the puma descended in a fast downward spiral, within what seemed like a few seconds, as the puma span into the palace grounds, it swooped upwards and landed, "this was the fastest descent I had ever made in a combat helicopter"... The door gunner opened the sliding doors as three people approached the puma, Paul shouted to me, "People pay good money for a ride like this" I laughed, within a split second the new passengers were in and belted up, weapons secured between their legs, from the look of them they were members of the SOF "the activity", long hair and unshaven,they were wearing civilian clothing, brown walking boots and carrying customized AR-15s, with Glock 23 pistols strapped to their legs.The puma lifted off this time hugging the ground and along the river bank, low level 50feet above the ground, until we were clear of Basra. Aggressive flying by the RAF pilots was a must, the terrorists and insurgents in the area had been taking pot shots with RPGs, as they had been coming into land and taking off. Surface to air missiles had also been fired at the British helicopters over the past few days. The pilots were now taking no chances. The puma ascended to 1000 feet for the rest of the flight time to camp wolf Kuwait. We touched down at camp wolf, Kuwait a little after 0900hrs in the morning, we de-bussed, a nod of take care to our travelling companions and we made our way over to the flight office. I hooked up with some British officers who were heading out and staying in the same hotel as us, the Crown Plaza, Kuwait City. After loading our personal kit into their SUV, the Military officers drove us to the hotel. We checked in and had our kit sent up to the rooms, I confirmed in a phone call to Adnan Abou Ayyash our flight timings and hotel reservations, all was in order, we were flying out to Riyadh early the next morning. I told the Dr that I would be with him by mid-day, his personal driver would pick us up from the Sherington Hotel and drive us to the meeting. I told Dr Adnan, I would give him a curtsey call when I had landed safely in Saudi Arabia. He asked what Iraq was like, I answered interesting, he asked if I was safe there, as safe as I can be... I finished the call with look after yourself and we will talk tomorrow. The next day, we got to the airport early, I expected a delay because of the extra security. After navigating through all the security, we boarded the plane. I looked around, we were the only westerners on board and we were the only ones wearing western clothes. We settled in and were in the air within 30mins, the flight was only afew hours from Kuwait to Riyadh. I started going through my notes and files, by now I had a good overview off all that had been going on at the al-Madina Bank....

Meeting with Adnan Abou AyyashSaudi Arabia

Adnan Abou Ayyash is a slip of a man.He is small in stature, but has an air of authority about him. He is very patent, but decisive. He is a very astute engineer and shrewd business man who is very old school. He had been fully aware that I had been working behind the scenes for him for some time and he also understood that I wanted my involvement in the case at that time kept confidential. He knew this was for security reasons. I went on to brief him on what my sources had found during the ongoing investigation. He asked my advice about putting a US company, Fortress Global, at work relating to the New York legal case; they were to work alongside Hughes Hubbard, the Paris based legal firm dealing with other aspects of the case, both in Europe and the US. The two firms were known to me, they were professionals, as long as they were kept an eye on and reported back to me and Adnan at regular intervals with updates and reports, it would be a good idea. I asked that my involvement was kept secret and on a need to know basis. Only a few people including the four people in the room would know of my involvement.

"I was to become Adnan Abou Ayyahs's Special Adviser, "Intelligence Officer" Head of his security and close confident..."

Adnan Abou Ayyahs made Anthony Stephen Malone, the Sole Liaison between the Chairman of the Bank of Madina and all Government Agencies, Task Forces and Government Investigations. This letter of Authority gave Anthony Stephen Malone permission to liaise with all International Intelligence Agencies and to view all "Documents" relating to the Banks and permission to interviwe all witnesses and to procure "Documents, Evidence" connected to the Bank of Madina.

(See Offical Document of Authority Signed by Adnan Abou Ayyahs)

My first question I put straight to him. What had he been thinking about putting Rana Koleilat and Ibriham Abou Ayyash, Adnan's brother, in charge of the bank and all the money init, without a board of advisers appointed by himself, to oversee and report back to him once a month. He answered, "I made a grave mistake, I trusted them". "It was a straight honest answer". I continued in my normal subtle way of straight questioning, no time for foreplay. He was assessing me as I was also trying to weigh him up, was he telling me the truth, was he just an innocent party in all this or was he the mastermind behind two banks that were funding and helping International Terrorism. He pleaded his innocence, I told him straight, that if he ever lied to me in any way I would just walk away from him and the investigation. I also wanted to find out just how deep and wide the money laundering was within the bank and I wanted the names within Syrian Intelligence who were involved. Also on my to do list were the names and detailed information of all the front companies being used by terrorist groups that were using the banks. This date was of major strategic importance and would help bring down and pull apart international terrorist networks from within and in doing so could save a lot of American and British lives...

I went on with the briefing to Adnan Abou Ayyash in his board room at his international headquarters in Riyadh. I went through a broad spectrum of topics and subjects that involved the bank, I did not divulge all the information I had in my files or had been privy to in Iraq. When I had visited the American Intelligence in Iraq he had slipped a copy of a file into my bag. (A little thank you for saving American soldiers lives).

Elite Group International the front company name registered in the Middle-East and used for security reasons, for Deniable Covert Operations and High Risk Intelligence Tasks, had uncovered that there had been rampant fraud and money laundering by officials at Lebanese Al-Madina Bank. The money laundering involved $3.5 million to Al-Shaheed (confirmed; front organisation for the terrorist organisation, Hezbollah based in Lebanon) including; money laundering to a convicted international terrorist who used the money to buy military night vision goggles for terrorist activity, this equipment was also being used against American and British troops on the ground in Iraq and Afghanistan, various Syrian military and intelligence officers (Head of Syrian Intelligence who I had met) and

"Uday, Qusay the sons of Saddam Hussein, the Bin Laden family and several infamous other people and HVTs all banked and held multiple accounts at the banks".

These were so called black accounts that Rana had set up off the books. These were accessed by using pass books and key passwords. (One of the Black Accounts that had been within the bank had used the password "Name of a Shopping Mall in Beruit" as a password) J had confirmed this at a later date, he was amazed that I had information like this... The al-Madina bank also was laundering money for Iraq's central bank when Saddam Hussien was in power, witness statements have indicated that the UN oil for food program when manipulated, channelled funds into accounts held at the al-Madina bank. EGI uncovered evidence of a cover-up by the Syrian- backed Lebanese Central Bank. The cover-up stems from the collapse of the Al- Madina Bank and the sudden halt of an investigation by the Central Bank. Lebanon had recently returned to international banking after years of being blacklisted for this precise activity. Evidence demonstrated that former Al-Madina Bank executive Rana Koleilat, who is currently incarcerated in Brazil, was the ring leader of a corrupt enterprise that, at its peak, involved dozens of bank employees who were paid off with luxury vehicles; BMWs, Mercedes and luxury houses, apartments and villas. Another way that Rana was paying people off was to give them credit cards, that they ran up large amounts of credit on them. Rana would then pay the cards off using bank money. Also large sums of bank money was stolen and laundered without the knowledge of the Bank board of directors, several of whom had originally been charged in the case. Some of Saddam's Iraqi Gold had also found its way in the banks vaults and many deals were done within the bank to sell Gold for international currency. The currency was transferred to several countries including; Central and South America, Africa, Singapore, Russia (St Petersburg, Moscow) and across Europe including; Cyprus, France, Britain, Germany. Funds were deposited into accounts ran by front companies overseen by terrorist groups and organisations. Senior Lebanese and Syrian officials held black accounts within the bank and they could access funds internationally by using the International accounts set up across Europe by Rana. **(Even in 2018 Rana would not reveal to an International Investigation any of these details, this was because senior members of several Governments were implicated and they had all threatened to silence her, kill her, if she did. Rana had dirt, evidence on all of them so as long as she did not talk or release evidence, she would remain alive)...**

EGI had brought to attention to the massive corruption at Al-Madina Bank that contributed to international terrorist financing and instability in the Middle East. EGI, formed and passed on a copy of all findings to relevant intelligence agencies, these include the CIA, FBI, MI6, DST and US military Intelligence, all Special Task Forces were also informed of all that been uncovered regards all relevant data, both tactical and strategic, this was down to one simple fact; the money from over 100 accounts from the bank was being used to fund international terrorist operations and the growing insurgency in Iraq and Afghanistan. During the investigation names of engineering companies based in Saudi Arabia and Dubai being used to facilitate the travel of known terrorist were uncovered, as well as over twenty names of known (CIA List) Al Qaeda and Iraqi insurgents. These named people also held many accounts at the bank of Al Madina.

Our source also uncovered, during a one-month period ending in January 2003, Koleilat used Al-Madina funds to pay $941,000 to the brothers of Gen. Rustum Ghazali, then the powerful Chief of Syrian Intelligence in Lebanon. Citing a confidential source, that the following March, Koleilat arranged a $300,000 "donation" for General Ghazali from bank funds. She also moved $100,000 in

November 2002, through an account at a sister bank of Al-Madina's to a Lebanon bank account of Mustapha Tlass, then the minister of defense and the deputy Prime Minister of Syria.

Our sources also found other "questionable" deals. In 2002, Rana Koleilat transferred, at no cost, a lavish Beirut apartment to a close friend of Khaled Kaddour, identified as the office manager for Syrian Lt. Col. Maher Assad. Assad is the brother of Syrian President Assad. Koleilat also used bank funds, the report said, to buy a villa from Elias Murr, then Lebanon's interior minister and the son-in-law of Lebanese President Lahoud. Koleilat paid $10 million for the property and placed it in the name of her boyfriend. Fortress Global says when the villa was later taken over by Lebanese authorities, the investigators, it was valued at $2.5 million.Rana Koleilat at her height of corruption, managed to live a pretty nice life. She travelled by private jets, took along her servants and hairdresser and stayed at exclusive hotels in London, Park Lane and Paris, George 6. Back home, in Beirut, Lebanon, she lived in a three-story penthouse. To anyone who asked how she lived so well, she replied that she had a "rich Egyptian uncle". Through extensive international research by EGIs human resources network and interviewing over 50 former al-Madina bank employees, no rich Egyptian uncle was ever found or traced. My sources also informed me and were waiting for confirmation that one of Ranas relatives had been killed in the past by the Columbian drug cartels for a business deal gone bad some years before, this involved money laundering, his body was found cut up in a bin. There were other large numerous questionable payments by Koleilat to various officials of the Lebanese and Syrian governments. Rana Koleilat acted as the ringleader of a corrupt enterprise that included her brothers Bassel and Taha, her boyfriend Moawad, her aunt Ayyas and other officers, managers and employees of Al-Madina Bank. In the beginning as early as November 1999, Koleilat is alleged to have executed a series of forgeries designed to transfer funds into "dummy" accounts at the bank controlled by her and others. This was done by fake investors, who took out large loans. By November 2002, Dr. Abou Ayyash had unwittingly transferred $670 million into one such account. Eventually, Dr. Abou Ayyash would infuse an additional $470 million of his own funds into the Al-Madina Bank in a fruitless effort to avert a liquidity crisis allegedly brought on by Rana Koleilat and her cohorts.Mohammed Ousaily: fake prince, fake bank guarantee, he wanted $50 million, he also told me and sent me details of documents, that cite that the Saudi Royal family and one of the Former kings wives had her name on a Saudi Arabian company buying arms for Iraq, Saddam Hussien. Copies had been seen and certain aspects of the arms deals had checked out. He was trying to blackmail Adnan Abou Ayyash, he had threatened to go to the newspapers with the documents, Rana gave him files of more documents from the al Madina bank the night before she was smuggled out of Lebanon using her British passport.(See Photograph) She left instructions that they were to be used against Adnan Abou Ayyash.

The passport that Brazilian police found being used by Lebanese woman Rana Abdel Rahim Koleilat, when they arrested her in Sao Paulo, Brazil 2006. The British Embassy in Beirut has confirmed that they issued the passport to an Irish citizen...

A list of other HVAs of the bank was also identified by the banks chairman.

List of Yachts, that were brought by Al-Madina Bank.

To   :   Mr. Anthony Malone,
                       elitegroupinternational

CC   :   Mr. Paul D

From   :   Dr. Adnan Abou-Ayyash

Date   :   November 30, 2005

Subject   :   List of Motor Yachts (M/Y)

According to your request, please find below the list of M/Y connected with our project.

(1) Madina BZA (azimuth 25 meters owned by Ibrahim Abu Ayyash worth 3 Million Euro.

(2) Madina 15 Wissam (azimuth 17 meters owned by Ibrahim Abu Ayyash) worth 550,000 U.S.D.)

(3) Madina 9 (cranchi 10 meters owned by Ibrahim Abu Ayyash worth 400,000 U.S.D.

(4) Zeina (techno marine 33 meters owned by Taha Kolaylate (Rana's brother) worth 15 million Euro.

(5) Thaipan (sun seeker 23 meters owned by Bassel Kolaylate (Rana's brother) worth 2.5 million Euro.

(6) Lea (cranchi 12 meters owned by Salim Dada worth 500,000 USD.)

Please keep me posted about the progress of your work.

With my regards,
Dr. Adnan Abou-Ayyash

Reey Moward, asked the chairman of the bank via Rana to have money sent to the Cheq Republic to buy a hotel, this hotel has also been linked to the al-Madina bank and further money laundering and illegal arms deals and HVT meetings.

Akram, former credit controller in the bank of al-Madina, had moved sensitive documents from the al-madina bank and kept them in a safety deposit box in a bank in North Lebanon. Rana had summoned him to a late night meeting at one of her villas, she wanted the documents from him. Expense money was sent by EGI by western union $10.000 in Akram in his girlfriend's and mother's names. To secure these documents and files Akram sent copies of cheques made out in Ranas name, from Barclays Bank UK and Royal Bank of Scotland.

The below article published in Lebanon highlights the details of the Banks situation and political fallout in Lebanon and the way it effected International banking.

The Al-Madina Bank Scandal
by Gary C. Gambill and Ziad K. Abdelnour

During the last six months, Lebanese public attention has been fixated on the country's largest banking scandal in over three decades. That the collapse of Bank Al-Madina in mid-2003 should attract such concern is not surprising. Relative to the overall size of its economy, Lebanon has the largest banking sector in the world, with deposits of roughly $40 billion in more than 70 private banks. While other sectors of the economy have languished in recent years, Lebanon's bank secrecy laws and open market economy have continued to make it attractive to capital. When a bank fails in Lebanon, people demand answers - the collapse of Intra Bank in 1966 brought down nearly a dozen other institutions and caused a major economic crisis.

And the collapse of Al-Madina was no ordinary bank failure - over a billion dollars of depositors' assets simply disappeared and informed sources say that the bank was involved in laundering billions of dollars from the Russian mafia, Saudi Islamic associations and the former Iraqi regime of Saddam Hussein. It is difficult to imagine a scandal more threatening to the reputation of Lebanon's much-touted banking system.

However, rather than seeking to shore up the reputation of the country's financial sector by prosecuting those responsible for criminal wrongdoing to the fullest extent of the law, the Lebanese government has tried to cover up the scandal and intimidate journalists investigating it. When the perpetrators of a major crime in Lebanon enjoy such blanket immunity from prosecution, the hand of Syria is usually involved. Syrian protection allows Subhi Tufaili, a former secretary-general of Hezbollah who came under indictment in January 1998 after his henchmen killed several Lebanese soldiers, to make public appearances today without fear of arrest.

In the case of Al-Madina, however, the criminals are not terrorist fugitives, but belong to a special class of postwar *nouveaux riches* who have come to dominate most sectors of the economy in Syrian-occupied Lebanon. Whether their business is banking or stolen cars, the most important and necessary ingredient of success for aspiring entrepreneurs in Lebanon today is not cost efficiency or marketing savvy, but political protection, obtained through tacit partnerships with Syrian military and intelligence officials in Lebanon (or with Lebanese politicians close enough to Damascus to impart such protection themselves). In return, a large portion of the windfall profits that accrue to those who circumvent the law with impunity invariably finds its way into Syrian pockets.

A Tale of Two Families

Rana Qoleilat

Al-Madina and its subsidiary, United Credit Bank (UCB), are owned by two Druze brothers with dual Lebanese-Saudi citizenship from the town of Baakline, Adnan and Ibrahim Abu Ayash. Adnan, an engineer by profession, made his fortune in Saudi Arabia owing to his friendship with Nasser al-Rashid, an influential advisor to King Fahd. In 1984, he purchased Al-Madina from its Saudi owners and appointed his brother deputy chairman.

Beginning in 1998, evidence of money laundering and other illicit activity at Al-Madina began coming to the attention of Lebanon's ostensibly independent bank regulatory authorities. Most of the suspicious transactions were carried out by a woman named Rana Qoleilat, a file clerk from a humble family in Lebanon (her father was a building superintendent) who rose to become Ibrahim's chief aide and was given power of attorney to carry out transactions on behalf of the two brothers. How she attained this position has been the matter of considerable dispute, but apparently her central role in the bank's repeated violations of the credit and banking code was intended to allow the Abu Ayash brothers to plausibly deny knowledge of any wrongdoing (they later made precisely this claim).

Rana was richly rewarded for her work at the bank and funnelled millions of dollars to her brother, Taha (and, to a lesser extent, his twin brother Bassel), who became the biggest depositor in Al-Madina and enjoyed dizzying success as an entrepreneur. Rumours of Taha's shady business dealings abounded, both in Lebanon and abroad (in 2001, Belgium froze his assets on suspicion of money laundering). Meanwhile, he accumulated a large portfolio of assets in Lebanon, including the luxury Sheraton-Coral Beach Hotel in Beirut, several hotels in Mount Lebanon, a luxury car rental with a fleet of over 180 vehicles, and seven yachts. According to informed Lebanese sources, however, the Qoleilat family's fortune was mainly a front for assets owned secretly by high-level Lebanese and Syrian officials.

Many of the suspicious transactions at Al-Madina were purchases of real estate. The bank would purchase assets at an inflated price, on the condition that the sellers deposit their earnings in Al-Madina. The depositor would then receive a passbook that is properly signed, stamped and issued, but *not* recorded in the bank's books. The bank offered substantially inflated interest on such deposits, which the beneficiaries could regularly cash at the bank. The interest payments, however, were paid out from special funds not carried on the books of the bank. In other cases, real estate would be purchased with one or more post-dated checks (also unrecorded in Al-Madina's books) drawn on the Central Bank, but not actually presented for collection because they were paid on maturity from the same special funds, in effect yielding a similarly inflated interest rate. Many of these inflows and outflows were disguised by filing false documentation with the Banking Control Commission (BCC), an independent administrative body set up in 1967 to monitor private banks - meaning that, in effect, the bank was guilty of money laundering.

According to an informed Lebanese source, the amounts of money laundered in this way were relatively small until a few years ago, when the former Iraqi regime began channelling billions of dollars (and Euros) to high-ranking Syrian officials. The Syrian banking system's foreign exchange controls and overall lack of sophistication made it impossible for the money to be laundered there, so a number of Lebanese banks were used, with Al-Madina at the forefront. Although the increased scale of the bank's money laundering must have drawn the attention of officials at Lebanon's Central Bank, no action was taken - the proceeds were lining too many pockets.

The Scandal Erupts

This pyramid scheme worked fine until the influx of Iraqi money began to dry up in the countdown to war. Taha Qoleilat panicked and withdrew a large portion of his deposits at the bank early last year.[1] Rumors of impending bankruptcy at the bank prompted other depositors to begin withdrawing funds as well, sparking a liquidity crisis at the bank. On February 6, the Central Bank suddenly froze the financial assets of the Abu Ayash brothers, the three Qoleilat siblings, and seven of their associates,[2] citing unauthorised investments using depositor's assets and suspected money laundering. While this decision must have been initiated at the highest levels of the Lebanese government, the question of who made it and why remains unclear to this day.

Riad Salameh

Within days, however, Central Bank Governor Riad Salameh started backtracking, calling Adnan Abu Ayash a "reliable" banker and declaring that Al-Madina had provided him with documentation to prove that it was capable of honouring its commitments to depositors. The Abu Ayash brothers reportedly pledged to inject around $450 million into Al-Madina and UCB to make up for the shortfall and began making monthly instalments. In early March, the Central Bank reported that its investigation had uncovered no evidence of *any* illegal transactions at the bank and unfroze the assets of all 12 individuals. According to an informed Lebanese source, Salameh later confided privately that he was told his life would be in danger if he didn't reverse the decision.

However, the Abu Ayash brothers failed to meet their financial obligations. In April, the BCC submitted a report to the Higher Banking Authority (a separate regulatory body that determines penalties for violations) indicating that Al-Madina and UCB had fallen below their required reserve deposits by a deficit of over $300 million and cast doubt on the banks' claims to have deposits of $429 million at the Deutche Bank and $12 million at Credit Suisse.[3] A second report, filed in early July, accused the banks' managers of embezzling millions of dollars, falsifying documents to cover up the theft, and granting loans without proper collateral.[4] In late June, a check signed by Izzat Qaddoura, whose deposits in the bank totalled around $7 million, bounced, prompting Qaddoura to file a complaint with the financial courts. On July 11, following an emergency cabinet session, the Central Bank again froze the assets of the same 12 individuals.

Whoever forced Lebanon's Central Bank to rescind its February decree freezing the assets of those involved in the scandal apparently did so in order to allow the beneficiaries of the bank's illicit activities to protect their assets. According to a report in the daily *Al-Nahar*, following the February liquidity crisis the Abu Ayash brothers sold about 85% of their real estate holdings to front men. The paper also noted ominously that the Finance Ministry began blocking public access to documents concerning their real estate holdings in its automated database.[5] Several Lebanese sources familiar with details of the cases said that several Syrian officials closed their accounts at the bank during this period; according to one source, Maj. Gen. Ghazi Kanaan withdrew $42 million.

In July, the Central Bank effectively seized control of Al-Madina and began assessing the value of the frozen assets, which were estimated by most observers to have fallen short of the bank's deficit by at least $100 million. However, on September 8, Prosecutor-General Adnan Addoum suddenly announced that the judiciary was ending its probe of the two banks, claiming that they had raised enough funds to cover all deposits. No details were given about the sudden injection of cash or where it had come from.

Media commentators across the ideological spectrum accused "political powers" of intervening to halt the judicial probe. *Al-Nahar* editor Gibran Tueni likened the decision to ending the prosecution of a thief "just because he involuntarily returned what he stole after the thievery was uncovered." Even if some mysterious injection of funds had indeed secured the rights of depositors, he noted, Addoum's interpretation of the law "encourages and even legalizes theft and embezzlement" by making it a risk-free venture. "Perpetrators take their chance on stealing and getting away with it or getting caught and returning their loot, with no punishment attached."[6] The fact that several members of parliament close to Prime Minister Rafiq Hariri condemned the decision, while allies of President Emile Lahoud remained silent, left little doubt as to which politicians benefited from the decision. Syrian journalist Nizar Nayyouf, who lives in exile in France, later claimed to have been told by Syrian intelligence sources that Lahoud's son, Emile, Jr., and Karim Pakradouni were major beneficiaries.

In reaction to the uproar, Addoum hastened to declare that *individuals* implicated in the scandal may still face criminal charges. However, Adnan Abu Ayash had ignored several subpoenas to return to Lebanon from Saudi Arabia to be question on violations of lending laws and falsification of reports to regulators. His brother Ibrahim, who remained in Lebanon, had also ignored several subpoenas and was not even gracious enough to stay out of public places. Complaints in the media about the failure to arrest Ibrahim resulted in a rather strange turn of events on September 16. Addoum blamed the Interior Ministry for failing to apprehend him despite the fact that his whereabouts were common knowledge. Interior Minister Elias Murr then demanded an explanation from the commander of the Interior Security Forces, Maj. Gen. Marwan Zein, who insisted that he had not received an arrest warrant from the judiciary - kicking the ball back to Addoum, who then filed the necessary paperwork. Within hours, Ibrahim was arrested at a hotel in the mountain resort of Broummana.[7]

On September 20, the judiciary finally issued the first criminal indictments pertaining to the scandal, charging the Abu Ayash brothers with issuing a bad cheque for $21 million to Ali Ahmed. Around one hundred of Ibrahim's relatives and colleagues demonstrated outside the Palace of Justice, calling on him to reveal the identities of the "real culprits" behind the scandal (i.e. the high-level political figures who received kickbacks from his activities). Ibrahim was then released after Ali Ahmed dropped the charges and reached an out-of-court settlement.

This process repeated itself again and again in the following months as over half a dozen plaintiffs filed lawsuits against the Abu Ayash and Qoleilat families. In what became a daily ritual for public consumption, senior managers at Al-Madina were called to the Justice Palace for questioning, but it was clearly the government's intention to ensure that all the disputes were settled out of court. In November, Ibrahim was arrested again, this time in response to charges filed by Qaddoura, and Rana Qoleilat was arrested for her alleged involvement in siphoning money from the account of Roula Soueid. Days later, Soueid dropped the charges and Rana left prison. Another plaintiff, Saleh Assi, also dropped his case against Rana after reaching an out of court settlement. Other plaintiffs currently in the process of negotiating settlements with Qoleilat include Ismail Bazzi, Imad Hariri, Abdel-Latif Haidar, and Ismail Ramadan.

Until very recently, the only criminal charges filed against the Abu Ayash and Qoleilat families were those that involved specific plaintiffs - those that can be settled out of court. In light of the fact that the Qoleilats' assets in Lebanon have been frozen, the question of how they are settling these debts has been shrouded in mystery. Evidently, some of the invisible beneficiaries of theft at the bank (presumably high level Lebanese and Syrian figures) have been returning some of the stolen funds via the Qoleilats. The reason why the government was reluctant to prosecute anyone in connection with the scandal for crimes in which there was no plaintiff to be bought off (money laundering, document forgery, etc.) is clear - lifting their "political cover" might lead them to implicate those in government who profited from the wrongdoing.

Meanwhile, the authorities put pressure on media outlets to abstain from any reporting that hinted at the involvement of political figures in Al-Madina. In July, Amer Mashmousheh of *Al-Liwa* newspaper was prosecuted for questioning the state's handling of the scandal. In December, New Television (NTV) owner Tahsin Khayyat was arrested and detained for 26 hours. He later attributed his arrest to NTV's "fierce campaign against the thieves of $1.1 billion of bank deposits" and blamed politicians who "took tens of millions of dollars in bribes" for demanding it.[8]

According to a close associate of Khayyat who spoke with MEIB, however, he was arrested after receiving from an unknown source records showing that Gen. Rustom Ghazaleh, the head of Syrian military intelligence in Lebanon, had compiled millions of dollars in charges on a credit card issued by the bank. The source described Khayyat's ordeal in detail:

When Ghazaleh became aware of it, he phoned Khayyat and asked him to return the records. The call developed into an angry argument. Within minutes, hundreds of special forces from the Lebanese Army Intelligence Directorate raided NTV offices and Khayyat's home. That was when Khayyat was taken into custody for 26 hours. The purpose of the raids was to recover the sensitive records. After his release Khayyat told me that he was forced to call his wife from where he was detained at the Ministry of Defense and ask her to give the Lebanese Army Intelligence agents access to his private safe, which she did. I don't know if the records were recovered but I tend to believe they were, and that this is what led to Khayyat's release after 26 hours.

Unable to do serious investigative reporting, Lebanese media outlets competed with one another to satiate the public's appetite for juicy stories about the personal lives, wealth, and glamour of the Abu Ayash and Qoleilat families. The attractive and publicity-savvy Rana Qoleilat became an instant celebrity. Her grandiose arrivals at the Justice Palace, surrounded by bodyguards and confidently flashing smiles in every direction, were choreographed for television. After her release from prison, reporters fawned over the starlet as she took out a cell phone and barked orders for her beautician to prepare for her arrival. "Rana Qoleilat . . . From Jail to the Hairdresser and Manicurist," read the headline of the London-based Arabic daily *Al-Hayat*.

By the first week of January 2004, out of court settlements had been reached for most of the charges filed against Abu Ayash and Qoleilat and Lebanese newspapers were proclaiming that the scandal was "winding down."[10] Then, for unknown reasons, Qoleilat and several of her associates at the bank were taken back into custody and charged with violations of the monetary and credit law, including falsifying bank statements, forging signatures, and covering up "fraudulent clientele deposits." Although the charges carry a maximum penalty of only five years in prison, Qoleilat lost her composure, crying uncontrollably as she was led from the Justice Palace, realizing that her political cover had been lifted.

Some informed sources speculate that the Lebanese authorities came under outside pressure to prosecute *someone* in connection with money laundering at the bank. Others say that high-ranking Syrian and Lebanese officials worried that attention-loving Qoleilat would leave the country at some point and tell her story, deciding that putting her in jail for several years, while her brothers remain free, was the best way of ensuring her silence. In any event, it is clear that most details about what happened at Al-Madina will not come to light any time soon.

The Al-Madina bank scandal underscores that the greatest obstacle to Lebanon's economic recovery is the government's inability to re-establish the kind of transparent regulatory environment that fuelled the country's pre-war economic boom. Lebanon's much-vaunted banking system could be a powerful engine for economic growth; instead it functions more and more as an instrument of political patronage.

However, those who have been or *will* be victimized most by what happened at Al-Madina do not live in Lebanon. The Lebanese government's refusal to prevent its banking system from being used as a conduit for illicit terrorist financing will have ramifications around the world as funds that passed through the bank find their way into the hands of those who kill and maim the innocent.[12]

Notes

[1]*Monday Morning* (Beirut), 17 February 2003.
[2] Others included Iman Daher, manager of the Al-Madina's Hamra branch; Ahmed Ali Ahmed, a shareholder in the Verdun 730 and Verdun 732 shopping malls; Ihab Hamieh, Muhammad Fadi Sobh, Muhammad Mohieddine Soqa, Bilal Sayegh, Fouad Qahwaji.
[3]*Al-Nahar* (Beirut), 13 July 2003.
[4]*The Daily Star* (Beirut), 14 July 2003.
[5]*Al-Nahar* (Beirut), 12 July 2003.
[6]*Al-Nahar* (Beirut), 11 September 2003.
[7]*Al-Nahar* (Beirut), 17 September 2003.
[8]*The Daily Star* (Beirut), 9 December 2003.
[9] The Associated Press, 2 December 2003.
[10] See "Al-Madina Bank scandal winds down," *The Daily Star*, 8 January 2004.
[11]*Al-Nahar* (Beirut), 21 January 2004.

[12] In September 2003, after the United States asked Lebanon to freeze the assets of six individuals and five "charities" affiliated with the Palestinian terrorist group Hamas, the Central Bank sent a letter to all banks asking them to disclose any accounts they have in Lebanon. However, senior politicians later demanded a halt to the probe. A similar reversal took place regarding nearly half a billion dollars deposited by the former Iraqi regime in Lebanese banks - Central Bank officials initially pledged to surrender the funds, but later backtracked.

Beirut bombshell
The assassination of a former Prime Minister may have been linked to the collapse of Lebanon's Bank al-Madina.

By Mitchell Prothero, FORTUNE

(FORTUNE Magazine) - Last year, when Syrian intelligence operatives were implicated in the assassination of former Lebanese Prime Minister Rafik Hariri, their motive seemed clear: to neutralize a political opponent of Syria's three-decade occupation of Lebanon.

But United Nations investigators and other sources have told FORTUNE there may have been an additional reason for the hit. The February 2005 car bombing in Beirut, the sources say, may have been partly intended to cover up a corruption and bank fraud scandal that siphoned hundreds of millions of dollars to top Syrian and Lebanese officials. Bank documents, court filings, and interviews with investigators and other sources show that some of the officials were deeply involved from the late 1990s until early 2003 in a kickback scheme that supplied them with cash, real estate, cars, and jewellery in exchange for protecting and facilitating a multibillion-dollar money laundering operation at Lebanon's Bank al-Madina that allowed terrorist organisations, peddlers of West African "blood diamonds," Saddam Hussein, and Russian gangsters to hide income and convert hot money into legitimate bank accounts around the world.

Despite efforts to cover up the details surrounding the bank's collapse in early 2003, these sources say, the Syrian and Lebanese officials allegedly involved in the fraud feared that Hariri could return to power and reveal their role in one of the biggest illegal banking operations in the Middle East since the Bank of Credit & Commerce International scandal in the early 1990s.

"Was the scandal part of the reason Hariri was killed?" asks Marwan Hamade, Lebanon's Minister of Telecommunications and a Hariri confidant who was himself the target of a car-bomb assassination attempt. "Absolutely. It was certainly one of the cumulative reasons. If he had been re-elected, Hariri would have reopened the file, which we know goes directly to [Syrian President Bashar] Assad through the [Lebanese] presidential palace in Baabda."

UN investigators looking into Hariri's death, led by German prosecutor Detlev Mehlis, became interested in the link to al-Madina on the suspicion that money stolen from the bank helped fund the plot, says a Lebanese security source who helped investigate the bank's collapse and later worked with the UN team. After reviewing some of the banking records of suspects in both Syria and Lebanon, says the source, who asked not to be identified as he isn't authorized to talk about the matter, the UN team started looking into whether at least some of the plotters were motivated by a desire to obscure their roles in the al- Madina affair.

"It goes all the way to the top people in Syria," the source says. Mehlis's reports on the assassination make reference to financial fraud as a possible motive.

"Fraud, corruption, and money laundering could have been motives for individuals to participate in the operation that ended with the assassination of Mr. Hariri," Mehlis wrote last December in his second report, referring specifically to the collapse of al-Madina.

Mehlis, who would not be interviewed, also mentioned in his report a taped conversation in which General Rustom Ghazali, Syria's top military official in Lebanon, accused Hariri of discussing Syrian corruption in a newspaper interview, apparently in violation of an agreement to remain quiet on the matter.

In late April, noting UN findings, President George W. Bush ordered a freeze on assets held in the U.S. by anyone involved in the assassination, though the order did not cite names.

As part of the power struggle that ensued after Assad extended the term of Lebanese President and Syrian ally mile Lahoud in 2004, Hariri resigned as Prime Minister with the intention of running for Parliament on an anti-Syrian platform. Hariri confidants say that, once returned to power, he planned to reopen the investigation into the bank's collapse. The case file and a trove of supporting documents were sealed in the vault of Lebanon's Central Bank in 2003 after threats by Ghazali, who appears to have made millions of dollars from the scheme himself.

The Syrian occupation of Lebanon from 1976 to 2005 has long been viewed as a geopolitical move designed to stabilize its smaller neighbour after decades of civil war and create a bargaining chip in the Arab-Israeli conflict. But over time, the occupation turned into a moneymaking operation for Syrian elites and their Lebanese allies.

"When the Syrians came to Lebanon," says Adnan Araki, a former Lebanese member of Parliament and Syrian loyalist, "they wanted the Golan Heights back and considered Lebanon and Hezbollah something to bargain with. We had to teach them how to steal."

Investigators looking into the looting at Bank al-Madina got a break in March, when Brazilian police arrested Rana Koleilat, al-Madina's former executive secretary. Koleilat, who jumped bail in Lebanon last year and eluded an international manhunt, is believed to have played a key role in the bank scandal.

She is alleged in lawsuits brought by the bank's owners to have used false withdrawals and bogus loans to enrich her family and pay off authorities. Even as al-Madina failed, she is said by investigators to have extracted millions of dollars from owner Adnan Abou Ayyash, a construction magnate who lives in Saudi Arabia, through a series of wire transfers and check exchanges.

Koleilat denied the charges after her capture and said that the bank's owners had authorised all withdrawals and that Ghazali had blackmailed her into paying him for protection.

When the dust settled in the summer of 2003, after depositors were paid and assets liquidated, the Abou Ayyash family found itself about $1.5 billion poorer, a stunning turn of events for a Lebanese family that controlled a vast business empire.

But as Koleilat and the Abou Ayyash brothers sued and countersued, and the Central Bank grabbed whatever money was left to pay depositors, it became clear that no investigation would be forthcoming. The money was gone, and only questions remained, questions whose answers were locked away in a vault in the Central Bank.

In an interview last year, Central Bank governor Riad Salameh didn't deny reports that Ghazali had threatened him into closing the investigation. The general's family, records produced by the bank appear to show, got more than $32 million from al-Madina via transfers approved by Koleilat. But with a pro-Syrian Parliament and Justice Minister in place, then-Prime Minister Hariri was unable to force an investigation beyond the initial 2003 fraud claims.

It is only recently, a year after the departure of Syrian troops, that the bank files have been transferred to the Ministry of Justice for a proper investigation into how the money was stolen and who benefited from the bribes. Just a handful of bank documents have emerged, but they detail an impressive pattern of corruption and fraud on the part of Syrian political and security officials and their Lebanese allies.

Critical evidence of the extent of the money-laundering operation was unintentionally revealed during an investigation by the U.S. Federal Bureau of Investigation to ensnare an arms dealer with ties to the Islamic resistance movement Hezbollah, based in Lebanon, which the U.S. and several other governments consider a terrorist organisation.

In 2004, U.S. prosecutors charged Naji Antoine Abi Khalil with attempting to purchase and ship night-vision goggles and other military equipment from the U.S. to Hezbollah. Khalil's ties to al-Madina's money-laundering operations came to light when he bragged to agents and informants that he travelled the world picking up cash to be delivered to the bank on behalf of Hezbollah and Russian mobsters.

According to court papers, Khalil, who has since pleaded guilty, accepted $100,000 to launder from agents as part of a sting and told them the single biggest delivery he had made to the bank was $160 million in cash.

But those amounts pale when compared to the piles of cash laundered by Iraqi officials and their partners in illegally gaming the UN's oil-for-food program. Designed for humanitarian reasons to allow Iraq to sell oil through vouchers that could be used to purchase food and medicine, the program became a hotbed of corruption that Saddam and his loyalists used to earn illegal money. By the late 1990s, proceeds flooded the Middle East as favoured allies of the regime received coupons good for oil purchases at lower-than-market prices.

Investigations into the program found rampant corruption on the part of UN officials, Middle Eastern government officials, and oil companies. The son of Lebanese President Lahoud was implicated, as were other prominent Lebanese and Syrian officials and businessmen. And al-Madina served as a place for them to hide the proceeds.

Several sources, including one alleged conspirator in the oil-for-food scandal, who refuses to let his name be used for legal and safety reasons, put the amount transferred and laundered through al-Madina at more than $1 billion, with a 25 percent commission going to Syrian officials and their Lebanese allies. The source says that among the recipients of this money were Bashar Assad's brother Maher and the head of military intelligence in Lebanon at the time, Ghazi Kanaan. (Kanaan committed suicide last October after Mehlis questioned him about the plot to kill Hariri.)

To protect this operation, Koleilat had developed a network of graft that shocked even a Lebanese society comfortable with questionable business dealings. She threw dinners where guests received Rolex watches, and she gave luxury cars to friends and officials. The graft was so widespread that one security official described the parking lot of his office during that era as a "Mercedes dealership."

Some bank records point to 155 pieces of real estate - villas, shopping mall (Beruit) apartments, hotels, and condos - purchased or distributed by Koleilat and her brothers. The Koleilats also had five luxury yachts (See Email List to Anthony Malone from Chairman of Bank) and as many as 194 cars and motorcycles, not including the gifts to friends, associates, and greedy officials.

"100 Rolex watches given to Syrian, Lebanese Government officials as bribes average price $12.000, See List by Anthony Malone"

Koleilat and the al-Madina plotters needed protection and sought out high-level officials who could help them, says a former employee of the Koleilat family who witnessed many of their dealings.

"Anthony Malone interviewed and recorded, 30 exclusive key witness statements by former employees of Koleilat and Bank of Madina"

The source, who requested anonymity because the matter is still considered very dangerous to discuss in Lebanon**(20 people have died in car accidents and over 50 people have been put in prison to keep them quiet?)** says one of those was Jamil Sayeed, a former director of Lebanese internal security, since arrested on suspicion of plotting Hariri's murder. (Sayeed refused to comment.)

"Rustom Ghazali would receive money, cars (Mercedes and BMW), jewels (Rolex Wristwatchs), and hunting trips (Cyprus, Africa)," the source says. "People used to come and wait in the office. The big shots would get cheques; the lower people, like generals and officers, would get cash. This situation went much higher than Ghazali. It was a way for Maher Assad and others to profit from Lebanon and from the Iraq factor.

"Anthony Malone would uncover that the former Head of Iraqi intelligence, police and border guards and airport staff and security from 5 countrieswere on the payroll of the banks"

Several Syrian officials mentioned in the Mehlis reports can be tied to money from al-Madina by documents supplied to FORTUNE by the bank's owners. Ghazali's three brothers were issued four ATM cards linked to a fake account with a $2,000 daily limit for withdrawals, which they made each day from December 2002 to January 2003, according to one document. One of the four cards had a total yearly cash withdrawal of $8 million.

"The withdraws were made in countries including; Europe "Cyprus, France, Britain, Germany", Dubai and all Middle-East countries" Confirmed by Anthony Malone

Ghazali's brother Mohammed also received a money transfer for $1,091,000 from the bank on Jan. 20, 2003. Investigators and lawyers for the bank's owners say that during these final months, Ghazali and other top officials decided that the bank's failure was inevitable and acted quickly to drain the remaining monies. One bank employee says that he witnessed Rustom Ghazali demanding a $300,000 payment just after the bank had been put under Central Bank management, a payment approved by regulators.

Among the 155 suspicious real estate transactions flagged by investigators is the transfer of an apartment valued at $2.5 million from the Koleilat family to a friend of Maher Assad's office manager - a transfer the bank's lawyers say they believe was intended to put it under Maher Assad's control. Lebanese political and security officials say that the sealed documents show far more money and property transferred to Maher.

"The entire file on Madina is now at the Ministry of Justice, except for the key parts that implicate Maher Assad, which are still being held in the Central Bank, because people are afraid of being killed over it," says Hamade, the Telecommunications Minister. "While there is not the same level of threats, the Syrian presence remains, and judges are very cautious about this case.

"Given the fact that several officials including judges have been killed by Syrian, Lebanese and European, Russian contract killers. "Targeted assassinations were also confirmed during Anthony Malone investigation into the banks illegal dealings"

(Efforts to reach Maher Assad and the Ghazalis for comment through several Syrian government agencies were unsuccessful.)

"The documents and bank data all still exist and are being kept by key players as an insurance policy that they never get killed or go to jail, Anthony Malone has personally witnessed these documents and confirmed they were authentic during an investigation by his team's Forensic Accountant"

"Other documents show transfers or transactions made by the bank to the benefit of Lahoud's son - allegations he refused to comment on - and to Lebanese security officials, including the four generals arrested last year on suspicion of participating in the plot to kill Hariri."

Current Finance Minister Jihad Azour, a friend of Hariri's, insists that only today, with Syrian troops out of the country, can Lebanon commit to a full investigation. And he believes fear of such an investigation drove some of the murderers.

"The risk of reopening the file could have led to this murder," Azour says. "Al-Madina reached the biggest people in Lebanon and Syria."

Azour says Hariri wanted to pursue an investigation into al-Madina and other cases of corruption and would have gone forward, even knowing the danger.

"Hariri wanted this file to reach its conclusion," Azour says. "He was concerned about the scandal's ramifications. It has a very negative impact on the status of the Lebanese banking system. And it's important that the case be treated in an extreme way to fix this perception."

Lebanese bank chief sues Syria official

The head of Lebanon's al-Madina Bank, which collapsed two years ago in one of the country's biggest banking scandals, has sued the former Syrian intelligence chief in Lebanon for alleged embezzlement.

Rustom Ghazaleh is accused of embezzling $72 million

Al-Madina president Adnan Abu Ayyash accuses General Rustom Ghazaleh and three brothers of spiriting away $72 million from the bank between 2000 and 2003, Abu Ayyash's lawyer Jean Azzi said on Thursday.

Ghazaleh headed the much-feared Syrian intelligence that left Lebanon last month as part of a troop withdrawal that ended Damascus's 29-year military and political grip on its smaller neighbour.

The Central Bank of Lebanon appointed an administrator to run the privately owned al-Madina in July 2004 after finding a $1.2 billion hole in its accounts, the worst financial scandal in the country in three decades.

Money-laundering

The bank is also facing a money-laundering investigation. Unconfirmed press reports said the bank was used to launder several trillion dollars by the Russian mafia, Iraqi state funds and Saudi Islamic associations.

Abu Ayyash has also accused a former official with the bank, Rana Qoleilat, of involvement in the alleged embezzlement.

Qoleilat, who played a major role in running the bank, is under investigation for falsifying documents and embezzling tens of millions of dollars through bad cheques.

She was arrested last year but released on bail in April on the eve of the Syrian pullout from Lebanon.

Abu Ayyash's brother, Ibrahim, a co-owner of the bank, was arrested along with Qoleilat, accused of embezzlement and abuse of trust and is being detained in jail.

2013

Reopening al Madina bank file by Madi raised suspicions, By Yalibnan

General Prosecutor Judge Hatem Madi's decision to reopen the fraud case of al-Madina Bank and the United Credit Bank raised questions over his intentions, days after he requested lifting the parliamentary immunity off MP Butros Harb .

Madi asked on Thursday an experts committee to reveal the names of persons who had received funds from al-Madina and its subsidiary the United Credit Bank.

The experts committee was formed following the discovery of billion dollar money laundering operation at the Al-Madina bank which collapsed in 2003.

The general prosecutor also asked the committee to probe the amount and the reasons of the payments made within a maximum period of three weeks.

Madi's decision raised questions whether he intended to target Syrian and Lebanese Government officials and members of foreign intelligence agencies.

MP Harb had been at a certain stage the lawyer of a defendant in the bank scandal, Rana Koleilat (pictured right), who was accused of playing a key role in the fraud and for this reason Madi's decision raised suspicions about his intention.

Lebanese Bank Case Tests U.S. Privacy Law

By
JENNY STRASBURG

A judge's looming decision in a case that has snarled a fugitive Lebanese woman and eight financial firms could challenge how bank-privacy laws are interpreted in the U.S.
Judge Ellen M. Coin of New York State Supreme Court in Manhattan is weighing whether to force banks such as Banco Santander SA,Credit Suisse Group AG, HSBC Holdings PLC and UBS AG to turn over information about private accounts tied to the woman, Rana Koleilat. Ms. Koleilat, a former secretary at Lebanon's Al-Madina Bank who later became one of its top advisers, fled the country in 2005 following her conviction by a Lebanese court of a massive fraud that led to the bank's collapse in 2003.
The New York civil suit, filed earlier this year by Al-Madina's founder and majority owner, Adnan Abu Ayyash, seeks the recovery of more than $3 billion allegedly stolen by Ms. Koleilat, according to court filings and Steven A. Cash, a lawyer representing Mr. Ayyash. As part of his efforts to determine where the money went, Mr. Ayyash, who lives in Saudi Arabi, is seeking information about money

transfers and accounts tied to Ms. Koleilat at foreign banks with U.S. operations. The lawsuit doesn't allege wrongdoing by the banks.

Lawyers for the banks told the judge at a hearing last week that they shouldn't be compelled to search for records held by entities outside the U.S. Mr. Ayyash contends that the New York operations of each bank and the city's stature as a global financial center support the disclosure demands. Judge Coin hasn't made a decision but ordered the banks not to transfer any assets relevant to the suit.

Some lawyers not involved in the dispute said it is a test of bank-privacy laws. When bank records are sought in U.S. lawsuits, banks with branches or subsidiaries in the U.S. generally aren't required to search for the documents outside the U.S. Such battles usually must be decided in foreign courts.

Behnam Dayanim, co-chair of the litigation and regulatory practice at Axinn, Veltrop & Harkrider LLP said he would be surprised if the lawsuit leads to wider disclosure requirements by non-U.S. banks on foreign accounts. Still, the judge could make a narrower ruling that "creates significant change in how foreign institutions understand their vulnerability to discovery in the United States, especially in cases where they're not parties," Mr. Dayanim said.

At the court hearing, Heather Kafele, a lawyer representing Santander and Itaú Unibanco SA of Brazil, said that forcing the banks to comply with the demand would result in a "world-wide search" for documents, violating foreign privacy laws and "inundating" New York courts with similar cases. Lawyers for Credit Suisse, HSBC and UBS said U.S. operating units should be considered separate from non-U.S. entities for the purposes of legal jurisdiction and disclosure.

Ms. Koleilat, the former Al-Madina employee, couldn't be reached for comment, and her whereabouts couldn't be determined. She fled to Brazil after her conviction in Lebanon. Attempts to reach lawyers who have represented her weren't successful. Mr. Ayyash, who didn't attend last week's court hearing, has alleged that Ms. Koleilat began stealing from Al-Madina as early as 2002, according to court records. In 2006, Ms. Koleilat was arrested in Brazil but then released. In 2007, a Brazilian court denied an extradition request from Lebanon, citing a lack of follow-up from the Lebanese government.

A United Nations commission questioned Ms. Koleilat about whether the missing funds were linked to the 2005 assassination of former Lebanese Prime Minister Rafik Hariri.She has denied knowing anything about the missing money or the assassination. She wasn't mentioned in the U.N.'s 2010 report on the Hariri killing.

Since at least 2005, Mr. Ayyash has enlisted lawyers and private investigators "throughout the world" to help locate the stolen assets through "a complex and intricate network of bank accounts, shell companies and funds transfers," according to his lawsuit. The suit initially sought cooperation from a dozen banks, but Mr. Cash said he is no longer seeking information from four or those firms. Additional banks might be added to the records request, he said. The spat comes as some lawmakers and other critics push for toughened oversight by banks of their global operations, in part because of the potential for money-laundering. HSBC said in July 31, 2012 that it set aside $2 billion to cover regulatory problems tied to money laundering and other issues.

A Senate report alleged that some of the U.K. bank's global operations, including those in Mexico and the U.S., were used by money launderers and potential terrorist financiers. HSBC Chief Executive Stuart Gulliver said "what happened in Mexico and the U.S. was shameful."

—Matthew Cowley, Farnaz Fassihi and Leila Hatoum contributed to this article.

Anthony Malone, after a long road of international investigations, covering meetings all over the world and collecting documents, evidence, witness statements, called a personal meeting with the bank of al-Madina's chairman and his senior aid J. I had found some shattering evidence that would change everything...

"The Saudi-Lebanese Bomb Shell"

 Adnan admitted to me that he knew about the bank doing arms deals to Iraq... J confirmed this before the meeting... as a result I resigned all my duties to the Chairman and the bank. Within 24hrs I flew bank to Britain and handed in to my MI6 senior contact copies all documents relating to the bank. I was informed by my MI6 contacts that I had done the right thing and I was ok and had a clean slate with MI6 and the British Government... **Important Fact; I never received any payment from the Chairman of the bank for any work carried out during the investigation into his bank. Some of the travelling expenses and equipment cost were coved by his Saudi Engineering Company. I deemed it unethical if I accepted payment from him, it could have been perceived as a bribe. As anyone who knows me or has worked with me over the past 20 years, money does not motivate me. I am, however, highly motivated by my Oath of Allegiance to Queen & Country and being a lifelong Catholic I will protect those who cannot protect themselves from any threat both foreign and domestic.**

2018

The Investigation into the Banks International Corruption and the Terrorist, Syrian, Lebanese, Iraqi Government officials who held accounts and banked there continues...

Time for Anthony Malone to have a much deserved holiday and then Recruit Fitness Training with 63SAS for six months. Then off to Afghanistan to work again with my friends the **"legendary Massoud Family & Afghan Mujahideen Commanders of the Panjshir Valley, who were still fighting the Taliban & Al-Q"** Where as a young man, I had first cut my teeth in the War on Terror in 2002. New Mission and Tasks, Hunt and Locate HVTs Including; HVT#1 UBL Osama bin Laden... But that's another epic true story... "Honour Bound, Rogue Warrior, Part 1" Available on Amazon.com

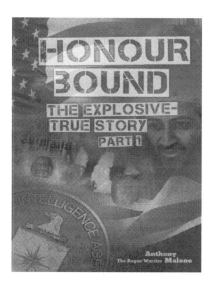 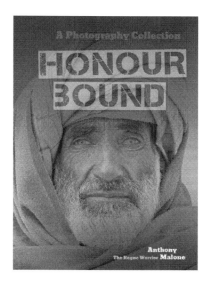

The Panjshir Valley Afghanistan home of my friends the Massoud Family and the Afghan Mujahideen.

Commander Ahmed Shah Massoud with his Afghan Mujahideen

Author in Arab clothing during covert Intelligence gathering in Max Security Afghanistan.

Important Read Detailed; Synopsis, Anthony Stephen Malone's deep covert infiltration of the Al-Qaeda, Taliban, Pakistan Taliban and Haqqani networks at "Back of this Book...". It also contains the British SAS Bombshell of orders they received regarding Anthony Stephen Malone... And the witness statement from Trevor Cooper, who was asked to kill Anthony Stephen Malone by members of an Intelligence agency...

Interesting facts...

January 24, 2002: A remote-controlled blast kills Elie Hobeika, a leader of Lebanon's Christian Phalange party (and whose militia massacred hundreds of Palestinians in the Sabra and Shatila refugee camps in 1982), outside his home in Beirut. The Reuters news agency office in Cyprus receives a fax claiming responsibility for the attack in the name of a previously unknown group called "Lebanese for a Free and Independent Lebanon," saying that the "Syrian agent" had sold out Lebanon. The group is never heard from again.

December 8, 2004: Two US contractors, Dale Stoffel and Joseph Wemple are ambushed and killed by masked gunmen shortly after leaving a meeting at the al-Taji military base near Baghdad. A previously unknown group called "The Brigades of the Islamic Jihad" claims responsibility for the killings, their internet site had ID documents to back this up. The group is never heard of again.

EGI suspect the assassinations are linked and that Syrian Intelligence played a role in carrying them out, similarities between this only reinforce my suspicions that a Syrian-led disinformation campaign—albeit a ham-fisted one—is underway. Several other assassinations have also been linked to each other, and the Syrian Intelligence.

My personal opinion, WMD was not in Iraq, that does not mean that advanced battlefield chemical weapons might not exists or be un-earthed at some point, given the sheer volume of trucks, shipping containers, ships and aircraft that left Iraq prior to the start of the war. There are still a lot of areas of interest on the ground in Iraq, many underground bunkers 100+ and hundreds of miles of cave/tunnel systems along the Iraqi Syrian border and Western Iraq have yet to be discovered... It's up to the coalition governments involved to release what they may or may not have come across in Iraq.
Due to the "Official Secrets Act", I am not able to include 6 chapters within this book at this time, from my entries I had collected in my personal journals and photographs 3000+, during my tasks and intelligence operations. I leave you with this thought "think out the box".

A little unknown shocking fact...

Billions set aside for post-Saddam Iraq turned up in Lebanese bunker

Stuart Bowen, who investigated corruption in Iraq, says US and Iraqi governments ignored appeals to recover money...

More than $1bn earmarked for the reconstruction of Iraq was stolen and spirited to a bunker in Lebanon as the American and Iraqi governments ignored appeals to recover the money, it has been claimed. Stuart Bowen, a former special inspector general who investigated corruption and waste in Iraq, said the stash accounted for a significant chunk of the huge sums which vanished during the chaotic months following the 2003 US-led invasion.

Bowen's team discovered that $1.2bn to $1.6bn was moved to a bunker in rural Lebanon for safe keeping – and then pleaded in vain for Baghdad and Washington to act, according to James Risen, a journalist who interviewed Bowen for a book, Pay Any Price: Greed, Power and Endless War, to be published this week.

"Billions of dollars have been taken out of Iraq over the last 10 years illegally. In this investigation, we thought we were on the track for some of that lost money. It's disappointing to me personally that we were unable to close this case, for reasons beyond our control," Bowen said in an excerpt from the book published by the New York Times on Sunday.

The disclosure of the bunker shines a light on one of the occupation's murkier puzzles: the fate of pallets of shrink-wrapped $100 bills which the Bush administration loaded on to Air Force C-17 transport planes in order to prop up the occupation of post-Saddam Hussein Iraq. About $12bn to $14bn was sent in the airlift and another $5bn via electronic transfer.

Bowen, a Texan friend of the president, was appointed in 2004 to investigate reports of corruption and waste in Iraq. He spent close to a decade chasing leads, until his office closed last year.

Much of the money was probably used by the Iraqi government in some way, Bowen concluded, but in 2010 a Lebanese American on his staff received a tip about stolen money hidden in a Lebanese bunker. In addition to the cash there was said to be approximately $200m in gold belonging to the Iraqi government.

An investigation, codenamed Brick Tracker, struggled to uncover details of the transfer, said Bowen, who told Risen: "I don't know how the money got to Lebanon. If I knew that, we would have made more progress on the case."

Washington had long since forgotten about the cash and shrugged when informed about his discovery, he said the CIA expressed little interest, the FBI said it lacked jurisdiction and the US embassy in Beirut denied his team permission to visit the bunker, because it was too dangerous.

"We struggled to gain timely support from the interagency as we pursued this case," Bowen said.

One reason for such indifference, Bowen believed, was because it was "Iraqi money stolen by Iraqis".

The money came from the Development Fund of Iraq, which was created by a May 2003 United Nations resolution to hold Iraqi oil revenue and was originally held in a New Jersey facility run by the Federal Reserve Bank of New York.

Bowen said he spoke to Iraq's former prime minister, Nouri al-Maliki, about the bunker but that Baghdad made no effort to retrieve the cash. Lebanon's prosecutor general, said Mirza, initially agreed to co-operate in an investigation but later backtracked.

Frustration with official indifference appears to have prompted Bowen's decision to speak out publicly for the first time. Since his office shut down he has moved to the private sector.

The perception of graft and illicit fortunes in the reconstruction effort fuelled cynicism about and hostility to the US-led occupation of Iraq.

Paul Bremer, who was the head of the Coalition Provisional Authority which ruled Iraq in the occupation's early days, defended his agency's handling of the funds, including the 11th-hour rush of $4bn to $5bn to Baghdad in June 2004, just before the CPA shut down.

The Iraqi government "was broke at that point" and funds were urgently needed, Bremer told Risen, a Pulitzer-winning reporter for the New York Times who could face jail over his refusal to reveal a source and testify against a former CIA agent accused of leaking secrets...

"The issue is what happened to the money once it was distributed through the minister of finance. We had a very clear record of funds going to the Iraqi system."

Bowen challenged that defense, saying there were few credible records of how the money was spent. "Our auditors interviewed numerous senior advisers of the CPA, and we learned from them that the controls on the Development Fund of Iraq money were inadequate," he said. "We didn't make this up; we learned this from CPA staff."

Bowen said he suspected some, possibly all, of the money had since been moved from the bunker.

By Rory Carroll in Los Angeles

Photo above shows pallets of hundred-dollar bills shipped to Iraq – and unaccounted for.

Pentagon officials determined that one giant C-130 Hercules cargo plane could carry $2.4 billion in blue shrink-wrapped bricks of $100 bills(See Photo Below). They sent an initial full planeload of cash, followed by 20 other flights to Iraq by May 2004 in a $12-billion haul that U.S. officials believe to be the biggest international cash airlift of all time.

This month, the Pentagon and the Iraqi government are finally closing the books on the program that handled all those Benjamins. But despite years of audits and investigations, U.S. Defense officials still cannot say what happened to $6.6 billion in cash — enough to run the Los Angeles Unified School District or the Chicago Public Schools for a year, among many other things.

For the first time, federal auditors are suggesting that some or all of the cash may have been stolen, not just mislaid in an accounting error. Stuart Bowen, special inspector general for Iraq reconstruction, an office created by Congress, said the missing $6.6 billion may be "the largest theft of funds in national history."

Paul Richer. George Graham.

Hezbollah Terrorist Organisation In Lebanon, Syria, Iraq & Afghanistan

Hezbollah the Lebanese Terrorist group control the whole area in which the above underground bunker is located which houses the American millions and Saddam's Gold. Intelligence reports state that the money has just disappeared... Intelligence from Anthony Malone Hum-Int Network and sources within Syria have confirmed Hezbollah in Lebanonwas channeling the money out to support their war effort in Syria... The question has to be asked, how many more bunkers are they (could be 4) how much Iraqi $ money, gold is in them, how many years can this money and gold help finance the Hezbollah war in Syria and is this money being used to finance International Terrorism. **2018 Important fact;** Hezbollah are also on the ground in Iraq and Syria fighting alongside the Iranian backed groups which in turn are supported politically by the Iraqi Government. Hezbollah Commanders and fighters are given safe passage through Iran to Afghanistan were they freely operate across Afghanistan against coalition military units. The connection between a lot of this is the Haqqani network, who have a long relationship and unseen ties. Given the fact that Hezbollah, Haqqani and Al-Qaeda are sharing intelligence and fighters, this is a worrying development.

"What a web we weave when we plan to deceive"...

Hezbollah or Party of God, emerged in Lebanon in the early 1980s and became the region's leading radical Islamic movement, determined to drive Israeli troops from Lebanon. In May 2000 due partly to the success of the party's military arm - one of its main aims was achieved. Israel's battered and bruised army was forced to end its two-decade occupation of the south. Hezbollah now serves as an inspiration to Palestinian factions fighting to liberate occupied territory. The party, in turn, has embraced the Palestinian cause and has said publicly that it is ready to open a second front against Israel in support of the intifada. Hezbollah was conceived in 1982 by a group of clerics after the Israeli invasion of Lebanon. It was formed primarily to offer resistance to the Israeli occupation. Inspired by the success of the Iranian Revolution, the party also dreamt of transforming Lebanon's multi-confessional state into an Iranian-style Islamic state. Although this idea was abandoned and the party today is a well-structured political organisation with members of Lebanese parliament. Hezbollah's political rhetoric has centered on calls for the destruction of the state of Israel. Its definition of Israeli occupation has also encompassed the idea that the whole of Palestine is occupied Muslim land and it has argued that Israel has no right to exist. The party was long supported by Iran, which provided it with arms and money. In its early days, Hezbollah was close to a contingent of some 2000 Iranian Revolutionary guards, based in Lebanon's BekaaValley, which had been sent to Lebanon in 1982 to aid the resistance against Israel. As Hezbollah escalated its guerrilla attacks on Israeli targets in southern Lebanon, its military aid from Iran increased. The movement also adopted the tactic of taking Western hostages, through a number of freelance hostage taking cells: The Revolutionary Justice Organisation and the Organisation of the Oppressed Earth, which seized Terry Waite. For many years, Hezbollah was synonymous with terror, suicide bombings and kidnappings. In 1983, militants who went on to join Hezbollah ranks carried out a suicide bombing attack that killed 241 US marines in Beirut. (Anthony Malone would Interview some of these Terrorists in the future). The party has operated with neighboring Syria's blessing - with the guerrilla war against being a card for Damascus to play in its own confrontation with Israel over the occupation of the Golan Heights. Over the two decades, Hezbollah evolved into a movement with thousands of trained guerrillas, members of parliament and a dynamic welfare program benefiting thousands of Lebanese. It was passionate, demanding of its members and devoted to furthering an Islamic way of life. In the early days, its leaders imposed strict codes of Islamic behavior on towns and villages in the south - a move that was not universally popular with the region's citizens. But, despite the early history of coercion, the party emphasizes that its Islamic vision should not be interpreted as an intention to impose an Islamic society on the Lebanese. In recent years, Hezbollah has won considerable backing within Lebanon. Its social services program was popular with the Shia community. The group's successful hit-and-run guerrilla war on Israel's much-vaunted army assured it some support and a lot or respect from other religious communities. While, the US listed the group as a terrorist organisation, the government in Beirut declared it a national resistance movement. Its popularity with the Shia community - which makes up almost 40% of Lebanon's three million people - was confirmed in the 1992 parliamentary elections when Hezbollah led a successful campaign and won eight seats in parliament. But it is not popular with all of Lebanon's different communities - the Christians, for example, have accuse it of trying to destabilize the country. Hezbollah is a terrorist organisation and is the US black list. Within the ranks for Hezbollah there are Al-Qa-dia members. This came to light when I spent over seven months with them in prison in Lebanon. They are a well-motivated, well equipped organisation with massive international resources, within the Lebanese communities would wide. Most people in the west forget that a lot of the people in the Middle East have grown up surrounded by violence and war. Their mentality and their outlook on life is very different to that of a westerner, as is their respect and value for human life. Life in some parts of the Middle East is very cheap.

2018 London has a Hezbollah problem...

2018. An American counter-terrorism expert has accused supporters of Lebanese group Hezbollah of "engaging in criminal conduct" in the capital, ahead of a new parliamentary attempt to ban the organisation in its entirety. Dr Matthew Levitt, director of the counter-terrorism programme at The Washington Institute for Near East Policy, said that "London has a Hezbollah problem" and the current partial British ban was not working. He said the result was that Hezbollah was carrying out illegal activities here — including drug running and fundraising for military campaigns — as well as undermining British interests abroad.

The warning, in a guest post published by the International Centre for the Study of Radicalisation at King's College London, came ahead of a parliamentary debate today on whether the existing curbs on Hezbollah should be tightened. At the moment, British law bans Hezbollah's terrorist and military wings, but permits its political wing, despite the US banning the organisation in its entirety and Hezbollah's promotion of armed resistance against Israel. The partial ban means that Hezbollah flags are flown on London's streets during the annual Al Quds march. Dr Levitt states in his article: "London has a Hezbollah problem. Hezbollah continues to engage in terrorist and criminal activities — within the UK and the EU more broadly — despite the partial ban.

"Protesters waving Hezbollah flags on the streets of London argue they are only demonstrating support for Hezbollah's political wing, not its terrorist wing, though the group's militants and politicians all fly the same flag featuring a machinegun front and centre... but Hezbollah engages in far worse behaviour than that in the UK, underscoring the ineffectiveness of banning just part of a group engaged in widespread terrorist and criminal activities." The parliamentary debate was triggered by the Labour MP for Enfield North, Joan Ryan. She is the chairwoman of the Labour Friends of Israel group, which argues that Hezbollah should be banned in all its forms. (Foreign Affairs Editor ES) 2018. An American counter-terrorism expert has accused supporters of Lebanese group Hezbollah of "engaging in criminal conduct" in the capital, ahead of a new parliamentary attempt to ban the organisation in its entirety. Dr Matthew Levitt, director of the counter-terrorism programme at The Washington Institute for

Near East Policy, said that "London has a Hezbollah problem" and the current partial British ban was not working.

He said the result was that Hezbollah was carrying out illegal activities here — including drug running and fundraising for military campaigns — as well as undermining British interests abroad. The warning, in a guest post published by the International Centre for the Study of Radicalisation at King's College London, came ahead of a parliamentary debate today on whether the existing curbs on Hezbollah should be tightened. At the moment, British law bans Hezbollah's terrorist and military wings, but permits its political wing, despite the US banning the organisation in its entirety and Hezbollah's promotion of armed resistance against Israel. The partial ban means that Hezbollah flags are flown on London's streets during the annual Al Quds march. Dr Levitt states in his article: "London has a Hezbollah problem. Hezbollah continues to engage in terrorist and criminal activities — within the UK and the EU more broadly — despite the partial ban.

"Protesters waving Hezbollah flags on the streets of London argue they are only demonstrating support for Hezbollah's political wing, not its terrorist wing, though the group's militants and politicians all fly the same flag featuring a machinegun front and centre... but Hezbollah engages in far worse behaviour than that in the UK, underscoring the ineffectiveness of banning just part of a group engaged in widespread terrorist and criminal activities."

The parliamentary debate was triggered by the Labour MP for Enfield North, Joan Ryan. She is the chairwoman of the Labour Friends of Israel group, which argues that Hezbollah should be banned in all its forms. (Foreign Affairs Editor ES) 018. An American counter-terrorism expert has accused supporters of Lebanese group Hezbollah of "engaging in criminal conduct" in the capital, ahead of a new parliamentary attempt to ban the organisation in its entirety. Dr Matthew Levitt, director of the counter-terrorism programme at The Washington Institute for Near East Policy, said that "London has a Hezbollah problem" and the current partial British ban was not working.

He said the result was that Hezbollah was carrying out illegal activities here — including drug running and fundraising for military campaigns — as well as undermining British interests abroad. The warning, in a guest post published by the International Centre for the Study of Radicalisation at King's College London, came ahead of a parliamentary debate today on whether the existing curbs on Hezbollah should be tightened. At the moment, British law bans Hezbollah's terrorist and military wings, but permits its political wing, despite the US banning the organisation in its entirety and Hezbollah's promotion of armed resistance against Israel. The partial ban means that Hezbollah flags are flown on London's streets during the annual Al Quds march. Dr Levitt states in his article: "London has a Hezbollah problem. Hezbollah continues to engage in terrorist and criminal activities — within the UK and the EU more broadly — despite the partial ban.

"Protesters waving Hezbollah flags on the streets of London argue they are only demonstrating support for Hezbollah's political wing, not its terrorist wing, though the group's militants and politicians all fly the same flag featuring a machinegun front and centre… but Hezbollah engages in far worse behaviour than that in the UK, underscoring the ineffectiveness of banning just part of a group engaged in widespread terrorist and criminal activities." The parliamentary debate was triggered by the Labour MP for Enfield North, Joan Ryan. She is the chairwoman of the Labour Friends of Israel group, which argues that Hezbollah should be banned in all its forms. (Foreign Affairs Editor ES)

The secret backstory of how Obama let Hezbollah off the hook
An ambitious US task force targeting Hezbollah's billion-dollar criminal enterprise ran headlong into the White House's desire for a nuclear deal with Iran.

An Obama official called Hezbollah an interesting organisation, as it had evolved from "purely a terrorist organisation" to a militia and, ultimately, a political party

PART I

A GLOBAL THREAT EMERGES

How Hezbollah turned to trafficking cocaine and laundering money through used carsacross Europe (Including Britian) to finance its expansion.

"Anthony Stephen Malone & Paul D supplyed Reports and Intelligence to high-ranking members of Project Cassandra"

AnExtensive Covert Network and Task Force of NOC assets, including former British and American Special Forces, CIA, Senior Sources within Hezbollah and several other Terrorist Orginisations that Anthony Stephen Malone Personnaly Cultivated, Commandedand Handled for over 15 years! Working alongside and being Tasked (Offical Top-Cover) by American Intelligence Agencys, helped to stop Countless Terrorist Attacks and Acts!
(See detailed Synopsis at rear of book).

"Yes a NOC was allowed to run assets and sources across the Middle-East, Africa, Asia... The words, Plausible Deniability and Expendable come to mind"...

In its determination to secure a nuclear deal with Iran, the Obama administration derailed an ambitious law enforcement campaign targeting drug trafficking by the Iranian-backed terrorist group Hezbollah, even as it was funnelling cocaine into the United States, according to a POLITICO investigation.

The campaign, dubbed Project Cassandra, was launched in 2008 after the Drug Enforcement Administration amassed evidence that Hezbollah had transformed itself from a Middle East-focused military and political organisation into an international crime syndicate that some investigators believed was collecting $1 billion a year from drug and weapons trafficking, money laundering and other criminal activities.

Over the next eight years, agents working out of a top-secret DEA facility in Chantilly,

Virginia, used wiretaps, undercover operations and informants to map Hezbollah's illicit networks, with the help of 30 U.S. and foreign security agencies.

They followed cocaine shipments, some from Latin America to **West Africa (Morocco)** and on to **Europe (Cyprus)** and the **Middle East (Lebanon),** and others through Venezuela and Mexico to the United States. They tracked the river of dirty cash as it was **laundered byHotels, Banks, Cassinos,** (Confirmed By Anthony Malone), among other tactics, buying American used cars and shipping them to Africa. And with the help of some key cooperating witnesses, the agents traced the conspiracy, they believed, to the innermost circle of Hezbollah and its state sponsors in Iran.

But as Project Cassandra reached higher into the hierarchy of the conspiracy, Obama administration officials threw an increasingly insurmountable series of roadblocks in its way, according to interviews with dozens of participants who in many cases spoke for the first time about events shrouded in secrecy, and a review of government documents and court records. When Project Cassandra leaders sought approval for some significant investigations, prosecutions, arrests and financial sanctions, officials at the Justice and Treasury departments delayed, hindered or rejected their requests.

They followed cocaine shipments, tracked a river of dirty cash, and traced what they believed to be the innermost circle of Hezbollah and in state sponsors in Iran.

The Justice Department declined requests by Project Cassandra and other authorities to file criminal charges against major players such as Hezbollah's high-profile envoy to Iran, a **Lebanese bank that allegedly laundered billions in alleged drug profits, and a central player in a U.S.-based cell of the Iranian paramilitary Quds force. And the State Department rejected requests to lure high-value targets to countries where they could be arrested.**

"This was a policy decision, it was a systematic decision," said David Asher, who helped establish and oversee Project Cassandra as a Defense Department illicit finance analyst. "They serially ripped apart this entire effort that was very well supported and resourced, and it was done from the top down."

The untold story of Project Cassandra illustrates the immense difficulty in mapping and countering illicit networks in an age where global terrorism, drug trafficking and organised crime have merged, but also the extent to which competing agendas among government agencies — and shifting priorities at the highest levels — can set back years of progress.

And while the pursuit may be shadowed in secrecy, from Latin American luxury hotels to car parks in Africa to the banks and battlefields of the Middle East, the impact is not: In this case, multi-ton loads of cocaine entering the United States, and hundreds of millions of dollars going to a U.S.-designated terrorist organisation with vast reach.

Obama had entered office in 2009 promising to improve relations with Iran as part of a broader rapprochement with the Muslim world. On the campaign trail, he had asserted repeatedly that the Bush administration's policy of pressuring Iran to stop its illicit nuclear program wasn't working, and that he would reach out to Tehran to reduce tensions.

The man who would become Obama's top counterterrorism adviser and then CIA director, John Brennan, went further. He recommended in a policy paper that "the next president has the opportunity to set a new course for relations between the two countries" through not only a direct dialogue, but "greater assimilation of Hezbollah into Lebanon's political system."

By May 2010, Brennan, then assistant to the president for homeland security and counterterrorism, confirmed in a speech that the administration was looking for ways to build up "moderate elements" within Hezbollah.

317

John Owen Brennan was the Director of the Central Intelligence Agency from March 2013 to January 2017. He has served as chief counterterrorism advisor to U.S. President Barack Obama; his title was Deputy National Security Advisor for Homeland Security and Counterterrorism, and Assistant to the President

Offical CIA Photograph.

"Hezbollah is a very interesting organisation," Brennan told a Washington conference, saying it had evolved from "purely a terrorist organisation" to a militia and, ultimately, a political party with representatives in the Lebanese parliament and Cabinet, according to a Reuters report.

"There is certainly the elements of Hezbollah that are truly a concern to us what they're doing," Brennan said. "And what we need to do is to find ways to diminish their influence within the organisation and to try to build up the more moderate elements."

In practice, the administration's willingness to envision a new role for Hezbollah in the Middle East, combined with its desire for a negotiated settlement to Iran's nuclear program, translated into a reluctance to move aggressively against the top Hezbollah operatives, according to Project Cassandra members and others.

John Brennan, who would become Obama's top counterterrorism adviser and then CIA director, went further than the president in improving relations with Iran.

Lebanese arms dealer Ali Fayad, a suspected top Hezbollah operative whom agents believed reported to Russian President Vladimir Putin as a key supplier of weapons to Syria and Iraq, was arrested in Prague in the spring of 2014. But for the nearly two years

Fayad was in custody, top Obama administration officials declined to apply serious pressure on the Czech government to extradite him to the United States, even as Putin was lobbying aggressively against it.

Fayad, who had been indicted in U.S. courts on charges of planning the murders of U.S. government employees, attempting to provide material support to a terrorist organization and attempting to acquire, transfer and use anti-aircraft missiles, was ultimately sent to Beirut. He is now believed by U.S. officials to be back in business, and helping to arm militants in Syria and elsewhere with Russian heavy weapons.

Project Cassandra members say administration officials also blocked or undermined their efforts to go after other top Hezbollah operatives including one nicknamed the "Ghost," allowing them to remain active despite being under sealed U.S. indictment for years. People familiar with his case say the Ghost has been one of the world's biggest cocaine traffickers, including to the U.S., as well as a major supplier of conventional and chemical weapons for use by Syrian President Bashar Assad against his people.

And when Project Cassandra agents and other investigators sought repeatedly to investigate and prosecute Abdallah Safieddine, Hezbollah's longtime envoy to Iran, whom they considered the linchpin of Hezbollah's criminal network, the Justice Department refused, according to four former officials with direct knowledge of the cases.

The administration also rejected repeated efforts by Project Cassandra members to charge Hezbollah's military wing as an ongoing criminal enterprise under a federal Mafia-style racketeering statute, task force members say. And they allege that administration officials declined to designate Hezbollah a "significant transnational criminal organisation" and blocked other strategic initiatives that would have given the task force additional legal tools, money and manpower to fight it.

Former Obama administration officials declined to comment on individual cases, but noted that the State Department condemned the Czech decision not to hand over Fayad.

Several of them, speaking on condition of anonymity, said they were guided by broader policy objectives, including de-escalating the conflict with Iran, curbing its nuclear weapons program and freeing at least four American prisoners held by Tehran, and that some law enforcement efforts were undoubtedly constrained by those concerns.

The Justice Department, they pointed out, never filed corresponding U.S. criminal charges against the suspects arrested in Europe.

But the former officials denied that they derailed any actions against Hezbollah or its Iranian allies for political reasons.

"There has been a consistent pattern of actions taken against Hezbollah, both through tough sanctions and law enforcement actions before and after the Iran deal," said Kevin Lewis, an Obama spokesman who worked at both the White House and Justice Department in the administration.

Lewis, speaking for the Obama administration, provided a list of eight arrests and prosecutions as proof. He made special note of a February 2016 operation in which European authorities arrested an undisclosed number of alleged members of a special Hezbollah business affairs unit that the DEA says oversees its drug trafficking and other criminal money-making enterprises.

Project Cassandra officials, however, noted that the European arrests occurred after the negotiations with Iran were over, and said the task force initiated the multinational partnerships on its own, after years of seeing their cases shot down by the Justice and State departments and other U.S. agencies.

The Justice Department, they pointed out, never filed corresponding U.S. criminal charges against the suspects arrested in Europe, including one prominent Lebanese businessman formally designated by the Treasury Department for using his "direct ties to Hezbollah commercial and terrorist elements" to launder bulk shipments of illicit cash for the organisation throughout Asia, Europe and the Middle East.

A former senior national security official of the Obama administration, who played a role in the Iran nuclear negotiations, suggested that Project Cassandra members were merely speculating that their cases were being blocked for political reasons. Other factors, including a lack of evidence or concerns about interfering with intelligence operations could have been in play.

"Under the Obama administration … these [Hezbollah-related] investigations were tamped down for fear of rocking the boat with Iran and jeopardizing the nuclear deal"
"What if the CIA or the Mossad had an intelligence operation ongoing inside Hezbollah and they were trying to pursue someone … against whom we had impeccable [intelligence] collection and the DEA is not going to know that?" the official said. "I get the feeling people who don't know what's going on in the broader universe are grasping at straws."

(Anthony Stephen Malone can confirm their was several ongoing operations at that time, some were long standing NOC Tasks and other offical operations against Hezbollah by several countrys Inteligence Services...)

The official added: "The world is a lot more complicated than viewed through the narrow lens of drug trafficking. So you're not going to let CIA rule the roost, but you're also certainly not going to let DEA do it either. Your approach to anything as complicated as Hezbollah is going to have to involve the interagency [process], because the State Department has a piece of the pie, the intelligence community does, Treasury does, DOD does."

Nonetheless, other sources independent of Project Cassandra confirmed many of the allegations in interviews with POLITICO, and in some cases, in public comments.

One Obama-era Treasury official, Katherine Bauer, in little-noticed written testimony presented last February to the House Committee on Foreign Affairs, acknowledged that "under the Obama administration ... these [Hezbollah-related] investigations were tamped down for fear of rocking the boat with Iran and jeopardizing the nuclear deal."

As a result, some Hezbollah operatives were not pursued via arrests, indictments, or Treasury designations that would have blocked their access to U.S. financial markets, according to Bauer, a career Treasury official, who served briefly in its Office of Terrorist Financing as a senior policy adviser for Iran before leaving in late 2015. And other "Hezbollah facilitators"arrested in France, Colombia, Lithuania have not been extradited — or indicted — in the U.S., she wrote.

Bauer, in an interview, declined to elaborate on her testimony.

David Asher, for one, said Obama administration officials expressed concerns to him about alienating Tehran before, during and after the Iran nuclear deal negotiations. This was, he said, part of an effort to "defang, defund and undermine the investigations that were involving Iran and Hezbollah," he said.

"The closer we got to the [Iran deal], the more these activities went away" — David Asher, who helped establish and oversee Project Cassandra
"The closer we got to the [Iran deal], the more these activities went away," Asher said. "So much of the capability, whether it was special operations, whether it was law enforcement, whether it was [Treasury] designations — even the capacity, the personnel assigned to this mission — it was assiduously drained, almost to the last drop, by the end of the Obama administration."

With much fanfare, Obama announced the final agreement on implementation of the Iran deal on Jan. 17, 2016, in which Tehran promised to shelve efforts to build a nuclear weapons program in exchange for being released from crippling international economic sanctions.

Within months, task force officials said, Project Cassandra was all but dead. Some of its most senior officials, including Jack Kelly, the veteran DEA supervisory agent who created and led the task force, were transferred to other assignments. And Asher himself left the task force long before that, after the Defense Department said his contract would not be renewed.

As a result, the U.S. government lost insight into not only drug trafficking and other criminal activity worldwide, but also into Hezbollah's illicit conspiracies with top officials in the Iranian, Syrian, Venezuelan and Russian governments — all the way up to presidents Nicolas Maduro, Assad and Putin, according to former task force members and other current and former U.S. officials.

The derailment of Project Cassandra also has undermined U.S. efforts to determine how much cocaine from the various Hezbollah-affiliated networks is coming into the United States, especially from Venezuela, where dozens of top civilian and military officials have been under investigation for more than a decade. Recently, **the Trump administration designated the country's vice president, a close ally of Hezbollah and of Lebanese-Syrian descent, as a global narcotics kingpin.**

Meanwhile, Hezbollah — in league with Iran — continues to undermine U.S. interests in Iraq, Syria and throughout wide swaths of Latin America and Africa, including providing weapons and training to anti-American Shiite militias. And Safieddine, the Ghost and other associates continue to play central roles in the trafficking of drugs and weapons, current and former U.S. officials believe.

"They were a paramilitary organisation with strategic importance in the Middle East, and we watched them become an international criminal conglomerate generating billions of dollars for the world's most dangerous activities, including chemical and nuclear weapons programs and armies that believe America is their sworn enemy," said Kelly, the supervisory DEA agent and lead coordinator of its Hezbollah cases.

"If they are violating U.S. statutes," he asked, "why can't we bring them to justice?"

Kelly and Asher are among the officials involved in Project Cassandra who have been quietly contacted by the Trump administration and congressional Republicans, who said a special POLITICO report April 24 on Barack Obama's hidden Iran deal concessions raised urgent questions about the need to resurrect key law enforcement programs to counter Iran.

That won't be easy, according to former Project Cassandra members, even with President Donald Trump's recent vow to crack down on Iran and Hezbollah. They said they tried to keep the project on life support, in hopes that it would be revived by the next administration, but the loss of key personnel, budget cuts and dropped investigations are only a few of many challenges made worse by the passage of nearly a year since Trump took office.

"Sources evaporate. Who knows if we can find all of the people willing to testify?" —Jack Kelly, the veteran DEA supervisory agent
"You can't let these things disintegrate," said Kelly. "Sources evaporate. Who knows if we can find all of the people willing to testify?"
(Anthony Stephen Malone and his entire network with all documents from al Medina Bank and his covert NOC network within Hezbollah are willing to talk again to elements within the United States Government. They know how to get hold of him).

Derek Maltz, who oversaw Project Cassandra as the Head of the DEA's Special Operations Division for nine years ending in July 2014, put it this way: "Certainly there are targets that people feel that could have been indicted and weren't. There is certainly an argument to be made that if tomorrow all the agencies were ordered to come together and sit in a room and put all the evidence on the table against all these bad guys, that there could be a hell of a lot of indictments."

But Maltz said the damage wrought by years of political interference will be hard to repair.

"There's no doubt in my mind now that the focus was this Iran deal and our initiative was kind of like a fly in the soup," Maltz said. "We were the train that went off the tracks."

Project Cassandra had its origins in a series of investigations launched in the years after the 9/11 attacks which all led, via their own twisted paths, to Hezbollah as a suspected global criminal enterprise.

Operation Titan, in which the DEA worked with Colombian authorities to explore a global alliance between Lebanese money launderers and Colombian drug trafficking conglomerates, was one. Operation Perseus, targeting Venezuelan syndicates, was another. At the same time, DEA agents in West Africa were investigating the suspicious flow of thousands of used cars from U.S. dealerships to car parks in Benin.

Meanwhile, in Iraq, the U.S. military was probing the role of Iran in outfitting Shiite militias with high-tech improvised explosive devices known as Explosively Formed Penetrators, or EFPs, that had already killed hundreds of U.S. soldiers.

All of these paths eventually converged on Hezbollah.

This wasn't entirely a surprise, agents say. For decades, Hezbollah — in close cooperation with Iranian intelligence and Revolutionary Guard — had worked with supporters in Lebanese communities around the world to create a web of businesses that were long suspected of being fronts for black-market trading. Along the same routes that carried frozen chicken and consumer electronics, these businesses moved weapons, laundered money and even procured parts for Iran's illicit nuclear and ballistic missile programs.

As they pursued their investigations, the DEA agents found that Hezbollah was redoubling all of these efforts, working urgently to raise cash, and lots of it, to rebuild its south Lebanon stronghold after a 2006 war with Israel had reduced it to rubble.

Hezbollah mostly left the United States alone, in what was clearly a strategic decision to avoid U.S. retaliation.

Dating back to its inception in the early 1980s, Hezbollah, which translates to "Party of God," had also engaged in "narcoterrorism," collecting a tariff from drug dealers and other black-market suppliers who operated in territory it controlled in Lebanon and elsewhere. Now, based on the DEA's extensive network of informants, undercover operatives and wiretaps, it looked like Hezbollah had shifted tactics, and got directly involved in the global cocaine trade, according to interviews and documents, including a confidential DEA assessment.

"It was like they flipped a switch," Kelly told POLITICO. "All of a sudden, they reversed the flow of all of the black-market activity they had been taxing for years, and took control of the operation."

Operating like an organised crime family, Hezbollah operatives would identify businesses that might be profitable and useful as covers for cocaine trafficking and buy financial stakes in them, Kelly and others said. "And if the business was successful and suited their current needs," Kelly said, "they went from partial owners to majority owners to full partnership or takeover."

Hezbollah even created a special financial unit that, translated into English, means "Business Affairs Component," to oversee the sprawling criminal operation, and it was run by the world's most wanted terrorist after Osama bin Laden, a notoriously vicious Hezbollah military commander named Imad Mughniyeh, according to DEA interviews and documents.

Mughniyeh had for decades been the public face of terrorism for Americans, orchestrating the infamous attack that killed 241 U.S. Marines in 1983 in their barracks in Lebanon, and dozens more Americans in attacks on the U.S. Embassy in Beirut that year and an annex the year after. When President Ronald Reagan responded to the attacks by withdrawing peacekeeping troops from Lebanon, Hezbollah claimed a major victory and vaulted to the forefront of the Islamist resistance movement against the West.

Members of the Lebanese Hezbollah parade with a mock missile. Over the next 25 years, Iran's financial and military support for Hezbollah enabled it to amass an army with tens of thousands of foot soldiers, more heavy armaments than most nation-states and approximately 120,000 rockets and ballistic missiles that could strike Israel and U.S. interests in the region with devastating precision.

Hezbollah became an expert in soft power, as well. It provided food, medical care and other social services for starving refugees in war-torn Lebanon, winning credibility on the ground. It then evolved further into a powerful political party, casting itself as the defender of poor, mostly Shiite Lebanese against Christian and Sunni Muslim elites. But even as Hezbollah was moving into the mainstream of Lebanese politics, Mughniyeh was overseeing a secret expansion of its terrorist wing, the Islamic Jihad Organization. Working with Iranian intelligence agents, Islamic Jihad continued to attack Western, Israeli and Jewish targets around the world, and to conduct surveillance on others — including in the United States — in preparation for future attacks.

Hezbollah mostly left the United States alone, in what was clearly a strategic decision to avoid U.S. retaliation. But by 2008, the Bush administration came to believe that Islamic Jihad was the most dangerous terrorist organisation in the world, capable of launching instantaneous attacks, possibly with chemical, biological or low-grade nuclear weapons, that would dwarf those on 9/11.

While the DEA had quickly proven itself adept at working on the global stage, few people within the U.S. government thought of it as a legitimate counterterrorism force.

By funding terrorism and military operations through global drug trafficking and organised crime, Mughniyeh's business affairs unit within Islamic Jihad had become the embodiment of the kind of threat the United States was struggling to address in the post-9/11 world.

The DEA believed that it was the logical U.S. national security agency to lead the interagency effort to go after Mughniyeh's drug trafficking networks. But within the multipronged U.S. national security apparatus, this was both a questionable and problematic assertion.

Established by President Richard Nixon in 1973 to bring together the various anti-drug programs under the Department of Justice, the DEA was among the youngest of the U.S. national security agencies.

And while the DEA had quickly proven itself adept at working on the global stage — especially in partnerships with drug-infested countries desperate for U.S. help like Colombia — few people within the U.S. government thought of it as a legitimate counterterrorism force.

In the final years of the Bush administration, though, the DEA had won the support of top officials for taking down two major international arms dealers, a Syrian named Monzer al-Kassarand the Russian "Lord of War," Viktor Bout. And thanks to supportive Republicans in Congress, it had become the beneficiary of a new federal law that empowered its globe-trotting cadre of assault-weapon-toting Special Operations agents.

The statute allowed DEA agents to operate virtually anywhere, without permission required from other U.S. agencies. All they needed to do was connect drug suspects to terrorism, and they could arrest them, haul them back to the United States and flip them in an effort to penetrate "the highest levels of the world's most significant and notorious criminal organisations," as then-Special Operations chief Derek Maltz told Congress in November 2011.

As they crunched the massive amounts of intel streaming into the DEA's Counter Narco-Terrorism Operations Center in Chantilly, Virginia, the agents on Operation Titan, Perseus and the other cases began to connect the dots and map the contours of one overarching criminal enterprise.

* * *

PART II

EVERYWHERE AND NOWHERE

From its headquarters in the Middle East, Hezbollah extends its criminal reach to Latin America, Africa, Europe (Britian) and the United States.

On Feb. 12, 2008, CIA and Israeli intelligence detonated a bomb in Imad Mughniyeh's car as he was leaving a celebration of the 29th anniversary of the Iranian revolution in Damascus, Syria. He was killed instantly. It was a major blow to Hezbollah, but soon after, wiretapped phone lines and other U.S. evidence showed that his criminal operation was busier than ever, and overseen by two trusted associates, according to interviews with former Project Cassandra officials and DEA documents.

One was financier Adham Tabaja. The other, the interviews and documents reveal, was Safieddine, the key link between Hezbollah — which was run by his cousin, Hassan Nasrallah and his own brother Hashem — and Iran, Hezbollah's state sponsor, which saw the group as its strategic ally in defending Shiite Muslims in the largely Sunni Muslim states that surrounded it.

Investigators were also homing in on several dozen key players underneath them who acted as "superfacilitators" for the various criminal operations benefitting Hezbollah, Iran and, at times, their allies in Iraq, Syria, Venezuela and Russia.

But it was Safieddine, a low-key, bespectacled man with a diplomatic bearing, who was their key point of connection from his base in Tehran, investigators believed.

The Colombia and Venezuela investigations linked him to numerous international drug smuggling and money laundering networks, and especially to one of the biggest the DEA had ever seen, led by Medellin-based Lebanese businessman Ayman Joumaa.

People pray over the coffin of assassinated Hezbollah leader Imad Mughniyeh. Ayman Saied Joumaa's network rang alarm bells in Washington when agents discovered he was working with Mexico's brutal Los Zetas cartel to move multi-ton loads of cocaine directly into the United States, and washing $200 million a month in criminal proceeds with the help of 300 or so used car dealerships. The network would funnel huge amounts of money to the dealerships to purchase used cars, which would then be shipped to Benin, on Africa's west coast.

As the task force investigators intensified their focus on Safieddine, they were contacted out of the blue by Asher, the Defense Department official, who was at Special Operations Command tracking the money used to provide ragtag Iraqi Shiite militias with sophisticated weapons for use against U.S. troops, including the new and lethal IED known as the "Explosively Formed Penetrator." The armor-piercing charges were so powerful that they were ripping M1 Abrams tanks in half.

(See Anthony Malone, Report of IED/Shape Chargers made in Iran and used by Incurgents in Iraq, Syria, Afghanistan. Report given to JSOC and American Military Intelligence "WD" in Afghanistan, Report by Anthony Malone confirmed locations in Iran).

"Nobody had seen weapons like these," Asher told POLITICO. "They could blow the side off a building."

Asher's curiosity had been piqued by evidence linking the IED network to phone numbers intercepted in the Colombia investigation. Before long, he traced the unusual alliance to a number allegedly used by Safieddine in Iran.

"I had no clue who he was," Asher recalled. "But this guy was sending money into Iraq, to kill American soldiers."

"I had no clue who he was. But this guy was sending money into Iraq, to kill American soldiers" — David Asher on Abdallah Safieddine

Thanks to that chance connection, the Pentagon's then-head of counternarcotics, William Wechsler, lent Asher and a few other Defense Department experts in tracking illicit money to the DEA to see what they might find.

It was a fruitful partnership. Asher was accustomed to toiling in the financial shadows. During his 20-plus years of U.S. government work, his core expertise was in exposing money laundering and schemes to avoid financial sanctions by rogue nation states, terrorist groups, organized-crime cartels and weapons proliferation networks.

Usually, his work was strictly classified. For Project Cassandra, however, he got special dispensation from the Pentagon to build networks of unclassified information so it could be used in criminal prosecutions.

Asher and his team quickly integrated cutting-edge financial intelligence tools into the various DEA investigations. With the **U.S. military's help, agents translated thousands of hours of intercepted phone conversations from Colombia in Arabic that no one had considered relevant until the Hezbollah links appeared.**

When the translations were complete, investigators said, they painted a picture of Safieddine as a human hub of a criminal enterprise with spokes emanating **from Tehran outward into Latin America, Africa, Europe and the United States via hundreds of legitimate businesses and front companies.**

Safieddine did not respond to requests for comment through various intermediaries including Hezbollah's media arm. A Hezbollah official, however, denied that the organization was involved in drug dealing.

"Sheik Nasrallah has confirmed lots of times that it is not permitted religiously for Hezbollah members to be trafficking drugs," the official said. "It is something that is preventable, in that we in Islam have things like halal [permitted] and haram [prohibited]. For us, this is haram. So in no way is it possible to be done."

The accusation that Hezbollah is involved in drug trafficking, the representative said, "is part of the campaign to distort the image of Hezbollah as a resistance movement against the Israelis. Of course, it is possible to have Lebanese people involved in drugs, but it is not possible for them to be members of Hezbollah. This is absolutely not possible."

Asked about Safieddine's role in the organization, the official said, "We don't usually expose the roles everyone plays because it is a jihadi organization. So it is a little bit secret."

Safieddine's cousin Nasrallah, the Hezbollah leader, has publicly rejected the idea that Hezbollah needs to raise money at all, through drugs or any other criminal activity, because Iran provides whatever funds it needs.

Safieddine himself, however, suggested otherwise in 2005, when he defiantly refuted the Bush administration's accusations that Iran and Syria supplied Hezbollah with weapons. Those countries provided "political and moral" support only, he told Agence France-Presse. "We don't need to arm ourselves from Tehran. Why bring weapons from Iran via Syria when we can procure them anywhere in the world?"

"Hezbollah operates like the Gambino crime family on steroids, and he is its John Gotti" —
John Kelly on Abdallah Safieddine

Safieddine may have been right. Agents found evidence that weapons were flowing to
Hezbollah from many channels, including networks that trafficked in both drugs and weapons.
And using the same trafficking networks that hummed with drugs, cash and commercial
products, agents concluded, Safieddine was overseeing Hezbollah efforts to help Iran procure
parts and technology for its clandestine nuclear and ballistic missile programs.

"Hezbollah operates like the Gambino crime family on steroids, and he is its John Gotti," said
Kelly, referring to the infamous "Teflon Don" crime boss who for decades eluded justice.
"Whatever Iran needs, Safieddine is in charge of getting it for them."

The Bush administration had made disrupting the networks through which Iran obtained parts
for its weapons of mass destruction programs a top priority, with then-Deputy National
Security Adviser Juan Zarate personally overseeing an interagency effort to map out the
procurement channels. A former Justice Department prosecutor, Zarate understood the value of
international law enforcement operations, and put DEA's Special Operations Division at the
center of it.

But even then, other agencies were chafing at the DEA's role.

A Series of Roadblocks

Much of the early turbulence stemmed from an escalating turf battle between federal law
enforcement and intelligence agencies over which ones had primacy in the global war on
terrorism, especially over a so-called hybrid target like Hezbollah, which was both a criminal
enterprise and a national security threat.

The "cops" from the FBI and DEA wanted to build criminal cases, throw Hezbollah operatives in prison and get them to turn on each other. That stoked resentment among the "spooks" at the CIA and National Security Agency, who for 25 years had gathered intelligence, sometimes through the painstaking process of having agents infiltrate Hezbollah, and then occasionally launching assassinations and cyberattacks to block imminent threats.

Further complicating the picture was the role of the State Department, which often wanted to quash both law-enforcement actions and covert operations due to the political backlash they created. Hezbollah, after all, was a leading political force in Lebanon and a provider of human services, with a sincere grass-roots following that wasn't necessarily aware of its unsavory actions. Nowhere was the tension between law enforcement and diplomacy more acute than in dealings with Hezbollah, which was fast becoming a key part of the Lebanese government.

Hezbollah supporters fly balloons to mark the anniversary of the end of the 2006 war with Israel. Distrust among U.S. agencies exploded after two incidents brought the cops-spooks divide into clear relief.

In the waning days of the Bush administration, a DEA agent's cover was blown just as he was about to become a Colombian cartel's main cocaine supplier to the Middle East — and to Hezbollah operatives.

A year later, under Obama, the State Department blocked an FBI-led Joint Terrorism Task Force from luring a key eyewitness from Beirut to Philadelphia so he could be arrested and turned against Safieddine and other Hezbollah operatives in a scheme to procure 1,200 Colt M4 military-grade assault rifles.

In both cases, law enforcement agents suspected that Middle East-based spies in the CIA had torpedoed their investigations to protect their politically sensitive and complicated relationship with Hezbollah.

The CIA declined to comment on the allegation that it intentionally blew the cover of a DEA agent or any other aspect of its relationship with Project Cassandra. The Obama State Department and Justice Department also declined to comment in response to detailed requests about their dealings with Hezbollah.

But the tensions between those agencies and the DEA were no secret. Some current and former diplomats and CIA officers, speaking on condition of anonymity, portrayed DEA Special Operations agents as undisciplined and overly aggressive cowboys with little regard for the larger geopolitical picture. "They'd come in hot to places like Beirut, want to slap handcuffs on people and disrupt operations we'd been cultivating for years," one former CIA case officer said.

"They refused to accept no for an answer. And they were often given no for an answer" — FBI terrorism task force supervisor

Kelly and other agents embraced their swashbuckling reputation, claiming that more aggressive tactics were needed because the CIA had long turned a blind eye to Hezbollah's criminal networks, and even cultivated informants within them, in a misguided and myopic focus on preventing terrorist attacks.

The unyielding posture of Kelly, Asher and their team also rankled some of their fellow law-enforcement agents within the FBI, the Justice Department and even the DEA itself. The more Kelly and Asher insisted that everyone else was missing the drug-crime-terror nexus, the more others accused them — and their team out at Chantilly — of inflating those connections to expand the task force's portfolio, get more funding and establish its importance.

After a few years of working together on the Hezbollah cases, Kelly and Asher had become a familiar sight in the never-ending circuit of meetings and briefings in what is known as the "interagency process," a euphemism for the U.S. national security community's efforts to bring all elements of power to bear on a particular problem.

From outward appearances, the two made an unusual pair.

Kelly, now 51, was a streetwise agent from small-town New Jersey who cut his teeth investigating the Mafia and drug kingpins. He spent his infrequent downtime lifting weights, watching college football and chilling in cargo shorts.

Asher, 49, speaks fluent Japanese, earned his Ph.D. in international relations from Oxford University and has the pallor of a senior government official who has spent the past three decades in policy meetings, classified military war rooms and diplomatic summits.

Both were described by supporters and detractors alike as having a similarly formidable combination of investigative and analytical skills, and the self-confidence to match it. At times, and especially on Project Cassandra, their intensity worked to the detriment of their careers.

"It got to the point where a lot of people didn't want to have meetings with them," said one FBI terrorism task force supervisor who worked often with the two. "They refused to accept no for an answer. And they were often given no for an answer. Even though they were usually right."

"We should also not forget about the 100's of used car companies in the states — some of them owned by Islamic Extremists — which are part of this network" — Jack Kelly

An early flash point was Operation Titan, the DEA initiative in Colombia. After its undercover agent was compromised, DEA and Colombian authorities scrambled to build cases against as many as 130 traffickers, including a Colombian cartel leader and a suspected Safieddine associate named Chekry Harb, nicknamed El Taliban.

For months afterward, the Justice Department rebuffed requests by task force agents, and some of its own prosecutors, to add narcoterrorism charges to the drug and money-laundering counts against Harb, several sources involved in the case said. Agents argued that they had evidence that would easily support the more serious charges. Moreover, Harb's prosecution was an essential building block in their larger plan for a sustained legal assault against Hezbollah's criminal network.

Its centerpiece would be a prosecution under the Racketeer Act, a powerful tool used by the Justice Department against sophisticated international conspiracies, including the Mafia, drug cartels and white-collar corporate crimes. A RICO case would give the task force the ability to tie many seemingly unconnected conspiracies together, and prosecute the alleged bosses overseeing them, like Safieddine, participants say.

It would also allow authorities to seize potentially billions in assets, they say, and to use the threat of far longer prison terms to wring more cooperation out of Harb and others already charged or convicted.

After the Justice Department's final refusal to bring narcoterrorism charges against Harb, Kelly sent an angry email to the DEA leadership warning that Justice's "obstruction" would have "far reaching implications including threats to our National Security" given Hezbollah's mushrooming criminal activity.

Of particular concern: A 25–year-old Lebanese man that Kelly described as the network's "command and control element," according to the email.

The young man was not only in contact "with Joumaa and some of the other top drug traffickers in the world" but also "leaders of a foreign [country's] black ops special forces; executive leadership of Hezbollah; and a representative of a company which is most likely facilitating the development of WMDs."

"We should also not forget," he added, "about the 100's of used car companies in the states —

some of them owned by Islamic Extremists — which are part of this network." In interviews, former task force officials identified the young man as Safieddine's son, and said he acted as his father's liaison in Beirut.

A man inspects a field of Cannabis plants in the Hezbollah-controlled Bekaa valley. All of that information was shared with other law enforcement and intelligence agencies — and the White House — via the DEA's Chantilly nerve center. But by early 2009, Obama's national security team batted down Project Cassandra's increasingly urgent warnings as being overly alarmist, counterproductive or untrue, or simply ignored them, according to Kelly, Asher, Maltz and other participants in and out of government.

By following the money, though, Asher had become convinced that the task force wasn't overhyping the threat posed by Hezbollah's criminal activities, it was significantly underestimating it. Because Hezbollah's drug trafficking was bankrolling its Islamic Jihad military wing and joint ventures with Iran, as Asher would later testify before Congress, it represented "the largest material support scheme for terrorism operations" the world had ever seen.

As proof, Asher would often bring PowerPoints to interagency drug and crime meetings, showing how cash reserves of U.S currency in Lebanon had doubled, to $16 billion, in just a few years, and how shiny new skyscrapers were popping up around Beirut, just like Miami, Panama City, Panama, and other cities awash in drug money.

Privately, Asher began to tell task force colleagues, the best way to take down the entire criminal enterprise — especially such a politically sensitive one as Hezbollah — was to go after its money, and the financial institutions assisting it. Their first target would be one of the world's fastest-growing banks, the Beirut-based Lebanese Canadian Bank and its $5 billion in assets.

Blocked efforts, missed opportunities

Asher knew how to successfully implode the financial underpinnings of an illicit, state-sponsored trafficking network because he'd already done it, just a few years earlier, as the Bush administration's point man on North Korea. In that case, he used the post-9/11 PATRIOT Act to cut off Pyongyang by going after Banco Delta Asia, a Macau-based bank that made illicit financial transactions on behalf of the North Korean regime.

In Beirut, Asher and his team worked with an Israeli intelligence operation to penetrate the Lebanese bank's inner workings and diagram its Byzantine money flows. They gathered evidence showing how Joumaa's network alone was laundering $200 million per month in "bulk proceeds of drug sales" through the bank and various money exchange houses, according to Justice and Treasury department documents.

Much of the freshly laundered cash, the records show, was then wired to about 300 U.S. used-car dealers to buy and ship thousands of vehicles to West Africa.

"Right now, we have 50 FBI agents not doing anything because they know their Iran cases aren't going anywhere" — Jack Kelly on what a Justice Department official told him about the chilling effect of Obama's rapprochement with Iran

Task force agents also documented how Safieddine was a financial liaison providing Hezbollah — and, of potentially huge significance, Iran — with VIP services at the bank, including precious access to the international financial system in violation of U.S. sanctions, according to those records.

By then, the task force was working closely with federal prosecutors in a new Terrorism and International Narcotics Unit out of the Justice Department's Southern District of New York. The Manhattan prosecutors agreed to file criminal charges against the bank and two senior officials that they hoped to turn into cooperating witnesses against Hezbollah and Safieddine, several participants said.

Federal authorities filed a civil action against the bank in February 2011 and later seized $102 million, ultimately forcing it to shut down and sell its assets without admitting wrongdoing. But the Justice Department never filed the criminal charges, and also stymied investigations into other financial institutions and individuals that task force agents targeted as part of the planned case, they say.

The Obama White House said privately that it feared a broader assault on Lebanese financial institutions would destabilize the country. But without the threat of prison time, complicit bank officials clammed up. And without pressure on the many other financial institutions in Lebanon and the region, Hezbollah simply moved its banking business elsewhere.

Soon afterward, Kelly said, he ran into one of the unit's top prosecutors and asked if there was "something going on with the White House that explains why we can't get a criminal filing."

"You don't know the half of it," the prosecutor replied, according to Kelly. "Right now, we have 50 FBI agents not doing anything because they know their Iran cases aren't going anywhere," including investigations around the U.S. into allegedly complicit used-car dealers.

Justice Department officials involved, including then-U.S. Attorney Preet Bharara and other prosecutors, declined requests to discuss the bank case or others involving Hezbollah.

Former U.S. Attorney Preet Bharara | Justin Lane/EPA

That October, Asher helped uncover a plot by two Iranian agents and a Texas-based Iranian-American to hire Mexican cartel gunmen to assassinate Saudi Arabia's U.S. ambassador in a crowded Washington cafe. A month later, prosecutors indicted Joumaa, accusing him of working with Mexico's Zetas cartel and Colombian and Venezuelan suppliers to smuggle 85 tons of cocaine into the U.S., and laundering $850 million in drug proceeds.

Task force agents hoped those cases would win them the political support needed to attack the Hezbollah criminal network and its patrons in Tehran. Instead, the opposite appeared to be happening.

DEA officials weren't included in the Justice and FBI news conference on the assassination plot, and claim it was because the Obama White House wanted to downplay the drug-terror connection. And Joumaa's indictment didn't mention Hezbollah once, despite DEA evidence of his connections to the group dating back to 1997.

By the end of 2012, senior officials at the Justice Department's National Security and Criminal divisions, and at the State Department and National Security Council, had shut down, derailed or delayed numerous other Hezbollah-related cases with little or no explanation, according to Asher, Kelly, Maltz and other current and former participating officials.

Agents discovered "an entire Quds force network" in the U.S., laundering money, moving drugs and illegally smuggling Bell helicopters, night-vision goggles and other items for Iran, Asher said.

"We crashed to indict" the elite Iranian unit, and while some operatives were eventually prosecuted, other critically important indictments "were rejected despite the fact that we had excellent evidence and testifying witnesses," said Asher, who helped lead the investigation.

In Philadelphia, the FBI-led task force had spent two years bolstering its case claiming that Safieddine had overseen an effort to purchase 1,200 military-grade assault rifles bound for Lebanon, with the help of Kelly and the special narcoterrorism prosecutors in New York.

Now, they had two key eyewitnesses. One would identify Safieddine as the Hezbollah official sitting behind a smoked-glass barricade who approved the assault weapons deal. And an agent and prosecutor had flown to a remote Asian hotel and spent four days persuading another eyewitness to testify about Safieddine's role in an even bigger weapons and drugs conspiracy, multiple former law enforcement officials confirmed to POLITICO.

Some Obama officials warned that further crackdowns against Hezbollah would destabilize Lebanon.

Convinced they had a strong case, the New York prosecutors sent a formal prosecution request to senior Justice Department lawyers in Washington, as required in such high-profile cases. The Justice Department rejected it, and the FBI and DEA agents were never told why, those former officials said.

Justice Department officials declined to comment on the case.

Kelly had been searching for an appropriate DEA code name to give to collaborating agencies so they could access and contribute to task force investigative files. He found it while reading the Erik Larson book "In the Garden of Beasts," in which the former U.S. ambassador to Germany named his U.S. speaking tour about the growing Nazi menace after the famous mythological figure whose warnings about the future were unheeded.

Now the project had its name: Cassandra.

Standing down on Hezbollah

After Obama won reelection in November 2012, the administration's pushback on Hezbollah drug cases became more overt, and now seemed to be emanating directly from the White House, according to task force members, some former U.S. officials and other observers.

One reason, they said, was Obama's choice of a new national security team. The appointment of John Kerry as secretary of state was widely viewed as a sign of a redoubled effort to engage with Iran. Obama's appointment of Brennan — the public supporter of cultivating Hezbollah moderates — as CIA director, and the president's choice of the Justice Department's top national security lawyer, Lisa MonacoLisa Monaco, as Brennan's replacement as White House counterterrorism and homeland security adviser, put two more strong proponents of diplomatic engagement with Iran in key positions.

Another factor was the victory of reformist candidate Hassan Rouhani as president of Iran that summer, which pushed the talks over a possible nuclear deal into high gear.

The administration's eagerness for an Iran deal was broadcast through so many channels, task force members say, that political appointees and career officials at key agencies like Justice, State and the National Security Council felt unspoken pressure to view the task force's efforts with skepticism. One former senior Justice Department official confirmed to POLITICO that some adverse decisions might have been influenced by an informal multi-agency Iran working group that "assessed the potential impact" of criminal investigations and prosecutions on the nuclear negotiations.

The victory of reformist candidate Hassan Rouhani as president of Iran pushed the talks over a possible nuclear deal into high gear| Abedin Taherkenareh/EPA

Monaco was a particularly influential roadblock at the intersection of law enforcement and politics, in part due to her sense of caution, her close relationship with Obama and her frequent contact with her former colleagues at the Justice Department's National Security Division, according to several task force members and other current and former officials familiar with its efforts.

Some Obama officials warned that further crackdowns against Hezbollah would destabilize Lebanon. Others warned that such actions would alienate Iran at a critical early stage of the serious Iran deal talks. And some officials, including Monaco, said the administration was concerned about retaliatory terrorist or military actions by Hezbollah, task force members said.

"That was the established policy of the Obama administration internally," one former senior Obama national security official said, in describing the reluctance to go after Hezbollah for fear of reprisal. He said he criticized it at the time as being misguided and hypocritical.

"We're obviously doing those actions against al Qaeda and ISIS all the time," the Obama official said. "I thought it was bad policy [to refrain from such actions on Hezbollah] that limited the range of options we had," including criminal prosecutions.

Monaco declined repeated requests for comment, including detailed questions sent by email and text, though a former White House subordinate of hers rejected the task force members' description of her motives and actions.

The couriers were lugging suitcases stuffed with as much as $2 million each, and the task force was on the tail of every one of them.

The White House was driven by a broader set of concerns than the fate of the nuclear talks, the former White House official said, including the fear of reprisals by Hezbollah against the United States and Israel, and the need to maintain peace and stability in the Middle East.

Brennan also told POLITICO he was not commenting on any aspect of his CIA tenure. His former associates, however, said that he remained committed to preventing Hezbollah from committing terrorist acts, and that his decisions were based on an overall concern for U.S. security.

For their part, task force agents said they tried to work around the obstacles presented by the Justice and State Departments and the White House. Often, they chose to build relatively simple drug and weapons cases against suspects rather than the ambitious narcoterrorism prosecutions that required the approval of senior Justice Department lawyers, interviews and records show.

At the same time, though, they redoubled efforts to build a case and gain Justice Department support for it.

Their ace in the hole, Kelly and Asher said they told Justice officials, wasn't some dramatic drug bust, but thousands of individual financial transactions, each of which constituted an overt criminal act under RICO. Much of this evidence grew out of the Lebanese Canadian Bank investigation, including details of how an army of couriers for years had been transporting billions of dollars in dirty U.S. cash from West African car dealerships to friendly banks in Beirut.

The couriers would begin their journeys at a four-star hotel in Lome, Togo, lugging suitcases stuffed with as much as $2 million each, Kelly said. And the task force was on the tail of every one of them, he said, thanks to an enterprising DEA agent who had found a way to get all of their cellphone numbers. "They had no idea what we were doing," Kelly said. "But that alone gave us all the slam-dunk evidence we needed" for a RICO case against everyone involved in the conspiracy, including Hezbollah.

Such on-the-ground spadework, combined with its worldwide network of court-approved communications intercepts, gave Project Cassandra agents virtual omniscience over some aspects of the Hezbollah criminal network.

And from their perch in Chantilly, they watched with growing alarm as Hezbollah accelerated its global expansion that the drug money helped finance.

Both Hezbollah and Iran continued to build up their military arsenals and move thousands of soldiers and weapons into Syria. Aided by the U.S. military withdrawal from Iraq, Iran, with the help of Hezbollah, consolidated its control and influence over wide swaths of the war-ravaged country.

Iran and Hezbollah began making similar moves into Yemen and other Sunni-controlled countries. And their networks in Africa trafficked not just in drugs, weapons and used cars but diamonds, commercial merchandise and even human slaves, according to interviews with former Project Cassandra members and Treasury Department documents. Hezbollah and the Quds force also were moving into China and other new markets.

But Project Cassandra's agents were most alarmed, by far, by the havoc Hezbollah and Iran were wreaking in Latin America.

A threat in America's backyard

In the years after the 9/11 terrorist attacks, when Washington's focus was elsewhere, Hezbollah and Iran cultivated alliances with governments along the "cocaine corridor" from the tip of South America to Mexico, to turn them against the United States.

The strategy worked in Bolivia, Ecuador and Venezuela, which evicted the DEA, shuttering strategic bases and partnerships that had been a bulwark in the U.S. counternarcotics campaign.

In Venezuela, President Hugo Chavez was personally working with then-Iranian president, Mahmoud Ahmadinejad, and Hezbollah on drug trafficking and other activities aimed at undermining U.S. influence in the region, according to interviews and documents.

"If we had gotten our hands on either of them, we could have taken down the entire network"
— Kelly on the extradition of a top Venezuelan official and a drug kingpin

Within a few years, Venezuelan cocaine exports skyrocketed from 50 tons a year to 250, much of it bound for American cities, United Nations Office of Drugs and Crime statistics show.

And beginning in 2007, DEA agents watched as a commercial jetliner from Venezuela's state-run Conviasa airline flew from Caracas to Tehran via Damascus, Syria, every week with a cargo-hold full of drugs and cash. They nicknamed it "Aeroterror," they said, because the return flight often carried weapons and was packed with Hezbollah and Iranian operatives whom the Venezuelan government would provide with fake identities and travel documents on their arrival.

From there, the operatives spread throughout the subcontinent and set up shop in the many recently opened Iranian consulates, businesses and mosques, former Project Cassandra agents said.

But when the Obama administration had opportunities to secure the extradition of two of the biggest players in that conspiracy, it failed to press hard enough to get them extradited to the United States, where they would face charges, task force officials told POLITICO.

One was Syrian-born Venezuelan businessman Walid Makled, alias the "king of kingpins," who was arrested in Colombia in 2010 on charges of shipping 10 tons of cocaine a month to the United States. While in custody, Makled claimed to have 40 Venezuelan generals on his payroll and evidence implicating dozens of top Venezuelan officials in drug trafficking and other crimes. He pleaded to be sent to New York as a protected, cooperating witness, but Colombia — a staunch U.S. ally — extradited him to Venezuela instead.

The other, retired Venezuelan general and former chief of intelligence Hugo Carvajal, was arrested in Aruba on U.S. drug charges. Carvajal "was the main man between Venezuela and Iran, the Quds force, Hezbollah and the cocaine trafficking," Kelly said. "If we had gotten our hands on either of them, we could have taken down the entire network."

Walid Makled, alias the "king of kingpins," was arrested in Colombia in 2010 on charges of shipping 10 tons of cocaine a month to the United States .

Instead, Venezuela was now the primary pipeline for U.S.-bound cocaine, thanks in part to the DEA's success in neighboring Colombia. It had also become a strategically invaluable staging area for Hezbollah and Iran in the United States' backyard, including camps they established to train Shiite militias.

And at the center of much of that activity was the Ghost, another suspected Safieddine associate so elusive that no photos of him were said to exist.

Project Cassandra agents came to regard the Ghost as perhaps the most important on-the-ground operator in the conspiracy because of his suspected role in moving drugs, money and munitions, including multi-ton loads of cocaine, into the United States, and WMD components to the Middle East, according to two former senior U.S. officials.

Now, he and Joumaa were living in Beirut, and Project Cassandra agents were so familiar with their routines that they knew at which cafe the two men gathered every morning to drink espresso and "discuss drug trafficking, money laundering and weapons," one of the two former officials said.

The Ghost was also in business with another suspected Safieddine associate, Ali Fayad, who had long been instrumental in providing weapons to Shiite militias in Iraq, including through the deadly IED network that had killed so many U.S. troops, the former officials believed.

Now, they had information that Fayad, a joint Lebanese and Ukrainian citizen, and the Ghost were involved in moving conventional and chemical weapons into Syria for Hezbollah, Iran and Russia to help President Assad crush the insurgency against his regime. Adding to the mystery: Fayad served as a Ukrainian defense ministry adviser, worked for the state-owned arms exporter Ukrspecexport and appeared to have taken Bout's place as Putin's go-to arms merchant, the former officials said.

So when Fayad's name surfaced in a DEA investigation in West Africa as a senior Hezbollah weapons trafficker, agents scrambled to create a sting operation, with undercover operatives posing as Colombian narcoterrorists plotting to shoot down American government helicopters.

Hezbollah's network moved "metric ton quantities of cocaine [to] launder drug proceeds on a global scale, and procure weapons and … explosives" — Excerpt of a Confidential DEA assessment

Fayad was happy to offer his expert advice, and after agreeing to provide them with 20 Russian-made shoulder-fired Igla surface-to-air missiles, 400 rocket-propelled grenades and various firearms and rocket launchers for $8.3 million, he was arrested by Czech authorities on a U.S. warrant in April 2014, U.S. court records show.

The Fayad sting — and his unprecedented value as a potential cooperating witness — was just one of many reasons Project Cassandra members had good cause, finally, for optimism.

* * *

PART III

A BATTLE AGAINST ENEMIES FAR AND NEAR

As negotiations for the Iran nuclear deal intensify, the administration pushes back against Project Cassandra.

More than a year into Obama's second term, many national security officials still disagreed with Kelly and Asher about whether Hezbollah fully controlled a global criminal network, especially in drug trafficking and distribution, or merely profited from crimes by its supporters within the global Lebanese diaspora. But Project Cassandra's years of relentless investigation had produced a wealth of evidence about Hezbollah's global operations, a clear window into how its hierarchy worked and some significant sanctions by the Treasury Department.

A confidential DEA assessment from that period concluded that Hezbollah's business affairs entity "has leveraged relationships with corrupt foreign government officials and transnational criminal actors ... creating a network that can be utilized to move metric ton quantities of cocaine, launder drug proceeds on a global scale, and procure weapons and precursors for explosives."

Hezbollah "has at its disposal one of the most capable networks of actors coalescing elements of transnational organized crime with terrorism in the world," the assessment concluded.

Some top U.S. military officials shared those concerns, including the four-star generals heading U.S. Special Operations and Southern commands, who warned Congress that Hezbollah's criminal operations and growing beachhead in Latin America posed an urgent threat to U.S. security, according to transcripts of the hearings.

"The intelligence community fundamentally doubted the intel" from the DEA, the subordinate recalled.

In early 2014, Kelly and other task force members briefed Attorney General Eric Holder, who was so alarmed by the findings that he insisted Obama and his entire national security team get the same briefing as they formulated the administration's Iran strategy.

So task force leaders welcomed the opportunity to attend a May 2014 summit meeting of Obama national security officials at Special Operations Command headquarters in Tampa, Florida. Task force leaders hoped to convince the administration of the threat posed by Hezbollah's networks, and of the need for other agencies to work with DEA in targeting the growing nexus of drugs, crime and terror.

The summit, and several weeks of interagency prep that preceded it, however, prompted even more pushback from some top national security officials. Monaco, Obama's counterterrorism adviser, expressed concerns about using RICO laws against top Hezbollah leaders and about the possibility of reprisals, according to several people familiar with the summit.

They said senior Obama administration officials appeared to be alarmed by how far Project Cassandra's investigations had reached into the leadership of Hezbollah and Iran, and wary of the possible political repercussions.

As a result, task force members claim, Project Cassandra was increasingly viewed as a threat to the administration's efforts to secure a nuclear deal, and the top-secret prisoner swap that was about to be negotiated.

Monaco's former subordinate, speaking under on condition of anonymity, said the White House did not attempt to curb DEA-led efforts against Hezbollah because of the Iran deal. But the subordinate said the White House felt a need to balance the drug agency's interests with those of other agencies who often disagreed with it.

"The intelligence community fundamentally doubted the intel" from the DEA, the subordinate recalled. "I spent so much time trying to get them to work together."

Nonetheless, after the meeting in Tampa, the administration made it clear that it would not support a RICO case, even though Asher and others say they'd spent years gathering evidence for it, the task force members said.

In addition, the briefings for top White House and Justice Department officials that had been requested by Holder never materialized, task force agents said. (Holder did not respond to requests for comment.) Also, a top intelligence official blocked the inclusion of Project Cassandra's memo on the Hezbollah drug threat from being included in Obama's daily threat briefing, they said. And Kelly, Asher and other agents said they stopped getting invitations to interagency meetings, including those of a top Obama transnational crime working group.

Lebanese women affiliated to Hezbollah student movements parade through Beirut marking the religious festival of Ashura.

That may have been because Obama officials dropped Hezbollah from the formal list of groups targeted by a special White House initiative into transnational organized crime, which in turn effectively eliminated DEA's broad authority to investigate it overseas, task force members said.

"The funny thing is Tampa was supposed to settle how everyone would have a seat at the table and what the national strategy is going to be, and how clearly law enforcement has role," Jack Riley, who was the DEA's chief of operations at the time, told POLITICO. "And the opposite happened. We walked away with nothing."

Willfully blind to the threat

After the Tampa meeting, Project Cassandra leaders pushed – unsuccessfully, they said – for greater support from the Obama administration in extraditing Fayad from the Czech Republic to New York for prosecution, and in locating and arresting the many high-value targets who went underground after hearing news of his arrest.

They also struck out repeatedly, they said, in obtaining the administration's approval for offering multimillion-dollar "rewards for justice" bounties of a type commonly issued for indicted kingpins like Joumaa, and for the administration to unseal the secret indictments of others, like the Ghost, to improve the chances of catching them.

And task force officials pushed the Obama team, also unsuccessfully, to use U.S. aid money and weapons sales as leverage to push Lebanon into adopting an extradition treaty and handing over all of the indicted Hezbollah suspects living openly in the country, they said.

"There were ways of getting these guys if they'd let us," Kelly said.

Frustrated, he wrote another of his emails to DEA leaders in July 2014, asking for help.

The email stated that the used-car money-laundering scheme was flourishing in the United States and Africa. The number of vehicles being shipped to Benin had more than doubled from December 2011 to 2014, he wrote, with one dealership alone receiving more than $4 million.

And despite the DEA's creation of a multi-agency "Iran-Hezbollah Super Facilitator Initiative" in 2013, Kelly said, only the Department of Homeland Security's Customs and Border Patrol was sharing information and resources.

"The nuclear negotiations are on their own. They're standing separate from anything else" — Secretary of State John Kerry to reporters

"The FBI and other parts of the USG [U.S. government] provide a little or no assistance during our investigations," Kelly wrote in the email. "The USG lack of action on this issue has allowed [Hezbollah] to become one of the biggest transnational organized crime groups in the world."

Around this time, people outside Project Cassandra began noting that senior administration officials were increasingly suspicious of it.

Douglas Farah, a transnational crime analyst, said he tried to raise the Project Cassandra investigations with Obama officials in order to corroborate his own on-the-ground research, without success. "When it looked like the [nuclear] agreement might actually happen, it became clear that there was no interest in dealing with anything about Iran or Hezbollah on the ground that it may be negative, that it might scare off the Iranians," said Farah.

Asher, meanwhile, said he and others began hearing "from multiple people involved in the Iran discussions that this Hezbollah stuff was definitely getting in the way of a successful negotiation," he said. One Obama national security official even said so explicitly in the same State Department meeting in which he boasted about how the administration was bringing together a broad coalition in the Middle East, including Hezbollah, to fight the Islamic State terrorist group, Asher recalled.

Indeed, the United States was seeking Iran's help in taking on the Islamic State. As the nuclear deal negotiations were intensifying ahead of a November 2014 diplomatic deadline, Obama himself secretly wrote to Iran's supreme leader, Ayatollah Ali Khamenei, to say the two countries had a mutual interest in fighting Islamic State militants in Iraq and Syria, The Wall Street Journal reported.

Kerry, who was overseeing the negotiations, rejected suggestions that the nuclear deal was linked to other issues affecting the U.S-Iranian relationship.

"The nuclear negotiations are on their own," he told reporters. "They're standing separate from anything else. And no discussion has ever taken place about linking one thing to another."

The Obama team "really, really, really wanted the deal" — Former CIA officer on how intelligence operations were also impacted by negotiations with Iran
But even some former CIA officials said the negotiations were affecting their dealings in the Middle East and those of the DEA.

DEA operations in the Middle East were shut down repeatedly due to political sensitivities, especially in Lebanon, according to one former CIA officer working in the region. He said pressure from the White House also prompted the CIA to declare "a

moratorium" on covert operations against Hezbollah in Lebanon, too, for a time, after the administration received complaints from Iranian negotiators.

"During the negotiations, early on, they [the Iranians] said listen, we need you to lay off Hezbollah, to tamp down the pressure on them, and the Obama administration acquiesced to that request," the former CIA officer told POLITICO. "It was a strategic decision to show good faith toward the Iranians in terms of reaching an agreement."

The Obama team "really, really, really wanted the deal," the former officer said.

As a result, "We were making concessions that had never been made before, which is outrageous to anyone in the agency," the former intelligence officer said, adding that the **orders from Washington especially infuriated CIA officers in the field who knew that Hezbollah "was still doing assassinations and other terrorist activities."**

That allegation was contested vehemently by the former senior Obama national security official who played a role in the Iran nuclear negotiations. "That the Iranians would ask for a favor in this realm and that we would acquiesce is ludicrous," he said.

Obama holds a press conference on the Iran deal

Nonetheless, feeling that he had few options left, Asher went public with his concerns at a congressional hearing in May 2015 saying, "the Department of Justice should seek to indict and prosecute" Hezbollah's Islamic Jihad Organization as an international conspiracy using the RICORICO case statute. That was the only way, he testified, for U.S. officials to "defeat narcoterrorism financing, including that running right through the heart of the American financial system," as Hezbollah was doing with the used-cars scheme.

The nuclear deal was signed in July 2015, and formally implemented on Jan. 17, 2016. A week later, almost two years after his arrest, Czech officials finally released Fayad to Lebanon in exchange for five Czech citizens that Hezbollah operatives had kidnapped as bargaining chips.

Unlike in the case of Bout, the former arms trafficker for Putin, neither Obama nor other senior White House officials made personal pleas for the extradition of Fayad, task force officials said. Afterward, the U.S. Embassy in the Czech Republic issued a statement saying, "We are dismayed by the Czech government's decision."

For the task force, Fayad's release was one of the biggest blows yet. Some agents told POLITICO that Fayad's relationships with Hezbollah, Latin American drug cartels and the governments of Iran, Syria and Russia made him a critically important witness in any RICO prosecution and in virtually all of their ongoing investigations.

"He is one of the very few people who could describe for us the workings of the operation at the highest levels," Kelly said. "And the administration didn't lift a finger to get him back here."

One senior Obama administration official familiar with the case said it would be a stretch to link the Fayad case to the Iran deal, even if the administration didn't lobby aggressively enough to have Fayad extradited to the United States.

"I guess it's possible that they [the White House] didn't want to try hard because of the Iran deal but I don't have memories of it," said the former official. "Clearly there were things that the Obama administration did to keep the negotiations alive, prudent negotiating tactics to keep the Iranians at the table. But to be fair, there was a lot of shit we did during the Iran deal negotiations that pissed the Iranians off."

Afterward, Czech President Milos Zeman told local media he had freed Fayad at the personal request of Putin, a close ally of both the Czech Republic and Iran, who had lobbied hard for his release in a series of phone calls like the ones Project Cassandra officials were hoping Obama would make.

Russian President Vladimir Putin and his Czech counterpart Milos Zeman
A week later, European authorities, working with the DEA and U.S. Customs and Border Patrol, arrested an undisclosed number of Hezbollah-related suspects in France and neighboring countries on charges of using drug trafficking money to procure weapons for use in Syria.

In announcing the arrests, the DEA and the Justice Department disclosed for the first time the existence of Project Cassandra, as well as its target, the drug-and weapons-trafficking unit known as Hezbollah's Business Affairs Component. In a news release, DEA also said the business entity "currently operates under the control of Abdallah Safieddine" and Tabaja.

Jack Riley, the DEA's acting deputy administrator, said in the news release that Hezbollah's criminal operations "provide a revenue and weapons stream for an international terrorist organization responsible for devastating terror attacks around the world."

Riley described the operation as "ongoing," saying "DEA and our partners will continue to dismantle networks who exploit the nexus between drugs and terror using all available law enforcement mechanisms."

But Kelly and some other agents had already come to believe that the arrests would be a last hurrah for the task force, as it was crumbling under pressure from U.S. officials eager to keep the newly implemented Iran deal intact. That's why Project Cassandra members insisted on including Safieddine's name in the media releases. They wanted it in the public record, in case they had no further opportunity to expose the massive conspiracy they believed he had been overseeing.

A last hurrah

The news release caused a stir. The CIA was furious that Project Cassandra went public with details of Hezbollah's business operations. And the French government called off a joint news conference planned to announce the arrests. Kelly, who was already in Paris awaiting the news conference, said European authorities told him the French didn't want to offend Iran, which just 11 days after the nuclear deal implementation had agreed to buy 118 French Airbus aircraft worth about $25 billion.

"Given the group's ever-lengthening criminal rap sheet around the world, designating it as a TCO [Transnational Criminal Organization] has become an open-and-shut case" — Matthew Levitt

Two weeks later, after firing off another angry email or two, Kelly said he was told by his superiors that he was being transferred against his wishes to a gang unit at DEA headquarters. He retired months later on the first day he was eligible.

Several other key agents and analysts also transferred out on their own accord, in some cases in order to receive promotions, or after being told by DEA leaders that they had been at the Special Operations Division for too long, according to Kelly, Asher, Maltz and others.

Meanwhile, the administration was resisting demands that it produce a long-overdue intelligence assessment that Congress had requested as a way of finally resolving the interagency dispute over Hezbollah's role in drug trafficking and organized crime.

It wasn't just a bureaucratic exercise. More than a year earlier, Congress – concerned that the administration was whitewashing the threat posed by Hezbollah – passed the Hizballah International Financing Prevention Act. That measure required the White House to lay out in writing its plans for designating Hezbollah a "significant transnational criminal organization."

The White House delegated responsibility for the report to the office of the director of National Intelligence, prompting immediate accusations by the task force and its allies that the administration was stacking the deck against such a determination, and against Project Cassandra, given the intelligence community's doubts about the DEA's conclusions about Hezbollah's drug-running.

"Given the group's ever-lengthening criminal rap sheet around the world, designating it as a TCO [Transnational Criminal Organization] has become an open-and-shut case," Matthew Levitt, a former senior Treasury official, said of Hezbollah in an April 2016 policy paper for a Washington think tank.

Agents from Project Cassandra and other law enforcement agencies "investigate criminal activities as a matter of course and are therefore best positioned to judge whether a group has engaged in transnational organized crime," wrote Levitt, who is also a former FBI analyst and author of a respected book on Hezbollah. "Intelligence agencies are at a disadvantage in this regard, so the DNI's forthcoming report should reflect the repeated findings of law enforcement, criminal courts, and Treasury designations."

As expected, the administration's final report, which remains classified, significantly downplayed Hezbollah's operational links to drug trafficking, which in turn further marginalized the DEA's role in fighting it, according to a former Justice Department official and others familiar with the report.

Once the Obama administration left office, in January 2017, the logjam of task force cases appeared to break, and several task force members said it wasn't a coincidence.

An alleged top Hezbollah financier, Kassim Tajideen, was arrested in Morocco — seven years after Treasury officials blacklisted him as a sponsor of terror — and flown to Washington to stand trial. Asher said task force agents had kept his case under wraps, hoping for a better outcome in whatever administration succeeded Obama's.

The Trump administration also designated Venezuelan Vice President Tareck Aissami as a global narcotics kingpin, almost a decade after DEA agents became convinced he was Hezbollah's point man within the Chavez, and then Maduro, regimes.

Ironically, many senior career intelligence officials now freely acknowledge that the task force was right all along about Hezbollah's operational involvement in drug trafficking. "It dates back many years," said one senior Directorate of National Intelligence official.

"They are a global threat, particularly if the Trump relationships turn sour" Meanwhile, Hezbollah — in league with Iran, Russia and the Assad regime — has all but overwhelmed the opposition groups in Syria, including those backed by the United States. Hezbollah continues to help train Shiite militants in other hotspots and to undermine U.S. efforts in Iraq, according to U.S. officials. It also continues its expansion in Latin America and, DEA officials said, its role in trafficking cocaine and other drugs into the United States. And it is believed to be the biggest trafficker of the powerful stimulant drug Captagon that is being used by fighters in Syria on all sides.

Progress has been made on other investigations and prosecutions, current and former officials said. But after an initial flurry of interest in resurrecting Project Cassandra, the Trump administration has been silent on the matter. In all of the Trump administration's public condemnations of Hezbollah and Iran, the subject of drug trafficking hasn't come up.

In West Africa, satellite imagery has documented that the Hezbollah used-car money-laundering operation is bigger than ever, Asher told lawmakers in recent testimony before the House Foreign Affairs Committee.

And Hezbollah continues to scout potential U.S. targets for attack if it decides Washington has crossed some red line against it or Iran. On June 1, federal authorities arrested two alleged Hezbollah operatives who were conducting "pre-operational surveillance" on possible targets for attack, including the FBI headquarters in New York and the U.S. and Israeli embassies in Panama.

"They are a global threat, particularly if the Trump relationships turn sour" with Iran, Syria and Russia, said Magnus Ranstorp, one of the world's foremost Hezbollah experts.

The June arrests "bring into sharp focus that the Iranians are making contingency plans for when the U.S. turns up the heat on Iran," said Ranstorp, research director of the Center for Asymmetric Threat Studies at the Swedish National Defence College, who is in frequent contact with U.S. intelligence officials. "If they think it requires some military or terrorist response, they have been casing targets in the U.S. since the late 1990s."

An Iranian man holding a Lebanese Hezbollah flag walks past an anti-US mural depicting the Statue of Liberty on the wall of the former US embassy in Tehran 2009 | Behrouz Mehri Ranstorp said U.S. intelligence officials believe that Hezbollah's U.S.-based surveillance is far more extensive than has been publicly disclosed, and that they are particularly concerned about the battle-hardened operatives who have spent years on the ground in Syria.

"The U.S. intel community is very concerned about this," Ranstorp said. Hezbollah's agents "have become extremely sophisticated and good at fighting."

Maltz, the longtime head of DEA Special Operations, who retired two months after the Tampa summit in 2014, has lobbied since then for better interagency cooperation on Hezbollah, to tackle both the terrorist threat and the criminal enterprise that underwrites it.

Turf battles, especially the institutional conflict between law enforcement and intelligence agencies, contributed to the demise of Project Cassandra, Maltz said. But many Project Cassandra agents insist the main reason was a political choice to prioritize the Iranian nuclear agreement over efforts to crack down on Hezbollah.

"They will believe until death that we were shut down because of the Iran deal," Maltz said. "My gut feeling? My instinct as a guy doing this for 28 years is that it certainly contributed to why we got pushed aside and picked apart. There is no doubt in my mind." By JOSH MEYER

Throughout Anthony Stephen Malone International Investigation into the Bank of Madina& Other Tasks "Project Cassandra Operators" would Liaisewith Anthony Stephen Malone and his Team/Assets in Afghanistan, Iraq, Syria, Kuwait, Lebanon, Russia, Somalia, Libya,Morocco & Columbia... All roads always lead back to Hezbollah...Haqqani Network... and Al-Qaeda... (Copys of Intelligence Reports are safe with a British Solicitor and are avalible for Reference by American Agencies)

Elite Team Leader, Middle-East, Africa & Asia
(Thankyou Bro, Looking forward to another 15 years!)

Acknowledgements

There are so many people to be eternally grateful to for their concern and invaluable support during my time on operations and Taskings. It would be impossible to name them all. If I have inadvertently omitted anyone, I can only apologies profusely.

Thank you to the 101st ABD combat camera team in Iraq for the use of some of their photographs. It was an Honour spending time with you all. "Air Assault".

Special acknowledgements go to Nicki and Maria, who kindly agreed to help with editing of the early drafts, without their help this would not have been possible. My incredible and supportive family, Patrick, Veronica and Maria, all of whom campaigned endlessly for my freedom and with great dignity, I am extremely proud of their efforts and their fight for justice. Pat "RIP" and Ian thank you for your continued support, Karen and Family, also Sami, for all their support and encouragement, 'Esperance'. During some challenging times.

Nicki (Big Smiles) keep on going after the bad guys and looking good doing it! John, thanks for being a friend, keep up the great photographs, if I need help cutting down a tree I will call you! Sheila and Angela for their unwavering support for myself and other military veterans.

Greg, Jane, Steve, John, Mike, Sara and Scott CIA, keep up the good work and thank you for your service, help and support. B & W, B, M, DEA keep on doing whatever you all do! "It was Emotional". C enjoy Life after being an action Girl.

Trevor Cooper, Graham H (SBS), Mike (Para Reg) and Brian D, Troy H, NJ, James, Tom thanks for everything boys. (Once a soldier always a soldier) hold yours heads high boys, we made a difference.

My Best Regards to Paul Downs, PJ, Paul D, Stev Boy and CJ we kicked ass in Iraq and Syria, Paul hope you liked the Puma Extraction! Have a beer mate, you helped save a lot of lives.

A special thank you to Jane and Alissa for covering my ass and saving my life in Syria, Iraq. Thank you. I hope this book answers some of your questions! I will always class you both as good friends, (a ray of sunshine).

I am indebted to my friends in Afghanistan, Peter Jouvenal and Major Bill Shaw MBE, who supported me through some dark times. Also Kevin Stainburn and Tim Ward for their kindness, support and much needed food supplies without your help in Afghanistan I would not have made it. Thank you.

Major Bevan Campbell RIP, who without his help, friendship and advice, I could well have been killed many times during operations. You are an incredible human being and I am proud to call you not just my friend, but a True Brother. We did something Very Special....!! (Remember the Pale Horse in 'The Book'...) RIP Brother until we meet again. (Your Video Evidence will make you a Rockstar!)

Werner (RIP) and Hannelie, whose support made all the difference, I knew that I was doing God's work, thank you for all your prayers, I know you're at peace up in heaven with your two children, you are all in my prayers, I will never forget....!!

Julian Lebanon, who kept us in supplies when we were getting no food – even with the guards "taxing" it – it still meant that we could at least eat a little better.

Ursula Campbell, thank you also for all your kind words and support for my family and I.

Phil Young, who shared his horrific experiences of his time in Pul-i-Charkhi prison and backed it up with detailed statements, I wish you all the best for the future.

Tanya, whose kindness and prayers helped me see the light, keep your chin up, you're one in a million Doll.

Amanda Lindhout, you're still an action girl who I admire and I always will. Keep up the great and important work you're doing in Somalia, one woman can make a difference. I am proud to have met you and call you a friend. Thank you for your support.

Paula Daly, thank you for everything, you're a rock star. (Forces for Their Future) Veterans Charity.

I would also like to thank MP Colonel Bob Stuart and Colonel Dave Reynolds for their concern and help. Sir Peter Gibson OBE, MP Colonel Patrick Mercer MBE and MP Alex Cunningham, for their support and advice. Sir David Richards GCB, CBE, DSO, ADC, Gen, (former chief of the defence staff), thank you for your support and advice. Bob Morrison (Rox) C&S for their help, support and messages of encouragement.

I would also like to thank HRH Queen Elizabeth II, HRH Prince's Charles, Harry and William, for their correspondences and best wishes. Also the Right Honorable David Cameron, MP, The former Prime Minister, for his responses to my correspondence. I would also like to thank the Chief of Staff of the British Army for his advice and best wishes.

A special thank you to 'Sharpy' my operations manager Cyprus, Lebanon who told me that "failure was not an option", well mate, I helped to take down Osama bin Laden and stopped in excess of 100 terrorist attacks, saving hundreds of lives, I hope I did you proud.

Big thanks to J in Lebanon, Daz and Jane (British military Cyprus) thank you for your friendship, enjoy retirement in the Northeast of England.

I would also like to thank the soldiers and officers from 101st Airborne Division who served in Iraq and Afghanistan, thank you for all of your letters of support, it was an honour working alongside you all. A big thank you to Robert Woodward, USA for the use of his Photographs in my book, mate you're a rock star and fellow Airborne Brother, when we meet again the Victory Cigars are on me.

My special thanks to General David Petraeus, Brigadier General Michael Lennington and Brigadier General Joe Anderson, these men are all Paratroopers and outstanding fighting men and true military leaders, it was an honour spending time with you in Iraq, Stay Safe gentlemen. David, remember "one man came make a difference", we did.

Malcolm in Lebanon, Sami in Jordan Intelligence, Colonel Hayatt (Afghanistan), Wali Massoud (Afghanistan), Hayatt (France-Baghdad), for all your help and support.

Members of the British Army, Parachute Regiment, Troy Holden, 3 Para and Special Forces SAS/SBS, for all their help, support and best wishes, your messages of encouragement kept me going.

CIA, Jane and all her operators and personnel, RSO's who I had dealings with and operated with across the Middle-East, Afghanistan, Africa and Europe. Keep up the good work (Stay Safe).

Ken, Walter, John and the rest of the CSSP team, thank you for covering my back when the political crap started from the British FCO, "We did make a difference", American, British, Canadian ISAF lives were saved, you should all be very proud of what we did.

All the Red Cross staff and personnel, Martin, who I met in Pul-iCharkhi, Afghanistan and across the Middle-East and Africa, you are all amazing people who do a job that save lives every day, I owe you my life as do countless others, thank you.

Members of the International press, Nadine (Mail on Sunday), Travis (Afghanistan), Deborah Haynes (Times), Solomon (New York Times), Abraham (CNN), Adam Nathan (Sunday Times) for your help on the Iraq task. Donna MilesAmerican Forces Press Service for the article on David Petaeus in Iraq.

British Legal team, Karen Todner, Alison Walker, for all their support, help and advice, through some very challenging times. FTI (Fair Trials International), Rachel for all her work, help and advice while I was in Afghanistan. Trudy Kennedy MBE, FCO, thank you for trying to help me in Pul-i-Charkhi, I wish you the best for the future. A very special thank-you to Jan Everleigh, FCO, who was the one person at the UK Embassy (Kabul) to really make a "difference" for ALL UK and Commonwealth Nationals – if only there were more of you out there.

Mitch Albert (Canadian), thank you for all your help, support, guidance, stay safe my friend.

Colin B. Thankyou for all your help and support. It ment alot and was good to talk to someone who understands the situation. Regards, Stay Safe.

My Best regards to Paul Jenkins, thank you for all your help advice and guidance, the next bottle of red wine is on me!

To anybody else who helped in any small way with the campaign, added a name to the petition, sent a message, letter, or made the effort to come and visit me, I truly appreciate your support. I could never have got through this without you...

Regards, Stay Safe, Anthony Stephen Malone

RIP; My Life Long Brother Major Bevan Campbell, Airforce Intelligence SA. "I Still Have Your Back Bro... Thankyou for saving My Life so Many Times!" Rest Easy Soldier until we meet in Valhalla!".

Bibliography

References and details from the below publications have been used within my manuscript to ensure my writing is as accurate and as detailed as possible for the reader. References from news articles have been used within my manuscript and reports, the sources of these articles were: The Guardian, New York Times, Sunday Times and American CNN. I would like to thank them all for helping me to ensure that my manuscript was as accurate and detailed as possible.

3 Para – Patrick Bishop

A hell for heroes – Theo Knell

An ordinary soldier – Doug Beattie

Apache - Ed Macy

Arabian Sands – Wilfred Thesiger

Body of Lies – David Ignatius

Bush at war – Bob Woodward

Genghis Khan – Ata-Malik Juvaini

Helmand – Diaries of front-line soldiers

In the company of soldiers – Rick Atkinson

Kill Switch – Major Bill Shaw MBE

Military Intelligence Blunders – Colonel John Hughes Wilson

Sand Strom – Lindsey Hilsum

Seven pillars of Wisdom – T. E. Lawrence

Tajikistan – Bradt

Task Force Black – Mark Urban

Task Force Dagger – Robin Moore

The Assassins' Gate – George Packer

The fall of Baghdad – Jon – Lee Anderson

The Forgotten Palestinians – Ilan Pappe

The Great war of Civilization – Robert Fisk

The Middle-East – Bernard Lewis

The occupation of Iraq – Ali a Allawi

The war against Saddam – John Simpson

Through our enemy eyes – Michael Scheuer

Exclusive: Future publications by Anthony Stephen Malone

Honour Bound - Rogue Warrior Operating Behind Enemy Lines Exclusive Photography Collection

Tracking & locating Osama bin Laden UBL (The target package)

International Terrorism (Exclusive perspective from within an International terrorist networks)

-

Synopsis of Anthony Stephen Malone deep covert infiltration of the Al-Qaeda, Taliban, Pakistan Taliban and Haqqani networks from within Iraq Syria and Afghanistan (Continuation of counter-terrorism and intelligence work carried out between 2002-2007)"

A)   Between 2007 and 2010 Anthony Malone infiltrated the Al-Qaeda, Pakistan Taliban, Haqqani terrorist networks up to leadership level and their trusted inner circles. This task was requested and ordered by senior American military intelligence stationed in Afghanistan. American senior officers also confirmed that Anthony had top-cover from the American Military/Government. This was for future protection against the British Foreign Office, who at a later date would try and accuse Anthony of being a terrorist and member of the Al-Qaeda, Pakistan Taliban terrorist network.

B)   Conservatively over 150 international terrorist attacks were stopped and disrupted by Anthony covertly feeding intelligence back to American military intelligence (W D, CSSP/American Military intelligence and Col Ken McKellar) Major Campbell has confirm this fact in video interview...

C)   Infiltrating the "Talib Jan" (he ordered the bombing of the "Finest" shopping centre, just across the road from the UK Embassy) suicide bombing network being coordinated from within Pul-i-Charkhi Prison Afghanistan, Anthony stopped over 100 suicide and IED attacks on ISAF American and British soldiers in Afghanistan by infiltrating and disrupting the terrorist network. Senior Afghan NDS Security Service officers confirmed information on Talib Jan and the terrorist network operating out of Pul-i-Charkhi prison. The story also printed in the British Daily Telegraph newspaper.

D)   Disrupting and stopping of terrorist attacks also included; the disruption of attacks in several county's including, Kurdistan, America, Saudi Arabia, Iraq, Yemen, Somalia, UAE, Europe and Cyprus.

E)   Anthony identified, while under deep cover within the Al-Qaeda, Pakistan Taliban terrorist network:

- Weapons and explosives shipments.
- Hostage locations.
- HVT and safe house locations.
- Terrorist leaders travel plans and routes.
- International terrorist financing systems, including "bank account numbers" and names of front companies used for money laundering.
- Intelligence concerning the identification and location of IED factories and international terrorists involved in bomb making across the Middle-East and the terrorist areas of operations.

F)   Anthony worked closely with the British SAS Chief of Staff and his Blade Teams, resulting in several terrorist training camps being located in Afghanistan and Pakistan. This intelligence resulted in Air strikes on the camps, a large number of terrorists killed and future terrorist attacks on America and Britain stopped. (Confirmed in meeting between Sergeant Trevor Cooper, Anthony's operations manager, and SAS Major in Hereford UK). Other task's received from SAS COS included updates and reports of locations of other HVT's and terrorist leaders including, Mullah Omar. (Copy of original reports available, Sergeant Trevor Cooper and members of Special Forces are also available to be discreetly interviewed).

G)   Anthony's deep infiltration also uncovered the Pakistan Taliban plans to detonate a large car bomb in Times Square New York. Intelligence covertly passed back to American Military Intelligence helped stop the 4x4 car bomb, parked in Times Square, before it detonated in a heavily populated area in New York City.

H)   Al-Qaeda plans to attack HRH Queen Elizabeth II, and members of the British Royal Family at Buckingham Palace, were intercepted and passed onto British SOCA/NCA in Afghanistan; Anthony gave this information to SOCA/NCA employee Troy Heldon, long term SOCA/NCA contact and professional contact. Troy had passed training with Anthony for the Parachute Regiment 15 years earlier. Troy had also previously driven Anthony, covertly, to meetings within military bases with SOCA/NCA in Afghanistan. (Troy Heldon is a witness to the above facts and information, interview also available).

I)   Al-Qaeda operational note book containing hundreds of real names and contact phone numbers used within the Al-Qaeda, Pakistan Taliban international terrorist network. A copy of this critically important note book was sent by Anthony to British Prime Minister David Cameron at 10 Downing Street London. A copy of the note book was also sent to the Director of MI6 at that time. (Copy of photographs of notebook and other exclusive photographs of inside Afghan Pul-i-Charkhi Maximum security prison are available) Important note; The original note book belonged to AKA Hussien Laghmani, the god-son of 2011 Al-Qaeda leader Al-Z, Hussien was the Quartermaster for AL-Qaeda, Pakistan Taliban and Lashkar e-Taiba operations, including the procurement of Stolen American Stinger missiles. Hussein was responsible for organising the ordinance for Lashkar e-Taiba, used in the Mumbai attack.

J)   Anthony's covert intelligence reports were shown to Col Bob Stewart (MP) by Sergeant Trevor Cooper and B. Within 15 minutes of reading the reports, Col Bob Stewart arranged for the reports to be taken into an official meeting at MOD HQ Whitehall London with senior MOD officials (all the above were present at the meeting) Copy of reports available. Report included photographs, names, car registration numbers and contact numbers of Pakistani Taliban suicide bombers living in London, UK.

K)   During Anthony's deep infiltration of the Al-Qaeda network within the Prison environment, over several years, he was officially tasked by American Military Intelligence ("Major" Walter Downs). Tasking's included the tracing, tracking and locating of Al-Qaeda leaders hiding in Pakistan, several Senior Al-Qaeda Commanders were located, including Al-Qaeda No 1 HVT, UBL. This comprehensive target package was personally handed to American Military Intelligence, W D, by Anthony. This included; Location of UBL villa in Abbottabad, Pakistan:

- UBL was also living and slept on the 3rd floor with one of his wives.
- Other sensitive information and intelligence including military mission options and recommendations.

- Phone numbers of trusted couriers used by the terrorist network between Afghanistan and Pakistan.
-

Anthony and Major Campbell's Personal Diaries confirm the date and location of UBL 8 months before UBL was targeted and killed by American Seal Team 6 at the above location). An "Index List" given to an American lawyer, also confirmed the Location of UBL, as well as a list of intelligence reports handed by Anthony to American Military Intelligence. Major Campbell was witness to the "Index List" being handed over personally by Anthony to the lawyer. The America lawyer confirmed that she personally handed the "Index List" to W D, senior American Military Intelligence. (Chain of evidence for locating UBL). "Jeff" (pseudonym) the CIA Head of Humint (Human intelligence), based out of the American Embassy (Kabul), was also updated during a covert brief between Anthony and Jeff, which took place in Pul-i-Charkhi Prison. Major Campbell was witness to this meeting as well. (See Video) Anthony personally updated Jeff on the location of UBL being located in a villa in Abbottabad Pakistan, this was 8 months before UBL was killed by American Special Forces, Seal Team 6.

L)   Major terrorist attack on Kandahar Air Field (KAF) was disrupted from within Pul-i-Charkhi Prison. Hours before the attack, Anthony shorted the electric mains box in the prison block, this while the Al-Qaeda and Taliban were charging their mobile phone, Sat-Com's/phones and laptop computers, all of which were being used to help coordinate the attack. This resulted in reducing the terrorist Command and Control ability, which resulted in a failed terrorist attack, having the overall effect of leaving the attack disorganised and disjointed. Following the attack, intelligence "confirmed" that the British PM, David Cameron, was sitting on-board a fully fueled military C130 transport aircraft, a mere 400 meters from one of the terrorist attacks which managed to infiltrate the airfield, and made their way to the runway.

M)   Anthony identified and located the main terrorist IED factory and terrorist safe house at Al-Hatera Western Iraq. After an American military Special Forces mission against the target, attacks of American troops diminished within this area.

N)   Malone used the extensive international terrorist network within Pul-i-Charkhi prison, and beyond, to trace and track American Stinger missiles and other SAMs (Surface to Air Missiles). Other military hardware including weapons grade plutonium and other material that terrorist groups were trying to obtain for dirty bombs also became a priority for Anthony and his team, who were directly involved in the counter proliferation of such material. (See report of meeting with American Major set up by Tim SAS Special Forces Operations liaison officer, Bagram Air base Afghanistan).

O)   GPS co-ordinates, and other terrorist Commanders tactical and strategic information was passed by Anthony to B, who in turn passed information directly to Col Ken (American Military Intelligence). Col Ken also acknowledged the risk of this task and telephoned B to thank him for passing on such critically time-sensitive information, which had saved American and British lives.

P)   Anthony ascertained the date and time of a high number of terrorist attacks planned on American soldiers. An example of this was the planned multiple IED attack and sniper ambush on American soldiers (Senior American Intelligence Operatives) visiting Pul-i-Charkhi prison. The attack had been planned and put in place for 1500hrs, location; the Bridge just off Jalalabad Road backing onto the ISAF American base. The attack was disrupted; the American patrol and prison visit were rescheduled. Again American lives were saved. Within the week Anthony had identified a major IED factory, located in shipping-container company on the Jalalabad Road. This terrorist IED factory was poised to launch several attacks on British and American soldiers patrolling along the Jalalabad road from their Forward Operating Bases (FOB). They also planned to use some of these IED's to attack soldiers from the American 101st Airborne Division, based in Eastern Afghanistan. The attacks were stopped, IED factory located and destroyed by American Special Forces. Message passed back to Anthony from American military "Job Well Done".

Q)   Anthony was tasked by American Military Intelligence and Senior British SAS officers and handed over material on several other highly sensitive subjects; this material is confidential due to ongoing military and international intelligence operations.

R)   Anthony ran and cultivated the covert investigation into the Bank of Al Medina letter of autherisation by the Chairman of the Bank (see photograph of document). The investigation included confirming all ties to internation terrorist organisations from within the bank and their bank account's front companies. Anthony Malone was the sole liaison between the chairman of the bank and all government agencies including DEA, CIA, FBI, MI6, DoD and French DST. Anthony Malone and his NOC assets across the Middle East, Europe and Asia helped to map out the criminal infrastructure of Hazbolla's global network. Interesting facts and connections between AQI Haqina netweok, Al Shabab Somalia, Russian Mafia and Mexican Central American drug cartels. Links between all names was confirmed during the covert investigation. Links between other international banking institutions were also uncovered: examples HSBC; Royal Bank of Scotland; Barclays Bank. The value of the fraud was in excess of 1.3 billion USD.

"In 2007 after Anthony Malone located Taliban Leader Mullah Omar and other senior Terrorist Commanders, The British SAS Bomb Shell. The SAS regiment was ordered officially by senior British Intelligence/FCO/Government members to ignore and disregard, not to act on, check, confirm or follow up on any and all Intelligence from Anthony Malone and the Elite Team. Due to internal Government politics, Anthony Malone was making certain elements within British Intelligence look very bad... Members of the SAS who had met with or had worked on the Intelligence provided by Anthony Malone and his Team were not happy or impressed with this order... American and British soldiers died and were injured as a direct result of this order... Question, Who gave the order and why...?"

Members of the Elite Team all senior former British Military, were turned away from handing in a file to MI6 HQ which contained the detailed report including photographs of several suicide bombers on route to Europe and Britain.

"British MP Colonel Bob Stewart confirmed the above and the contents of the report to SKY News, Lisa Holland".

Colonel Bob Stewart had after hearing that the team had been turned away from MI6 HQ London. Unforgivable gross incompetence by MI6. Colonel Stewart had walked the Elite Team into MOD HQ in Whitehall, into a meeting within 30min of reading the report with senior Military staff who acted upon the report... The only question Colonel Stewart asked was who was the source of the report, "Anthony Malone". Terrorist attacks were stopped as a result of this report and Colonel Stewart's swift actions. My question is, why would elements within the British Government Intelligence/FCO not want to be given a report...? What are they trying to hide...?

"What do the families of killed and injured British and American Soldiers think of the British Governments actions..? Please feel free to write to the British Prime Minister and the American President, asking them this question...Please post their responses... I can confirm that both of the above and HRH Queen Elizabeth II, HRH Prince Charles, Harry and William, have all received copies of my book!"

Written Statements and detailed video interviews with all team members including; former Special Forces and Major Campbell, ex-SAAF Intelligence, confirming the above points is available via my British legal team.

Major Bill Shaw MBE can also confirm Al-Qaeda-Pakistan Taliban attacks planned, coordinated and commanded from within Pul-i-Charkhi Prison Afghanistan. (See Legal Statement).

American Military Commanders overseeing intelligence from Anthony Stephen Malone 2007-2014

1)   Colonel Ken M CSSP/American Military Intelligence.

2)   Senior Intelligence officer W D/American Military Intelligence.

3)   J Head of American Hum-Int (Human Intelligence) operating out of American Embassy Kabul, under the Command of G RSO (Regional Security Officer, CIA Station head). 2015 G is now Head of the CIA "Clandestine Unit" Based at CIA HQ.

4)   Brigadier General XXXXXX, Commander of "ISAF" Forces in Afghanistan.

5)   XXXXX XXXXX, Commander American Central Command (CENTCOM) & Head of the American CIA (Central Intelligence Agency).

Senior British SAS Officers

Major,XXXXXXXX Military SAS Chief of Staff British Embassy Kabul and A&B Blade Team Commander Afghanistan.

Confidential Contact numbers are available for all the above.

Official British Legal Statement with Regard SAS - CIA - Colonel Bob Stewart MP

During 2006 and 2007 I worked with Anthony Malone in Kabul, Afghanistan, Middle-East as his Operations Manager my responsibilities were to meet with clients, plan assignments and ensure the safety of the team and client.

During this period I was heavily involved with attending meeting at Bagram airport (US BASE) just outside Kabul, on several occasions I attended meeting with high ranking US officers with regards to weapon buy back projects that we took part in, during my time with Anthony Afghanistan I wrote several reports detailing weapons, equipment (vehicles, communications, Helicopter part, surface to air missile systems) that had been located in various locations in Afghanistan.

Along with this information we obtained information on suicide bombers who were to be deployed to the UK to carry out attacks I attempted to meet with the British Ambassador in Afghanistan to relate this information back to the UK, he was not interested at this time.

I was then tasked by Anthony Malone to return to the UK and hand over the information that we had to the relevant agencies, this proved somewhat impossible to get a meeting I then contact Lt Col Bob Stewart with this information, who assisted with setting up a meeting with MOD Whitehall, where the following attended the meeting TREVOR COOPER – GRAHAM HILLIARD – LT COL BOB STEWART and Lt Col Richards, in the meeting where several other high ranking officers from the MOD from the rank of Colonel and above, Both Graham and myself spent several hours being interviewed by the MOD, my report was taken away and acted on.

Several weeks after I returned from Afghanistan I noticed a black Range rover sitting outside my house, this had happened for two consecutive days, on the morning of the second day I approached the vehicle to see two men sitting inside reading the New York Times and USA today, I asked why they was watching me and following me around, they asked me if I thought that Anthony Malone had gone over the Taliban and if they proved it would I take him out, kill him, as I could get close enough, I told them that he had not turned and referred them back to General David Petraeus who was the Head of CIA. These men never returned.

I met with E H former Chief of staff British SAS Afghanistan. SAS Chief of Staff he confirm GPS of the terrorist training camp in Pakistan was good that Anthony Malone had passed on during covert intelligence Tasking's in Iraq, Afghanistan/Pakistan was accurate, the SAS officer also confirmed that the terrorist training camps had been destroyed by airstrikes.

SAS Chief of Staff also confirmed American/British airstrikes had destroyed several other IED factories and terrorist camps based on Intelligence submitted by Anthony Malone and his team.

Also Chief of Staff personal opinion was: "the way that the Elite team and Anthony had been treated by the British Government due to politics was disgraceful".

Sergeant, Trevor Cooper

British Secret Intelligence Service MI6

The motto: 'Semper Occultus' Always secret? refers to the ethos of the Secret Intelligence Service.

The Secret Intelligence Service, sometimes known as MI6, originated in 1909 as the Foreign Section of the Secret Service Bureau, under RNR Commander, later Captain, Sir Mansfield Cumming, which was responsible for gathering intelligence overseas. By 1922 Cumming's section had become a separate service with the title SIS. Cumming signed himself 'C'; his successors have done so ever since. The Special Operations Executive (SOE) was established in 1940, partly from the then Section D of SIS. After the War it was disbanded and some of its members were reabsorbed into SIS. With the passing of the Intelligence Services Act, SIS was placed on a statutory footing under the Foreign & Commonwealth Secretary to whom it is responsible for all aspects of its work. The Act defines the functions of the Service and the responsibilities of its Chief, as well as establishing control and oversight arrangements. The Service's principal role is the production of secret intelligence in support of Her Majesty's Government's security, defense, foreign and economic policies within the framework of requirements laid upon it by the JIC and approved by Ministers. It meets these JIC requirements for intelligence gathering and other tasks through a variety of sources, human and technical, and by liaison with a wide range of foreign intelligence and security services. Specific operations are subject to longstanding procedures for official and ministerial clearance. As the CIA is known as "The Company," SIS is known internally as "The Firm" and to other agencies as "The Friends." SIS is based at 85 Albert Embankment, Vauxhall Cross in London (known to those who work there as "Legoland"). MI6 also paid for a number of telephones located in a busy street in south London (Borough High

Street in Southwark, opposite the Police Station) which has been identified as the spy training centre. The main training centre is FortMonckton, a Napoleonic fort on the south coast at Gosport in Hampshire. What is thought to have been MI6's former City of London office is located in an office block in the Square Mile. After the devastating attacks ripped throw central London on 7th July 2005 and the suicide attack in Manchester. The British intelligence services both foreign and domestic, set up specialized teams of highly trained operatives, to track down, locate and deal with al-Qa'dia and the growing threat of returning ISIS from Syria and international, home grown terrorism. The next terrorist attack in Britain, Europe and America is not a case of if, but when...

I wonder if the founder of SIS/MI6 would have been impressed by his beloved services actions by turning away from MI6 HQ London, a group of Former British Soldiers trying to hand in a file (From Afghanistan) that contained details of several Suicide Bombers International Terrorists coming into and some already in Britian. Turned away due to gross incompetence and FCO/MI6 internal politics... (See Sergeant Trevor Cooper Statement). Luckly my friend British MP Colonel Bob Stewart, Saved the day!

The British Military and Security Services are the best in the world, but are we Lions led by Donkeys... Led by Politicians out of touch with the people of Britain. Politicians are so focused on their own jobs and rewards, being politically correct and tree huggers... They need to be reminded that they are all civil -servants, that are there to service the people of Britain...

SAS soldiers storm the Iranian Embassy in London during the seige in May 1980

SAS Hero & War Veteran Bob Curry (Photo of SAS during the Iranian seige above) was left homeless & left to live in a hostel by his local council (This really could happen to any military veteran). While returning ISIS, Immigrants & Convicted Terrorists are given large cash payouts, big council houses & fully paid benefits, paid legal aid and free healthcare...

"I think it's about time the British Prime Minister got a grip of her Government Departments, they are a disgrace; their utter betrayal of the British Military, the Covernant & the British people & our values is both Disgusting & Shocking... I am just saying what alot of people are thinking...

As a once Homeless Military Veteran myself, you may be shocked to learn that fact, I can speak from firsthand experience, this can happen to anyone. The fact that so many (2500+) former British Soldiers & Service personnel are homeless & living on the streets of Britain is scandalus & highlights what the British Government think of Veterans who once served & Protected this Country. Another very sad & disturbing fact is that soldiers with Mental Health Problems & PTSDdue to their military service, take their own lives after being repeatedly let down & neglected by NHS & Government. This is the Governments "Dirty Little Secret". My personal message to the British Prime Minister & Her Government, stop bluffing your case, "Talk is Cheap" Action by you, your Office & Government is urgently required"...

"A big thankyou from all the Military & Veterans families too, HRH Prince Harry for speaking out for Military Veterans & his incredible work he continues to carry out for Military Veterans".

Piers Morgan, Good Morning Britain & British Journalist, you earned 100 cool points from Soldiers & Veterans everywhere by your actions On & Off camera in your support & attitude towards Bob Curry. It meant so much to so many of us that someone not just took an interest but really cared.

February 2018 we can confirm that Bob Curry has now been given a bungalow to live in by Hereford County Council. We all wish Bob the very best for the future. Thank you to everyone who has helped him aswell.

Thank you

"A Large donation from this books profits go to Military Charities & Veterans both in Britain & America".

Please follow me on my Official Facebook Page, Books by Anthony Stephen Malone & receive Exclusive updates on Books, Photographs, Reports & Interviews. Also please write a book review on Amazon.com Anthony Stephen Malone Book buying page, bottom of page, this will help spread the word about this book, the more people that read the book the better.

Regards

Stay Safe

Anthony Stephen Malone (Airborne)

<u>Equipment List Placed in all Elite (Operational) GMC's 4 x 4s in Lebanon-Syria-Iraq-Kurdistan</u>

All equipment below to be tested and checked into 4 x 4 prior to start of daily tasks by elite team leaders.

Vehicle to be checked over night before deployment on any task.

Bull bar, (Black) and tow bar SOP.

<u>Car – Kit/box</u>

Large Box (wood/plastic) all tools to be placed into box, (box will move with the team if 4x4 is changed, due to operational circumstances)

Two Spare wheels, (place on roof rack/or rear door mount)

Tow-rope (5ton kinetic pull)

Sand plates x 2 (Metal)

2 ton Jack (X 2) High lift Jack

Jump Leads

Spare car batteries, (fully charged) Min of one

Tool kit (Heavy duty bag, adjustable spanners, pliers, hammer, screw drivers/assorted, socket/set).

Heavy duty X bar (fixed to inside of lid of box)

Heavy working gloves, fire resistant x 1

2 x (s) bottle motor oil

1 x (s) bottle Break fluid

Torch and spare batteries / taped to inside top of box lid* batteries to be reversed in torch

Axe (small)* clipped to inside of box lid

Shovel (multi-tool)

Vehicle Med-pack (large), spare med supplies for on the ground, IV's etc (bear in mind children's injuries) (1000 water pure taps)

1 x box, US, MREs, rations, spare food supplies for on the ground, wrapped in waterproof/tarpaulin.

Spare bottled water 1LT X 18

Blankets x 2

Jerry can 2 x water, (plastic) black

Jerry can 2 x fuel, (not plastic, check seals before use)

3 feet plastic hose/pipe, to funnel fuel

Plastic funnel, for fuel transfer (long neck, flexible)

Croc clips, to run power off spare batteries, (recharge for computers and sat-phone etc) from Thruyra company (accessories bag)

4 x cartons / cigarettes Marlborough red and lights, (gifts)

Stove/cooker, 5 fuels (for hot tea/food) runs on all fuel, diesel, petrol, etc.

Tea box, plastic container, (tea/coffee/powdered milk/sugar/packet soups)

Black Titanium pot set (wrapped in cotton bag, no noise)

Water proof bags /bin bags x 10

Heavy/strong, black tape x 1 duck tap

Plastic ties/clips x 20 assorted box cable ties

Epoxy glue (comes in two tins)

Maps/silver compass/GPS 12XL

Spare goggles, in protective bag (if windows go down, sand storms)

Spare sat-phone charger x 1

Orange air panel, 4x4feet, (friendly fire panel)

Spare fuses (taped to inside of lid)

Spare bulb lights (hard boxed and taped to inside of box lid)

Spare starter motor (for auto 4X4 GMC ETC)

Sand bags mil X 20, empty

Spare Fan belt

Spare cam belt

Liquid foam (No Flat), fill tires with foam will not go flat, (fill spare tires) put in before task.

Prolong (oil fluid, 1 LT per vehicle) put in Prior to start of Task.

Assailing rope, 50meters, black and figure of eight and sling

Tracker to be fitted to Elite Group Vehicles (Elite and Mil trackers)

Inferred Strobe (Can only be seen using Night Vision Equipment, used to ID the team 4x4 or to direct in an airstrike onto an Enemy location)

Fire Fly (Used to Guide in Helicopters onto our location in times of emergency)

If the vehicle is to be armored while on the ground, plate the floor, roof, back of all seats, doors and grill.(this will increase the weight x 2 of the vehicle, check suspension and ground clearance).

Nuclear Biological Chemical EQT, S10 respirators, 15, anthropen injections, "anti nerve agent".

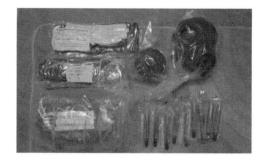

Anthony Stephen Malone Personal NBC kit taken into Iraq Picked up from Syrian Safe House

<u>Specialist List of camera equipment used during Middle East Operations.</u>

Grays of Westminster
40, Churton Street
Pimlico

London SW1V 2LP
England
Tel: 0207-828 4925
Fax: 0207-976 5783
www.graysofwestminster.co.uk

INVOICE

Elite Group International

1 x Nikon D2H Kit
1 x Nikon F6 body
3 x EN-EL4 batteries
14mm f/2.8D AF Nikkor
60mm f/2.8D AF Micro- Nikkor
200-400mm f/4G VR IF-ED Nikkor
1 x SB-800 Speedlight
4 x 512mb Lexar Professional memory cards
1 x Lowepro Dryzone backpack large
1 x Nikon Coolpix 8400 & spare EN-EL7 battery
Nikon case for above
1 X Lexar 1GB Professional memory card

Total cost including VAT £11,195.00

VAT no. 503 1317 05GB

Glossary

Acronyms, keywords, names, abbreviations, intelligence and military terminology, synopsis of terrorist groups and Arabic glossary. Including Islamic customary prayers and phrases.

Al-Qaeda, Haqqani, ISIS, Hezbollah and other terrorist groups and networks operate across the globe and are involved with numerous personalities, organizations and ethnic groups, crossing all geographic boundaries. The following navigational aid is meant to assist the reader of this book-report, in maintaining focus, gain in-depth knowledge, and to use for future reference.

101st:	American 101st Airborne Division (Air-Assault) paratroopers, Commanded in Iraq 2003, by General David Petraeus, who later became the Director of the American CIA. (See Petraeus).
11/3:	March 2004, Madrid. Al-Qaeda detonated ten nearly simultaneous bombs in four packed passenger trains. Killing 191 people and wounding more that twelve hundred.
21/9:	September 21st, 2013. Al-Shabab, Somali terrorist group, with close links to Al-Qaeda, Boko Haram and Nigerian Taliban. Al-Shabab terrorists attacked the Israeli owned Westgate shopping mall in Westland's, Nairobi, Kenya. Killing 70+ and injuring 300+. Casualties included; Kenyan, British, American, Australian and Netherland nationalities. The nationality of Al-Shabab terrorists killed and captured during terrorist attacks and operations, included; European and American. The 21/9 terrorist attack in Kenya was a real game changer to the international terrorist threat from Al-Shabab, Al-Qaeda coming out of East Africa, against soft Western targets across Africa and beyond. (See AlShabab/Al-Shaab and Modern Warfare).
22nd SAS:	British Special Forces 'Special Air Service Regiment'. SAS Headquarters is based at "Stirling Lines", Hereford, United Kingdom.
2IC:	Second in Command.
3-Para:	British military, 3rd Battalion the Parachute Regiment (Elite Paratroopers). Part of 16 Air-Assault, Brigade. Based in Colchester, United Kingdom.
7/7:	July 7th 2005, terrorist attacks on the public transport system in London, United Kingdom. Casualties, 56 killed 700+ injured. (See Modern Warfare-July 7th 2005).
9/11:	September 11th 2001, Al-Qaeda, Attacks on America, including New-York, Twin Towers, The Pentagon and Flight UA93. Casualties; 2752+ killed, thousands injured. (See September 11th 2001).

A-10:	(See Thunder bolt, Warthog).
A2:	British Army standard assault rifle, ammunition 5.56mm, previously known as the SA80. The A2 can be fitted with the standard iron open sights or the SUSAT, (Sight Unit Small Arms Trillux) the ACOG sight is also interchangeable. The A2 can be fitted with a 40mm under-barrel grenade launcher and other tactical attachments.
Abbottabad:	City in North East Pakistan, home of the Pakistan military academy and location where "Osama bin Laden" was traced, tracked then killed by American Special Forces, "Seal team 6", on 2nd May 2011, under the Executive order of the President of the United States of America.
Abdul Aziz:	Saudi born, educated in Medina, holy city located in Southern Saudi Arabia. Abdul Aziz is an Al-Qaeda commander-AQAP and has strong ties to the Haqqani network in Afghanistan and Pakistan. Abdul Aziz is personally responsible for killing American soldiers in Afghanistan and was also one of the top insurgent Commanders in Iraq. (See Haqqani network) (Interviewed by Anthony Malone in Afghanistan).
Abu Dhabi:	Capital city of the United Arab Emirates "UAE". (See Dubai).
Abu-Yahyia-Al-Libi:	Second in Command of the Al-Qaeda network/group.
AC130:	American/British Hercules aircraft, specially converted C-130-gunship also known as Spectre and Combat Talon. AC-130's are operational across the Middle-East, Afghanistan and Africa. (See Spectre).
ACP:	Afghan Chief Prosecutor. The ACP works within the Afghan Ministry of Justice. From 2007 to 2014+, the ACP was personally responsible for
	changing the prison files in return for money, "from terrorist convictions to drugs convictions", of a large number of Al-Qaeda and Taliban terrorists, prisoners. This resulted in a large number (50+) of Terrorists walking free from Afghan prisons. The Afghan justice system, Afghanistan Government; is one of the most corrupt in the world according to the United Nations. (See Haqqani network and Hussein Laghman).
Afghan:	National from Afghanistan.
Africom:	American military Africa command.
Airborne Initiative:	British Paratroopers ability to think on their feet, training, knowledge, experience and initiative, all put together in a volatile or intense situation

and/or environment. The ability to stay focused and deal with any situation or potential problem, "Think outside the box". (See 3 Para).

AK-47:
Russian Kalashnikov assault rifle, fires 7.62 X 39 ammunition, named after the Soviet inventor, "favoured weapon of terrorists". The AK-47 also appears on several terrorist flags, including Lebanese Hezbollah.

Akrotiri-RAF:
British RAF base, located in Western Cyprus in the Mediterranean. British long range fighter planes and bombers, surveillance assets are located at RAF, Akrotiri. The base is also the staging location for British forces operating across the Middle-East, North Africa and is a major logistics hub for British forces being deployed internationally.

Aleppo:
Also known as Halab, second largest city in Syria. Strategically located along the ancient silk route, 300km north of Damascus, close to the geographic borders of Lebanon and Turkey.

Al-Jazeera:
Arabic news/TV channel based in Qatar (Arabic version of CNN).

Al-Manama:
Capital of Bahrain, Bahrain is also the operational home of the American 5th Naval fleet, strategically located to cover the Middle-East.

AL-Q:
Al-Qaeda -Al-Qae'da- Al-Qa'dea- Al-Qaida, originally, Arabic word meaning "The Base", (See Osama bin Laden). (Anthony Malone

interviewed several members, Commanders of Al-Qaeda in Afghanistan).

Al-Shabab/Al-Shaab:
Terrorist group located in Somalia, with strong ties to Al-Qaeda and the "Haqqani", network in Pakistan-Afghanistan and Boko Haram, Nigerian Taliban. Al-Shabab receives funding and logistics from the Al-Qaeda leadership-network, in Arabia (Al-Qaeda in the Arabian peninsula-AQAP) and the Al-Qaeda leadership-supreme council in Pakistan, Afghanistan and Yemen. High jacking shipping and kidnapping-ransoming international nationals is a major contributor to Al-Shabab funding. AlShabab facilitates Al-Qaeda weapons shipments, training camps and safe houses across Somalia and East, Western Africa. Al-Shabab claimed responsibility for the 21st September 2013 terrorist attack on the Westgate shopping mall in Nairobi, Kenya. 70+ Killed including woman and young children. Killed nationals included; Kenyan, British, American, Australian and Netherlands and over 300 injured. It is reported that
British, European, American and Canadian nationals are members of the Al-Shabab group in Somalia and British and American nationals were reported to be among the terrorists who attacked the Westgate shopping

mall in Kenya. (See 21/9 White Widow, Haqqani Network). (Anthony Malone interviewed members of Al-Shabab in Lebanon and Somalia).

Amman: Capital city of Jordan.

Ammo: Ammunition.

AMOJ: Afghan Ministry of justice.

ANA: Afghan national army.

Ankara: Capital city of Turkey.

ANP: Afghan national police.

AO: Area of operation.

AP: Associated press.

Apache AH64D/AH-MK1:   American, British helicopter gunship. (The British apache AH-MK1 cost £46 million each). The Apache is the most technically advanced helicopter in the world. The AH MK1-British Army Apache attack helicopter is built by Agusta Westland, all are fitted with the longbow radar. (See Longbow), (Anthony Malone interviewed Apache pilots in Iraq and Afghanistan).

APC: Military armoured personnel carrier.

Apostles: Special Iraqi unit, set up by British military-Special Forces, as part of TF14 (Task Force 14). Originally formed with a dozen Iraqi's, so the unit was immediately christened the Apostles. They were used for everything from interpreting for the SBS and SAS, their Blade teams, on covert and sensitive missions and operations. Their singular advantage in all these missions was their natural ability to blend into the indigenous population and remain undetected for long periods of time. (See Task Force Black).

AQAP: Al-Qaeda in the Arabian Peninsula, (See Strait of Hormuz).

AQI: Al-Qaeda in Iraq. In 2013 AQI moved into Syria and became ISIS (Islamic
                             State of Iraq and al-Sham) ISIS joined the fight against the Assad regime
                             as part of an increasingly sectarian conflict, pitting Sunni rebels against

an Alawite and Shia-dominated regime. (Anthony Malone interviewed
AQI members in Iraq and Afghanistan).

AQIM: Al-Qaeda in the Maghreb (franchise of Al-Qaeda).

Arab Afghans: The term originally used to describe the non-Afghan Muslims who fought alongside the Afghan insurgents in the 1979-1989 Jihad. This group included not only Arabs, but also Muslims from a virtually every country in the world with a Muslim population. Estimates of the total number of Afghan Arabs are all over the map, ranging from 5,000 to 100,000. Since the Soviets withdrew in 1989, a steady flow of non Afghan Muslims, still known as Arab Afghans, Mujahedeen class, Tier 2 insurgents are trained at camps in and across Afghanistan, Pakistan. These fighters are now reported to be fighting in Syria, Iraq, Pakistan,
Lebanon, Yemen, Philippines, Kashmir, Chechnya, Uzbekistan, Indonesia, Bangladesh, Sudan, Western China and the Balkans and Sudan, Somalia, Kenya, Libya, Algeria, Mali. 'Osama bin Laden' is the most well-known Arab fighter. (See Haqqani network).

Arab Spring: When a young, unemployed man named Mohammed Bouazizi set fire to himself in the central Tunisian town of Sidi Bouzid in December 2010, few imagined the firestorm of change his desperate suicide would ignite across the region. Within months, the dictatorships of Egyptian President Hosni Mubarak had been overthrown in a popular uprising. Within a year, leaders of other Islamic countries, Libya and Yemen had been swept aside. Syria which also started as a peaceful uprising had become a full-scale armed insurrection, when faced with the brutal dictatorship of the Bashar Al-Assad's regime. Over the past years millions of Syrian people/refugees have been forced to flee their home towns and villages across Syria, fleeing to refugee camps in Turkey, Lebanon and Jordan. The refugee camp in Jordan, (Zaatari), is estimated to be housing one million Syrian refugees, Men-women-children. The Arab spring had turned into an Arab winter. The Hezbollah terrorist group based in Lebanon now openly fights on Bashar Al-Assad's regimes side in the Syrian Civil-War against the FSA, Free Syrian Army and its splinter groups including; Jabhat Al-Nusra, a group with links to the Al-Qaeda Network, these groups form the opposition to the Bashar Al-Assad's Government of Syria. With the escalation in violence on all sides of the Civil- War, 150,000+ people killed so far, the body count rises daily... and over 2 million people displaced-refugees. The UN is officially calling the Syrian conflict a Humanitarian disaster. With terrorist groups including; Hezbollah, Al-Shabab, Al-Qaeda and Haqqani network, now tactically and strategically exporting International terrorism on a Global scale. The Arab Spring has turned into an Arab winter and evolved into an Arab Terror. World leaders hold their breath for the next major terrorist attack on a Western Target, not if, but when. (See Glossary, Zaatari, CW- Chemical weapons, Al-Shabab, Hezbollah, AQAP, Haqqani Network).

Asa'ib-Ahl-Al-Haq: Also known as "The league of the righteous", An Iraqi political and
terrorist group closely linked to Lebanon Hezbollah and the Iranian revolutionary guard. Asa'ib-Ahl-Al-Haq, gained notoriety in Iraq with a string of high level attacks on American and British forces, including: shooting down a British Lynx military helicopter and a RAF Hercules. They are also responsible for the Kidnapping and murder of British nationals. (See Iraq Hezbollah).

Ashgabat: Capital   city   of Turkmenistan.

Asmara:
Capital city of Eritrea.

A-Team: The Standard twelve-man teams that make up Special Forces.

Atlas Mountains: Located in Eastern Morocco. Area of interest to Western intelligence, HVT's and terrorist leaders have been known to stay in Bedu and tribal encampments, scattered across the mountains and valleys of the Atlas mountain range.

ATO: Air tasking order; the means of distributing joint firepower assets around the battlefield in a prioritised and fair as possible method.

Atropine: Anti-nerve agent injection used by British and American armed forces. (See Glossary, Chemical weapons).

AWT: Annual weapons test - Yearly official certification for handling/carrying weapons.

Ayman Zawahiri: Leader of the Al-Qaeda group and network. (See Al-Qaeda-Haqqani).

B-1/lancer: American supersonic strategic bomber, Call/sign "Bone", used for the B1.

B-2/Spirit: American strategic stealth bomber.

B-52:	Also known as the Stratofortress; a USAF heavy bomber.
B6 – B7:	High level of armour on a civilian 4X4 vehicle. Example: B6 armoured Toyota land cruisers, used by NGO's, Diplomatic services, and private military companies PMC's, worldwide.
Baghdad Cafe:	Isolated cafe resting point in the middle of the Syrian Desert, located between the towns of Tadmor and Del-e-Zore, only one road in area, located at the junction of the main highway that leads to Iraq and the Syrian - Iraq remote border crossing point. The Baghdad cafe is 100km from the nearest town, its isolation makes it the perfect meeting location for transiting insurgents and terrorists. The Bedu also inhabit the surrounding desert. (See Glossary, Tadmor).
Baghdad:	Ancient Capital city of Iraq, Located on the banks of the Tigris River.
Bagram Airbase:	Large American military airbase and logistics hub, located in Northern Afghanistan. Bagram is also the location of one of the American Governments, "Black prisons" used to house terrorist suspects. (See Glossary, KAF-Black prison).
Balad TSF:	Iraqi town and location North of Baghdad, American military airbase and HQ-"JSFOC", for Taskforces and Special Forces including British Taskforce Black. Balad was also the location of the TSF, (temporary screening facility) interrogation centre of terrorists, foreign fighters and insurgents captured in Iraq. American DOD, Department of Defense, Rendition flights also emanated from "Balad", airbase, to locations worldwide. (See Glossary, Extreme Rendition-Black prison).
Barnard Lewis:	A world-respected authority on Islamic and Middle-Eastern history. (See Acquired reading list).
Barrett .50 Calibre:	American .50 calibre sniper weapon, effective up to 1 mile, (depending on the skills of the shooter), for engaging enemy targets and HVT's, can also be used for stopping soft skinned vehicles. It is reported that Taliban and Al-Qaeda fighter's use captured .50 calibres in Afghanistan, Pakistan, Iraq, Syria and Somalia. (See Glossary, Dragonov Russian sniper weapon).
Bastion Camp:	Main British military base, headquarters and logistic hub for British forces operating in Helmand province, Southern Afghanistan. 10,000 British Military personnel were based out of Bastion at the height of the

Afghan conflict. Bastion is also the location of the airfield that supports military operations across Helmand. (KAF is also used in a supporting role). Apache MK1 are also stationed at Bastion, used as force protection; Bastion base is the size of Reading City, England and is the biggest British military base outside of Great Britain. (See KAF).

Battle group:	A military battalion-sized fighting force.
Bedouin:	Nomad tribe, also known as the Bedou or Bedu, nomads who live, inhabit the deserts of the Arabian Peninsula and old Persia, (Syria, Iraq, Jordan, Saudi Arabia, Yemen, Iran and Afghanistan).
Beirut Marine Barracks 1983:	Lebanon 1983, suicide bomber attack on the American Marine barracks. 241 American marines killed, 75 injured. 58 French paratroopers killed and 6 civilians killed. The same year 1983, American Embassy bombing killed 17 Americans, 32 Lebanese, 14 visitors and 1 suicide bomber, 120 other people were injured. (Anthony Malone interviewed one of the terrorists responsible for the attacks in Lebanon).
Beirut unload:	A rough and ready way of firing at something without risking the life of the firer, the firer stands behind cover and places, holds the weapon"AK-47" over or around a wall and fires a full magazine of ammunition, in the rough direction of the intended target, name derived from the methods of firing Ak-47's used in Beirut, Lebanon.
Beirut:	Capital city of Lebanon. Location of many terrorist meetings, several prominent terrorists Commanders live in and across Lebanon (See Phoenicia Hotel).
BEK:	British Embassy Kabul.
Bekaa Valley:	Also known as Al-Biqa, Geographic location in Southern Lebanon; the terrorist group "Hezbollah" stronghold close to the Syria border. The ancient town of Baalbak is located in the Al-Biqa valley. (See Hezbollah).
Bill Shaw (Major) MBE:	Bevan and I go 'back-a-ways'. Little did we know that we'd end up together in the hell-holes of Afghanistan doing what we "did". Bevan served in the SADF/SANDF, leaving as a Major, prior to working as a Security Consultant in Africa, Europe and Asia. He was "convicted" on narcotics charges, and finally "Pardoned by Pres. Hamid Karzai" and released

"Unconditionally" after spending 6 years 3 months and 8 days (2292 days) – possibly the longest serving "Westerner" in an Afghan prison to date.

Bill Shaw joined the cadets at fourteen and, after enlisting in the regular army at seventeen, saw service in many countries including Northern Ireland, Hong
Kong, Bosnia, Cyprus, New Zealand, Africa, Kuwait, Iraq, Germany, Spain, Argentina and Colombia throughout his twenty-eight year career. Rising through the ranks, he was promoted to Major and awarded the MBE from the Queen before leaving the Military to protect British and foreign diplomats in Iraq and Afghanistan. Bill Shaw was wrongfully arrested and imprisoned in Afghanistan, including; Pul-iCharkhi prison for four months and five days=128 days. Bill Shaw was released when all charges against him were dropped. As Andy McNab said, "An honourable military man treated in the most dishonourable way".

Bin Laden, Osama - UBL: UBL is the abbreviation used by the CIA for Osama bin Laden. Born in
1957, the youngest son of Muhammed bin Laden. Educated at King,
Abdul Azziz University, he fought in the Afghan jihad and organised the
Al-Qaeda group to assist armed Muslim insurgents around the world. Al-
Qaeda franchises are in several countries including; Saudi ArabiaYemen-Iraq-Pakistan-Afghanistan-Syria, and across North-West Africa.
Following the precedent set by the medieval Muslim military leader Saladin, bin Laden declared a defensive jihad against what he called the crusaders – predominately Christian Western countries led by the
United States-in the summer of 1996. Bin Laden was killed in Abbottabad Pakistan by American Special Forces "seal team 6" during a military operation 2rd May 2011. Bin Laden's body was buried at sea by the US Government. (See Al-Qaeda, AQAP, Haqqani network, AlShabab-Strait of Hormuz).

Biometrics: Authentication, Identification by characteristics or traits, technology, method implemented by Intelligence agencies and law-enforcement to identify high value targets, (HVT's) and terrorist suspects. Biometrics is also used to uncover and find terrorist suspects who are trying to hide behind cover identities and false names. (See Glossary, Sleepers).

Black Facility:	Deniable base or military facility used for Special Operations in countries across the Globe. (See Balad TSF, Black prisons, Black op's).
Black hawk MH-60:	American military standard transport helicopter, which can be armed. (Also used by several other countries, including, Saudi Arabia, Turkey and Israel). (See Mogadishu Battle).
Black on Black op's:	Two countries, Black operational military teams, tasked-ordered to eliminate, (capture or kill each other). (See Black op's).
Black Op's:	Military operations/missions that are off the books, no official record. The Government's official stance if a mission goes wrong or military personnel are captured, complete" Plausible Deniability". Serial numbers of weapons used on "Black Operations" are often filed off, to stop tracing and identification. (See Glossary, Sanitise).
Black prison:	Western government's unofficial terrorist prisons-located world –wide.
Black widow:	Chechnya woman suicide bomber.
Blade teams:	British Special forces teams (SAS).
Bleed out-Blow back:	Political and Intelligence term meaning, reaction-repercussion following an event or action. (For example see 21/9 Kenya attack by Al-Shabab).
Bletchley Park:	British Second World War, code-breakers. The modern equivalent is GCHQ. (See Glossary, GCHQ).
Boko Haram:	Islamist terrorist group based in Northern Nigeria. Has close links to AlShabab and AQAP, a franchise of Al-Qaeda. Many Boko Haram fighters are trained in Somalia by Al-Shabab. (See Al-Shabab).
Bounty:	Money paid out by the American Government/CIA, for the capture or killing of HVT's, known terrorists. A bounty can also be given for information leading to the death or capture of a HVT, terrorist.
Bowe Bergdahl:	American soldier captured in Afghanistan by the Taliban in 2009. Reported to be held by the Haqqani network, along the tribal belt, area of "Waziristan", situated along the Pakistan Western border. Bowe Bergdahl is officially listed and reported as an American POW, Prisoner of War. (Would later be released and returned to America)

Broken arrow:	American military communication "Code Word" stating-American military position being over ran by the enemy.
Burka:	Full body-length clothing worn by women in the Middle-East and Islamic countries/Muslims. According to Islamic law, this is to protect their modesty.
Buzkashi:	A game in which a dead goat is placed in the centre of a field and surrounded by horsemen from two opposing teams. The object of the game is to get control of the carcass and move it to the scoring area. In some games there are no teams; every player is out for himself.
C/S:	Call-sign.
C:	Commander, historically the letter "C" is used by the head of British MI6, to sign all official correspondence.
C-130:	A 4 propeller military fixed wing transport plane used by several countries to move troops and equipment. (See AC-130).
C-17:	Boeing C-17 Globemaster III – Large US Air Force strategic/tactical transport plane.
C4:	American military grade plastic explosives. (See Semtex).
Cairo:	Capital city of Egypt. (See Muslim Brotherhood).
Calibre:	The inside diameter of the barrel of a weapon. (See M4).
Camp Bastion:	British Headquarters of military operations in Helmand, Afghanistan. (See Bastion-camp).
Camp Chapman:	American FOB (Forward Operating Base) located along the Afghanistan, Pakistan border. It is also reported American "Drones" are operated from this location. A suicide bomber posing as an Intelligence source, killed several members of the CIA within Camp Chapman during a planned meeting. This was the biggest single loss of life for the American CIA in the Afghanistan conflict (See Glossary, Pakistan Taliban).
Camp Moorhead:	American Special Forces camp, Afghan commando training school, rangers training area and LZ landing zone, located 40km outside Kabul, Afghanistan. (See Glossary, Photographs).
Camp X-Ray/Delta:	The names designated by American authorities to areas that house International Al-Qaeda terrorists, within Guantanamo bay prison, located in Eastern Cuba.
CAP:	Combat air patrol.
CAS:	Close air support.

Case Officer:	Also known as a handler, someone who oversees Hum-Int (Human Intelligence Assets). A case officer is normally a very experienced CIA/NSA/MI6, operator who cultivates and develops intelligence assets. (See Glossary, Handler-Trade craft-CIA).
Casevac:	Casualty Evacuation. (See T-1).
Cat:	Counter-Action-Team, Normally a heavily armed four man team, travelling in an armoured 4X4. Sometimes used in conjunction with a close protection team.
CBRN:	Chemical - Biological – Radiological – Nuclear.
CCT:	Combat camera team.
CCT:	Combat Controller, an Air force CAS specialist.
CDS:	Chief of defence Staff.
Cedars-Mountains:	Mountain range located in Eastern Lebanon (Home of Hezbollah training camps and safe houses).
Cell:	Small team or group of people.
Centcom:	American military-Central Command.
Chai:	Afghan green or black tea.
Chemical Weapons- CW:	When dealing with Chemical weapons the important point to remember when assessing a threat is the "Delivery means" of the weapon. There are two categories, battle field chemical weapons and WMD. Are the Chemical weapons adapted to be used for; Artillery-Rockets-Mortars or Air delivery means using aircraft-helicopters? VX-nerve agent that can kill in seconds has been confirmed as part of Syrians chemical weapons stockpile. Syrin gas has been confirmed, (by Britain-America –France and the UN), as being used in 2013, by one of the sides in the Syrian civil war. It is reported and confirmed by American and Russian Government sources that Syria has over 1000 tons of chemical weapons, including VX and other deadly nerve agents-spread over 42+ sites across Syria. (See Glossary, Dirty Bomb).
Chief of station:	MI6 head of deployed country office or Embassy MI6 sub-office. (See Glossary, COS).
Chinook CH-47 /MH-47:	Large military twin-turbine, tandem-rotor heavy transport helicopter, used by British and American forces. The Chinook MH-47 is specially modified for use by "Special operations forces".
CI:	Counter insurgency,

CIA/CTC:	CTC-Counter-terrorism centre, the unit within the American CIA focused on terrorism.
CIA/NOC/OCO:	(See NOC-OCO).
CIA:	American Central Intelligence Agency "HQ Langley, Virginia" (see NOCOCO-Trade craft CIA-Camp Chapman).
CII:	Counter Iranian influence. (See Iraq Hezbollah).
CJOTF:	Combined Operations Task Force.
Classified:	A security classification given or assigned to an official British Government document-report. Other classifications include: Top-Secret and Eyes only Alpha
Claymore:	American military anti-personnel mine, homemade IED's/claymores are used by terrorists groups, including Taliban, Al-Shabab and Al-Qaeda. Also suicide bombers strap homemade claymores to their bodies, (packs of small steel ball bearings), to inflict maximum death and casualties. (See Glossary, 21/9 and IED).
Cleaner/clean-up team:	Terminology used to describe a cleaner or clean-up team, used for detailed site exploration of a specific location or target area. (Example Captured terrorist training camp or safe house) Information, evidence is collected to be assessed, analysed for intelligence.
Cluster fuck:	Military term used to describe a messed up situation, made famous by the American actor, Clint Eastwood in the war movie "heartbreak ridge".
C-Mock/Nineveh:	Hotel used as CIA location Mosul Iraq "Nineveh", Located within the grounds of one of Saddam Hussein's old palaces. (See Task Force 121).
CN:	Counter narcotics.
CO:	Commanding Officer, found in a military unit-Lieutenant Colonel in charge of a Regiment, Battalion.
Coalition:	National military forces working together as one force. (See ISAF).
COB:	Contingency operating base.
COBRA:	Cabinet office briefing room "A", The British Government "Cobra", meetings are called in times of national emergency or domestic, foreign crises.

COK:	Capture or kill-order given as part of military briefings in relation to HVT's/known terrorists.
Collateral Damage:	Military / Political term used to describe damage or fallout – Civilian casualties, during military action and operations. (See Modern Warfare).
Comanche:	American military RAH-66 stealth helicopter. (Similar to the Military helicopters used in the mission to kill Osama bin Laden 2nd May 2011).
Command wire:	Method used by terrorists to detonate an explosive charge or IED (Improvised Explosive Device). This method of detonation was used by the IRA or PIRA in Northern Ireland during the troubles. Former IRA bomb makers/instructors have been reported in terrorist training camps around the world, including, Lebanon Hezbollah, Al-Qaeda in Iraq, Afghan-Taliban, Pakistan-Taliban and Kandahar-Al-Qaeda. Former IRA, personnel have also been reported instructing the Al-Shabab terrorist group in Somalia and Jabhat Al-Nusra in Syria.
Comms:	Communications.
Compartmentalise:	Isolated-independent units within a network-breaking down a network into independent cells that do not have contact with each other. Compartmentalise is a security tactic, used by Western Intelligence agencies and terrorist groups to keep the whole-overall information on a subject or operation secret.
Coord:	Coordinate/coordination.
COS:	Chief of Staff "British military".
Counter-Intel:	Counter Intelligence.
Coup d'état:	A sudden violent overthrow of a Government. (Example Egypt 2013).
Cover Identities:	CIA: officers call "funny Names", false names used by intelligence personnel-sources, during operations to protect their true identity. (See Glossary, Trade craft-CIA).
Covert Op:	Clandestine military action/tasking or intelligence operation. (See NOC and Special Forces).
Cow:	Taliban-Al-Qaeda slang for the British-American military Chinook helicopter.
Coy:	Company.

CP:	Check point.
CP:	Counter Proliferation.
CPO:	Close protection officer.
CQB:	Close quarter battle.
CQMS:	Company quartermaster sergeant.
Crap-Hat:	To be elite requires someone to be crap, in the eyes of the ultras of the British Parachute Regiment that designation applies to everyone else in uniform. The phrase "Crap-Hat" is used for all in uniform who do not belong to the British elite Parachute Regiment. Para's have an aggressive attitude of superiority, which comes from physical wellbeing, due to their training. Al-Qaeda -Taliban fear the soldiers from the Parachute Regiment-confirmed by "Saladin" and other senior Taliban- Al-Qaeda Commanders.
Crocodile hunting:	Term used by security operatives to hunt HVT's, terrorists. Throughout the Middle-East and Africa. (See Glossary, Bounty-CIA).
Cruise missile:	Ballistic-long range missile. Examples; Tomahawk (US)-Storm Shadow (UK). Cruise missiles have been used in Pre-emptive strikes against enemy/terrorist targets across the Middle-East and Africa. TLAM, Tomahawk land attack missile, a subsonic cruise missile that attacks targets on land, and can be fitted with a conventional unitary warhead, (TLAM\C), a nuclear warhead, (TLAM\N), or a sub-munition dispenser (TLAM\D).
Crypo:	Cryptographic-Secure codes which enable encoded secure communication.
CSA:	American central support agency.
CSSP:	American prison mentors located in Afghanistan. Most members of the CSSP team are former or serving members of American military intelligence.
CT:	Counter-Terrorism.
CTC:	Counter-terrorism command, the UK police unit leading the domestic counter-terrorism effort, created in 2002.
CTR:	Close target reconnaissance.

Damage limitation:	Political-intelligence-military term "containment" of a damaging situation after it has happened. Controlling the flow of outgoing information relating to a given situation or incident. Objective to minimise the damage-potential fallout, caused by the incident-situation.
Damascus:	Ancient Capital city of Syria. Damascus is the oldest continually inhabited city in the world. (See Syria).
Dasht-e-Margo:	"Desert of death", located in Southern Afghanistan.
DAT:	Defence attaché.
David Ignatius:	A prize-winning columnist for the Washington Post has covered the Middle-East and the CIA for more than twenty-five years. David Ignatius is one of the Authors who inspired Anthony Malone to write his manuscript. (See Reading list).
David Petraeus (General):	American military 4 star general and paratrooper. Also former head of CENT-COM (American Military Central Command) and former Director of the American CIA. (See Glossary, for overview see Petraeus).
De Oppresso Liber:	Latin for "Free the Oppressed"; the creed of the U.S. Army Special Forces, the Green Berets.
DEA:	American drug enforcement agency.
Dead drop:	One way static drop location point for information and important messages. (See Trade craft).
De-Brief:	Official briefing "post" evaluation of an operation/mission or tasking. Comprehensive statement of account-actions-information and intelligence gained. De-briefs can be given written or orally.
Del-e-Zore/Deir ez-Zur:	Town, located in central Syria, strategically placed on the banks of the Euphrates River, the town has two bridges and a small airport-airfield. Al-Qaeda-terrorist training camps and safe houses are located close to the town. Strategical geographic location, the town is used by Al-Qaeda leaders and other terrorist group commanders, for tactical, strategic and operational planning of covert meetings. Del-e-Zore is on one of the main routes used by Al-Qaeda groups to transport weapons and fighters between Lebanon, Iraq, Iran, Afghanistan and Pakistan. (See TadmorPalmyra).
Delta:	American Special Forces "Delta force" (1st Special Forces Operational Detachment-Delta).
Dems:	Demolitions.

Denied area of operations:	An operational area either behind enemy lines or in hostile country, were the operation is unauthorised and without permission (See Glossary, Black Op's and Covert Operations).
Desert Hawk:	Small British UAV-Drone.
Det:	Detachment.
DFID:	British department of international development.
DG:	Director general, the head of MI5, the UK's domestic security service.
DGSE:	General Directorate of external security, (French; Direction Generale De La securite exterieure), French foreign intelligence service.
DHS:	American, department of homeland security.
DIA:	Defence Intelligence Agency, the U.S. military's CIA.
Diego-Garcia (DG):	American naval support facility and USAF base, located on "DG" island in the Indian Ocean. American strategic B1-B2-bombers have launched tactical and strategic raids-missions across the Middle-East and Afghanistan from "DG". Rendition flights also go through this location. (See B2).
Diplomacy:	Handling of international relations. (See Gunship diplomacy).
Dirty bomb:	WMD, connected to components-conventional explosives, objective of a dirty bomb is to disperse a selection of WMD material over a tactical or strategic area. Example: City or population area. Al-Qaeda- Jabhat AlNusra and other terrorist groups in Syria, Iraq, Afghanistan, Pakistan, and Sudan have tried to acquire dirty bomb "radioactive" material. Chemical weapons could also be used as components in a dirty bomb. (It is reported that Syria has "VX" nerve agent amongst its large stock pile of chemical weapons. It is also reported that Syria has the world's biggest stock pile of chemical and biological weapons. 1000 tons of CW, over 42+ sites across Syria. Confirmed-agreed figures by the American and Russian Governments. Western Governments including Britain, France, America, and their intelligence services are rightly worried and concerned that terrorist groups operating in and across Syria are trying to acquire CW to export out of Syria to be used against Europe, American and Israeli targets. (See Glossary, Chemical weapons and Jabhat Al-Nusra).
DIS:	British Defence Intelligence Staff, intelligence unit of the UK Ministry of Defence, functioning similarly to the American DIA.
Dish dash:	Loose Kaftan-style outfit worn by many Afghan and Arab men.

Diwan:	"Arabic" room set aside for the use of gentlemen wishing to chew "Khat" (See Glossary, Khat).
Diyah:	"Arabic" blood money.
DNA:	Deoxyribonucleic-Acid, a substance storing genetic information. DNA testing and profiling is used to locate and positively identify terrorist suspects (See Glossary, Nucleic acid).
Doha:	Capital city of Qatar.
Double tap:	Military tactic, of firing two rounds from a weapon in quick secession into an enemy's head or body to kill or immobilise the target.
Dragunov:	Russian sniper rifle-used by Taliban, Al-Shabab and Al-Qaeda fighters across the Middle-East, Afghanistan-Pakistan and Africa. Terrorist sniper teams normally operate in twos, one sniper and one spotter, similar, MO (Modus operandi) to British and American military forces snipers.
Drone (UAV):	Unmanned aerial vehicle-aircraft "Predator, Rapture or Reaper", remotely piloted by an operator (sometimes in a different country) can be armed with hellfire missiles. Used widely for reconnaissance and surveillance.
Drone strike-CIA:	CIA signature drone strike, also known as airstrikes on HVT's, high value targets, and terrorists. Drone strikes have been carried out in countries including: Somalia, Yemen, Iraq, Afghanistan, Pakistan, Sudan and Syria.
Dry hole:	Location-person, viewed-monitored-searched, no useable intelligence found. Also has the meaning of an empty location, nobody found.
DU:	Depleted Uranium.
Dubai-UAE:	Dubai, in the UAE (United Arab Emirates) is an oil rich ultra-modern city which has risen from the deserts of the UAE. Dubai is a banking and financial hub for international business, with an appointed "Trade free zone" in the heart of the city. Dubai has mixed old with new, with the old "souks" markets, establishing themselves as tourist's attractions. There is also an indoor ski centre and international airport, which act as a major attraction and transport hub for travellers across the Middle-East and beyond. Dubai has been called the playground for the oil rich Arabs. The Dubai Banking sector is also the destination of choice for major money transfers, cash deposits, (suitcases full of money) out of Afghanistan,

Iraq, and Pakistan. Many Islamic "NGO's" bank in Dubai and money transfers are facilitated to many known terrorist front

companies around the globe. (See Glossary, Madrasah).

Dushanbe:	Capital city of Tajikistan.

Dushka: Nickname of the DShK-Soviet built Anti-aircraft machine gun-12.7mm, (equivalent to the American .50cal) and common amongst terrorist groups across the Middle-East and Africa.

Duty of care: Official term used to describe the responsibility towards an intelligence source or an individual who comes under their official responsibility. Duty of care also applies to "Hum-Int" (Human Intelligence Sources) or assets operating behind enemy lines or in hostile environments. Duty of care-includes, keeping the source safe and relocation after source extraction. (See Glossary, Wit-Sec).

DZ: Parachute Drop Zone.

ECHR: European Court of Human Rights.

EF: Enemy Forces.

EIJ or Al-Jihad: Egyptian Islamic - jihad Islamic movement, the group has a strong presence in the Persian Gulf, Yemen, United Kingdom, Pakistan, Afghanistan and Europe. The EIJ has also developed a cadre of excellent insurgent commanders across the Middle-East, Islamic world Jihad's. The EIJ has very strong links to the Al-Qaeda leadership and network. (See Glossary, Haqqani Network).

ELZ: Emergency landing zone for helicopters or aircraft.

Empta: O-Ethyl Methylphosphonothioic acid, a dual-use chemical used for pesticides and as a precursor in the synthesis of nerve agent. (See Glossary, VX-nerve agent-Chemical Weapons).

EOD: Explosive Ordnance Disposal.

EQT: Equipment.

ESB: External Security Bureau, Sudan's intelligence service.

ETA/ETD: Estimated Time of Arrival – Estimated Time of Departure.

EUCOM: European Command.

E-Vac:	Emergency medical evacuation.
Extreme rendition:	Transfer of prisoners between countries without "Habeas Corpus" legal due-process. (See Glossary, Balad TSF).
Eyes on-mark one eye ball:	Term used to describe or referring to a clear line of sight on a person or target.
F/F:	Foreign Fighter, brought into a country to fight for Al-Qaeda, Taliban, Haqqani network and Al-Shabab. (See Haqqani network).
F3 Classification:	Official British Military intelligence classification, given to a "Hum-Int", source, to protect the sources personal identity. (See Glossary, grade "A" sources).
FAC:	Forward Air Controller.
Falcon view:	Classified American military satellite imagery.
Farm:	Nickname for the CIA American-tactical and strategic training facility. (See Glossary, Trade craft-CIA).
Farsi:	Language of Northern Afghanistan.
FBI:	American "Federal Bureau of Investigation".
FCO:	British Foreign and Commonwealth Office "HQ London England".
FIBUA:	Fighting In Built Up Areas.
Firm:	Nickname referring to the British Intelligence Service "SIS", "MI6".
FO:	Forward Observer.
FOB:	Forward Operating Base.
Force 84:	British Special Forces Task Force, operating in Afghanistan.
Fox:	The Fox is the codename for Saladin, an Al-Qaeda, Taliban Commander, originally from Eastern Afghanistan. (Interviewed by Anthony Malone in Afghanistan).
Friendly fire:	Also known as "Blue on Blue" when your own military or friendly forces open fire on their own side by mistake.

Front company:	Legitimate legal companies set up for ML (Money laundering) and moving assets and money around the world. Used by terrorist groups and drug cartels to hide their proceeds of illegal activity. Also used to apply for travelling visas, this facilitates the movement of HVT's and terrorists between countries. (See Glossary, Dubai).
FSA:	Free Syrian army. Armed opposition group, made up of several factions- Fighting against the Government of President Assad of Syria. (See Syria).
FSB:	Russian Secret Service, previously known as the KGB.
G1:	Senior American military intelligence officer.
Gaza Strip/West Bank:	Palestinian territories within the disputed country borders of Israel. AlQaeda and other affiliated terrorist groups operate within the Gaza Strip and the West Bank. The Rafah crossing point is the only public crossing point to and from Egypt from the Gaza Strip. Smuggling tunnels are scattered across the Egyptian, Gaza border, these are used to transport weapons and other black market material into Gaza. (See Glossary, AQAP).
Gazelle:	British reconnaissance military helicopter.
GCHQ:	British Headquarters for gathering electronic intercepts from all over the world and electronic intelligence analysis (SIS). A modern version on the British World War Two, Bletchley Park "code breakers". SIS and MI5 staff work alongside GCHQ linguists who are there to translate interpret, "Sigint" (Signal Intelligence).
GHQ:	General Headquarters, British Army.
Gitmo:	The American military abbreviation for Guantanamo bay prison Cuba.
Glock:	9mm pistol, favoured by American DEA, intelligence agencies, law enforcement and close protection teams. Can be fitted with silencer, noise suppresser (A Glock 23, can chamber a .40mm round/bullet, this gives it more stopping power).
GMG:	Grenade Machine Gun.
GMLRS:	Guided Multiple Launch Rocket System.
GMT:	Greenwich Mean Time.
GOI:	Globalisation of Intelligence.

Going Native/Deep Cover:	Term to describe a person who has immersed themselves in the local culture and population. He or she looks, speaks, acts like a local. More local than the locals, can blend in to the local environment without drawing any undue attention. The term is used to describe undercover intelligence operatives working across the middle-east to infiltrate terrorist groups and networks. (See Glossary, Trade craft-CIA).
Golan Heights:	Disputed geographic area of land between Syria and Israel. The town of Katzrin is the capital of Golan.
GPMG:	General Purpose Machine Gun.
GPS:	Global Positioning System.
Grade "A" Source:	In intelligence source deemed by the British and American intelligence services to be an impeccable source of accurate actionable intelligence, information from an grade "A", source can be actioned without authenticating, if deemed time sensitive and of extreme high value.
Grey man:	Term used to describe a person who blends into their environment and surroundings, without drawing any un-due attention. A person who does not stand out in a crowd.
Grey Fox:	Codename for the American military special forces/CIA operations team/unit. Trained to dispose of, assassinate enemy personnel, during the Vietnam War. (See task Force 121-363 Afghanistan).
Guantanamo:	Official terrorist prison ran by America Government, located in Cuba.
GUB:	Guided bomb unit-Smart bomb.
Guerrilla warfare:	Unconventional warfare; a hit-and-run method of warfare used to inflict maximum damage with a minimum of weaponry and manpower. (See also UW-unconventional warfare).
Gun run:	A military term for a fighter plane or helicopter gunship, diving close to the ground and using its cannon and machine guns to strafe the enemy position on the ground.
Gunship Diplomacy:	Seeking diplomacy through the threat of direct or indirect force.
GWOT:	Global War on Terror, the abbreviated term given to President George Bush's post-9/11 strategy for countering Al-Qaeda.

Habeas Corpus:	The right to a legal hearing and legal due-process. (See Rendition).
Hamas:	Palestinian organisation based in the Garza strip and West bank. Fiercely opposed to Israel.
Handler:	Intelligence officer, CIA/NSA/MI6, case officer who handles human assets' and "Hum-Int" (Human Intelligence). A good handler cultivates and develops intelligence sources. (See Glossary, Trade craft-CIA).
Haqqani network:	International terrorist network, many of its members and fighters are drawn from Afghan Taliban-Pakistan Taliban-Kandahar Al-Qaeda and the old Haqqani resistance network based in Khost Eastern Afghanistan. The Haqqani network has strong ties to the Al-Qaeda network, Afghan Taliban, Pakistan Taliban and Lebanese Hezbollah. Haqqani network fighters have been reported in Syria, Iraq, Afghanistan, Pakistan, Yemen, and Somalia, training Al-Shabab and across North Africa. (Members interviewed by Anthony Malone in Afghanistan) (See Glossary, Hussein Laghman).
Haqqani-Jalauddin:	A major Afghan insurgent Commander and Pashtun tribal leader, who had close ties to Osama bin Laden and continues to have very strong ties to the Al-Qaeda network. Haqqani also has very strong links to the Pakistan Taliban and the Pakistan ISI. At one time Haqqani was the Taliban's Minister of tribal affairs. (See Glossary, Saladin-Haqqani network).
Hassake:	City located in North East Syria. Mainly Arab-Kurdish influenced. Stopover point for known insurgents, terrorists travelling from PakistanAfghanistan-Iran-Iraq, to Lebanon. (See Hezbollah and Haqqani network).
Hawala:	Un-official, Islamic money transfer money system, used throughout the Middle-east, Africa, and Europe. Also used extensively by Terrorist groups to transfer money between countries without a trace or accountability. (See Glossary, Dubai).
HE:	High Explosive (ammunition).
Heat:	High Explosive Anti-Tank (ammunition).
Heckler & Koch/H&K:	German weapons Production Company, who manufacture a wide variety of specialist weapons, including the MP5k submachine gun designed for close quarter battle, used by clandestine operators and Special Forces. (See Photographs).
Hekmatyar-Gulbuddin:	An Afghan Pashtun leader of the "Hisbi Islami", Islamist group. Exceptionally talented political opportunist, attracting funding

from Iran and Saudi Arabia. Has very close ties to the Pakistan Taliban and the Afghan Taliban. It is reported that he also has major ties and unofficial support for the Pakistan ISI. The American CIA gave funding to Hekmatyar during the Soviet Jihad in Afghanistan. (See Glossary, Haqqani network).

Hellfire Missiles: AGM-114k Sal (semi-active laser) hellfire II, is a laser-guided hellfire missile fitted to the Apache and UAV-Predator drone.

Helio: Military slang for "helicopter". Also chopper, Huey, hawk, bird, Slick.

Heroin: Narcotic mass produced in Afghanistan. A powerful, addictive drug narcotic farmed and produced by Taliban and Warlords across Afghanistan. The illegal narcotics trade helps fund the Taliban and AlQaeda terrorist operations across the Middle-East and beyond. (See Glossary, Hezbollah).

Hezbollah-Hizballah: Lebanon based terrorist group, backed by Iran, with links to Al-Qaeda.
Its fighters are involved in terrorist activity and operations across the
Middle-East, Including: Lebanon, Syria, Iraq, Afghanistan, Pakistan and
North Africa. Hezbollah training camps have been found in Syria, Iraq,
Pakistan, Afghanistan. Hezbollah were the first terrorist group to use
IED's in the Middle-East, "against Israel". Hezbollah have exported their
IED knowledge to other terrorist groups including the Afghan, Pakistan Taliban and Al-Qaeda in Iraq. Hezbollah facilitate and run terrorist training camps in the mountains of Eastern Lebanon-sponsored by Iran. Iranian Republican Guard/Iranian Special Forces have been seen teaching and instructing within the Hezbollah training camps. It is reported that elements within the Hezbollah originally facilitated
Taliban and Al-Qaeda illegal narcotics Laboratories in the mountains of North Eastern Lebanon. The product-narcotics (Afghan Heroin) is transported from Afghanistan, through the Taliban Al-Qaeda network of safe houses and established routes from Afghan, Iran, Iraq, Syria and Lebanon, then distributed by Land, Sea and air, to international locations including Europe and America. There are also links between Hezbollah and Al-Shabab in Somalia. (See IH-Iraq Hezbollah) (Members interviewed by Anthony Malone in Cyprus-Lebanon-Syria-Iraq and Afghanistan).

Hind/MIL-Mi24:	Russian made heavily armed helicopter gunship, used by several Middle-East countries, including; Syria, Iraq, Afghanistan and Iran. The MIL-Mi24 is also in active military service across several African countries.
Hindu Kush:	Mountain range-located in Northern Afghanistan.
Hisbi Islami:	(See Hekmatyar-Gulbuddin).
HMG:	Her Majesty's Government (Great Britain) reference to the Government of the United Kingdom.
Home grown:	Term used to describe home grown terrorists, who are born in places like Britain, American, Canada and France, who become terrorists against their own Government and country.
HUM-INT:	Human intelligence-sources. (See Handler).
Hum-vee	Also known as "hummer", American military 4X4, used extensively by the American military throughout the Middle-East. Can be heavily armoured and mounted with heavy machine guns and "TOW" anti-tank missiles (normally houses a four man crew, one riding top cover).
Hussien Laghman:	God son of Ayman Al-Zawaniri, the leader of the Al-Qaeda network. Hussein is a member of the Pakistan ISI and major player/negotiator between Al-Qaeda and the Taliban. He also acts as their fixer and quartermaster. Hussein is also responsible for organizing safe transportation of known terrorists between countries, including airplane tickets, passports and money transfers, secret hideaways in strange cities, cell phones and computers. Hassien has also been arrested in the past for selling SAM's (Surface to Air Missiles) and other weapons to the Pakistan, Afghan Taliban. The Chief prosecutor in Afghanistan (Afghan Ministry of Justice) has been paid money by Hussein and members of the Taliban network, for the changing of Taliban prisoner's official files, from terrorist charges to narcotics/drug charges and in doing so a large number of known Taliban terrorists have walked free from British mentored Afghan prisons. (See ACP and Haqqani network) (Interviewed by Anthony Malone in Afghanistan).
HVT:	High Value Target- The target indication of a terrorist's standing/value.
I.L.:	"Index list" Document-list of content of intelligence-source reports.
I.R.	Illum, Infer-red illumination.

IA:	Intelligence Analyst.
Ibrahim Al-Asiri:	Saudi born chief bomb maker for Al-Qaeda in the Arabian peninsula, "AQAP". Reported to be operating in Syria, Yemen, Afghanistan, Pakistan and Somalia. (See AQI and Jabhat Al-Nusra).
Ideology:	Ideas that form the basis of a political or economic theory, Al-Qaeda and Islamic fundamentalist ideology is a major modern threat to Western countries national security. (See Modern Warfare, Al-Shabab).
IDF:	Israeli defence force. (See Mossad).
IED:	Improvised explosive device. (See Ibrahim Al-Asiri- Command wireshape charge).
IH:	Iraqi Hezbollah; Hezbollah have exported their fighting experience, fighters, and knowledge of IED's and guerrilla warfare-GW, to terrorist training camps in Iraq-Syria-Afghanistan-Pakistan. Hezbollah facilitate terrorist safe houses in several countries including; Iraq-LebanonCyprus-Afghanistan-Pakistan. (See Glossary, Hezbollah/Asa'ib Ahl-Al Haq).
Iman:	"Arabic", a Muslim who leads prayers in a mosque and a person of authority in the Muslim community.
IMAO:	Improvise-Modify-Adapt-Overcome (See Glossary, Trade craft-CIA).
Infidels-Kufr:	Term used by some Muslims to describe none Muslims.
INMARSAT:	International maritime satellite telephone/radio.
Intel:	Intelligence. (See hum-int).
Interpol:	International European police headquarters, located in Lyon, France.
Intifada:	Palestinian uprising against Israel.
IRA:	Irish republican army (see Glossary, PIRA).
IRBM:	Intermediate-Range Ballistic Missiles.
IRG:	Iranian Revolutionary Guard.
IRT:	Immediate Response Team.
ISAF:	The UN-mandated International Security Assistance force, based in Kabul, Afghanistan. Members include: America, Britain,

ISI:	Canada, Germany, France, Turkey, Italy and many others. Pakistani Inter-Service Intelligence agency, vicious enemies of the Afghan Northern Alliance and Pakistan's version of the Russian old KGB or modern FSB. The Pakistan ISI has reported strong links to the AfghanTaliban, Pakistan-Taliban and Al-Qaeda. Some elements within the Pakistan ISI openly support the Taliban. Members of the Pakistan ISI are in prison in Afghanistan-due to them trying to sell "Surface to Air" missiles to the Taliban, (See Haqqani network). (Anthony Malone interviewed members of ISI, operating in Afghanistan).
Islam:	The Muslim religion.
Islamabad:	Capital city of Pakistan.
ISOF:	Iraqi Special Operations Force (See Glossary, Apostles).
ISOFAC:	Isolation facility where Special Forces teams prepare for combat missions and remain until they deploy.
Istanbul:	Strategically located city in Turkey. Previously known as, "Constantinople". Also known as the gateway to the West.
ISTAR:	Intelligence, signals (surveillance) target acquisition and reconnaissance.
J1 – J2:	American military intelligence officer, also used as intelligence liaison officer between friendly country's military units (See Glossary S1-G1RSO).
Jabhat Al – Nusra:	Syrian based terrorist group, with strong links to Al-Qaeda-Pakistan Taliban and the Haqqani network. Jabhat Al – Nusra, are logistically and financially supported by Al-Qaeda in Iraq "AQI" which in turn are supported by the Al-Qaeda supreme council in Pakistan. Europeans include: Commonwealth nationals; British, Canadian, Sweden also German nationals have been reported fighting for Jabhat Al-Nusra in Syria (See Glossary, AQAP, AQI and Iraq).
Jalalabad-Jbad:	Provincial capital city located in Jalalabad province, Eastern Afghanistan. Geographic location close to the border of Pakistan, and close to the volatile and turbulent tribal area of Waziristan (Western Pakistan). Jalalabad is historically on the major trade-transit route from Pakistan to Afghanistan. In modern times this route is used by the Taliban and the insurgency to transport fighters and weapons between Pakistan and Afghanistan. These Taliban fighters launch attacks against British and American (ISAF) soldiers across Afghanistan. Taliban safe houses and training camps are also located on the outskirts of Jalalabad city and the border area. The city and the

area have a reputation for being "Lawless" the "Wild West" with corrupt Afghan Government officials. (You can rent an Afghan, but you cannot buy one) is an old saying used by local Afghan's (See Glossary, Haqqani network).

Jambia: "Arabic" curved dagger much favoured by Yemenis and the tribes of Arabia. (See Glossary, AQAP).

Janes: Janes military books, CD and reports, give comprehensive, highly detailed, technical background information on all aspects of modern warfare.

JDAM: Joint Direct Attack Munitions; an upgrade kit that turns conventional bombs into GPS-navigated bombs with an INS (internal navigation system) kit that is retrofitted to the bombs. JDAM-equipment bombs can navigate to a target over fifteen miles away, regardless of weather conditions.

Jebel: General Arabic word for mountains.

Jerusalem: Capital city of Israel.

JFACC: Joint Forces Air Component Command.

JIC: Joint Intelligence Committee, the UK Government committee wherein intelligence gathered by the intelligence agencies is pooled.

Jihad: Islamic holy war against "infidels" declared by Islamic fundamentalists.

Jihadists: Fighters in a Jihad, "Islamic holy war".

JOC: Joint Operational Command.

JSFOC: Joint Special Force Operational Command.

JSOC: Joint Special Operations Command. (See Glossary, Balad).

JTAC: Joint Tactical Air Controller.

JTAC: Joint Terrorism Analysis Centre, the UK multi-agency "clearing house" for terrorism-related intelligence.

July 7th 2005: United Kingdom-London, home grown, Al-Qaeda inspired suicide bomber attacks on the London public transport system, one bus and four underground stations. 56 killed and 700+ injured. Al-Qaeda leader Zawahire, then Osama bin Laden's deputy claimed credit for the attacks (See 7/7 and Haqqani network Pakistan).

K2: American ultra-secret Special Forces operations and staging base.

Located in Uzbekistan, close to the Turkmenistan border. K2 has played an important role in the "War on terror". Tactical and strategic military operations and missions have been launched from this location across the Middle-East and Afghanistan. (See Glossary, Task forces 121-323).

Kabul: Capital city of Afghanistan.

KAF: Kandahar airfield "American and British operational military airbase, located in Southern Afghanistan" close to the historic city of Kandahar.

Kaftan: Loose Dish dash-style outfit worn by many Afghan and Arab men.

Kalima Tayyab   'La Ilaha Ill Allah Muhammadur Rasool Allah' (There is no god only Allah, Muhammad is the Rasool (Messenger) of Allah) is also known as Kalima Tayyab. Kalima Tayyab is the testification of faith in Islam. A person cannot be considered to be a Muslim if he/she does not believe in the words of this Kalima.

Kandahar Al-Qaeda: Extremist group within the Al-Qaeda network. (See LOA).

Kandahar/Qandahar: Historic Afghan City located in Southern Afghanistan, is also the spiritual home of the Taliban.

Karachi-Pakistan: Major city-transport hub located on the coast in Southern Pakistan. It is also a known transit route for Taliban and International terrorist suspects in and out of Pakistan-Afghanistan.

Kefraya red: Red wine produced in the Bekkaa valley Lebanon. (See Hezbollah).

Kerman: City located in Southeast Iran. Key location on the Taliban and Al-Qaeda smuggling routes from Afghanistan to Iraq, Syria and the West. Also the location of the compound that houses members of the "Bin laden" family. Iranian factory made IED's and explosive shape charges are made, transported into Afghanistan to be used against British and American (ISAF) forces. (See Glossary, IED-Shape charge).

Kevlar: Bullet resistant material, offering different degrees of ballistic protection against projectiles/bullets. Used in body armour and ballistic plating. (See Glossary, B6-B7).

KGB: The committee for State Security, (Russian; Komitet Gosudarstvennoy Benzopasnosti) foreign-intelligence service of the Soviet Union, created in 1954, disbanded in 1991.

Khartoum: Capital city of Sudan.

Khat: Mildly narcotic leaf which can be chewed, popular in Yemen and Somalia.

KIA:	Killed in action; to be killed on the battlefield.
Killing House:	Live firing training area and location, used by Special Forces to practice CQB, close quarter battle and hostage release.
Kuwait city:	Capital city of Kuwait, oil rich, modern Muslim country. With borders to Iraq-Saudi Arabia and the Persian Gulf.
Langley-CIA:	Langley, Virginia. The headquarters of the American CIA (See Farm).
Lase:	To highlight or "Paint" a laser signature on a target, so that a laserguided bomb may use its guidance system to home in on it. (See Glossary, Smart bomb).
Lashkargah:	Provincial Capital city of Helmand province Southern Afghanistan.
LAV:	Light armoured vehicle.
Leakers:	Terrorists-insurgents, that are attempting to escape, (Leak), from the target area.
Lilly white:	Disposable, untraceable "pay as go" mobile phone. (See Trade craftCIA).
Little bird:	American military Kiowa helicopter can be heavily armed with a wide verity of heavy machine guns and rockets /missiles. (See Night Stalkers).
LN:	Local National.
LOA:	Lions of Allah: Al-Qaeda, special operations team (See Kandahar Al-Q).
Locstats:	Location Status.
LOE:	Limit of Exploitation.
Lone wolf:	Completely independent fighter, operator (Plan's their own missions).
Lonely Planet books:	Impeccably researched and published books that specialize in travelling across the Middle-East and worldwide. A wealth of information required for day to day travelling in foreign countries (See Acquired reading list).
Long:	Assault rifle or long barrelled weapon (A "short" would be a pistol).
Longbow-Apache:	The Longbow radar is the Apache helicopter, fire control radar, it looks like a large Swiss cheese and sits on top of the main rotor system. (See Glossary, Apache Helicopter).
Loya Jirga:	Islamic council of tribal representatives, meeting to discuss political and tribal issues.
M/L:	Money Laundering (See Dubai-Front companies).

M/O:	"Latin" Modus operandi.
M-4A1:	A shorter version of the M-16A2 assault rifle, with a collapsible stock and a heavier barrel, favoured by Special Forces, Security operators and vehicle crews. Includes a removable carrying handle and rails for mounting scopes and night-vision devices. Often includes an underbarrel 40mm M203 grenade launcher or shotgun (See Photographs).
Madrasah:	An Islamic school house used for "Educating", Taliban and A-Qaeda, in fundamentalist Islamic practices-Common throughout Pakistan. A large number of Madrasah's are funded from Saudi Arabia, and NGO's who operate out of Dubai (See Dubai and Money laundering).
Man-pad:	Any man-portable, surface to air missile, including the Soviet SA-7 and the US military stinger missile. (See SAM).
Mark Urban:	Highly respected British TV reporter-journalist and author. Mark Urban's writing and books are impeccably researched, his writing inspired Anthony Malone to write his manuscript (See acquired reading list).
Massoud:	Ahmad Shah Massoud-Former Commander of the Afghan Northern Alliance. Was killed by Al-Qaeda on the 8th September 2001, by a suicide bomber posing as part of a TV camera crew, 3 days before 9/11. Anthony Malone interviewed in Afghanistan Wali Massoud, former Afghanistan Ambassador to Britain and America (See Northern Alliance).
Mecca or Makkah:	City in Saudi Arabia, and religious capital for the Sunni Muslims and place of pilgrimage.
Medevac:	Medical Evacuation.
Medina:	Islamic holy city in Saudi Arabia.
Mercenary:	A person who is paid to fight and kill for money (See PMC).
Mert:	Medical emergency response team.
MIA:	Missing in Action.
Michael Scheuer:	Former American CIA intelligence operative, veteran of 22 years; and former head of "Alec Station" (1996-99) appointed head of "Islamic Extremist Branch", of the counter terrorism centre CTC- "Osama bin

Laden" unit. Michael Scheuer is academically qualified and trained as a historian. Michael Scherer's book, "Through our Enemies eyes" inspired Anthony Malone to infiltrate the Al-Qaeda network, to stop terrorist attacks and later to write his manuscript in order to pass on his knowledge (See Glossary, acquired reading list).

Millbank: Term used to describe MI5 headquarters location. Located along
                           Millbank road, London United Kingdom.

MOB: Main Operating Base (See Glossary, Bastion camp).

MOD: British Ministry of Defense.

Modern Warfare-Urban Siege: Terrorism-Modern Warfare-Urban Siege, Examples: Syria-Hamma, Mumbai-India, 7/7 attacks-London, Westgate Mall-Kenya. It is now and forever the day after September 11th 2001, 9/11 terrorist attacks. Modern warfare has evolved like a living organism, into the modern age. Wars and battles are not fought on the battlefields, open deserts or rolling hillsides with clear enemy lines. The modern and next generation of warfare is being fought (urban warfare), amongst our homes, city streets and shopping malls. Suicide bombers and armed Islamic insurgents-terrorists groups storming public buildings, killing unarmed civilians, women and children, off duty soldiers in Capital cities. "Urban Siege" is the new terrorist tactic, hostage taking and summary executions of none Muslim men, women and children. Suicide bombers detonating during morning rush hour, in busy Western city coffee shops, boutiques, and during sporting events, covered by live TV broadcasts and cameras. The horrific images beamed live across the

Globe in full uncut graphic colour. People watching the aftermath of Chemical Weapon attacks on TV over their lunch time meal. The modern internet-tweeter-multi-media gives terrorism a 24/7, global platform of extensive coverage on the world stage. Extreme violence, death and horrific carnage are just a mouse click away. I.T, computers and multi-media are the new weapons, tools used by terrorist groups and organisations, bringing violence and terrorist ideology into our homes, offices and lives. Children and young adults have access to the internet, unlimited violence, beheadings, Al-Qaeda propaganda videos that glorify the Islamic Jihad, and the killing of none Muslims. Children and adults are being desensitized, nightly news programs show violent Jihad almost every night, no one is surprised at yet another foreign terrorist attack or suicide bombing, 10 dead, 50 dead, 100 dead and these are just the empty numbers to the faceless viewer. It's only when the local shopping mall disappears in a fireball or local bus or train is running late, due to a suicide bomber blowing themselves up, making modern warfare/terrorism's horrific scenes of death a shocking reality, and not just on the TV screens or laptops. Terror is the fundamental core of terrorism, when families are too scared to go to the local shopping mall, cinema, or train station. This should give us all pause for thought. It's been just over 12 years since the 9/11 terrorist attacks on America. What will the next 12 years in modern warfare/terrorism evolve into? Chemical weapon, VX nerve agent attacks, Dirty Bombs, whole Western cities disappearing due to a terrorist attack. All makes for one hell of a potent bedtime story and an ongoing troubling concern for Western Governments and leaders (See Glossary, Arab Spring Unconventional Warfare, Al-Shabab 21/9 attacks).

Mog or Mogadishu:	Capital city of Somalia. Location of the 3rd – 4th October 1993 battle for Mogadishu "Black Hawk Down". Casualties: 18 American soldiers killed, 80 injured and estimated three thousand Somalian guerrillas killed.
MOG:	Mobile operations group.
Mohammed Naim:	Official spokesman for the Taliban, from their new offices in Qatar.
Mosquito:	Taliban and Al-Qaeda slang for the British-American, Apache attack helicopter. (See Apache).
Mossad:	Israeli intelligence services headquarters located, Tel-Aviv (Mossad are one of the best intelligence services in the world).
Moukhabarat:	Jordanian secret police or intelligence services/headquarters located in in Amman city.
MP:	Member of Parliament.
MSST:	Military Stabilisation Support Team.
Mujahideen-Muj:	Afghan opposition groups fought the Soviets during the Soviet invasion and each other in the Afghan civil War-plural for the word Mujahid meaning "Struggler or Fighter". Anthony Malone interviewed key Mujahedeen Commanders and leaders across the Middle-East and Afghanistan (See Glossary, Massoud).
Mullah Omar:	Spiritual leader of the Afghan Taliban (See Taliban).
Muscat or Masqat:	Capital city of Oman.
Muslim Brotherhood:	Egyptian political group/organisation, with strong links to Al-Qaeda and other extremist groups across the Middle-East, Afghanistan, Pakistan and Iraq. The political arm of the Brotherhood is called, "freedom and Justice" (See Glossary, EIJ).

415

Napalm:	A highly flammable form of petrol used in military munitions-firebombs.
Narghilehs:	Arabic, "smoker's water pipe" flavours of tobacco include, apple, orange and grape.
NATO:	North Atlantic Treaty Organisation.
NBCW:	Nuclear-Biological-Chemical-Warfare.
NDS:	Afghanistan National Directorate of Security-Afghan Security Services.
Net:	Military radio network.
Network:	Inter-connected groups, teams or cells of International terrorists. Many networks are International-global.
NGO:	None Government Organisation.
Nicosia:	Capital city of Cyprus.
Nigerian Taliban:	Franchise of the Pakistan Taliban, close links to "Boko Haram", the Islamist terrorist group operating across Northern Nigeria (See AQIM).
Nightstalkers:	Nickname of the 160th Special Operations Aviation Regiment (SOAR), the air transportation and support component to the American Special Forces (See Glossary, Special Forces-Delta).
Nimrod MR2:	British RAF reconnaissance aircraft-jet, used as a spy/surveillance plane.
NOC-CIA:	None Official Cover Operative-no diplomatic immunity. Full official deniability (See Glossary, Black Op's, and Trade Craft-CIA).
Noor:	Arabic word for "light".
Northern Alliance:	Officially titled the "United front military forces", the Mujahedeen or freedom fighters of Northern Afghanistan (See Glossary, Panjshir valley, Massoud).
NSA:	American National security agency. The American agency for gathering electronic and "signals" intelligence, surveillance; equivalent of the UK's GCHQ, based in Cheltenham.
Nucleic Acid:	Either of two, substances, DNA or RNA, present in all living cells. (DNA is used to positively identify bodies of HVT's-terrorists suspects after airstrikes, and military operations-missions (See DNA and field craftCIA).
N-U-T-S:	Second World War, American Paratroopers response, when asked to surrender by a German officer, who had the Paratroopers surrounded. N-U-T-S; was the official written response to the Germans.

(Paratroopers never surrender...They fight till the last man and then some). N-U-T-S; was the same responses that Anthony Malone (former Paratrooper) gave the Taliban/Afghan authorities when they tried torturing him to sign a confession, that said he was working for the American military intelligence. Anthony Malone's response was N-U-T-S... he was not a prisoner of war; he was a prisoner at war. Anthony Malone also gave the answer "Donald Duck" when asked by his interrogators who he worked for; this made him laugh, but got him another beating. (See Ill-treatment Statement by Anthony Malone).

NVG:
Night Vision Goggles-Night sights that are magnify light by 40.000 times.

OCO-CIA:
Official Cover Operative, covered with diplomatic immunity.

ODA:
Operational Detachment Alpha; Another term used in place of "ATeam", to describe the Special Forces, standard twelve-man team (See Glossary, A-Team).

OEF:
Operation Enduring Freedom.

OP:
Observation Post.

Op's:
Operations room, Op's officer, or literally a military operation.

Operator:
Highly experienced security or intelligence personnel.

Op-sec:
Operational security.

OSCT:
Office for security and counter-terrorism in the UK home office department, coordinating all UK counter-terrorism activity.

Osprey MV22A:
American Military aircraft, used for combat and rescue operations in Iraq-Libya-Afghanistan-West Africa. The CV22-B is the Special Forces variant. (See Glossary, Nightstalkers).

Palmyra:
(See Glossary, Tadmor).

Panic/Strong room:
Emergency armoured room within a building or structure. Used as a last resort if building is being overrun by terrorist/insurgents. Normally fitted out with Emergency rations; food, water, spare weapons, ammunition, medical supplies and communication equipment. Strong rooms are also fitted in residences of VIP's and can be found within the super structures of oil tankers.

Panjshir Valley:
Afghan valley, located north of the Afghan capital Kabul. Formerly the strong hold of Ahmad Shah Massoud, Northern Alliance Commander. (See Photographs).

Para:	Term used to describe a member or soldier of the British military's elite Parachute Regiment. (See 3 Para).
Pashtun:	Tribe, language of Southern Afghanistan and the Western border area of Pakistan.
Pashtun-Walli:	Pashtun honour code.
Pax:	Person.
P-Company:	Pegasus company, grueling fitness tests used by the British military's Parachute Regiment to test suitable candidates for Parachute training and Airborne Forces. (See Glossary, 3 Para).
Persona Non Grata:	Latin-unwelcome person.
Peshawar:	City in Western Pakistan, often referred to as a lawless border town because of its proximity to the Afghanistan border. Peshawar is a major re-supply location on the route used by jihadists who fight British and American (ISAF) forces across Afghanistan (See Haqqani network).
Peshmerga:	Kurdish militia group, very well trained and equipped, located in Kurdistan- Northern Iraq. Peshmerga are fighting in Northern Syria to protect Kurdish people, towns and villages in the Syrian civil war. (Anthony Malone interviewed Peshmerga Commanders in Syria, Kurdistan and Iraq).
Petra:	Ancient Roman city, secreted away in a hidden valley and carved out of rock in eternal perfection. Located in Southern Jordan.
Petraeus-General:	General David Petraeus; American 4 Star military Commander, Petraeus Commanded the 101st Airborne Division (Air-Assault) paratroopers, in Iraq 2003. Highly regarded and respected by the men who serve under him, gained the reputation as a soldiers General. (Petraeus would never ask his men to do anything that he would not do himself), he spent most of his time on the ground, looking after the men under his Command. Petraeus believed that a good Commander always leads from the front, and was always first out of the door. Petraeus is credited for writing the counter insurgency strategy template for the American military and formulating the "Surge" in Iraq; part of the counter insurgency strategy. Petraeus's plans on dealing with the increasing Iraqi insurgency would become part of the overall American tactical and strategic plan on dealing with "unconventional warfare" in Iraq and the insurgency. Petraeus later became the Commander of "Centcom", American Centre Command and would also hold the prestigious post of Director

of the American CIA. Petraeus has political aspirations and with his extensive knowledge and a wealth of experience, will excel in the future. Petraeus has been awarded 44 separate military awards. General David Petraeus told Anthony Malone in Iraq "That a few good men can make a difference..." (See photographs).

Phoenicia –Beirut: Luxury hotel on the Beirut water front, overlooking the bay to Jounieh, popular location for Internatonal Press/Journalists and rich Arab's. Has been known as a meeting place for top Hezbollah and Al-Qaeda members, who book rooms or meet on the top floor wine bar and restaurant. (See Glossary, Hezbollah).

Phy-Ops: Psychological operations/ Psychological warfare.

PI: Politicalisation of intelligence. (See plausible deniability).

PID: Positively identify.

Pilgrim: Serving or former member of the British Special Forces (SAS) 22rd Regiment.

PIRA: (See Glossary, IRA).

PKM: Soviet-made light machine gun, fitted with bipod 7.62mm (Belt fed). Used throughout the Middle-East, Iran, Afghanistan, Pakistan and across Africa by terrorist groups.

Plausible deniability: Term used by politicians and intelligence services, "denied operations", to give top-cover, political protection to top civil-servants and politicians.

PLO: Palestine Liberation Organisation.

Plutonium: A radioactive metallic element used in nuclear weapons and reactors. (See Glossary, CW-Dirty bomb).

PM: Prime Minister.

PMC: Private military company, private corporate businesses who employ former professional soldiers and members of the Special Forces. Working on military style contracts, implementing their skills and field craft acquired during their official military service. PMC's are also licensed to carry firearms. But because they are private they do not come under military law.

Political spin doctor: Politicians and top civil servants who "Lie and manipulate true facts and information" for their own political agendas and/or personal gain. Example; Tony Blair's WMD in Iraq. The reason why Britain went to war in 2003...! (See plausible deniability and politicisation of intelligence).

Porton Down: British Military, Nuclear-Biological and Chemical warfare weapons training and research facility. (See Glossary, Chemical

	warfare-CW).
Post-One:	First Military check point outside American Embassies. Normally manned by American Marines.
PPIED:	Pressure-Plate Improvised Explosive Device. Tactic used by Al-Qaeda in Iraq and by the Taliban and Al-Qaeda in Afghanistan to kill British and American 'ISAF' soldiers (See Glossary, IED).
Profiling:	Comprehensive detailing of personal information and habits, enabling for a physiological pro-file to be formulated. This is a tactic used by Intelligence agencies to build strategies and tactics against terrorist groups and their international networks (See Glossary, Trade craft-CIA).
PSD:	Personal security detail.
Pul-i -Charkhi/Pul-e-Charrkhi:	Russian built prison in Afghanistan, houses thousands of Taliban and AlQaeda prisoners. One of the world's most notorious and dangerous prisons. Al-Qaeda and Taliban prisoners run the inside of the prison under strict Islamic 'Sharia law'. Ill-treatment, torture and murder is common place. (See separate comprehensive report on ill-treatment and torture, written by Anthony Malone).
Qamishle:	Syrian-Turkish, border town, located in North East Syria. Kurdish influenced. Known meeting location (Islamic Mosque's), transit point and over-night stop location for insurgents and terrorists from PakistanAfghanistan-Iraq-Lebanon-Saudi Arabia. (See Hassake).
QRF:	Quick-reaction force.
Quetta:	City in South Western Pakistan, located close to the Afghanistan border and in close proximity to the Afghan city of Kandahar. Quetta is also the base for the Taliban and Al-Qaeda supreme councils.
Qur`an:	Islamic holy book.
R&R:	Rest and recuperation.
RAF-British:	British Royal Air force.
Raw-Intel:	Information-intelligence, prior to it being analysed and receiving an official security classification. (See Glossary, Classification).
Recce:	Reconnaissance.

Rendition: Kidnapping a suspect and transporting the suspect between countries without "Habeas Corpus", legal due process, also known as "Extreme Rendition" (See Glossary, Balad TSF).

Right to Life: British High Court ruling in 2013, which stated-every British soldier has a right to life while serving in Afghanistan and on operational tours.

Riyadh: Capital city of Saudi Arabia.

RMP: Royal Military Police (See Glossary, Bill Shaw MBE).

RO: Radio Operator.

Robert Fisk: Respected international journalist and author, an authority on writing about the Middle-East. Robert Fisk has also interviewed Osama bin Laden and several other high profile political subjects and terroristsfreedom fighters (See acquired reading list).

ROE-Rules of engagement: Legal rules which military and Government personnel can use to engage the enemy and legally return fire to eliminate the enemy threat (See Glossary, Modern Warfare).

RPG: Soviet designed rocket propelled grenade/shoulder launch rocket with a powerful grenade warhead fitted to the front. Widely used by terrorist groups across the globe. Including the Afghan, Pakistan Taliban, AlQaeda and Al-Shabab.

RSM: Regimental Sergeant Major.

RSO: American Regional security officer, posted within the American Embassies world-wide, The RSO oversees all Intelligence in the region and reports information and Intelligence back to Washington DC, Pentagon and liaisons with other American intelligence agencies, including; CIA-NSA-DIA-DEA-FBI.

RST: Residential security team, works in conjunction with a close protection team/close protection officer.

RTI: Resistance to interrogation. Training carried out by all Special Operations Forces who operate in hostile countries and behind enemy lines (See Glossary, SERE).

RV: Rendezvous-Pre-arranged meeting or meeting place.
RW: "Rogue Warrior" Call sign, the name given to Anthony Malone

	by "elite team" members in 2006 during Special Forces training.
S/B:	Suicide bomber (See Glossary, UW -Unconventional warfare).
S-10:	British Military respirator issued to the British Military as part of PPE- Personal Protection Equipment, as protection against nuclear-biologicalchemical warfare (See Glossary, Porton Down).
S-2:	American military Command Staff, intelligence section.
SA:	Situation Awareness.
SA7/14:	Soviet-designed surface to air missiles, man-pads. (See Glossary, SAM, Stinger Missile).
Sabre:	The tactical operators in the SAS, so avoiding confusion with medical, administrative or other military personnel (See Task Force Black).
SADM:	Special Atomic Demolition Munition; Also known as a "Backpack nuke". (See Glossary, Dirty bomb).
SAF:	Small Arms Fire.
Safe house:	Term to describe a safe location or safe haven. (See Al-ShababHezbollah).
Saladin:	Historical Islamic military commander-Sultan Salahud bin Ayubi. (See Fox/Saladin, present day, Al-Qaeda Commander).
Salvo:	A simultaneous discharge of guns; a sudden series of aggressive statements or acts.
SAM:	Surface to air missile.
Sana/Sanaa:	Capital city of Yemen.
Sanitize:	Military reference to removing any identification that could "ID" a person by name, place, military unit or country of birth. Sometimes Special Forces are sanitized, prior to deployment on operations, so if captured by the enemy they are carrying no identifying or incriminating evidence. Al-Qaeda and some Taliban foreign fighters are sanitized before they carry out terrorist operations and attacks. Sanitized covert military teams or covert security operators give governments/politicians full "plausible deniability" (See Glossary, Black Op's-Trade craft CIA and Zeranjee).
SAP:	Security Advance Party.
SAS:	British Special Forces "Special Air Service" Regiment (See 22rd SAS).
Sat-Com:	Satellite Communications.

Sat-Nav:	Satellite Navigation.
Sayyid:	Arabic ruling class in Yemen, a title given to tribal or religious leaders who claim descent from the "Prophet Muhammad".
SBS:	British Special Forces "Special Boat Service".
Seal:	Sea, Air, Land; The American navy/marine Corps clandestine forces. (See Glossary, Delta Force).
Semtex:	Military grade plastic explosives, made in the Czech Republic, common throughout the old Soviet bloc countries. Libya was supplying the IRAPIRA with Semtex during the troubles in Northern Ireland. It is reported that Al-Qaeda has acquired large amounts of Semtex from several sources; including old Libyan weapons stores. (See IED-Shape charge).
September 11th 2001:	Al-Qaeda terrorist attacks on America, passenger airliners hijacked, including AA11 and UA175 were flown by Al-Qaeda terrorists into the Twin Towers, North and South, New York City. AA77 was hijacked and flown into the Pentagon. United American passenger airliner, UA93 came down in a field in Shanksville, Pennsylvania, when the passengers bravely fought back against the terrorist hijackers. The estimated casualties for 9/11 is 2752 people killed, thousands injured. (More people died in the 9/11 terrorist attacks than the number of people and American service personnel who died in the Second World War, Japanese attack on Pearl Harbour). This fact gives pause for thought. (See glossary, July 7th 2005, Al-Qaeda attacks on the United Kingdom).
SERE:	Survive-Evade-Resist and Extract, part of Special Forces Training. (See Glossary, Trade craft-RTI).
SF:	Special Forces.
SFC-SAS:	Special Forces Communicator-Military Communications and Signals Specialist.
Shabnama:	Night letters-Taliban propaganda leaflets distributed under the cover of darkness, typically slid under peoples doors. Threatening death, torture and public beheading.
Shape-charge:	Specialist explosive charge, used to breach or gain access to a building through a wall or reinforced entrance. The explosive charge is shaped so when detonated the blast penetrates a specific targeted area. The Taliban in Afghanistan are also using shape-charges within their improvised explosive devices, IEDs. To penetrate British and American armoured vehicles (See Glossary, IED).

Sharia:	Arabic law, practiced and observed by the Prophet Muhammad in his lifetime, enforced in certain countries in the Muslim world (See Glossary, Al-Shabab).
Sheikh:	Arab chief. (Anthony Malone body-guarded and interviewed Sheikh's in Iraq and Saudi Arabia).
Shia:	Minority branch of Islam, centered around Iran.
Shmac:	Arabic scarf, Arabs also wear as a head dress.
Shura:	Arabic for consultation.
Side arm:	Military-security terminology for a "pistol".
Sig:	Sig Sauer 9mm pistol, Sig Sauer are issued to British Special Forces and are used by intelligence agencies and PMC's world-wide.
Sig-Int:	Signal Intelligence, intelligence gained from radio, telephone, text and e-mail intercepts (See Glossary, GCHQ-NSA).
Sinai:	Largely desert peninsular between Israel and Egypt, a lawless area of desert inhabited by local tribes and Bedu (See Glossary, Bedu).
SIS:	British Secret Intelligence Service, MI6, the UK's foreign intelligence service.
Sit-Rep:	Situation Report.
Slap & tickle:	Interrogation or torture.
Sleeper:	Terrorist operative laying low in Western society, hiding for months or years. Waiting undercover for orders to fulfil their mission.
Slush fund:	Unofficial or official sanctioned pool of money, sometimes located hidden in off-shore bank accounts, used to finance and support covert weapon purchases and covert military operations (See Glossary, Black Op's and Special adviser).
Small Arms:	Infantry light weapons/pistols, rifles and machine guns, weapons capable of being fired by a foot soldier on the move.
Snake-operation:	12 June 2003; American forces/Special forces, raided and destroyed a base for non-Iraqi mujahedin at Rawah, 20km north of the Euphrates River western Iraq, about 40km from the Syrian border. The attack killed more than eighty foreign Muslims in Iraq to fight the US-led occupation. Among the dead were Saudi's, Yemenis, Syrians, Afghans, Lebanese- Hezbollah and Sudanese. American Apache helicopter gunships and AC-130 Spectre gunship were on station during the operation (See photographs).

Snatch:	Lightly armoured British military Land rover. Used in operations in Northern Ireland-Iraq-Afghanistan-Africa. Snatch Land rovers have little protection against the Taliban IED's, as seen in Afghanistan. (See Right to life and IED).
SO19:	British police specialist firearms unit.
SOAR:	American, 160th Special Operations Aviation Regiment, (See Glossary, Nightstalkers).
SOCA:	British police, Serious Organised Crime Agency.
SOE:	Special operations executive. Exceptional British Second World War Special operations unit. Members operated behind enemy lines, working with résistance groups (See Glossary, unconventional warfare).
SOP:	Standard Operating Procedure.
Special adviser:	Term used to describe covert military-intelligence personnel, working or being assigned to a friendly group or official organisation, as a special adviser on subjects including: unconventional warfare (See OCO-CIA).
Spectre:	AC-130 Hercules military aircraft gunship, fitted with specialist armaments and weapons, can fly and fight in all weather conditions.
Spetsnaz:	Russian Military Special Forces. (See Hezbollah training camps Lebanon).
Spooks:	Term use to describe spies and intelligence operatives, (CIA-NSA-MI5-MI6).
SRR:	Special Reconnaissance Regiment, an independent Special Forces unit of the British army, specialising in close target reconnaissance (See Glossary, 22nd SAS).
Standby-Standby:	Warning call to watch out for something, action or movement is imminent.
State sponsored terrorism:	Terrorist groups and networks sponsored and supported, logistically and financially, by rogue Countries and Governments. Example; Iran backing the Lebanese Terrorist group Hezbollah.
Stinger:	American Surface to Air Missile (see SAM, man-pad).
Strait of Hormuz:	Geographic-strategic, an ocean location between the Arabian Sea and the Gulf of Oman. 60km wide, a bottle neck for

shipping-oil tankers. AlQaeda has targeted this location several times to date, including 2010, Japanese oil tanker the "M-Star", attacked-blast failed to breach the double hull of the oil tanker. Al-Qaeda's plan was to hijack and sink the oil tanker in the Strait of Hormuz, resulting in the world-wide disruption of shipping/carrying oil to Western countries, in doing so would have caused an environmental disaster. (See Glossary, Al-Qaeda, AQAP).

Suicide belt –vest:
Clothing worn by a suicide bomber incorporating explosives and detonators. Some suicide vests are detonated by remote control or mobile phone signal. The first recorded Suicide Bomber was during the Palestine - Israeli conflict (See Glossary, UW-Unconventional Warfare).

Sun Tzu:
Chinese strategist, "Art of War", wrote; "know your enemy and you will know yourself" (See Glossary, UW-Unconventional Warfare).

Sunni:
Majority branch of Islam.

Sun-ray:
Radio code word/keyword for British Military Commander-Commanding officer, during Military operations.

SWAT:
Special Weapons and Tactics (See Glossary, Trade craft-CIA).

Syria:
"The Land of Sham", strategically located Middle-Eastern country.
Capital is Damascus; the country has been ruled-dictatorship by the
Assad family for over 40 years. Syria borders, Iraq-Jordan-LebanonTurkey-Israel and the Mediterranean Sea. Russia has a naval base on the coast of Western Syria at Tartus. The Assad Government is backed by Iran and Russia, who supply large shipments of weapons, missiles, aircraft-helicopters and T72 main battle tanks. Syria has over 1000 tons of chemical weapons, the biggest stockpile in the world, including VXnerve agent. The Syria Government and Assad also backs and supports the Lebanese terrorist group Hezbollah, who fight under the flag of
Assad and the Syrian Government, During the Syrian Civil War the opposition group formed against the Assad Government is the FSA, Free Syrian army, an umbrella organisation with several splinter groups including; Jabhat Al-Nusra, a group with links to the Al-Qaeda network (See Glossary, Hezbollah-FSA-AQI).

T.E. Lawrence:
"Lawrence of Arabia" Author of "Seven pillars of wisdom", which is now acquired reading for British and American military officers at Sandhurst and West-point prior to being deployed to Islamic countries across the Middle-East, Afghanistan-Pakistan

and North-Africa. The lessons of cultural understanding and unconventional warfare in Arabia are as valid today as when they were written by T.E. Lawrence over 60 years ago (See acquired reading list by Anthony Malone).

T-1: Triage casualty code 1, needs to be in an operating theatre within an hour to be saved.

T-2: Triage casualty code 2, needs to be in an operating theatre quickly before they become T-1.

T-3: Triage casualty code 3, injured and needs medical help.

T-4: Triage casualty code 4, dead.

T62-T72: Russian main battle tank, used by many Middle-Eastern countries including; Iran, Iraq and Syria.

Tadmor-Palmyra: Ancient city located South Eastern Syria. Location of past Al-Qaeda safe houses and covert operational meetings between Hezbollah and the Pakistan Taliban, Haqqani network, AQI and Al-Qaeda in Iraq. Tadmor is in close proximity to the border of Iraq. (See Glossary, Del-e Zore).

Talib: Term used to describe a Taliban fighter or members of the Taliban.

Taliban: Meaning "Students". Extreme Afghan, Islamic fundamentalist group, with close links to Al-Qaeda-Pakistan Taliban and the Haqqani network. "Mullah Omar" is the spiritual leader of the Taliban. The Taliban supreme council is located in Quetta-city, Pakistan. (See Haqqani
network-Pakistan Taliban). (Anthony Malone interviewed Taliban members and Commanders in Afghanistan-Iraq).

Tango: Term used by Author to describe Taliban and Al-Qaeda terrorists in Puli-Charkhi prison Afghanistan.

Taqiyya: Arabic – Means lie, deceive, secrets, a tactic used by Middle-Eastern Muslim terrorist groups.

Task Force Black: British Special Forces taskforce in Iraq, who's mission was to hunt, capture or kill Al-Qaeda and members of other terrorist groups and networks operating within Iraq. (See Glossary, Task force 121-323).

Taskforce-121-145-323-626: Examples of Military Taskforces; joint British and American specialist Taskforces, made up of personnel from diverse and specialist backgrounds: including-CIA-NSA-MI6-SAS-SBS-Delt-Seals. Area of operations: Middle-East, Afghanistan and Pakistan. Task force codename '121' was set up in such a way that Delta and other elements of JSOC, could switch between Afghanistan and Iraq as required. (See Task force 84). (Anthony Malone interviewed and worked with members of the Task Forces in Iraq-Lebanon-Afghanistan).

Tasking-order:	An order or specific objective within an operation or mission.
Tawqeef:	Notorious and dangerous prison, housing 650+ Afghan Pakistan Taliban, Al-Qaeda prisoners, in the centre of Kabul, Afghanistan (See Glossary, Pul-i-Charkhi).
Tehran:	Capital city of Iran.
Terp:	Interpreter.
TF:	Task Force.
Thames House:	Location of British MI5, Intelligence services headquarters in London.
The Company:	Term use to describe the American "CIA".
Theatre:	Country or area in which troops are conducting operations.
Thermo baric:	Enhanced blast Hellfire missiles-Thermo baric means heat and pressure. (See Hellfire-Apache).
Thobe:	Arabic robe worn in the highlands of the Yemen and in Saudi Arabia.
TL:	Team leader.
TOC:	Tactical Operations Centre (See Op's room).
Top-cover:	Terminology used to describe military/political support-protection from senior Government officials.
Tornado GR4:	Royal Air Force, multi-roll strike warplane. GR4-Ground reconnaissance. ADV (F3)-Air Defence variants. IDS-Ground attack.
Tracer-Bullets:	Bullets that burn with a red, orange or green glow from 110m to 1.110m, so they can be seen, used for target indication and judging distances.
Tradecraft:	Term used to describe security and intelligence operators skills-training for operations and missions into hostile environments and countries. (See Glossary, Trade craft-CIA).
Tradecraft-CIA	Subjects included within tradecraft; Asset cultivation and development Physiological assessing-Deception-Profiling-Surveillance and counter surveillance-Communications-languages-Cultural understanding Weapons SWAT-Advance driving-Interrogation- Resistance to interrogation, and several other classified specialist subjects. (See Farm).
Transjorden:	Original name for the State of Jordan.
Trawling:	Searching an area for intelligence and information. (See

	Tradecraft-CIA).
Tusk:	Military call-sign for the American A10 Warthog-Thunderbolt, used for close air support, supporting combat troops on the ground and for destroying Taliban-insurgents, tunnel complexes across the areas of operation, or the theatre of war (See Glossary, A10).
UAE:	United Arab Emirates.
UBL:	The American CIA's abbreviation used by the agency for "Osama bin Laden".
UCO:	Undercover operative. (See NON-CIA).
Uday & Qusay:	Saddam Hussein's sons. Quay, Saddam's youngest son, was controlling Iraqi resistance and organising the Iraqi insurgency across Iraq prior to both brothers being located and killed by American forces in Mosul, Northern Iraq 2003. A black brief case found at the scene of their deaths confirmed that they were co-ordinating the insurgency in its infancy across Iraq. Plans, maps, money '$', bank information and several other countries passports, including; Syria and Lebanon were also found in the brief case, along with other highly sensitive intelligence, including planned attacks on American soldiers and General Petraeus. Uday and Qusay were also responsible for the Kidnapping, raping, torture, killing and murder of hundreds of their own people (See photographs of the fire fight when they were killed by American forces, also photographs of Udays & Qusay's gold plated AK-47 and MP-5).
UN HQ Iraq 2003 Bombing:	Suicide truck bombing of the Headquarters of the United Nations in Baghdad, Iraq. 22 Killed and over 100 injured.
UN:	United Nations.
Uranium:	A radioactive metallic element used as fuel in nuclear reactors. (See Glossary, Dirty Bomb-CW).
USAF:	United State Air force.
USAID:	United States Agency for International Development.
USSR:	Union of the Soviet Socialist Republics, the Soviet Union, disbanded in 1991.
Utrinque-Paratus:	Latin, "ready for anything", motto of the British Parachute Regiment. (See Glossary, 3 Para).

UW:	Unconventional Warfare, "guerrilla warfare".
UXO:	Unexploded Ordinance.
Vauxhall Cross:	Term used to describe MI6 Headquarters location, London-England.
VBD:	Vehicle Born Device (IED) car-bomb.
VCP:	Vehicle Check Point.
VR:	Vibration Reduction.
VX-nerve agent:	(See Glossary, chemical weapons).
Wadi:	Arabic, a riverbed, dry except in the rainy season (when it is a river).
Wahabi:	Muslim movement-tribe in Saudi Arabia. (Conservative reform of Islam), Osama bin Laden followed Wahabi beliefs, and teachings (Anthony Malone Interviewed Wahabi followers in Afghanistan-Saudi Arabia).
Wais Hudein:	Taliban military Commander-strong ties to Al-Qaeda, operates in Afghanistan, Pakistan and Somalia. (Interviewed by Anthony Malone in Afghanistan).
Walk-In's:	Un-announced-Unplanned "walk-in" meeting between a potential intelligence source and official authorities-intelligence personnel.
Warthog:	American A-10 fighter jet, ground attack aircraft, also known as the Thunderbolt-Tank buster. Fitted with the GAU8, Gatling gun.
Water boarding:	Term used to describe the use of water during terrorist suspect interviews-interrogation. "Simulated drowning", controversial tactic used by the American Government-intelligence agencies during interrogation sessions.
Waziristan:	Geographic area along the Western Pakistan border area to Afghanistan. Waziristan is also a Taliban and Al-Qaeda stronghold, cross-border Afghan attacks by the insurgency/terrorists are planned, prepared and launched from this location.
Wet-work:	Intelligence or mercenary terminology used as reference to eliminating or killing (See Glossary, PMC).
WGP:	Weapons Grade Plutonium.
White Widow:	British National; Samantha Luthwate, Al-Shabab Commander

	and wife of 7/7 suicide bomber Jermaine Lindsey (See Glossary, 21/9, Al-Shabab).
Wilfred Thesiger:	British gentlemen – epic explorer and traveller. Author of "Arabian Sands", the lessons of cultural understanding and travelling across the deserts of Arabia are as valid today as when they were written by Wilfred Thesiger over 60 years ago. The book "Arabian Sands" is now acquired reading for British and American military officers at Sandhurst and West-Point, prior to being deployed to Islamic countries across the Middle-East, Afghanistan-Pakistan and North-Africa (See acquired reading list by Anthony Malone).
WIT-SEC:	Witness Security protection program.
Wizard:	Military radio call-sign for the British Nimrod MR2 spy plane.
WMD:	Weapons of mass destruction (See Glossary, chemical weapons).
Yak:	Large animal, indigenous to the mountains of the Hindu Kush and the Himalayan.
Zaatari:	Refugee camp in Jordan, North of the capital, Amman, built to house Syrian displaced people/refugees fleeing the civil war in Syria. United Nations estimates that over one million people alone are in this refugee camp. People and children trafficking is a major problem within the camp. Child brides are also being sold to wealthy, Saudi men, who just use the young girls for sex then discard them, other human rights abuses "including rape", have been reported within the camp and to the Red-Cross.
Zahedan:	Iranian city located 50km from the Afghanistan-Pakistan border. Notorious for being on the smuggling-people, children-trafficking, human organ route from Afghanistan and Pakistan.
Zarqa:	Small town in Northern Jordan, close to the Syrian border. Zarqa mosque is a known meeting place for terrorists-insurgents from Iraq and Syria.
Zeranjee:	Provincial capital city in Nimruz province, Southern Afghanistan. Location for several Taliban, Al-Qaeda safe houses. Location of fighters moving from Iran, Iraq and Syria. Zeranjee is notorious for being on the smuggling people, children trafficking, human organ route from Afghanistan to Iran-Iraq-Syria-Turkey-Europe. These routes are also used to transport and smuggle HVT's (High Value Targets) "Terrorists" Taliban-Al-Qaeda leaders, between countries. These routes also facilitate the illegal narcotics trade "Drug Trade, Heroin" from and through Afghanistan-Pakistan-Iran-Iraq-Syria and Turkey and then internationally across the globe (See Haqqani network

	and Hezbollah).
ZPU-"Zeus":	Soviet, anti-aircraft gun, 14.5mm-Zpu 1 is single-barrelled, ZPU 2 has twin barrels and the ZPU 4 has quadruple barrels. The ZPU, are also called "Zeus", nickname given to them by Afghan and Arab fighters insurgents. Commonly seen being fixed onto the back of Toyota 4x4's by terrorist groups and freedom fighters across the Middle East, Afghanistan, Pakistan and Africa (See Glossary, Modern Warfare, AlShabab, Haqqani Network, and Taliban).

Examples of Middle-East, Afghanistan, Pakistan and African terrorist groups; Including Geographical areas of Known Active Operations.

Afghanistan Taliban:	(Afghanistan-Pakistan).
Pakistan Taliban:	(Pakistan-Global).
Hezbe-Islami:	(Afghanistan-Pakistan).
Hezbe-Islami-Nigeria franchise:	(Nigeria-Somalia-Kenya).
Al-Shabab/Al-Shaab:	(Somalia-Kenya-Ethiopia-Yemen-Global).
Al-Qaeda:	(Middle East-Afghanistan-Pakistan-Africa-Global).
Kandahar Al-Qaeda:	(Middle East-Afghanistan-Pakistan-Africa-Global).
(AQI) Al-Qaeda in Iraq:	(Middle East-Afghanistan-Pakistan-Africa-Turkey).
(AQAP) Global).	Al-Qaeda in the Arabian Peninsula: (Middle East-Afghanistan-Africa-
Nigerian Taliban:	(Africa, including; Somalia-Mai and Yemen).
Boko Haram:	(Africa-Nigeria-Mali).
Lions of Allah:	(Middle East-Afghanistan-Pakistan-Africa-Europe).
Haqqani Network	(Middle East-Asia-Africa-Europe).

Hezbollah: (Middle East-Afghanistan-Pakistan-Iran-Africa-and
                                        Europe-Global).

(IH) Iraq Hezbollah: (Iraq -Syria-Iran-Afghanistan-Pakistan-Somalia).

ISIS/ IS Islamic State   (HQ in Northern Syria, operates World-Wide)

Hamas: (Middle East-Gaza Strip-West Bank).

Muslim Brotherhood: (Middle East-Africa-Afghanistan-Pakistan-Global).

Jabat Al-Nusra: (Middle East (Syria)-Afghanistan-Pakistan-Africa).

Asa'ib-Ahl-Al-Haq: (Middle East (Iraq).

Arabic Glossary

Fatwa   A legal Islamic verdict or ruling (pl fatawa).

Fitna   Trial and tribulation.

Hadith   A narration recording a saying, action, tacit approval, habit or
                                        physical description of the Prophet (pl. Ahadith).

Halal	That which is permissible, lawful in Islam.
Haram	That which is impermissible, forbidden, unlawful in Islam. Iblis
	Satan, the devil, by his proper noun, equivalent to Diablo.
Jihad	Jihad can be manifested entirely peacefully as well as military-depending upon circumstance (See Jihad in main Glossary).
Jihadi	One who goes to extremes in the concept of Jihad, is excessively enthusiastic about it and holds a distorted idea of it that is more akin to terrorism, (Anglicised=Jihadist).
Jinn	A demon, spirit-like being created from smokeless fire.
Kufr	Disbelief, infidelity.
Kuffar	Non-Muslim, disbelievers, infidels (sing kafir).
Mujahid	One engaged in Jihad (pl.mujahidun-mujahidin).
Quran	(Pronounced=qur`an) Lit, the recital. The Holy book of Islam.
Shari`a-Shari`ah	The divine legislation of Islam (See Sharia main Glossary).
Sunni	An orthodox Muslim, one who adheres to the Prophets Sunna.
Shura	Council meeting of local elders.
Sura	Any one of the 114 chapters of the Qur'an.
Takfir	To accuse someone of major Kufr or disbelief = To eject a Muslim from the fold of Islam.
Takfiri	One who goes to extremes in performing Takfir.
Umma	The Muslim world community.

(Arabic key words and phrases are cross-referenced within the main Glossary)

Islamic Customary Prayers and Praises

'La ilaha ill-Allah, Muhammad-ur-rasool-ullah':

There is no God but God, and Muhammad is his prophet, this is the spoken declaration of faith, the words that make a Muslim a Muslim.

'Allah u Akhbar':

God is greatest, thanks for the God.

'Sal-Allahu 'Alayhi Wa Sallam`:

May Allah send (heavenly salutations of) peace and blessings upon him, 'said after mention of the Prophet Muhammad'.

Alayhi As-Salami:

'Upon him be the peace (of Allah)' After mentioning any Prophet of God`.

Radhi Allahu 'Anhu:

'Allah be pleased with him, after the mention of a companion of the Prophet`.

These prayers and praises have been given in their Arabic forms so as not to clutter the text with lengthy Latin transliteration and also to maintain flow for non-Muslims.

Printed in Great Britain
by Amazon

84316085R10249

PALMERTOWN PRESS

La Porte City, Iowa

ISBN 978-1-7320800-4-1